Edgework

The Sociology of Risk-Taking

D0145083

EDITED BY
STEPHEN LYNG

ROUTLEDGE
NEW YORK AND LONDON

Published in 2005 by
Routledge
Taylor & Francis Group
270 Madison Avenue
New York, NY 10016
www.routledge-ny.com

Published in Great Britain by
Routledge
Taylor & Francis Group
2 Park Square
Milton Park, Abingdon
Oxon OX14 4RN
www.routledge.co.uk

Printed in the United States of America on acid-free paper.

10 9 8 7 6 5 4 3 2 1

Edgework : the sociology of risk taking / edited by Stephen Lyng.
    p. cm.
Includes bibliographical references and index.
  ISBN 0-415-93216-5 (hardcover : alk. paper)—ISBN 0-415-93217-3
  (pbk. : alk. paper)
  1. Risk-taking (Psychology)—Social aspects. I. Lyng, Stephen, 1950-
BF637.R57E34 2004
302'.12—dc22

                                                              2004008211

Edgework

The Sociology of Risk-Taking

For My Mother and Father

Contents

Figures

Contributors

David Courtney is an Associate Professor of Art History and Art Criticism at Florida Atlantic University. He writes on contemporary European and American art for both European and American art publications such as *Tema Celeste*, *Arte Factum*, and *Sculpture*. His curatorial work includes: *Arnulf Rainer: The Autoportraits*; *Jan Schoonhoven*; *Dre Devens: Dutch Constructivist*; *Made in Florida*; among others. Dr. Courtney is a Francey and Martin L. Gecht Research Fellow.

Jeff Ferrell earned his PhD in Sociology from the University of Texas at Austin and is currently Associate Professor of Criminal Justice at Texas Christian University. He is the author of *Crimes of Style: Urban Graffiti and the Politics of Criminality* (Northeastern University Press, 1996), *Tearing Down the Streets: Adventures in Urban Anarchy* (Palgrave/Macmillan/St. Martin's, 2001/2002), and *Wreckage and Reclamation: Studies in Cultural Criminology* (New York University Press, forthcoming), and lead co-editor of four books: *Cultural Criminology* (Northeastern University Press, 1995), *Ethnography at the Edge* (Northeastern University Press, 1998), *Making Trouble* (Aldine de Gruyter, 1999), and *Cultural Criminology Unleashed* (Cavendish/Glasshouse, 2004). He is the founding and current editor of the New York University Press book series Alternative Criminology, and one of the founding and current editors of the journal *Crime, Media, Culture: An International Journal* (Sage, London). In 1998 he received the Critical Criminologist of the Year Award from the American Society of Criminology.

Mark S. Hamm is a Professor of Criminology at Indiana State University. He has published widely in the areas of terrorism, hate crime, and human rights. His most recent book is *In Bad Company: America's Terrorist Underground* (Northeastern University Press, 2002). Hamm is also the co-founder of the Teaching About 9-11 website (available at Stopviolence.com).

Lori Holyfield is an Associate Professor of Sociology at the University of Arkansas. Her dissertation topic and subsequent publications have been on the topic of commercial and non-commercial risk leisure. Her areas of research interest include the sociology of emotions, culture, and symbolic interaction. She has published works in journals such as the *Journal of Contemporary Ethnography, Social Psychology Quarterly, Symbolic Interaction, Sociological Spectrum, Annals of the American Academy of Political and Social Science,* and has book chapters on the topic of adventure in *Social Perspectives on Emotions,* and *Organizational Psychology.*

Lillian Jonas is the chief executive officer of Jonas Consulting Inc., an environmental consulting firm based in Flagstaff, Arizona. Her research interests focus on symbolic interaction, leisure, and the environment

Jennifer Lois received her Ph.D. in sociology from the University of Colorado-Boulder and is currently an assistant professor at Western Washington University in Bellingham, Washington. She studies in the areas of the sociology of emotions, gender, heroism, family, and social psychology, and is the author of *Heroic Efforts: The Emotional Culture of Search and Rescue Volunteers,* which is based on her six years of ethnographic research with a mountain-environment search and rescue group. She is currently studying homeschooling parents, specifically focusing on the social construction of motherhood, family, and education within the homeschooling subculture.

Stephen Lyng is a Professor of Sociology at Carthage College in Kenosha, Wisconsin. He has published research on the sociology of risk, medical sociology, work and leisure, and social movements in journals such as the *American Journal of Sociology,* the *Journal of Applied Behavioral Science, Social Forces, Symbolic Interaction,* and other professional journals and edited books. He is the author of two books, *Holistic Health and Biomedical Medicine: A Countersystem Analysis* (State University of New York Press, 1990) and *Sociology and the Real World,* coauthored with David Franks (Rowman and Littlefield, 2002).

William J. Miller earned his Ph.D. in Sociology from the University of Nevada, Las Vegas, and is currently an Associate Professor of Sociology and Criminal Justice at Carthage College. He is Chair of the Department of Sociology and Director of the Criminal Justice Program. He has published journal articles on a number of subjects including gambling, juvenile delinquency, state crime and homicide.

Dragan Milovanovic is professor of Justice Studies at Northeastern Illinois University. He received his Ph.D. at SUNY at Albany. He has authored, co-authored, or edited over sixteen books and has contributed regularly in scholarly journals in the area of postmodern criminology and law. His most recent books are *Critical Criminology at the Edge* (Praeger/Criminal Justice Press, 2003) and *An Introduction to the Sociology of Law,* 3rd Ed. (Criminal Justice Press, 2003). His forthcoming co-authored book is *The French Connection* (SUNY Press, 2004) and co-edited book, *Lacan: Topologically Speaking* (Other Press, 2004). He is editor of the *International Journal for the Semiotics of Law.*

Gerda Reith is professor of Sociology at the University of Glasgow, U.K. She is interested in "problematic" forms of consumption, especially those that are considered "addictive," or risky, such as gambling and drug taking, as well as the forms of consciousness and regulatory practices that develop around them. She is author of *The Age of Chance: Gambling in Western Culture* (London: Routledge, 1999 and 2002) and editor of *Gambling: Who Wins? Who Loses?* (New York: Prometheus Books, 2003).

Jonathan Simon is Professor of Law/Jurisprudence and Social Policy at the University of California, Berkeley. Simon is the author of *Poor Discipline: Parole and the Social Control of the Underclass, 1890–1990* (1993) and the co-editor of *Embracing Risk: The Changing Culture of Insurance and Responsibility* (with Tom Baker, 2002) and *Cultural Analysis, Cultural Studies, and the Law: Moving Beyond Legal Realism* (with Austin Sarat, 2003). His most recent book, *Governing through Crime: The War on Crime and the Transformation of America* is forthcoming in 2005 from Oxford University Press.

Gideon Sjoberg is professor of sociology at the University of Texas at Austin. Author of such books as *The Preindustrial City* (1960) and (with Roger Nett) *A Methodology for Social Research: With a New Introductory Essay* (1997), he is currently writing a book on bureaucratic capitalism and human rights as well as an essay (with others) on the logics in use in everyday life.

Charles W. Smith is a professor of sociology at Queens College, CUNY and a member of the doctoral program in Sociology at the CUNY Graduate School. He has spent the last forty years studying auction markets. He is the author of many books and articles including *Auctions: The Social Construction of Value* (Free Press/U of California Press: 1989), *Success and Survival on Wall Street: Understanding the Mind of the Market* (Rowman & Littlefield: 1999) and *Market Values in American Higher Education: The Pitfalls and Promises* (Rowman & Littlefield: 2000). He has been the senior editor of *The Journal for the Theory of Social Behaviour* since 1983.

Anna Zajicek is an associate professor in the Department of Sociology at the University of Arkansas. Her research interests focus on social inequalities, discourse, and social change.

Acknowledgments

This book would not have been completed without the encouragement of several individuals whose support and enthusiasm sustained me through the years I have devoted to this project. I owe a debt of gratitude to Joe Marolla for his efforts as Chairperson of my department at Virginia Commonwealth University to lighten the load of my teaching and administrative responsibilities at crucial points during the development of the book. I also thank David Bromley for his encouragement and useful advice on edited collections. I am especially grateful to David D. Franks for his unrelenting optimism about the outcome of this initiative and for his many substantive contributions to the ideas presented here. His critical reading of several key chapters raised the quality of the book considerably. Thanks also to Ilene Kalish and Salwa Jabado, my former and current editors at Routledge, for their encouragement, patience, and professionalism in helping me complete the book and to Misha Derrig for her diligence in preparing the index. Finally, I want to express my deepest gratitude to Gene P. Lyng and Victoria E. Lyng for all their affection and support and for passing on the love of adventure to their wayward child.

Part I
Introduction

Edgework and the
Risk-Taking Experience

STEPHEN LYNG

CONTENTS

This volume emerges out of a special kind of experience familiar to all who either practice or study edgework (or do both in some cases). This is the experience of *recognition*. Edgeworkers of various types always recognize one another, despite great differences in lifestyle and social location. The gonzo journalist Hunter S. Thompson, progenitor of the term "edgework," probably expressed it best when he explained to an interviewer how he won the confidence of the Hell's Angels motorcycle gang, the subjects of his first published book:

> I just went out there and said, 'Look, you guys don't know me, I don't know you, I heard some bad things about you, are they true?' I was wearing a fucking madras coat and wing tips, that kind of thing, but I think they sensed I was a little strange. . . . Crazies always recognize each other. I think Melville said it, in a slightly different context: 'Genius all over the work stands hand in hand, and one shock of recognition runs the whole circle round.' Of course, we're not talking about genius here, we're talking about crazies—but it's essentially the same thing. They *knew* me, they saw right through all my clothes and there was that

instant karmic flash. They seemed to *sense* what they had on their hands (Thompson, 1974, p. 78).

When people separated by divisions of age, gender, class, race, occupation, and intellectual temperament come together and discover deep-seated commonalities of personal experience, they often feel a sense of connection rooted in something basic to their souls. Such is the case with edgeworkers. Whatever else may distance them from one another, risk takers almost always recognize one another as brothers and sisters genetically linked by their desire to experience the uncertainties of the edge. And for students of voluntary risk taking, this sense of commonality among diverse groups engaged in very different kinds of risk taking suggests psychic influences traceable to social and cultural forces deeply imbedded in the modern way of life.

The contributors to this book belong to a variety of academic fields, ranging from sociology and criminology to law and art criticism. Despite the differences in our training and research interests, we have discovered through lengthy conversations, reading one another's work, and in some cases, introducing one another to our favorite edgework activities, that the risk experience is involved in a broader range of human endeavors than anyone might have previously imagined. Though it would seem that participants in extreme sports and street criminals have little in common with patrons of the high arts and academic scholars, the risk-taking dimensions of these and the other seemingly divergent enterprises discussed in this book account for similarities that are just beginning to be recognized. The studies undertaken here reveal a range of activities rooted in a common attraction to exploring the limits of human cognition and capacity in search of new possibilities of being. I am confident that if subjects from each of the social domains studied in this book were assemble in a room together, it would not be long before they recognized each other as members of the same tribe.

This appreciation of the multifaceted expression of edgework activities in contemporary Western societies has developed relatively recently. The first systematic analysis of risk taking conceptualized as edgework appeared a little over a decade ago with the publication of "Edgework: A Social Psychological Analysis of Voluntary Risk Taking" (Lyng, 1990). A small number of studies of risk taking activities such as high risk leisure sports and occupations existed prior to the publication of this article, but the edgework approach departed from the existing perspectives by conceptualizing risk taking as a form of boundary negotiation—the exploration of "edges," as it were. These edges can be defined in various ways: the boundary between sanity and insanity, consciousness and unconsciousness, and the most consequential one, the line separating life and death. Conceptualizing voluntary risk taking in these terms directs attention to the most analytically relevant features of the risk taking experience: the skillful practices and powerful sensations that risk takers value so highly.

The promise of this approach lies in the clear answer it offers to the central question raised by edgework practices as well as the important challenge it poses to find a distinctively *sociological* way of making sense of this answer. The question—why would anyone risk their lives when there are no material rewards for doing so?—can be answered simply. What draws people to "extreme" sports, dangerous occupations, and other edgework activities is the intensely seductive character of the experience itself. As the participants themselves report, they do it because "it's fun!" The challenge—to explain *how* life-threatening experiences come to acquire a seductively appealing character in the contemporary social context—requires a complex sociological theory of structure and agency in late modernity. Ongoing responses to this challenge are yielding a number of exciting new perspectives on voluntary risk-taking behavior.

Thus, the primary goal of the edgework approach is to connect the immediacy of the risk-taking experience to social structures and processes located at the levels of meso- and macro-social organization. The most promising conceptual developments in the study of edgework have explored the ways in which the risk-taking experience can be understood as either a radical form of escape from the institutional routines of contemporary life (variously conceived) or an especially pure expression of the central institutional and cultural imperatives of the emerging social order. This research program expands considerably the scope of issues important to the sociological study of risk. The chief implication of this approach is that the dangers we confront in contemporary Western societies arise not only as unanticipated consequences of the social and technological imperatives of industrialism, imposed on social actors by structural forces beyond their control, but also as consequences of risks actively embraced by some social actors in coming to terms with the institutional forces shaping their daily lives. Viewed in these latter terms, risk taking is an integral part of the very fabric of contemporary social life, pursued not as a means to an end, but as an end in itself.

Edgework as Escape and Resistance

The argument that edgework is a response to the over-determined character of modern social life was first articulated in the original study (Lyng, 1990), which emphasized the institutional constraints that edgeworkers seek to transcend through the pursuit of high-risk leisure activities and in some cases, dangerous occupations. Relying on a synthesis of Marxian and Meadian ideas relating to the dialectic between spontaneity and constraint in social action, this analysis reveals how institutional arrangements that give rise to "alienation" (Marx) and "oversocialization" (Mead) are implicated in the edgework response. The analysis directs attention to the opportunities that edgework provides for acquiring and using finely honed skills and experiencing intense sensations of self-determination and control, thus providing an escape from the structural conditions supporting alienation and oversocialization.

Other researchers have adopted this same general logic while identifying different institutional imperatives impelling the edgework response. Thus, for O'Malley and Mugford (1994), the transcendent character of edgework is found in the contrast it offers to growing disenchantment within the modern world. Relying on a Weberian interpretation informed by Colin Campbell's (1987) work on the "romantic ethic," O'Malley and Mugford argue that edgework "appears (to actors) as the natural 'alternative,' the 'other,' to be resorted to by those seeking to escape from, to resist, or to transcend mundane, modern rationality" (1994, 198). With additional references to Elias's (1982) study of the "civilizing" process of modernity, they locate edgework practices in the uncivilized spaces where actors resist the imperatives of emotional control, rational calculation, routinization, and reason in modern society.

Empirical studies of risk-taking activities also lend implicit support to the view that edgework serves as a vehicle of escape from social conditions that produce stunted identities and offer few opportunities for personal transformation and character development. For example, applications of the edgework concept to various high-risk leisure sports typically give expression to some version of the "weekend warrior" thesis, in which participants in these activities are seen as seeking a temporary escape from the stultifying conditions of work life and bureaucratic institutions. Similarly, studies employing a small-groups perspective often propose that risk taking generates qualities, such as group cohesion or personal character development, missing from the experience of people in certain social positions (Fine and Holyfield, 1996; Holyfield and Fine, 1997). This implies that groups organized around risk-taking and adventure activities provide a refuge for social actors confronting a formal institutional environment that does not fully meet their needs. As Holyfield and Fine note, "Today, adventure discourse surrounds the self. The undiscovered 'real' self (Turner, 1976) and the experience of all its emotional components are seen as necessary correctives to a 'world gone soft'" (1997, p. 358).

A substantive area where the themes of transcendence and resistance in risk taking are particularly prominent is in the study of criminal behavior from the phenomenological and cultural studies perspectives. Jack Katz's (1988) pioneering effort to apply a phenomenological perspective to the study of criminal action has helped spur an exciting body of research on criminal resistance and transcendence. Relying on data assembled through the use of ethnographic field methods, first-hand accounts of criminals, journalistic reports, and open-ended interviews, Katz focuses attention of the experiential "foreground" of crime, where criminals are embedded in the sensual immediacy of the criminal act. In contrast to earlier criminological theories, which assume a criminal disposition rooted in assessments of material gain or other forms of goal attainment, Katz posits that the attractions of crime have more to do with the rewards of the experience itself. Many criminal acts involve "sensual dynamics" that give the experience a deeply passionate, magical character. Katz's qualitative data indicate that criminal events are often experienced as transcendent realities that contrast markedly with the experiential patterns of everyday social life.

Complementing and extending Katz's work on the seductions of crime is a line of research conducted in the ethnographic/field research tradition of British and American cultural studies. The new "cultural criminology" introduced by scholars such as Jeff Ferrell and Clinton R. Sanders (1995) gives prominent attention to the role of the "adrenaline rush" in criminal endeavors and demonstrates how this and other experiential features of criminal action acquire political significance as forms of resistance. In his definitive study of graffiti writers, Ferrell (1993) makes a clear connection between the sensuality and aesthetics of the graffiti-writing experience and political theory and praxis: "When we look at graffiti writing in this way, we find its many nuances pointing toward an interesting conclusion: the politics of graffiti writing are those of anarchism. The adrenalin rush of graffiti writing—the moment of illicit pleasure that emerges from the intersection of creativity and illegality—signifies a resistance to authority, a resistance experienced as much in the pit of the stomach as in the head" (Ferrell 1993, p. 172). By experiencing pleasure and excitement in doing illicit edgework, graffiti writers demonstrate overt resistance to the "constraints of private property, law, and corporate art." Refusing to succumb to negative emotions of shame, guilt, or fear, law violators in the grip of the adrenaline rush and other edgework sensations thumb their noses at social control agents who seek to inculcate such negative emotions as a way to achieve their goals. Like other forms of anarchism, the illicit edgework of graffiti writers and other law violators inverts the emotional plane of normative transgression to express a type of visceral revolt (Ferrell 1993, p. 172).

Thus, in recognizing the seductive and enchanting qualities of criminal edgework, we face one of the great paradoxes of the late modern era. In a powerful expression of Emile Durkheim's insight about the nature of deviance, many crimes of the modern age can be understood as the inevitable flip-side of a rationalized, desacralized culture, one that produces by its own structural logic radical extremes of wealth and poverty, power and powerlessness—and the emotional contradiction of arrogance and humiliation that accompanies these extremes.

Edgework in the Risk Society

Although most analysts of voluntary risk taking have approached this phenomenon as a form of escape or resistance to the key structural imperatives of late capitalism, a separate line of inquiry identifies a basic consistency or even a degree of *synergy* between edgework practices and the institutional order of the "second modernity" (Beck, 1992). Following the work of Anthony Giddens (2000) and Ulrich Beck (1992) on the "risk society," one could argue that the skills, competencies, and symbolic resources deriving from leisure edgework have been increasingly in demand by the risk societies evolving in the last two hundred years. This is especially the case in the advanced postindustrial societies that have seen a dramatic restructuring of institutions that manage the risks since the 1980s. With the ascendancy of "neoliberal" or "post-Keynsian" political-economic policies in these societies (O'Malley and Palmer, 1996), the responsibility for risks has been increasingly directed away from organizations and collectivities and displaced on to individuals. As Jonathan Simon (this volume) points out, edgework and center work begin to blur in this context: "The polarity between institutional life and edgework collapses. Edgework is increasingly what institutions expect of people."

Framed in terms of the risk society model, the pursuit of risk becomes more than a response to the central imperatives of modern society. It is itself a key structural principle extending throughout the social system in institutional patterns of economic, political, cultural, and leisure activity. Thus, the insecurities of the risk society are reflected in almost every aspect of social life, from the dangers we confront in work and consumption to the uncertainties involved in leisure activities and the maintenance of our bodies and health (Reith, 2002).

In this analysis, the rise of hyperconsumption as a key economic imperative in the postwar era, along with related social and demographic changes, has contributed to the emergence of the risk-taking ethic in Western societies. Risk behaviors related to sexuality, substance use, motor vehicle operations, crime, and interpersonal conflict and violence have been particularly prominent in the subcultural patterns of postwar youth populations. These patterns became especially influential as the baby boom cohort moved into adolescence and adulthood and its consumption power began to have a powerful effect on the consumer market. The emergence of large numbers of young consumers with money to spend inspired marketing strategies that appealed to the particular consumer tastes of the youth market. One consequence of this change was the increasing exploitation of stylistic forms created by youth subcultures themselves, which brought attention to the high-risk lifestyles that produced many of these subcultural creations.

As an emerging cultural principle, the risk-taking ethic seems to accord with an increasing demand for edgework skills and perceptions in many different institutional sectors of the risk society. For instance, Mitchell Abolafia's (1996) description of Wall Street bond traders reveals the dominance of edgework skills among an occupational group that resides at the center of the formal economy of the postindustrial social system. Although Abolafia sees bond traders as the self-interested rational maximizers posited by game theorists, his description of their "hyper-rational gaming" strategies bears a much greater resemblance to edgework skills than any system of rational decision-making. He describes the importance bond traders attribute to being able to "feel the market" and maintain "vigilance," and their reliance on "intuitive judgment" (1996, pp. 232–238). These are precisely the kinds of embodied skills employed by individuals negotiating the life-and-death circumstances of edgework. Bond traders also describe the ineffable character of their experiences, as revealed in this quote from one of Abolafia's subjects: "Traders cannot put into words what they've done, even though they may be great moneymakers. They have a knack. They can't describe it" (1996, p. 236). Edgework skills are also reflected in the "identity tools" used by both bond traders and edgeworkers, such as the ability to control one's emotions, the valorization of self-reliance, and the sense of one's "nobility" as an accomplished risk taker (Abolafia, 1996, pp. 239–244).

Although it is tempting to classify bond trading as a distinct form of edgework governed by the same social–psychological dynamics involved in all other varieties of edgework, proponents of the risk society model would point out that bond trading is representative of many fully institutionalized roles that require values and skills supporting voluntary risk taking. In the emerging post-Fordist social universe, workers in most economic sectors are confronting demands for greater flexibility in the development and use of skills as well as declining long-term security in their employment contracts (Clarke, 1990). Temporary workers and contract laborers have become an expanding proportion of the labor force and work-related risks have steadily increased, in the form of higher probabilities of cyclical unemployment and forced periodic retooling of workers' skills and knowledge. Although one would expect that these changes would generate a largely negative response from workers, it is possible that some workers actively "embrace risk" (Baker and Simon, 2002) as an opportunity for greater variety and profit in their careers. Possessing the skills and perceptions of bond traders and edgeworkers—being vigilant and self reliant, trusting one's intuition, refusing to panic, and believing in one's survival skills—the post-Fordist employee may be attracted to the greater risks of the new economic reality.

Thus, from the perspective of the risk society model, the growing interest in the risk-taking experience is dictated by a structural imperative governing most institutional sectors, where uncertainties are increasing over time and new demands for risk management are being placed on those who occupy positions within these institutions. In this context, leisure experience more closely resembles work experience, whereas social life in general is characterized by increasing threats to psychic and physical well-being and increasing expectations that these threats will be managed through individual rather than collective action. As the "social safety net" is slowly unwoven at the same time that environmental, technological, and economic risks expand, the risk-taking ethic assumes greater cultural saliency.

The Edgework Paradox

In reviewing the two general sociological perspectives on edgework, it seems that we confront a paradox no less troubling than the core paradox represented by the very existence of edgework activities. In one perspective, edgework is seen as a means of freeing oneself from social conditions that deaden or deform the human spirit through overwhelming social regulation and control. In the other perspective, edgework valorizes risk-taking propensities and skills in demand throughout the institutional structures of the risk society. Thus, in one view, edgeworkers seek to escape institutional constraints that have become intolerable; in the other, edgeworkers strive to better integrate themselves into the existing institutional environment. These two ways of thinking about edgework seem mutually exclusive and contradictory, but then again, perhaps they are not. We must at least consider the possibility that people may, on one level, seek a risk-taking experience of personal determination and transcendence in an environment of social overregulation, whereas on another level they employ the human capital created by this experience to navigate the challenges of the risk society. The "second modernity" (Beck, 1992) may be a time of expanding risks in many domains, but this does not mean that the regulation of human behavior is any less extensive in this context, as Michel Foucault (1979) has so brilliantly demonstrated in describing the "technologies of domination" that pervade the present social order. Thus, the risk society and governmentality perspectives may capture two dimensions of the same social order in the late modern period.

The paradox of people being both pushed and pulled to edgework practices by opposing institutional imperatives reflects complexities in the contemporary experience of risk that we are just beginning to appreciate. One of the most remarkable things about the academic study of voluntary risk taking is how long it has taken social researchers to begin unraveling this complexity. The present volume is a response to this oversight, undertaken at least to begin the process of describing and understanding the variegated and evolving nature of the risk experience in the contemporary Western world. Each of the chapters in this collection examines a domain of social, cultural, economic, or political participation that reflects in some important way the growing influence of edgework practices. It is hoped that this examination will demonstrate the centrality of collective and personal edgework projects to our present way of life, even as observers both inside and outside of academia may continue to view these projects as largely marginal enterprises.

The twelve essays contained in this volume are grouped into pairs according to common conceptual or empirical themes covering a wide range of theoretical and substantive applications. The first pair of essays are devoted to theoretical elaboration and refinement of the edgework model in light of conceptual developments that have occurred in edgework research during the last ten to fifteen years. In "Sociology at the Edge: Social Theory and the Risk Taking Experience" (chapter 1), I attempt to move beyond the initial Marx–Mead formulation of edgework practices to consider other theoretical interpretations belonging to both the classical and postmodernist social theory traditions. Dragan Milovanovic's essay entitled "Edgework: A Subjective and Structural Model of Negotiating Boundaries" (chapter 2) achieves a much-needed analytical ordering of edgework activities, conceptualized in both experiential and structural terms. Milovanovic presents a typological framework inspired by important themes drawn from several theoretical traditions, including typological, chaos, constitutive, and postmodern theories. As both of these essays demonstrate, the challenge of fully accounting for the various permutations of the edgework experience developing within the dense structures of late modern society will require that we continue to push our theorizing beyond the limits set by any single metatheoretical tradition.

With the next pair of essays, the focus shifts away from theoretical abstractions to the domain of immediate experience. In "The Only Possible Adventure: Edgework and Anarchy" (chapter 3), Jeff Ferrell undertakes an experiential exploration of the genetic connections between edgework activities and anarchist projects both past and present. As one of only a few scholars who has conducted extensive field research on both edgework and anarchism, Ferrell is able to mine a rich body of ethnographic data to reveal the edgework attractions of anarchism and the anarchist foundations of edgework. Similarly, David Courtney draws on his deep understanding of the aesthetic experience, acquired through his work as a performer, art historian, and art critic, to shed light on the seductive qualities of edgework. In "Edgework and the Aesthetic Paradigm: Resonances and High Hopes" (chapter 4), he describes the phenomenological connections between two apparently divergent enterprises: the embodied encounter with high art and the embodied negotiation of high risk.

One of the continuing critical responses to edgework research is that it has yielded conceptual models rooted in the unique experience of white, middle-class, adult males, whose edgework activities have been studied most extensively. The next pair of essays respond to this important criticism by directing explicit attention to gender and age variations in the practice of edgework. In "Gender and Emotion Management in the Stages of Edgework" (chapter 5), Jennifer Lois uses her ethnographic study of voluntary rescue workers to develop a stage model of edgework, focusing on gender-specific strategies for managing the intense emotions involved in rescue work. William J. Miller also seeks to decenter edgework research by examining a form of risk taking more available to people who lack the financial resources of white, middleclass, adult males. In "Adolescents on the Edge: The Sensual Side of Delinquency" (chapter 6), Miller explores the convergences between the edgework model and Jack Katz's phenomenology of crime to construct an original model of juvenile delinquency. Miller's use of quantitative data to empirically validate his model also brings some methodological diversity into a line of research that has been largely dominated by qualitative studies.

In addition to the common themes that connect each of these pairs, the first six chapters align with the "edgework as escape or resistance" approach. By contrast, the last six chapters contribute to the second general approach. This is the perspective that sees edgework skills and sentiments converging with the key institutional demands of late modern society rather than deviating from them. Thus, in the fourth pair of essays, we seen how edgework has been pulled from the margins of the contemporary social order and integrated into the mainstream of institutional life. Lori Hoyfield, Lillian Jonas, and

Anna Zajicek describe part of the new "adventure industry" that has succeeded in marketing a version of the edgework experience to a growing population of consumers. "Adventure Without Risk Is Like Disneyland" (chapter 7) describes the techniques used by rafting guides to manage their own emotions and those of their clients to create the illusion of risk while maintaining the safety of their customers. Charles W. Smith offers another interesting combination of whitewater, edgework skills, and business practice in his essay "Financial Edgework: Trading in Market Currents" (chapter 8). Relying on his participant observation studies of whitewater kayaking and Wall Street stock market trading, Smith demonstrates that participants in these two enterprises employ similar skills in dealing with the risks created by the powerful "currents" they confront. This analysis contributes to a growing body of research that is beginning to seriously challenge rational choice models of trading behavior in high-risk financial markets.

The next pair of essays move even more decisively in the direction of an analysis that places risk taking at the center of the "post" or "late" modern social order rather than on its margins. One way to better understand the structural context of edgework practices is to bring a historical perspective into the analysis. Jonathan Simon and Gerda Reith both take up this task, with Simon focusing on the early the "risk society" of Victorian England and Reith describing the its most recent configuration in the late modern period. In "Edgework and Insurance in Risk Societies: Some Notes on Victorian Lawyers and Mountaineers" (chapter 9), Simon explains the ideological significance of one of the first "extreme" sports—mountaineering—to a profession that would play a pivotal role in establishing the political–legal arrangements for the emerging risk society of Victorian England. Reith describes the changing contours of the risk society 150 years after its first appearance. In "On the Edge: Drugs and the Consumption of Risk in Late Modernity" (chapter 10), she traces the extension of the risk-taking ethic beyond the sphere of work and production into the domain of consumption and leisure. In a socioeconomic system increasingly dependent on high levels of consumption, one of the greatest dangers one faces is the risk of uncontrolled consumption and the financial and psychological ruin that can result from this loss of control. Using recreational drug use as an exemplar for modern consumption patterns, Reith shows us how edgework beliefs, values, and skills, especially the injunction to "get as close to the edge as possible without going over," are coming to define a new cultural ideal in late modernity.

Finally, with the last pair of essays, the study of edgework takes a reflexive turn. As members of the same social order that we study, academic scholars must contend with the structural forces that have been the primary focus of attention in this volume. If we conceive of this social order in terms of the risk society model, as Gideon Sjoberg does in "Intellectual Risk Taking, Organizations, and Academic Freedom and Tenure" (chapter 11), then we can begin to see our greatest challenges as scholars arising from the restructuring of risk management in academic institutions by neoliberal political economic policies and other social and cultural trends of late modernity. Relying on an autobiographical case study of his academic career and other case materials relating to recent world events, Sjoberg explains the crucial role played by organizations in the distribution of risks, especially the risks involved in pursuing controversial scholarship within the academy. This analysis supports Sjoberg's assertion that the risk society theorists (Giddens, Beck) have not adequately attended to the organizational dimensions of risk distribution. Mark S. Hamm raises additional concerns about the changing character of academic institutions, and the implications that these changes have for maintaining academic freedom, with his own professional autobiography. In "Doing Terrorism Research in the Dark Ages: Confessions of a Bottom Dog" (chapter 12), he presents a penetrating account of the risks that one must assume as an intellectual edgeworker, both in the field and in the academy. In an analysis that concurs with Sjoberg's thesis about the role of organizations in risk taking, Hamm reveals that the greatest risk to one's career as an intellectual edgeworker may now come from the recently restructured "corporatized" university.

I started this essay by describing the shock of recognition that "runs the whole circle round" when edgeworkers of all stripes first confront one another. I wish to end it by suggesting that an ever-expanding population of people may experience this shock of recognition as the social and cultural world we inhabit imposes that curious mixture of risk and regulation ever more forcefully in our lives. Indeed, it is possible that the shock will gradually dissipate and recognition will eventually cease all together. We may be on the cusp of an era in which the terms "edgework" and "agency" will no longer be regarded as conceptual categories of academic reflection but will be treated as indistinguishable pursuits in a praxis of self-creation.

References

Abolafia, M. Y. "Hyper-Rational Gaming." *Journal of Contemporary Ethnography* 25(2) (1996): 226–250.

Baker, T., and Simon, J. *Embracing Risk: The Changing Culture of Insurance and Responsibility.* Chicago: University of Chicago Press, 2002.

Beck, U. *The Risk Society.* London: Sage, 1992.

Campbell, C. *The Romantic Ethic and the Spirit of Modern Consumerism.* Oxford: Basil Blackwell, 1987.

Clarke, S. "The Crisis of Fordism or the Crisis of Social Democracy?" *Telos* 83 (1990): 71–98.

Elias, N. *The Civilising Process.* Vol. 1: *The History of Manners.* Oxford: Basil Blackwell, 1982.

Ferrell, J. *Crimes of Style: Urban Graffiti and the Politics of Criminality.* Boston: Northeastern University Press, 1993.

Ferrell, J., and Sanders, C. R., eds. *Cultural Criminology.* Boston: Northeastern University Press, 1995.

Fine, G. A., and Holyfield, L. "Secrecy, Trust, and Dangerous Leisure: Generating Group Cohesion in Voluntary Organizations." *Social Psychology Quarterly* 59(1) (1996): 22–38.

Foucault, M. *Discipline and Punish: The Birth of the Prison.* Translated by A. Sheridan. New York: Vintage/Random House, 1979.

Giddens, A. *Runaway World.* New York: Routledge, 2000.

Holyfield, L., and Fine, G. A. "Adventure as Character Work: The Collective Taming of Fear." *Symbolic Interaction* 20(4) (1997): 343–363.

Katz, J. *The Seductions of Crime: Moral and Sensual Attractions in Doing Evil.* New York: Basic Books, 1988.

Lyng, S. "Edgework: A Social Psychological Analysis of Voluntary RiskTaking." *American Journal of Sociology* 95 (1990): 851–886.

O'Malley, P., and Mugford, S. "Crime, Excitement, and Modernity." In *Varieties of Criminology*, edited by G. Barak. Westport, CT: Praeger, 1994: 189–211.

O'Malley, P., and Palmer, D. "Post-Keynesian Policing." *Economy and Society* 25 (1996): 137–153.

Reith, G. "From Signs to Science: The Transformation of Chance and the Emergence of Risk in the Development of Modernity." Unpublished manuscript, 2002.

Turner, R. H. "The Real Self: From Institution to Impulse." *American Journal of Sociology* 81 (1976): 989–1016.

Vetter, C. "Playboy Interview: Hunter Thompson." *Playboy* November, 251 (1974): 75–90, 245–46.

Part II
Theoretical Advances in the Study of Edgework

1
Sociology at the Edge: Social Theory and Voluntary Risk Taking

STEPHEN LYNG

CONTENTS

The Absence of Voluntary Risk Taking in Social Theory

Looking at sociology at the beginning of the twenty-first century, it would appear that we have reached a crossroads. Just as the substantive focus of classical sociological theory was shaped by the formation of urban industrial societies during the nineteenth century, the newest areas of sociological interest reflect social transformations associated with the rise of post-industrial societies in the latter half of the twentieth century. Thus, though the "core" subfields of mainstream sociology align with classical theory's attention to production and social differentiation, new fields of study focus on such things as consumption and lifestyles, the body and emotions, and ineffability and irrationality. Because the founding theorists had little to say about these latter concerns (with some important exceptions), it is not surprising that many sociologists today are looking outside of the classical canon for guidance in analyzing these new issues.

The way that sociologists have approached the problem of risk reveals this tension between the classical and post-classical standpoints. Although risk was not a subject of special concern to Marx, Durkheim, Weber, and the other classical theorists, twentieth-century sociologists following in the classical tradition have defined the central issue in risk analysis as the social regulation of risks. Having ceded the problem of explaining why people choose to engage in risky behavior largely to psychologists and economists (see Heimer, 1988), the concerns of risk sociologists came to exclusively reflect mainstream sociology's paradigmatic focus on the institutional regulation of human behavior and the products of human invention. What these sociologists considered a novel application of this paradigmatic approach was an analysis of the institutional regulation of the risks endemic to contemporary societies. Thus, risk sociologists continue to see the regulation of risks as an inevitable problem of modern industrial societies, which produce increasingly dangerous technologies and social arrangements that place large populations of people at risk for death or injury (Perrow, 1999).

The study of edgework diverges significantly from this problem orientation. As a way of conceptualizing *voluntary* risk taking, the notion of edgework addresses a problem that has been largely off-limits for most sociologists of risk: understanding what motivates people to engage in high-risk behavior. The phenomenological orientation guiding the early studies of edgework (Lyng, 1986, 1990) yielded findings that have special relevance for this problem. What these studies revealed is that the motivations for engaging in high-risk behavior can be found in the experience itself. As demonstrated by the empirical research on a broad range of edgework activities, individuals are motivated to participate in such risky behavior because they find the experience to be seductively appealing. Those who venture close to the edge are attracted by embodied pleasures of such high intensity that they often have addictive consequences.

The edgework approach builds on a limited but insightful body of sociological literature on the subject of voluntary risk taking. In 1968, Samuel Klausner edited a collection of papers devoted to explaining *Why Man Takes Chances* (the volume's title) from a variety of disciplinary perspectives. Intellectual luminaries such as Jessie Bernard and Kenneth Burke joined other scholars from fields ranging from military science to literary criticism in offering insights about "stress-seeking" behavior, with Bernard and Klausner providing sociological treatments of the problem. A more important analysis of voluntary risk taking appeared the year before, with the publication in 1967 of Erving Goffman's essay "Where the Action Is." In the same way that Goffman anticipated so many other critically important social and cultural themes of postwar Western societies, he sensed the growing attraction of voluntary risk taking or "action," as he conceptualized it (1967, p. 185). However, apart from these brief explorations of the general significance of risk taking in the postwar era and a few studies of more specific high-risk endeavors (see Mitchell, 1983), there has been little recognition among social theorists of the growing importance of voluntary risk taking in late modernity.

We have to look outside of academic sociology to find significant attention to the growth of voluntary risk taking in recent decades. Hunter Thompson and other members of the so-called "new journalism" movement of the sixties and seventies, including writers like Tom Wolfe, Norman Mailer, Truman Capote, George Plimpton, and Rex Reed, were some of the first social observers to recognize the emergence of a new risk-taking culture. Despite some disagreement over the defining features of new journalism (cf. Wolfe, 1973), one of the most obvious connecting threads in this literature was the focus on topics relating to high-risk behavior (drug use, murder-robbery, street violence, etc.) and, most often, the risk-taking activities of youth subcultures (hippies, anti-war protestors, outlaw motorcycle gangs, etc).

This work undoubtedly played a part in stimulating sociological interest in voluntary risk taking. Since the 1960s, sociological analysis of voluntary risk taking has been conducted mostly by researchers interested in various dimensions of youth culture. It is noteworthy that the individual who coined the term "edgework," the self-proclaimed "gonzo journalist" Hunter S. Thompson, anticipated this line of social scientific research with his first published book, entitled *Hell's Angels* (1966). Although the book focused primarily on the most notorious motorcycle gang of the era, it also provided a somewhat idiosyncratic historical and cultural account of the general phenomenon of postwar motorcycle gangs. Thompson seemed to sense intuitively that the high-risk behavior of "outlaw bikers" would presage the growth of a broader range of risk-taking leisure pursuits as the baby boom generation moved into young adulthood. This is a pattern he captured in perhaps his best-known book, *Fear and Loathing in Las Vegas*, published in 1971.

The young working-class individuals who formed the early motorcycle gangs resembled members of various youth subcultures in the United States and Europe in their desire for experiential anarchy. For the Hell's Angels and other outlaw bikers, the desire was fulfilled not only in the reckless way that they rode their motorcycles but also in their sexual practices, alcohol and other drug use, and generally chaotic lifestyle patterns. Field research conducted by social scientists in the 1970s revealed similar patterns, reflecting the sensual attractions of edgework skills and emotions in adolescent crime and deviance. For example, in describing the special significance of violent exchanges to British juvenile delinquents, Willis (1977, p. 34) captured the distinctive edgework qualities of fighting:

> [Fighting] is one way to make the mundane suddenly *matter*. The usual assumption of the flow of the self from the past to the future is stopped; the dialectic of time is broken. Fights, as accidents and other crises, strand you painfully in 'the now'. Boredom and petty detail disappear. It really does matter how the next seconds pass. And once experienced, the fear of the fight and the ensuing high as the self safely resumes its journey are addictive.

Willis's reference here to alterations in the perception of time and self, the hyperreal quality of the event, strong emotion (fear), and the addictive "high" that participants experience could be taken as a rather typical description provided by skydivers, motorcycle racers, or firefighters in referring to their own particular forms of edgework. (See Lyng, 1990.) Accounts of other youth subcultures, such as the hipsters, beats, teddy boys, mods, and rockers, described by social scientists like Dick Hebdige (1979), also highlighted the important role of risk-taking behavior in the subcultural matrix, especially with respect to the use of drugs (1979, pp. 52–53).

With the growing prevalence of voluntary risk taking throughout second half of the twentieth century, sociology's omission in addressing this increasingly important social pattern became increasingly apparent. Thus, by the 1980s, public acknowledgments of the oversight began appearing in highly visible publication forums, such as James Short's Presidential Address at the American Sociological Association Meetings (1984) and Carol Heimer's article in the *Annual Review of Sociology* (1988). The need for a distinctively *sociological* account of the forces impelling people to seek out high-risk situations was beginning to be recognized.

Edgework and the Rationalization Process

The initial edgework study (Lyng, 1990) employed a critical social psychological perspective inspired by a promising but short-lived effort to marry elements of Marxian political economy with George Herbert Mead's social-psychological framework (Goff, 1980; Batuik and Sacks, 1981; Blake, 1976; Schwalbe, 1986). What made this synthetic framework attractive was the possibility it offered for analyzing voluntary risk taking in terms of both macro-level influences and the micro-dimensions of individually felt emotions and experiences. Although this approach offers a modernist interpretation of edgework with significant analytical potential, it does not exhaust the possibilities for exploiting the classical canon. A Weberian interpretation of the edgework phenomenon can be attempted, which perhaps could enrich our analysis of the structural "constraints" acting on members of modern Western societies, institutional forces that contrast so starkly with the "spontaneous" elements of risk-taking behavior. Though the Marx-Mead synthesis directs attention to the central importance of the "spontaneity/constraint" dialectic in understanding the unique character of the edgework experience (Lyng, 1990, pp. 866–869), alienated labor and the "generalized other" may not be the only imperatives implicated by the growing appeal of edgework.

For Max Weber, the emergent dynamic of modernity can be found in the expansion of formal rationality into almost every domain of social life. Where Marx saw the development of capitalism as the product of an immanent trans-formation of feudal productive forces into a new economic base for modern social institutions and culture, Weber regarded the capitalist economic sector as one facet of a larger social whole in which formal rationality had become the principal imperative. Weber offered a detailed examination of the complex and varied expressions of the rationality principle in different institutional realms, but he was also interested in understanding the origins of this principle (Weber, 1958) and how it would shape the subjective experience of modern social actors. Weber's view of the latter problem is embodied in his notion of "disenchantment." This idea refers to the steady erosion of meaning that fol-lows in the wake of the rationalizing forces of modernity. Though members of traditional societies experience enchantment in the form of the mystical quali-ties associated with religious practice and intimate connections with nature, these magical qualities of traditional life are lost in a rationalizing social world moving inexorably toward the "iron cage" of bureaucratic domination:

> No one knows for sure who will live in this cage in the future or whether at the end of this tremendous development entirely new prophets will arise, or there will be a great rebirth of old ideas and ideals, or, if neither, mechanized petrification, embellished with a sort of convulsive self-importance. For of the last stage of this cultural development, it might well be truly said: "Specialists without spirit, sensualists without heart; this nullity imagines that it has attained a level of civilization never before achieved" (Weber, 1958, p. 182).

The disenchanted world of formally rational social institutions offers little possibility for the vibrant experience of unexpected and unimagined sensual realities. In a highly rationalized system where almost nothing is left to chance, day-to-day existence is distinguished most by its closely regulated, predictable character. Consequently, though enchantment permeated the institutional practices of traditional societies in the form of rarified experi-ences mediated by religious and political authorities endowed with mystical powers, such experience is systematically excluded from the institutional practices of modern life.

Although Weber emphasized the disenchanting character of modern soci-ety, his thesis has been modified in the work of Colin Campbell (1987) and others (Ritzer, 1999) to take account of what some see as the enchanting char-acter of modern consumerism. Campbell argues that the spirit of consumerism can be traced to dimensions of Protestant religious practice overlooked in Weber's analysis. In contrast to Calvinist asceticism, some forms of Protestant religious practice emphasized the personal, mystical experience of God's grace and the intense emotion stimulated by this experience. These religious traditions gave rise to a "romantic ethic" and spawned a character type that became a counterpoint to the capital-accumulating miser inspired by Protestant ascetics. The romantic preoccupation with unfulfilled fantasies became the foundation of the modern consumption imperative: "romantic teachings concerning the good, the true and the beautiful, provide both the legitimation and the motivation necessary for modern consumer behavior to become prevalent throughout the contemporary industrial world" (Campbell, 1987, p. 206).

Campbell traces the opposition between the producing and consuming character types of modern capitalism to a symbiotic "sibling rivalry" between the rationalistic and romantic traditions (1987, p. 220). George Ritzer (1999) frames these opposing moments in terms of Weber's disenchantment–enchantment distinction. If members of modern Western societies confront rationalized institutional routines that have been stripped of any meaning by instrumental imperatives, perhaps their constrained, colorless worlds are re-enchanted in the "cathedrals of consumption" of late capitalism. Ritzer raises this possibility in describing the overwhelming diversity of consumption experiences that can be found in post-industrial societies today, ranging from shopping malls, chain stores, and "virtual" shopping centers, to cruise ships, casinos, and electronic mega-churches. Constituting what Ritzer defines as "the new means of consumption," these settings presumably create dream-like, magical encounters for consumers and provide them with enchanting alternatives to the drab world of bureaucratic experience.

Although there are strong reasons to question whether modern consumption practices actually lead to a re-enchantment of the dispirited worlds of contemporary Westerners (an ambivalence that Ritzer himself occasionally expresses), this thesis opens up some new possibilities for theorizing about edgework. One of the most distinctive features of contemporary risk taking is the expansion of risk opportunities within the realm of leisure consumption. The modern consumer confronts a plethora of possibilities for placing oneself in harm's way, from the broad range of "extreme sports" to "commercial adventure" (Holyfield, 1997) designed to build "character" or a sense of community (ropes courses, whitewater rafting, Outward Bound, etc.). Thus, risk taking is an ascendant theme in consumer culture, which may reflect the special function fulfilled by consumption practices within late capitalism. With the expansion of businesses that sell direct participation in risk taking and the growth of vicarious risk taking in spectator sports (NASCAR, Extreme Games, etc.), television programming, advertising, and the film industry, the marketing of edgework may be one of the more effective ways to re-enchant a disenchanted world.

In support of this argument, we could consider the "magical," seductive character of the edgework experience as revealed in data relating to a broad range of high-risk activities. These data suggest that commodified edgework may represent the purest form of enchantment that can be found in the consumer market today. Ritzer describes in detail the various ways in which the new means of consumption create spectacular environments and experiences for people looking to escape the stultifying environments of daily work life. But few of these settings and consumption activities can match the transcendent experience of edgework.

Consider, for example, the contrast between the manufactured "spectacle" of consumer settings and the spectacular character of the natural settings in which commercial adventure is often conducted. The spectacle of a Disneyworld fireworks display hardly compares with the spectacular panorama of canyon walls on a whitewater rafting trip, although it is certainly true that both environments possess a magical quality for observers. Moreover, what commercial edgework may offer customers is an opportunity to experience an active "personal spectacle" as opposed to the passive "collective spectacle" found within the cathedrals of consumption. Standing alone on the wheel strut of a skydiving plane waiting for the signal to jump is a breathtaking experience even though it may be an entirely personal one. In the increasingly individualized world of consumer culture being created by Internet commerce, home shopping television, telemarketing, and other technologies of personalized consumption, it is possible that consumer preferences are tending more towards personal spectacle as a substitute for the collective spectacles of mega shopping malls, theme parks, and casino-hotels.

Where commercial edgework connects most directly with other forms of spectacle as sources of re-enchantment is in its capacity to generate implosions of time and space. A key concept of Jean Baudrillard's postmodernist theory, the idea of implosion refers to the erasure of ontological distinctions through the collapse of previously separate experiential domains. As Ritzer (1999, p. 133) describes it, this involves a process of *dedifferentiation*, where distinct sectors of experience contract into an undifferentiated mass and earlier distinctions between things and places are dissolved. Baudrillard's conceptualization of implosion refers to a pattern of dedifferentiation that he sees as the central feature of postmodern culture: the collapse of the distinction between the real and the unreal in the overflow of simulations pouring from consumer culture. But the idea of implosion can also be applied to other kinds of contractions in people's perceptions of reality, including the dissolution of basic categories relating to time and space.

Ritzer directs attention to implosions brought about by the use of television and computer technologies that compress the space in which goods can be sold, innovations like infomercials, home shopping television, cybermalls, psychic hotlines, and telephone sex (1999, p. 149). Experienced by consumers as "phantasmagoric" in nature, these innovations hold great potential for re-infusing the world with the magical character it lost under the influence of the rationalizing forces of modernity (1999, p. 146). Ritzer also focuses on new consumer settings that compress time by creating a pastiche of elements from the past, present, and future, producing the "feeling of a *loss* of a sense of time, a dream-like state in which time ... seems not to matter" (1999, p. 159) or by manipulating spatial constraints to create a sense of infinite space (1999, p. 162).

Although these implosions may produce spectacular effects by challenging traditional perceptions of time and space boundaries, they cannot match the profound transformations of temporal and spatial boundaries experienced in the immediacy of edgework. Subjects report that significant alterations in perceptions of time and space occur in many different types of edgework (Lyng, 1990, p. 861). The experience of negotiating the edge typically results in a narrowing of the perceptual field in which participants become highly focused on those elements that determine success or failure. In this state, one's sense of the flow of events is radically transformed, and time passes either much faster or much slower than usual. Similarly, spatial boundaries are perceived differently as participants experience a sense of cognitive control over essential objects and a feeling of identity or sense of "oneness" with these objects. Thus, the implosion of time and space in the edgework experience gives it a mystical quality more pronounced than anything produced in other consumption settings.

In addition to implosion, other edgework sensations help to produce a sense of a transcendent reality. Participants often describe the experience of negotiating the edge as "more real" than the experience of everyday institutional routines. This sense of "hyperreality"[1] leaves them with deep feelings of authenticity and a reflective sense of their actions in these situations as being guided by their "true" selves. Thus, the edgework experience typically assumes an "other world" quality for participants. This is reflected in another persistent theme that emerges from the field data: the claim that the experience is essentially ineffable and can be fully understood only by actually participating in it (Lyng, 1990, p. 862).

Alterations in the experience of time and space and the hyperreal quality of edgework lifts participants out of the mundane reality of rational mediations and transports them to a world of sensual immediacy. This "other world" of commodified edgework may be a source of enchantment not unlike the other-world forces permeating the profane realities of premodern societies. Thus, if Ritzer is correct in asserting that the culture of consumption serves to return the magical quality to people's lives lost to the stultifying instrumentality of rational institutions, then we can extend his argument by claiming that leisure edgework represents one of the more powerful means of transcending the institutional world. One cannot help but harbor a certain amount of suspicion about the enchanting effects of Ritzer's cathedrals of consumption; are today's sophisticated consumers really enchanted by the manufactured spectacles of shopping malls, casinos, theme parks, and the like? The blank stares of many people in these environments would suggest otherwise. However, there can be no doubt about the awe-inspiring effect of the edgework experience, a theme that consistently shows up in participants' accounts. Considering the novelty and intensity of this experience, it is little wonder that so many participants claim to be "addicted" to their chosen form of edgework.

Edgework Beyond the Consumption Imperative

Ritzer's and Campbell's focus on the enchanting nature of consumption opens up some interesting theoretical possibilities for understanding voluntary risk taking in post-industrial, consumer society. However, some caution must be exercised in adopting an exclusive focus on consumption and leisure experiences as the primary means of re-enchanting the modern world. There is little doubt that the expansion of commodified edgework has been a prominent trend in Western societies during the past several decades. But to focus only on leisure edgework would be to ignore the growing impact of voluntary risk taking in social sectors outside of the consumer market. In addition to growing prominence of high-risk sports and other leisure activities, it appears that risk taking within the occupational sector has held an attraction for increasing numbers of people in late capitalism as well.

Evidence supporting this assertion is at best fragmentary and indirect. For example, we could consider that much of the popular print literature and electronic media devoted to risk-taking themes focuses on the lives of people who work in high-risk jobs: the day-to-day challenges of emergency rescue workers and medical personnel, fire and police workers, legal professionals involved in high-stakes litigation, private investigators, and the like. This evidence would suggest that the interest in these occupations is more vicarious than direct, but other trends point to an increased willingness to embrace risk taking in workplace settings where, in earlier times, risk avoidance was the rule.

A case in point is the evolution of new managerial philosophies in recent years that enjoin managers to work at or near the edge and to exploit risk and uncertainty to increase productivity and profits. Business ideologies reflected in works such as Thomas Peters' (1987) *Thriving on Chaos* promote an image of a rapidly changing world in which business organizations are permanently in revolution. In Peters' view, the old order of economics as a business discipline has passed. Although the old economics assumes fixity, predictability, and order, the new global economy is never stable. Today's customers are tomorrow's competitors, today's state-of–the-art is tomorrow's dinosaur, and today's bestseller is tomorrow's loss maker. Innovation, adaptation, and permanent flux characterize the new order. Peters' books, and those of like-minded authors, exalt an entrepreneurial capitalist order that seeks to promote risk, innovation, and enterprise.

A similar valorization of occupational risk taking can be seen in many of the high-yield investment approaches that have developed in the last two decades. In the 1980s we saw the junk bond market and corporate take-over and arbitrage movements. In the 1990s, it was the Internet-based industries and "dot com" revolution. Like the new managerial philosophy advanced by Peters and his associates, the business pioneers who developed these new investment strategies (individuals such as Michael Milken, Ivan Boesky, Warren Buffett, Carl Icahn, and Jeff Bezos) challenge the traditional business ethic of control and minimization of risk by extolling the virtue of high-stakes risk taking with a potential for extremely large returns. In seeking to explain the rise of these new high-risk business practices, it is tempting to attribute them to an extension of the entrepreneurial spirit that has always been the driving force in market systems. This explanation would emphasize the desire for profit maximization as the fundamental motive behind a new willingness to assume large risks. However, it is also possible that the new attitude toward risk has more to do with an emerging character structure (in the Weberian sense) than rational calculations of profit and reward. The theoretical advantage of adopting this Weberian emphasis is that it offers the potential for connecting behavior in the economic sector with similar patterns in other institutional domains, such as the commercial adventure practices discussed above and other forms of risk taking.

Such an interpretation would suggest that participants in these high-risk business enterprises are motivated much more by the "hunt" than the "kill." In other words, the most valued aspect of high-risk investment and business dealings may be the experiential character of the work rather than the financial reward. In the same sense that Weber's early mercantilists were inspired in their capital-accumulating ways by the value they placed on the ascetic experience rather than material greed, today's junk bond dealers and Internet day traders may also value the "adrenaline rush" of high-stakes dealings much more than the financial payoff. Thus, in this respect, they may have more in common with their fellow "adrenaline junkies" involved in non-business varieties of risk taking than they do with more traditional members of the business world. This would certainly suggest that their high-risk business dealings have the same magical, seductive character as leisure edgework activities. Both domains may serve as arenas of re-enchantment in an otherwise disenchanting social universe.

Expanding the scope of edgework activities even further, we can consider another domain of risk taking that offers transcendent possibilities for the disenchanted, one that overlaps the occupational and leisure activities described here. As field data on edgework reveals, the empowering sensations of the experience (self-actualization, feelings of omnipotence, control, etc.) often lead participants to search out additional opportunities for negotiating the edge. This is achieved by either expanding their risk activities into other arenas or by taking chances that they have avoided in previous risk experiences. One consequence of this tendency is that normative boundaries become blurred and actors become less sensitive to the line separating "unconstrained" practice and illegal conduct. It should be noted, for example, that many of the preeminent figures in the world of high-risk finance have been convicted of corporate crimes, in many instances paying large fines and actually serving prison sentences for their transgressions.[2] Thus, if these occupational edgeworkers are pulled so easily into the domain of illicit behavior in search of ways to raise the stakes and move closer to the edge, it is possible that the experiential distance between entrepreneurial risk taking and criminal conduct may be shorter than we often think. The more important implication is that criminal action could serve as yet another vehicle for re-enchanting the world. Indeed, recent theoretical developments in the study of crime and related empirical research lend strong support to this view.

Edgework, Enchantment, and the Criminal Experience

The study of crime has always presented researchers with challenging dilemmas. For all of the concern that academics, policy-makers, and the public have about crime, we seem to know very little about why people engage in criminal action or how they can be discouraged from doing so. Indeed, the long succession of theories about crime put forth by sociologists and criminologists in the twentieth century have proven unsatisfactory on either theoretical or practical grounds. What is common to all of these approaches is a predisposition to explain crime in terms of some rational calculus, as dictated by the rationalistic presuppositions of social science in general. Consequently, some critics have asked whether the inadequacy of previous approaches may be traced to this reliance on assumptions of rationality.

This is the position adopted by one of the most recent efforts to theorize about crime: the phenomenological perspective developed by Jack Katz (1988). A close examination of the sensual dynamics of the criminal experience reveals intriguing similarities with the edgework patterns described in the research on high-risk enterprises in the leisure and occupational domains. As noted in recent examinations of the convergence between Katz's study of crime and the edgework model (Lyng, 1993; O'Malley and Mugford, 1994), the central link between many forms of crime and voluntary risk taking is the inherently chaotic, anarchistic nature of these two domains of experience. In Katz's description of "stickup," we find perpetrators confronting highly fluid situations of unfolding suspense and uncertainty. Offenders cannot know in advance how much intimidation will be required to control their victims or whether bystanders will intervene in the action. When co-offenders are involved, it is unclear whether they will follow through on their assigned tasks or perhaps go too far in subduing victims (Katz 1988, p. 191). In fact, the general disposition of many criminals is to move towards temporal and social network arrangements that enhance the uncertainties involved in the illicit action (1988, p. 220). This implies that the more chaotic the situation, the more experientially appealing it is to the offender.

The centrality of chaos and uncertainty to these kinds of criminal enterprises indicates that they are clear instances of boundary negotiation along an edge separating order and disorder. Like other types of edgeworkers, these criminals appear to be drawn to the challenge presented by such circumstances to exercise control over a seemingly uncontrollable situation. Hence, chaotic circumstances are embraced because they become "provocation to manifest transcendent powers of control" (Katz, 1988, p. 220). Only in close proximity to this edge can perpetrators experience the distinctive implosions of time and space that signal the ontological shift to a transcendent reality:

> The chaos in the life of action lends a distinctive significance to those who respond by imposing a disciplined control through the force of their personality. This is the final, compelling appeal of the hardman—that he alone, in the face of chaos, embodies transcendence by sticking up for himself, literally and figuratively (Katz, 1988, p. 225).

Although the similarities between the foreground of criminal action and the edgework experience are striking, there are important differences between these two experiential realms as well. In contrast to their criminal counterparts, leisure edgeworkers typically do not undertake projects of *moral* transcendence. As noted in earlier work (Lyng, 1990, p. 857), the "edge" can be defined in several different ways (the line between life and death, between sanity and insanity, between an ordered and disordered social reality, etc.), and it is certainly possible to add the "normative edge" to the list of boundary conditions that can be negotiated in edgework. But clearly, it is the illicit nature of criminal action that sets this realm apart from the high-risk leisure and occupational activities described above (although, as noted earlier, in some instances licit edgework projects can easily evolve into illicit ones). Moreover, this difference is important for understanding the structural antecedents and emotional dynamics of criminal edgework.

In connecting the experiential foreground and the structural background in criminal action, Katz sees the emotional experience of humiliation as the lynchpin. Humbled by the prospect of entering a bureaucratic, technological society with limited resources and the stigma of lower class or minority status, aspiring criminals rely on emotional transformations as a way to escape:

> Running across these experiences of criminality is a process juxtaposed in one manner or another against humiliation. In committing a righteous slaughter, the impassioned assailant takes humiliation and turns it into rage.... The badass, with searing purposiveness, tries to scare humiliation off;... Young vandals and shoplifters innovate games with risks of humiliation, running along the edge of shame for its exciting reverberations. Fashioned as street elites, young men square off against the increasingly humiliating social restrictions of childhood by mythologizing differences with other groups of young men (Katz, 1988, pp. 312–313).

Although humiliation is the immediate emotional reality with which criminals must contend, this reality is directly tied to the broader sense of disenchantment engendered by the rational imperatives of the modern social order.
Thus, to understand the seductive appeal of illicit, criminal edgework, one
must appreciate the opportunity it offers for an "other world" experience—the
chance to experience an alternative reality circumscribed by sensual dynamics
that are radically different from those of mundane social reality. To be sure, it
is an alternative reality where strong emotions like rage can play a dominant
role, which is not usually the case in other types of edgework. But even in this
distinctive form, giving oneself up to the chaos of strong emotion, i.e., losing
control of oneself, has the immediate consequence of imploding time and
space distinctions. As O'Malley and Mugford (citing Katz) note, righteousness
and rage:

> "are plausible responses to humiliation precisely because they provide
> 'a blindness to the temporal boundaries of existence,' they take us out of
> time:… 'rage is mercifully blind to the future' because it 'focuses con-
> sciousness on the here and now' ([Katz] 1988, 30-1). This is its tran-
> scendence and its seduction: it is 'soothing' and a 'great comfort' — 'rage
> moves toward the experience of time suspended … this is the spiritual
> beauty of rage'" (1994, p. 192).

As this passage suggests, transcending humiliation through purposeful rage
produces a sense of time, space, and self that resembles the otherworld qualities of religious ecstasy. Thus, we see that the forces of rationalization in the
modern world have consequences that extend beyond the experience of disenchantment. For those who enter the iron cage (sometimes literally) as wards of
the state or other miscreants, disenchantment is combined with overwhelming humiliation. And for members of these groups, criminal edgework is a
much more relevant and accessible means to re-enchantment than the pursuit
of leisure edgework or postmodern consumption opportunities available to
more privileged social groups.

In concluding this section, it may be important to ask "in what ways does
the Weberian perspective take us beyond earlier interpretations to new
insights about the significance of edgework?" Responding to this question
would require us to consider the strength of Weber's focus on charactereology
as an organizing theme for theoretical discourse. (See Hennis, 1988.) This
focus is revealed most clearly in Weber's treatment of the "Protestant Ethic" as
the foundation of a character structure that could be related to the *Weltan-
schauung* or "spirit" of the modern period. Such an approach offers a powerful
alternative to psychological explanations of socially significant agents conceptualized in terms of modal personality types. Although explanations of behavior that focus on personality types often rely on tautological reasoning, the
analysis of character structures reveals how historically antecedent forces

shape individuals. Thus, it is possible in the Weberian framework to maintain the emphasis on human agency implied by personality theory without sacrificing analytical rigor.

Because most of the early attempts to explain voluntary risk-taking behavior relied on some expression of a "risk taking personality" (Klausner, 1968; Zucherman et al., 1964; see also Farley, 1991), the charactereological approach can perhaps be viewed as a sociological extension of this tradition. As we have seen, Campbell's Romantic Ethic serves as a counterpoint to the Protestant Ethic in the Weberian narrative on the emergence of bureaucratic–capitalist society. In a system in which "irrational exuberance" in consumption stands on equal footing with rational efficiency in production, it is necessary to analyze the opposing character structures that sustain this system. Moreover, if we can trace various "pathological" expressions of disciplined, self-regulated behavior in the modern era to the ascetic character structure, it is also possible to connect extreme expressions of emotionally charged, spontaneous behavior to the opposing romantic character structure. In the present analysis, it has been shown that licit and illicit forms of edgework may be the natural destination of a romantic character type that is increasingly alienated from rationalized production and consumption as means to self-realization.

This interpretation has the additional advantage of offering a unique way to think about the structural implications of the edgework pattern. Mirroring the polar character structures of bureaucratic–capitalist society, the Weberian approach focuses on the structural forces maintaining the dialectic between disenchantment and re-enchantment. Although the sense of disenchantment continues to grow with the steady rationalization of all sectors of modern societies, this process also creates the alternative pathways to re-enchantment. As O'Malley and Mugford (1994, p. 198) put it, the "same [rationalization/disenchantment] process separated out a world of the emotions, and delineated this in such a fashion that it appears (to actors) as the natural 'alternative', the 'other', to be resorted to by those seeking to escape from, to resist or to transcend mundane, modern rationality." Thus, the transcendent nature of edgework "appear[s], ironically, both as necessitated and made possible by the conditions of modernity" (1994, p. 198).

Postmodernist Interpretations of Edgework

While exploring possible readings of the edgework phenomenon within the classical theory tradition, we must remain cognizant of the broader metatheoretical framework to which these theories belong. Whatever the differences between the classical theorists, they share core modernist presuppositions about the direction of social change and the likely negative impact of many of these changes on human beings. In a world of increasing economic exploitation, technological deskilling, rationalization, and individualization and the resulting injuries of alienation, self-estrangement, and disenchantment, the risk experience offers an escape to a sensual universe of emotional intensity and self-determination. Thus, the source of the seductive appeal of edgework can be found in the contrast between the institutional constraints of modern societies and the intense emotions and spontaneity of high-risk situations.

Each of the classical social theorists offered a unique view of key structural principles governing the modernization process, but most accepted that these principles reflected in some way inevitable social differentiation driven by the forces of production. In arguing that consumption, not production, is now driving social and cultural change in contemporary Western societies, "postmodernist" theorists see this classical preoccupation with production as outmoded. As western economies shifted from a manufacturing base to dominance by culture industries, people's very sense of past, present, and future and their notions of self have been radically transformed. Hence, if the connection between the institutionally based experience and edgework is crucial for understanding the latter's appeal to risk takers, then a postmodernist analysis should yield a very different view of edgework activities.

Another focus of postmodern criticism is the classical theorists' faith in the liberating potential of reason. Although the modernist project may be driven by system imperatives that crushed the human spirit, the classical theorists shared in the belief that the force of reason can be employed to free people from such oppression (although Weber did anticipate some of the postmodern skepticism about the progressive potential of reason). In contrast to the modernist's assumptions about the progressive nature of human history and the special role played by the forces of reason in this progress, postmodernists view the very notion of "progress" directed by reason and rationality as the source of one of the most pernicious forms of oppression the modern world has ever known. Inspired by theorists like Michel Foucault, these postmodernist critics see the pursuit of progressive agendas by the agents of reason as leading to a decentralized system of control that profoundly *limits* rather than expands possibilities for human freedom. Armed with rigorously constructed definitions of "normality," "health," "well-being," and the like, knowledge experts impose categorical schemes that define anything outside of narrow ranges of the "normal" as requiring modification, either by human service professionals or by the afflicted actors themselves. Examined from the standpoint of such skepticism about modernist notions of the "normal" and the "progressive," the edgework phenomenon may assume entirely different significance for postmodernists than it does for modernist interpreters.

In light of these postmodernist critiques of modernist social theories, perhaps something may be gained by considering how perspectives associated with the former tradition can explain the increasing attraction to the risk experience in the (post)modern era. However, an important caveat must be issued before undertaking such an analysis: We must appreciate that the term "postmodernist social theory" is a misleading designation in many respects. In spite of recent efforts to identify a distinctive postmodernist tradition of social theorizing (Seidman, 1991), some commentators point to as many differences between theories often associated with the postmodernist "tradition" as similarities between them (Smart, 1993; Best and Kellner, 1991). Consequently, it may make more sense to examine how various themes developed in different strands of postmodernist thought are related to edgework activities. I will begin by examining edgework in the context of the postmodern world dominated by consumer culture.

Edgework, Desire, and the Culture of Simulation

The present focus is anticipated in the Weberian analysis previously discussed because both Campbell and Ritzer have attempted to broaden Weber's framework beyond the concern with rationalization and disenchantment to encompass consumption and re-enchantment as well. Ritzer in particular made an explicit attempt to wed some of Jean Baudrillard's ideas with Marxian and Weberian concepts in his analysis of the "new means of consumption." As noted above, this concept reflects the postmodernist concern with the blurring of boundaries seen as inviolable within the modernist worldview (distinctions between past and present, distant and immediate, the real and the simulated, etc.) under the influence of a consumer culture dominated by sophisticated media and merchandizing industries. For Ritzer, however, the collapse of these distinctions occurs within enchanted spaces created for the purposes of marketing consumer goods, spaces that attract people and their money because they offer an escape from the institutional constraints of modern social life. Hence, this analysis accords with the modernist view of postindustrial societies as alienating, rationalized, bureaucratized systems that deform human nature and compel people to look for avenues of escape in pockets of magical experience created by innovative merchants.

So how would a postmodernist analysis differ from Ritzer's synthetic perspective? A key difference may be that the realities constructed by consumer culture are not seen by postmodernists as governed by a romantic/consumer "ethic" that opposes the rational imperative of the formal system. Rather, in the postmodernist view, the formal system has been largely *transformed* by consumer culture. Consequently, the idea that members of postindustrial society seek to reclaim their humanity by temporarily escaping the system, or could find a destination for such an escape, makes little sense within the postmodernist framework.

Far from seeking to escape the system, the postmodern social actor moves in and out of experiential domains that generate multiple ontologies and create numerous opportunities for identity construction. In the decentered social universe of postmodern culture, there is no "authentic reality" or "true self" to be found, only variations in simulations and spectacles available to consumers for either direct or vicarious participation. The world of work may continue to require disciplined minds and bodies to meet the demands of rationally efficient economic institutions, but this world is a receding horizon in the lived experience of members of postmodern culture. Postmoderns find their most meaningful experiences in the realm of leisure consumption, and they participate in the disciplinary regimens of work only to generate the financial resources needed for deep-level engagement with the world of consumption.

Immersion in this world puts consumers in touch with the dominant social reality of the postmodern period, a reality in which emotions, irrationality, uncertainty, personal development, and mystical experience predominate over the elements of rationality emphasized by modernist theorists. Although the nonrational dimensions of human experience were derided and rejected by the agents of modern social institutions, they have come to occupy a privileged position within the life spaces of postmodernists, who harbor deep suspicion and mistrust of calculating reason and emotionless abstraction (Bauman, 1993, p. 33). In the simulated realities and grand spectacles choreographed by merchandizing and media agents, people find ample opportunity for emotionally charged, magical experiences that expand the range of possible identities and ontologies. Reason may have collapsed in this new social universe, but in the estimation of many postmodernist theorists, we are all the better for it.

Examined from this standpoint, edgework does not allow one to *transcend* the extant social reality of consumer society; the experience merely represents an extension of that reality. As noted in discussing Ritzer's ideas about the new means of consumption, the implosions of time and space that characterize edgework activities are not unique to this domain of human experience. Time and space implosions can also be readily experienced within the cathedrals of consumption and the virtual realities created by the market system. Consequently, in this interpretation, it makes little sense to emphasize the *contrast* between edgework and institutional routines because the nature of experience in these two domains does not differ in any fundamental way. Rather, it would be much more useful to consider edgework as a particular permutation of the structural logic embedded in the postmodern economy and culture.

And what is the character of this new structural logic? Here we can look again to Baudrillard for guidance. As one who has devoted much attention to conceptualizing the shift from production-based systems to a society dominated by consumer culture, Baudrillard is at his best in describing the changes brought about by the consumption revolution. For Baudrillard, the key to understanding this shift is to begin with how the body reproduces itself in socially mediated action. Although Marx sees the body's potential realized through the creative expropriation of material substance to satisfy human needs, Baudrillard looks to consumption practices that stimulate desire as the principle means of corporeal reproduction. In Baudrillard's view, consumer objects function not as responses to human needs but as "a network of floating signifiers that are inexhaustible in their ability to incite desire" (Poster in Baudrillard, 1988a, p. 3). In the consumption of commodities, objects are transformed into signs, and these become, in turn, the primary focus of human desire.

Thus, in contrast to the Marxian problematic employed by the original edgework analysis (Lyng, 1990) which emphasizes the skills acquired and practiced in edgework activities as a response to the de-skilling trends of modern capitalist economies, these activities serve a different purpose in Baudrillard's postmodern world. What makes edgework unique in the postmodern context is its function as a direct conduit to corporeal desire requiring no mediation by signified consumer objects or even socially situated thought (in the sense of Mead's "me"). In generating the pleasurable sensations associated with time and space implosions, a sense of omnipotence, and other intense feelings, edgework externalizes desire in a way similar to the sex act or ravenous food consumption. Indeed, it should come as no surprise that edgeworkers often draw parallels between these kinds of experiences, as revealed in the infamous skydiver maxim "Eat, Fuck, Skydive!" (Lyng and Snow, 1986).

Although edgework is distinctive as a means for achieving an unmediated expression of embodied desire, it nevertheless reveals the same refractory, self-referential character of other forms of corporeal reproduction in the consumer society. Baudrillard captures this latter dimension especially well in his descriptions of various social types he encountered in his travels across *America* (1988b). What he sees in the jogger, the body-builder, the break-dancer, the skateboarder with his walkman, and the intellectual working on his word processor is "the same blank solitude, the same narcissistic refraction" (1988b, 34). But the refraction he observes is cultural rather than psychological in nature:

> This is not narcissism and it is wrong to abuse that term to describe the effect. What develops around the video or stereo culture is not a narcissistic imaginary, but an effect of frantic self-referentiality, a short-circuit which immediately hooks up like with like, and in so doing, emphasizes their surface intensity and deeper meaninglessness (Baudrillard, 1988b, p. 37).

In sharing this self-referential quality, edgeworkers take risks not for purposes of achieving specific goals but only to demonstrate to themselves that they can survive the challenge. By cheating death, they affirm their own existence. As a form of fetishistic performance, edgework is undertaken so that the individual can say, "I did it!" What Baudrillard sees in this slogan is "a new form of advertising activity, of autistic performance, a pure and empty form, ... the joy engendered by a feat that is of no consequence" (1988b, p. 20).

When one occupies a cultural world in which death no longer has meaning, it becomes particularly important that death be postponed as long as possible.

Baudrillard addresses this problem in relation to the "omnipresent cult of the body," which refers to the postmodern preoccupation with preserving the youthful body and avoiding substandard performance of a body moving inexorably towards death. The "body is cherished in the perverse certainty of its uselessness, in the total certainty of its non-resurrection" (Baudrillard, 1988b, 35). These insights are especially applicable to edgework practices. Paradoxically, edgeworkers can be sure of their escape from death only by proving to themselves that they possess the capacity to resist it. Hence they must risk death to reaffirm their ability to escape its icy grip. This paradox is perhaps what edgeworkers reference when they say, "We go to the edge because it makes us feel alive."

Edgework as a form of self-referential, fetishistic performance may be best appreciated by relating it to Baudrillard's notion of the "hyperreality" produced by media-dominated postmodern culture. In the modernist interpretation, edgework is distinctive as a form of "authentic" experience that stands in stark contrast to the "artificial" character of institutional routines (Lyng, 1990, p. 881), whereas in Baudrillard's postmodern world, the real and authentic have given way to "simulations of simulations." The real exists only as something that can be reproduced or represented, but in postmodernity we find only that which has been already reproduced. As Baudrillard puts it, "the mirror phase has given way to the video phase" (1988b, p. 37). Video is both metaphorically and technologically at the center of the new postmodern hyperreality:

> Today, no staging of bodies, no performance can be without its control screen. This is not there to see or reflect those taking part, with the distance and magic of the mirror. No, it is there as an instantaneous, depthless refraction. Video, everywhere, serves only this end: it is a screen of ecstatic refraction. As such, it has nothing of the traditional image or scene, or of traditional contemplation; its goal is *to be hooked up to itself.* Without this circular hook-up, without this brief, instantaneous network that a brain, an object, an event, or a discourse create by being hooked up to themselves, without this perpetual video, nothing has any meaning today (Baudrillard, 1988b, p. 37; emphasis in original).

Perhaps there is no better illustration of this kind of hyperreality of edgework practices than the video-mediated world of BASE-jumpers and the Bridge Day Event (Ferrell et al., 2001). BASE-jumping is an offshoot of sport parachuting in which jumpers leap from the tops of **B**uildings (skyscrapers, etc.), **A**ntennas (radio towers, etc.), **S**pans (bridges, etc.), or **E**arth (cliffs, etc.). Usually an illegal activity, BASE-jumping is legally sanctioned one day each year at the Bridge Day Event in Fayette County, West Virginia. On the third weekend in October every year, about 300 jumpers from around the world show up to leap from the New River Gorge Bridge. As a part of an ongoing study of the complex subculture that has built up around BASE-jumping, the three-person research team of Ferrell, Milovanovic, and Lyng attended the Bridge Day festival for two consecutive years (1997 and 1998) to conduct a "situated ethnography" of this edgework event (see Ferrell et al. 2001, p. 182).

What they discovered was an event and a subculture in which the ever-present video probe functioned as a powerful tool for creating a multilayered hyperreality. At first glance, it would appear that negotiating the practical challenges of jumping off of fixed structures is central to the BASE-jumping enterprise. The challenges include developing the appropriate skills, acquiring and maintaining one's equipment, gaining access to jump sites, and carefully planning one's jumps. However, as much as these activities serve as a focal point for collective exchanges within the BASE-jumping network, an equally important part of their collective activity is devoted to producing, exchanging, and observing video recordings and other visual documentation of their edgework achievements. A leap from a skyscraper or other structure that is not videotaped by the jumper's friends and accomplices is a rare occurrence indeed. In fact, several simultaneous video recordings are usually made from multiple positions and angles to ensure the best material for editing a "final cut" of the jump. BASE-jumpers often wear body-mounted or helmet-mounted video cameras to capture the few seconds of actual free-fall that can be spliced with video recordings from other positions, such as the point of departure and the landing zone. Consonant with Baudrillard's assertion, the ultimate effect of the videotaping of these events is the creation of a "control screen," because jumps are often organized or staged to produce the most compelling video representations of these body performances.

Once created, jump videos become a central focus of subcultural activities. They are shared among members of the BASE-jumping network, watched repeatedly, and critiqued in terms of the jumping skills exhibited, the creativity involved in selecting jump sites, and the videographic techniques employed. Because most BASE-jumps are conducted illegally and therefore must be planned and executed surreptitiously, one could argue that the video representation of these events is a more fundamental component of subcultural interaction than the actual events themselves. Although strategic considerations (avoiding detection, making a quick getaway, etc.) limit the number of people who can be present during the actual jump, there is no limit to the number of people who can observe the video screening of the jump. As representations of edgework moments that are watched, rewound, replayed, studied in stop frames, critiqued, ridiculed, and celebrated by members of the BASE-jumping network, these videos function as devices for expanding or "elongating" the meaning of the jump experience (Ferrell et al., 2001).

Thus, although the ever-present video probe sustains a Baudrillardian hyperreality in virtually all forms of leisure edgework, BASE-jumping may be the most hyperreal edgework enterprise of all. This is certainly the conclusion one is likely to reach in observing the most public form of BASE-jumping, the once-a-year opportunity for legal leaps off the New River Gorge Bridge. Our ethnography of the Bridge Day festivities revealed multiple media loops (Manning, 1998) that intertwine to produce a dense web of reflexive video representation. For example, jumpers gather in the hotel headquarters the night before to watch their own video productions of illegal jumps, whereas local, national, and foreign television and film crews conduct interviews with some of the participants. The next day, these same film crews jockey for position in the "media pit" that has been set up at the bridge launch point by the event organizers. They are rotated through the pit at 15-minute intervals as they gather footage of the single- and multiple-person launches, whereas other crewmembers are dispatched to the landing site below the bridge to get additional footage. At day's end, most jumpers retire to hotel headquarters, where the after-event party gets underway, and where commercial venders of video and photography provide photographic proofs of each person's jump and take purchase orders. In the midst of all this activity, an official video of the entire day's jumping is running on several big-screen TVs for the amusement of a large crowd of onlookers. In a particularly striking example of the video "simulation of simulations," some in the party crowd videotape the official Bridge Day video, while foreign and domestic film crews looking for additional footage of the festivities videotape the videotapers!

As a multilayered hyperreality of mediated practices, BASE-jumping clearly reveals how the distinctions between the actual edgework experience and the mediated representation of it have become blurred within the context of postmodern consumer culture. Because all forms of leisure edgework take place within the same cultural context, they are all affected, to varying degrees, by this encasement in mediated practices and the resulting decentering of the actual experience. Moreover, in this interpretation, participants in edgework endeavors are increasingly motivated by the refractory culture that Baudrillard describes so well. In contrast to modernist preoccupations with the self-actualizing qualities of the experience, the postmodernist view highlights the self-referential nature of the mediated approach to conducting edgework. It suggests that the point of doing edgework is *not* to find one's authentic self; rather, it is observe oneself in a compelling video account of body performance.

BASE-jumping may represent the extreme case of mediated edgework that increasingly characterizes most forms of voluntary risk taking. However, though acknowledging the powerful insights that Baudrillard's approach offers, we must still consider what is missing in this account. Is it true that the ever-present video probe renders the actual edgework experience indistinguishable from the media representation of it? Is the meaning of the actual experience entirely superceded by the elongated meaning emerging from interactions dominated by the video control screen? In responding to these questions, I am inclined to agree with Arthur Frank (1995), who sees a fundamental methodological deficiency in Baudrillard's analysis of body performances. In Frank's view, Baudrillard's problem is his lack of *Verstehen* for the experience of embodiment:

> His eyes see scenes without the rest of him being embodied in these scenes. He is the remote control video probe from another world, seeing but never inquiring, incapable of joining in.... He cannot perceive [marathon running] as, in the full sense of the pun, a human race. He cannot hear runners talking to each other, much less drawing energy from their communal effort.... He is not wrong, only limited. In an urban space which denies embodiment, running a marathon may be 'publicity for existence,' but the action involved is less advertising, as Baudrillard calls it, than resistance. It is a communal ritual of shared embodiment, constituted in moments of shared intimacy of a sort which urban life rarely allows (Frank, 1995, p. 65).

This reaction to Baudrillard reflects the sentiments of a true participant observer.[3] What any participant observer of marathon running and other edge-work activities immediately recognizes as missing in Baudrillard's account are those fundamental aspects of the action that can be known only in its embodied experience. Does the video version of skydiving capture the viscerally and emotionally charged meaning of this experience for those who pursue it? Individuals who have participated in this activity (I among them) would state categorically that it does not. The only form of meaning that Baudrillard allows into his theoretical scheme is the cognitive meaning structures implicated by the Saussurian semiotics that inform his approach. What seems entirely lost to him is the possibility that meaning can assume other forms beyond the world of linguistic and visual signifiers, as suggested by the pragmatist notion of meaning as *behaviorally* based in the response of the "other" to one's actions. (See Mead's famous dictum on the meaning of the act.) Nor does he make room for the possibility of meaning rooted in emotion, a view that is now receiving strong support by recent advances in the neurosciences. (See Franks, 1999.) Thus, it is not surprising that the overriding feature of postmodern reality, for Baudrillard, is its meaning*lessness*. In a social universe in which almost all signs have been subjected to the powerfully transforming effects of endless simulations and other forces of consumer culture, it is undoubtedly true that the stability of cognitively based meaning has been profoundly shaken.

What is most troubling about Baudrillard's approach to bodily performance, however, is the absence in his analysis of any notion of the body as a site of potential resistance to cultural inscription. For Baudrillard, the search for the most powerful simulations of desire takes consumers into a black hole of meaninglessness, inertia, and apathy, where the body ceases to be reflected in consumer objects but rather becomes "a pure screen" for the display of a meaningless mix of dominating signs (Baudrillard, 1983, p. 133). In this hyperreal culture, corporeality vanishes as a form of resistance. However, though Baudrillard' generally disdains any notion of tension between culture and bodies, not all postmodernist theorists demonstrate this same disregard of the objective uncertainty of the body. One theorist often associated with postmodernist thought who maintains a keen awareness of the body's capacity for resistance is Michel Foucault. As I will now demonstrate, Foucault's approach to the body conceptualizes embodied resistance to cultural inscription in terms of what he calls the "limit experience," which bears a strong resemblance to edgework.

Edgework and the Limit-Experience

If Baudrillard's insights are limited by his failure to incorporate *Verstehen* into his method of inquiry, we can look to Foucault for a contrasting method of analysis, one that is deeply rooted in the personal experience of the analyst. Despite the tendency among many early commentators on Foucault's work to link him with poststructuralists, who sought to decenter the human subject and challenge the role of authorship in cultural texts, it became increasingly clear at the end of his life and career that all of his major studies were derived, in large part, from "direct personal experience" (Foucault, 1991, p. 8). With the publication of his book, *The Passion of Michel Foucault*, in 1993, James Miller can be credited with being the first to devote significant attention to the element of *Verstehen* in Foucault's philosophical method. Miller's careful examination of Foucault's corpus and interviews given by him at the end of his life yielded clear evidence of how his deep immersion in the experiences he wrote about (madness, sickness, deviance, illicit sexual practices) shaped his theoretical studies. Miller quotes Foucault as follows:

> 'Each time I have attempted to do theoretical work,' wrote Foucault, 'it has been on the basis of elements from my experience.'… Each of his books, as 'a kind of fragment of an autobiography,' could be approached as a 'field of experience to be studied, mapped out and organized,' precisely by reinserting the previously occluded dimension—of the author putting his 'nature,' and his knowledge to the test of his 'very existence' (1993, p. 31).

Consonant with these statements, Miller finds clear evidence in Foucault's final reflections on his career that "*all* of his work, for better or worse, had grown out of his personal fascination with experience" (1993, p. 31).

Miller's claims about the role of personal experience in Foucault's studies has helped to fuel significant debate among his interpreters about the ultimate goals of his work, the differences between the theoretical agendas of his early and late periods, and related matters. However, Miller's most provocative assertion about the French philosopher's life and work relates to the *kind* of experience that most attracted Foucault, both personally and intellectually. According to Miller, Foucault's personal and intellectual agendas were centered primarily on activities that he referred to as "limit-experiences." In these activities, Foucault deliberately push[ed] his body and mind to the breaking point, hazarding 'a sacrifice, an actual sacrifice of life … a voluntary obliteration.' … Through intoxication, reverie, the Dionysian abandon of the artist, the most punishing of ascetic practices, and an uninhibited exploration of sado-masochistic eroticism, it seemed possible to breach, however briefly, the boundaries separating the consciousness and unconsciousness, reason and unreason, pleasure and pain—and, at the ultimate limit, life and death—thus starkly revealing how distinctions central to the play of true and false and pliable, uncertain, contingent (Miller 1993, p. 30).

As noted at the end of this statement, the pursuit of limit-experiences served a specific theoretic-analytical goal that has been a persistent theme in all of Foucault's work. The "pliable, uncertain, contingent" nature of truth claims dominating in particular historical periods is a problem that Foucault takes up in each of his major studies. Drawing inspiration from the works of Fredrich Nietzsche, Maurice Blanchot, and Georges Bataille, Foucault embraced early on the method of exploring experience in its "negativity" by examining those domains of human existence that resist explanation in terms of rational standards of truth. This accounts for the substantive foci of many of his major books: insanity (*Madness and Civilization*, 1973), sickness (*The Birth of the Clinic*, 1975), crime (*Discipline and Punish*, 1979), and eroticism (*The History of Sexuality*, 1980). Although, on another level, Foucault made an important methodological shift during the completion of these works—the shift from archaeology to genealogy (see Dreyfus and Rabinow, 1982)—he continued throughout his career to focus on "negative" experience as a point of reference for uncovering the hidden dimensions of dominant discourses and institutional regimes. (See Lyng, 2002.) Each of these negative domains was treated as a "limit" to the prevailing order of institutions and discursive practices, as experiences that defy discursive understanding within the dominant discourse system.

And where does edgework fit into Foucault's project? The methodological shift in Foucault's career from archaeology to genealogy was also linked to a change in his approach to "negativity," with his theoretical interest in such negative domains as madness, crime, illness, and the like superceded by his personal experimentation with forms of transgression that strongly resemble edgework. The key to this "radical break" in his project (Rajchman, 1985) can be found in Foucault's turn in his later work to a different view of subjectivity. In his earlier, institutional analyses, his conception of subjectivity is best expressed in terms of his notion of "docile bodies." Although human beings are not capable of acting as unified, conscious selves, they do possess acting bodies (Warfield, 1999). However, their bodies are constituted from discourse systems and related discursive events and, once constituted, are left with no remainder. As Allan Stoekl (1992, pp. 190–191) notes, Foucault in the early stages of his career was "still very much operating in the Blanchotian-Bataillean tradition, apparently privileg[ing] language above all else, seeing everything—madness, sexuality, the various natural and human sciences—as nothing more than language (or "'discourse'")."

In his later work, however, the privileging of language gives way to an emphasis on the nondiscursive realm or the realm of "practices." Existing outside of language, the nondiscursive belongs to the "lived body," which is certainly shaped by disciplinary technologies but is not completely reducible to them. Thus, though Foucault holds in his early work "that 'everything is language' and [he] sees subjectivity and its relation to 'unthought' as essentially a problem (and illusion) within language, ... the later [work] recognizes the 'nondiscursive' realm, examin[ing] the specific political and social production of the fiction of subjectivity-objectivity" (Stoekl, 1992, p. 191). At issue here, of course, is the problem of agency and the possibility of establishing a standpoint from which to critically reflect on the structuring of experience by power-knowledge. For Foucault, the quest for critical knowledge of experience must begin with explorations of the lived body. As Dreyfus and Rabinow put it,

> If the lived body is more than the result of the disciplinary technologies that have been brought to bear upon it, it would perhaps provide a position from which to criticize these practices, and maybe even a way to account for the tendency towards rationalization and the tendency of this tendency to hide itself (1982, p. 167).

Thus, in his later work, Foucault proposes a genealogy of truth based on the body, but one that relies on the limit-experience as a vehicle for exploring the possibilities of the body. This project, which he undertook himself and encouraged others to embrace, involved experiments in self-creation through the process of transgressing limits. Consequently, where the subject had been only a linguistic construction in his earlier writings, he now saw subjectivity as a pragmatic goal to be attained as part of an "ethic of the self," a "method of fashioning oneself and investigating knowledge" (Warfield, 1999, p. 3). As Foucault expresses it,

> The critical ontology of ourselves has to be considered ... [as] a philosophical life in which the critique of what we are is at one and the same time the historical analysis of the limits that are imposed on us and an experiment with the possibility of going beyond them (quoted in Warfield, 1999, p. 3).

Although much has been written about Foucault's scholarship, in the form of exegeses and interpretations of a body of work that is both highly original and extremely challenging, it is not my goal here to contribute to the cottage industry of Foucauldian interpretation that has emerged in the decades since his death. However, having reviewed some of the more recent studies of the role of the limit-experience in his intellectual and personal life, I do want to suggest that we may find an implicit explanation of edgework practices within this branch of Foucauldian scholarship.

This would appear to some, perhaps, as a bit of a stretch, considering that the substantive focus of Foucault and his interpreters has been almost entirely on weighty philosophical issues of ontology, epistemology, ethics, and politics. After all, Foucault's references to the limit-experience in his published work and interviews relate primarily to its use as an analytical tool. Although Foucault's deep personal involvement in exploring limits through sado-masochistic sexual practices, along with his death from AIDS, has had a lurid appeal for many readers, it is clear that Foucault viewed his experimentation with limit-experiences as necessary for the realization of his intellectual goals as a philosopher. However, with an appreciation for the spirit of reflexivity that invigorates all of Foucault's work, I believe that he would regard his philosophical quest as a reaction shared by many, intellectuals and laypersons alike, who feel the impact of powerful cultural forces acting on them in the modern world.

To identify these cultural forces, we can look to those strands of Foucauldian thought that have received the greatest attention from social theorists. In an important modification and extension of the Weberian rationalization thesis (Dreyfus and Rabinow, 1982, p. 166), Foucault's career-long project was to trace the movement of reason in the modern world through the growth of the human sciences and their disciplinary technologies. By making the relationship between power and knowledge his primary point of focus, he goes well beyond Weber's iron cage notion to develop a "micro-politics of power" (Foucault, 1979). Foucault sees the relationship between power and knowledge as reciprocal in nature; knowledge is gained through the possession of power, but knowledge generates power by constituting subjectivity and morally regulating people in the process. Moreover, people are complicit in their own domination. As they internalize definitions of "normality," "health," and "well-being" derived from various branches of the human sciences, they align their subjectivities with the demands of existing institutional imperatives and delimit the possibilities for self-creation.

In describing this "disciplinary society," Foucault offers a vision of human domination that is much more disturbing than anything emerging out of modernist social theory. Moving beyond the worst Weberian nightmare, Foucault sees domination imposed through a system of micropowers that operates more deeply and efficiently than any previous system of overarching power. At the critical point in the modernist project when people became the object of knowledge, the range of human variability in thought and action became restricted to an unprecedented degree. This new system was "more regular, more effective, more constant, and more detailed in its effects" (Foucault, 1979, p. 80), undermining possibilities for the kind of collective unrest incited by the overtly coercive social control systems of the past.

However, at the same time that the technologies of surveillance and control have expanded and become more efficient, avenues of resistance to this panoptic system can still be found. This brings us back to the limit-experience and edgework.

It is beyond the scope of the present study to provide a comprehensive explanation of Foucault's rather complex theory of resistance. However, it is clear that the lynchpin of his approach to resistance is the practice of exploring limits, undertaken as personal commitment to freedom. The limit experience is, itself, an exercise in power but one that is "productive." As Warfield (1999, p. 2) puts it, "the subject is understood in relation to discourse and to oneself—the individual can create 'coercive, dominative,' productive relations with itself 'via the mediation of power-knowledge structures.'" Moreover, the variability of power-knowledge structures means that the pursuit of limit-experiences must be undertaken as an individual-level project:

> [T]he existence of limits cannot be said to be constant or identical across historical and social cleavages. Limits shift and decline, reappear and intensify in all manner of manifestations such that it is likely that each specific subject position will feature its own idiosyncratic set of limits. It is for this reason that ... that work with limits must be conducted at the level of the individual ... (Duff, 1999, p. 3).

As one delves deeper into the meanings assigned to the limit-experience by Foucault and his interpreters, it becomes clear that their conception does not refer to a practice that functions only as a philosopher's tool. In a poststructuralist extension of the Weberian analysis presented earlier, the exploration of limits or the "edges" between sanity and insanity, consciousness and unconsciousness, or life and death provides a way to break free of the rigidified subjective categories created by disciplinary technologies that circumscribe almost every aspect of human experience. This project is undertaken in an effort to discover new possibilities of embodied existence. If Foucault himself found this kind of experience to be not only analytically useful but also seductively appealing—and there is ample evidence to indicate that he did—then it is just as likely that *any* person confronting the constraints imposed by the disciplinary society could be potentially seduced by such an experience. As fully embodied practices, edgework or limit- experiences allow the individual to put his or her powers to work in discovering new ways of being. Because bodies can never be completely inscribed by power-knowledge arrangements, transgressing limits brings out corporeal potentials that have remained unrealized by existing disciplinary technologies. Thus, to explore limits or edges in this way is to take up "an ethic of the self"—a project of self-creation that draws on the indeterminacy of the body to identify new possibilities of being and doing.

In connecting the limit-experience and edgework, I want to highlight both commonalities and differences that exist between these two concepts and acknowledge that they may refer to experiences that are similar but not identical. In regard to commonalities, I would first point out that much of the empirical data collected on the edgework experience accords with Foucault's description of limit-experiences. For instance, it is clear that the notion of an "edge" or "boundary" condition is central to both conceptualizations. Miller's description of Foucault's limit-experiences, quoted above, refers to "boundaries separating the consciousness and unconsciousness, reason and unreason, pleasure and pain—and, at the ultimate limit, life and death" as the specific experiential domains that attracted Foucault. These are unquestionably the type of boundary conditions involved in edgework (Lyng, 1990, p. 857). On another level, Foucault's claim that limit-experiences involve the use of power as a response to the dominating affects of power-knowledge structures is borne out in edgeworker's' descriptions of the empowering consequences of their experiences. A Foucauldian explanation of the empowering character of edgework would direct attention to the specific power dynamics involved:

> The ideal power relationship, for Foucault, is one of agonism: a concept akin to a wrestling match whereby there exists strategic and capricious power relations. Foucault explains that if we conceive of power relations as "strategic games" of reciprocal interactions, we can nourish our active capabilities....[A]gonism is the most productive and liberating practice we can perform ... and relations of agonism ensure our ability to transgress limits and to resist congealed subjectivities (Warfield, 1999, p. 3).

In this interpretation, edgework is empowering because it involves the deployment of individual power against power-knowledge in a quest to discover what the body can do and be. Thus, the experience is not one of merely transcending the routines of institutional existence (as argued in the original analysis of edgework [Lyng, 1990]), but overcoming the very practice of subjectification and identity. As Foucault (1982 [in Dreyfus and Rabinow, 1982]) argues, what is employed in this negotiation of boundaries is the power to refuse individuality altogether and, in Martin Jay's words, "recapture the Dionysian oneness prior to individuation and alienation" (1998, p. 66).

Expanding on this general theme, it could be argued that most of the "edgework sensations" identified by previous empirical studies lend support to Foucault's conception of the limit-experience as a method for annihilating all the categories of existing power-knowledge arrangements, not only "congealed subjectivities" but categories of perception and experience more generally. Thus, alterations in the perception of time and space, ineffability, a sense of "flow," and similar sensations would emerge in the wake of an embodied encounter with indeterminate circumstances that cannot be ordered in terms of existing discursive categories. To quote Martin Jay again, "limit-experience means that there is no uncrossable boundary between subject and object, ego and alter, self and world" (1998, p. 74). Categorical distinctions that are taken as given in reality thus dissolve in the edgework experience, as new perceptual possibilities arise in the process of exploring boundaries. In addition, it is possible within the Foucauldian framework to redefine the sensations of "self-determination" or "self-actualization" reported by edgeworkers. Although these terms seem to refer to the amplification of a preexisting self, which would be at odds with Foucault's entire approach to subjectivity, they may actually signify the very process of self-creation that lies at the heart of his conception of the limit-experience. Thus, the experience of self-actualization indicates that edgework is, in its essence, "work carried out on ourselves by ourselves as free beings" (Foucault, 1984, p. 47).

On the basis on these considerations, we see that Foucault's notion of the limit-experience bears a strong resemblance to the idea of edgework. However, an examination of the recent work on the limit-experience also reveals important divergences between these two concepts. One key difference relates to how participants in edgework and limit-experience approach boundaries or limits in their respective projects. Because the edge explored by participants in high-risk sports and occupations is most often the line separating life and death, the principle goal in these endeavors is to get as close as possible to this line without actually crossing it. As noted in earlier studies, one of the defining features of these practices is a deep-seated preoccupation among edgeworkers with the issue of *control*, manifested most often as a desire to "control the seemingly uncontrollable" (Lyng, 1990, p. 872). Indeed, it could be said that the satisfaction edgeworkers derive from exercising personal control over chaotic circumstances may reflect their status as true "control freaks," although I have suggested that this tendency can be fully understood only in reference to the *lack* of control that people experience in their institutional lives. In any case, it is clear that the primary challenge in edgework is to use one's skills to approach, but not cross, the line between life and death, sanity and insanity, consciousness and unconsciousness, and similar limits.

By contrast, descriptions of limit-experience offered by Foucault and his interpreters indicate that this project is concerned primarily with movement *across* boundaries. As with edgework, this orientation towards boundaries reflects the kind of limits typically explored in the limit-experience. Although risking one's life and physical well-being are included among the pursuits conceptualized as limit-experiences (as indicated in Foucault's biography), the principal focus of these experiments in self-creation are normative boundaries—the lines separating normal and deviant, licit and illicit with regard to mental health, sexual orientation, sexual practices, and the like. Consequently, the goal of the limit attitude is not to *transcend* boundaries, in the sense of controlling the seemingly uncontrollable (or, at least, achieving the illusion of having done so), but rather to *transgress* boundaries. As Warfield points out, transgression does not imply transcendence:

> Foucault's discussion of transgression should not be understood as an idea of transcendence. To [transcend] limits in this sense would mean a final overcoming of these limits, and such a condition would no longer have possibilities for movement. Foucault does not, therefore, view transgression as 'a victory over limits' (1999, p. 3).

Warfield finds further elaboration of this point in Foucault's statement that

> "the limit and transgression depend on each other for whatever density of being they possess. [Transgression is an incessant, momentary transmutation that] crosses and recrosses a line which closes up behind it in a wave of extremely short duration" (Foucault, 1977, p. 34).

Boundary negotiation of this sort is not possible when one is conducting life-threatening forms of edgework because once you cross *this* line, you cannot return. However, in the case of pure transgression, crossing and recrossing boundaries is not only possible but also desirable as a strategy for self-creation.

It appears, then, that the essential difference between the concepts of limit-experience and edgework can be traced to the different kinds of limits that can be explored by embodied social actors. The line separating life and death is an "absolute" limit set by the physio-organic limitations of living things. The line separating normative and non-normative practices is a permeable limit set by the forms of power-knowledge that are never absolute but are always being assembled and disassembled in any historical period. Thus, Foucault's decision to emphasize transgression rather than death-defying edgework (although his biography does reveal his interest in the latter) reflects his belief that limits are conditions of possibility that can be explored only by engaging in experiments of self-creation. That is, "the limits of our knowledge are not to be simply understood as obstacles to better forms of knowledge, but conditions of possibility in gaining knowledge" of our corporeal potentials (Warfield, 1999, p. 3). Commitment to limit-experience, therefore, is rooted in the understanding that discourse is both oppressive and productive, but productive *only* through the transgression of limits.

The principal conclusion to be drawn from this discussion is that edgework and limit-experience are not synonymous concepts but are closely related ideas that may be distinguished either in terms of different degrees of generality or different substantive foci. Thus, if edgework is taken as the more general concept, referring to various forms of boundary negotiation ranging from "close encounters" to actually "crossing the line," then limit-experience would designate transgressions involving the crossing and recrossing of normative boundaries—what might be called "elicit edgework." Alternatively, if edgework is applied only to those forms of boundary negotiation where the consequence of failure is death or serious injury, then limit-experience would refer to nonlethal boundary negotiation in which one confronts the limits imposed by power-knowledge arrangements. However one chooses to connect these two ideas, establishing this link allows us to take advantage of a powerful perspective on the edgework practices of postmodern social actors.

Foucault's poststructuralist perspective thus provides an interpretation of edgework practices as "acts of liberation" in the face of the micro-politics of power operating in the modern world. Viewed in this way, it should come as little surprise that participation in edgework has steadily increased in the post-war period. As the boundaries of "normality" become increasingly delimited by the continued growth of the human sciences and popular discourses of improvement, the need for dramatic action to liberate the self becomes ever more urgent. Playing with boundaries in acts of transgression and transcendence, exploiting limits, and crowding edges may be the sole remaining form of resistance and one of the few possibilities for human agency that can be found in the disciplinary society. Foucault's conception of agency in this interpretation is particularly important because it pulls edgework from the margins of sociological concern and places it at the center of theoretical discourse in this field. We can now see agency as not just a theoretical issue to be debated but as a practical accomplishment, undertaken as part of an ethical/political agenda that incorporates edgework as its principal methodological tool. Few perspectives on edgework are as compelling as the Foucauldian perspective in indicating the central sociological and philosophical significance of this form of embodied social practice.

As I have indicated here, multiple interpretations of the edgework phenomenon are possible, reflecting in part the ongoing debate among social theorists about what constitutes the central structural imperatives of (post)modern society. Although the meaning of edgework varies in each of these interpretations, there can be little doubt about the visceral appeal that this practice acquires in the context of (post)modernity. In the pages that follow, the reader will find a diverse mix of empirical and theoretical studies that document and attempt to explain this phenomenon and, in doing so, speak to the growing importance of edgework as a key signifier of our age.

Notes

1. The meaning of the term "hyperreality," as used here, should not be equated with the meaning of this term in Jean Baudrillard's work. See Lyng, 1990, p. 861.

2. The stock fraud cases of Michael Milkin and Ivan Boesky are good illustrations from the 1980s. At this writing, corporate scandals associated with the Enron and Worldcom cases have yet to be completely resolved legally.

3. I have no direct knowledge that Frank's conclusions reflect his use of participant observation as a method of data collection.

References

Beck, U. *The Risk Society*. London: Sage, 1992.

Best, S., and Kellner, D. *Postmodern Theory: Critical Interrogations*. New York: Guilford Press, 1991.

Batuik, M. E., and Sacks, H. L. "George Herbert Mead and Karl Marx: Exploring Consciousness and Community." *Symbolic Interaction* 4(2) (1981): 207–223.

Baudrillard, J. "The Ecstasy of Communication" in *The Anti-Aesthetic: Essays on Postmodern Culture*, edited by H. Foster. Port Townsend, WA: Bay Press, 1983.

———. *Selected Writings*, edited by M. Poster. Stanford, CA: Stanford University Press, 1988 [a].

———. *America*. Translated by C. Turner. London: Verso, 1988 [b].

Bauman, Z. *Postmodern Ethics*. Oxford: Basil Blackwell, 1993.

Blake, J. A. "Self and Society in Mead and Marx." *Cornell Journal of Social Relations* 11(2) (1976): 129–138.

Campbell, C. *The Romantic Ethic and the Spirit of Modern Consumerism*. Oxford: Blackwell, 1987.

Capote, T. *In Cold Blood; A True Account of a Multiple Murder and Its Consequences*. New York: Random House, 1966.

Dreyfus, H. L., and Rabinow, P. *Michel Foucault: Beyond Structuralism and Hermeneutics*. Chicago: University of Chicago Press, 1982.

Duff, C. "Stepping through the Eye of Power: Foucault, Limits and the Construction of Masculinity." 1999. Available at www.qut.edu.au/edu/cpol/foucault/duff.html

Farley, F. "The Type T personality." In *Self-Regulatory Behavior and Risk Taking: Causes and Consequences*, edited by L.P. Lipsett and L.L Mitnick. Norwood, NJ: Ablex Publishers, 1991.

Ferrell, J., Milovanovic, D., and Lyng, S. "Edgework, Media Practices, and the Elongation of Meaning." *Theoretical Criminology* 5(2) (2001): 177–202.

Foucault, M. *Madness and Civilization: A History of Insanity in the Age of Reason*. Translated by R. Howard. New York: Vintage/Random House, 1973.

———. *The Birth of the Clinic: An Archaeology of Medical Perception*. Translated by A. M. Sheridan Smith. New York: Vintage/Random House, 1975.

———. *Language, Counter-Memory, Practice: Selected Essays and Interviews*. Translated by D. Bouchard and S. Simon, edited by D. Bouchard. Ithaca, NY: Cornell University Press, 1977.

———. *Discipline and Punish: The Birth of the Prison*. Translated by A. Sheridan. New York: Vintage/Random House, 1979.

———. *The History of Sexuality. Volume 1: An Introduction*. Translated by R. Hurley. New York: Vintage/Random House, 1980.

———. "How an 'Experience-Book' is Born" in *Remarks on Marx: Conversations with Duccio Trombadori*, translated by R. J. Goldstein and J. Cascaito, edited by J. Fleming and S. Lotringer. New York: Semiotext(e) 1991.

Frank, A. W. "For a Sociology of the Body: An Analytical Review." In *The Body: Social Process and Cultural Theory*, edited by M. Featherstone, M. Hepworth, and B. S. Turner. London: Sage, 1995: 36–102.

Franks, D. D. "Some Convergences and Divergences between Neuroscience and Symbolic Interaction." In *Mind, Brain, and Society: Toward a Neurosociology of Emotion*, edited by D. D. Franks and T. S. Smith. Stamford, CT: JAI Press, 1999: 157–182.

Giddens, A. *Runaway World*. New York: Routledge, 2000.

Goff, T. W. *Marx and Mead: Contributions to a Sociology of Knowledge*. London: Routledge and Kegan Paul, 1980.

Goffman, E. "Where the Action Is." In *Interaction Ritual: Essays on Face-to-Face Behavior*, edited by E. Goffman. Garden City, NY: Doubleday, 1967: 149–270.

Hebdige, D. *Subculture: The Meaning of Style*. London: Methuen, 1979.

Heimer, C. A. "Social Structure, Psychology and the Estimation of Risk" *Annual Review of Sociology* 14 (1988): 491–519.

Hennis, W. *Max Weber: Essays in Reconstruction*. London: Allen and Unwin, 1988.

Holyfield, L. "Generating Excitement: Experienced Emotion in Commercial Leisure." In *Social Perspectives on Emotion*, Vol. 4, edited by R. J. Erickson and B. Cuthbertson-Johnson. Greenwich, CT: JAI Press, 1997.

Jay, M. *Cultural Semantics: Keywords of Our Time*. Amherst, MA: University of Massachusetts Press, 1998.

Katz, J. *The Seductions of Crime: Moral and Sensual Attractions in Doing Evil*. New York: Basic Books, 1988.

Klausner, S. Z. "The Intermingling of Pain and Pleasure: The Stress Seeking Personality in Its Social Context." In *Why Men Take Chances*, edited by S. M. Klausner. Garden City, NY: Anchor, 1968: 137–168.

Lyng, S. "Edgework: A Social Psychological Analysis of Voluntary Risk Taking." *American Journal of Sociology* 95(4) (1990): 851–886.

———. "Disfunctional Risk Taking: Criminal Behavior as Edgework." In *Adolescent Risk Taking*, edited by N. Bell and R. Bell. London: Sage, 1993: 107–130.

———. "Gideon Sjoberg and the Countersystem Method." In *Studies in Symbolic Interaction*, edited by. N. K. Denzin. New York: JAI Press, 2002: 91–107.

Lyng, S., and Snow, D. "Vocabularies of Motive and High-Risk Behavior: The Case of Skydiving." In *Advances in Group Process*, Vol. 3, edited by E. J. Lawler. Greenwich, CT: JAI Press, 1986: 157–179.

Manning, P. "Media Loops." In *Popular Culture, Crime, and Justice*, edited by F. Bailey and D. Hale. Belmont, CA: West/Wadsworth, 1998: 25–39.

Miller, J. *The Passion of Michel Foucault*. New York: Simon and Schuster, 1993.

Mitchell, R. G., Jr. *Mountain Experience: The Psychology and Sociology of Adventure*. Chicago: University of Chicago Press, 1983.

O'Malley, P., and Mugford, S. "Crime, Excitement, and Modernity." In *Varieties of Criminology*, edited by G. Barak. Westport, CT: Praeger, 1994: 189–211.

Perrow, C. *Normal Accidents: Living with High-Risk Technologies*. Princeton, NJ: Princeton University Press, 1999.

Peters, T. J. *Thriving on Chaos: Handbook for a Management Revolution*. New York: Knopf, 1987.

Rajchman, J. *Michel Foucault and the Freedom of Philosophy*. New York: Columbia University Press, 1985.

Ritzer, G. *Enchanting A Disenchanted World: Revolutionizing the Means of Consumption*. Thousand Oaks, CA: Pine Forge Press, 1999.

Schwalbe, M. L. *The Psychosocial Consequences of Natural and Alienated Labor*. Albany, NY: State University of New York Press, 1986.

Seidman, S. "The End of Sociological Theory: The Postmodern Hope." *Sociological Theory* 9(2) (1991): 131–146.

Short, J. "The Social Fabric at Risk: Toward the Social Transformation of Risk Analysis." *American Sociological Review* 49 (1984): 711–725.

Smart, B. *Postmodernity*. London: Routledge, 1993.

Stoekl, A. *Agonies of the Intellectual: Commitment, Subjectivity, and the Performative in the Twentieth-Century French Tradition*. Lincoln, NE: University of Nebraska Press, 1992.

Thompson, H. S. *Hell's Angels: A Strange and Terrible Saga*. New York: Ballantine, 1966.

———. *Fear and Loathing in Las Vegas: A Savage Journey to the Heart of the American Dream*. New York: Warner, 1971.

Warfield, R. "Considering an Exercise of Self and Justice in the Later Foucault." *The Carleton University Student Journal of Philosophy* 18(1) (1999).

Willis, P. *Learning to Labor*. New York: Columbia University Press, 1977.

Weber, M. *The Protestant Ethic and the Spirit of Capitalism*. Translated by T. Parsons. New York: Charles Scribner's Sons, 1958.

Wolfe, T. 1973. *The New Journalism*. New York: Harper and Row, 1973.

Zucherman, M., E.A. Kolin, L. Price, and I. Zoob. "Development of a Sensation-Seeking Scale." *Journal of Consulting and Clinical Psychology* 28 (1964): 477–82.

2

Edgework: A Subjective and Structural Model of Negotiating Boundaries

DRAGAN MILOVANOVIC

CONTENTS

Introduction

Literature and research on edgework experiences has promised to illuminate not only a neglected area of study (experiences of those who confront various "edges" and "boundaries") but also to provide insights on the relation of the subject to structural factors. To a considerable degree, we all engage in edgework at some time. What varies is the intensity, duration, manner, and form. This chapter will build on some key earlier writings in developing a more integrated approach in understanding edgework experiences. Implicitly, it will criticize much of modernist analysis in its privileging the rational, logical component of the Cartesian dualism (mind, body). Deprivileged in modernist analysis is the more sensual, visceral, adrenaline rushes, excitement, and non-materialistic factors in confronting boundaries. Postmodern analysis attempts to resurrect the monistic and nomadic subject. Accordingly, this chapter will draw from topological and Lacanian theory, chaos theory, constitutive theory, and the works of Deleuze and Guattari on the "body without organs" in integrating structural and subjective factors behind edgework experiences. Its focus is more speculative; the goal is to push the scholarly investigation into a more holistic understanding of subjectivity in history and political economy. Much of what follows is an exercise in resituating discussion within the discourse of postmodern analysis.

We first provide an overview of theoretical developments. Second, we provide a five-dimensional state space within which edgework experiences may be provisionally located, and a typology of forms of edgework experiences. Third, we address topological models of interactions of the five dimensions. Fourth, and finally, we turn to the question of a constitutive account of subjects and structures.

Theoretical Developments

There have been several theorists who have contributed the primary material to an understanding of edgework experiences. David Matza, in *Becoming Deviant* (1969), building on Becker's (1963) classic study on becoming a marijuana user, explained how the subject confronts the "invitational edge" to deviance. He indicated the processes by which the subject is "pacified," becoming an object, and the subject of what the conditions suggest; in other words, a pacified subject is one that aligns itself with the dictates of circumstance. He explained how a "leap" is necessary to enter the invitational edge and how one shifts from the "outside" to the "inside" of some deviant activity. "Ban"—society's various norms, taboos and laws—while "bedeviling" the subject and providing a stamp of who they are, is also the basis of a conversion whereby the subject becomes cast into a particular type of deviant.

Jack Katz (1988), in *Seductions of Crime*, builds on Matza and indicates the seductive qualities of engaging in deviance. He argues for the "foreground factors" (as opposed to "background factors") to crime—the moral, sensual, and emotional. In his explanation of the "badass," "street elites," and "righteous slaughterer," it is escalating humiliation that leads to a state of "moral transcendence" whereby momentarily the subject becomes object, driven by a morality that seemingly provides an understandable explanation for his act. For righteous slaughter, this humiliation leads to rage, the very state in which the subject acts out in a violent episode.

Similarly, for the petty thief, shoplifter, or vandal doing sneaky thrills, it is the possible humiliation of being discovered that becomes a seductive force in challenging the rationally constructed world of legitimacy. The mundane everyday world provides the boundaries and edges that are approached. And it is the very approach to the edge that provides a heightened state of excitement and adrenaline rush. The thrill is in being able to come as close as possible to the edge without detection or apprehension, and the very avoidance of possible humiliation. Thus for Katz, some cross over the edge into chaos (righteous slaughter), while others attempt only to approach it as close as possible. For both, however, the edge, the boundary, is seductive.

Stephen Lyng (1990), a skydiver and skydive jump-plane pilot, was to follow with his insightful analysis of skydivers. They use the occasion of approaching the edge in demonstrating their abilities in extraordinarily demanding conditions where serious injury or death awaits even a slight hesitation or miscalculation. Lyng's edgeworker uses the occasion of approaching the edge to induce altered states where adrenaline rush is of the highest order, where high skills become operative to offset impending disaster. Unlike Katz's righteous slaughterer, who crosses the boundaries into a chaotic state, Lyng's edgeworker remains in control all the way. For Lyng, to enter too far into the boundary region, or to go over it, will likely produce "brainlock" and assured serious injury or death. The seductive quality is in the extreme rush experienced during the event and, subsequent to it, in the reflections on the accomplishments that have taken place under extreme conditions.

O'Malley and Mugford (1994) have provided the first thrust for a truly integrated approach in explaining edgework experiences. They suggest that we must look to history and current political economy in understanding the structural factors that provide the medium within which edgework experience can be understood. They draw from Campbell's (1983; 1987) study of Romanticists, who privileged the body over the rational. The mind–body dualism inherited from the Enlightenment all too often privileged the mind and the rational, reasoned, and orderly world. For the Romanticists, the emotional component was neglected. Thus personal expression, the cultivation of the emotional for self-realization, stood in direct opposition to the rational subject demanded by the emerging capitalist era. O'Malley and Mugford also draw from Elias's (1982) historical analysis of the "civilizing" process of modernity. It was during these times that modern man created various external and internal constraints to emotional expression.

For O'Malley and Mugford, the rise of capitalism privileged the rational while inducing the commercialization of human feelings. The modernist world was one where clock time, commodification, and the hyperreal replaced genuine emotional expression. And it is to these that the edgeworker reacts. Seductions arise as a response to the various boundaries and edges set up by society in historical and political economic conditions.

O'Malley and Mugford's call for a more genuine understanding of edge-workers pointed to a "phenomenology of pleasure."

Finally, Ferrell, Milovanovic, and Lyng (2001) provided a case study of edgeworkers in context. They studied basejumpers at an annual legal event held at Fayetteville, West Virginia, called "Bridgeday." At that time, hundreds of basejumpers from all over the world congregated to participate in the one-day event. Ferrell et al. studied being *in* the event. They noted the extensive use of technology (video equipment, chest- and helmet-mounted cameras, etc.), which contributed to the very definition of the activity itself. The social construction entailed coproduction. The basejumpers' constructions interacted with the journalistic accounts, which in turn interacted with the various video accounts and discussions, reflections, and critiques. The meaning of BASE-jumping at Bridgeday, therefore, could be best explained by a more "constitutive" approach indicating coproduction. Nomination—providing symbolic accounts of "what happened"—was a result of various attendees, reporters, participants, investigators, and TV representatives. Through various feedback "loopings," relatively stable symbolically constructed meanings emerged.

There have been several other studies that have focused on the excitement dimension of deviant activity. Each has implicitly criticized modernist understandings of the etiology of deviant behavior. These authors, however, only cursorily provided an alternative and explicit account of an underlying theoretical model. Similarly, the earlier-mentioned groundbreaking studies, while each in turn provides critical contributions to understanding edgework experiences, do not provide an explicit, comprehensive, and holistic framework in understanding edgeworkers, one that combines history, political economy, and an account of subjectivity. To this we now turn.

Typologically and Topologically Speaking

Building on the groundbreaking work of theorists mentioned in the previous section, we would like to offer a typology of edgework experiences that incorporates five factors. Each can be depicted with a boundary region. Then we will draw from topology theory (Ragland and Milovanovic, 2004), chaos theory (Milovanovic, 1997), and constitutive theory (Henry and Milovanovic, 1996) in mapping the various dynamics. In the final section we will turn to Deleuze and Guattari (1987) to show the relevance of their notion of the "body without organs" and how structure and agency interact in explaining edgeworkers. But ultimately, it is to Jacques Lacan (1977) that we turn for an understanding of how these dynamic forces are brought into stasis.

Typology of Edgeworker Forms

Five intersecting dimensions can be posited as necessary conditions in explaining edgeworkers (see Figure 2.1a). A provisional, one-dimensional typology of edgework experiences can also be presented (see Figure 2.1b). Situating edgeworkers along the five dimensions provides us a context for their activity.

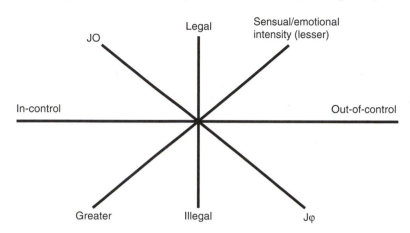

Fig. 2.1a State space of edgework experiences: Topological portrayal

First, socioeconomic structure and historical contingencies provide the background relevancies for edgeworkers. O'Malley and Mugford (1994) have provided valuable insights as to the necessity of situating edgework experiences. Present-day "hackers," for example, have only recently arrived with the computer revolution. Adrenaline Rush TV programming, reality TV programming, video gaming, and various workplace edgework all appear with technological advancements. And opportunities to commit specific forms of edgework are often structurally specific. There are differential life chances to engage in various forms of edgework. O'Malley and Mugford also suggest the importance of a historical understanding of which characteristics of being human are privileged over time. He shows that the "modern self" of the postenlightenment era privileges order, reason, rationality, and the mind. The Romanticists of the nineteenth century, however, were more interested in emotions, disorder, and the body. Thus, in the modern era, the grounds for possible expression of the emotional become more relegated to edgework type of experiences. Reflecting on Katz's stipulation that some calling ("moral transcendence") must be the basis for extreme display of emotions, O'Malley and Mugford say, "only in a society where there exist effective barriers to spontaneous expression of emotional extremes will a process of moral self-transcendence be called for" (1994, p. 199).

In-Control						Out-of-Control
Packaged edgework	Workplace edgework	Extreme sports	Sneaky thrills	Badass	Righteous slaughter	Transcendental experiences

Fig. 2.1b Typology of edgework experiences

Second, is the legal/illegal dimension. This incorporates formal definitions of crime (Henry and Lanier, 2001). Only with private property and laws against theft could we then talk about "sneaky thrills" in the form of shoplifting for excitement. Jeff Ferrell's (1996) graffiti writer and secretive basejumpers find themselves engaging in both the legal and illegal world in pursuing their activities; perhaps one of the sources of excitement is in fact to be able to overcome this added obstacle to their expressive activity. More recent Bridgeday events have had many voices expressing the call for "legalizing" their sport, perhaps not fully anticipating the regulations that would surely come.

Third, lesser and greater emotional intensity is a dimension that incorporates a feeling state—a visceral, sensual continuum. Reading detective fiction, a form of intellectual edgework, may provide excitement as Young (1996) argues, but arguably, it has a low degree of emotional intensity when compared with a police officer in hot foot-pursuit of a suspect, a basejumper leaping off a building in the middle of a city, or a hangglider pilot doing "loops."

Fourth is the dimension of in- and out-of-control. We have already seen with Katz that the "righteous slaughterer" goes over the edge, crosses a boundary, loses control, and acts out a violent resolution to his moral dilemma. On the other hand, we have seen that with Lyng's skydiver, it is being in control that is of a premium as one approaches the edge; going beyond is a sure ticket to serious injury or death.

Fifth, and finally, is the dimension dealing with what Jacque Lacan (1977) referred to as *jouissance*. Or as Lacan, punning, would say, *j'ouir sens* (I hear enjoy sense). This depicts the subject's capacity to make sense of her/his activity. Jϕ stands for phallic *jouissance*. It appears at the confluence of the symbolic (the sphere of discourse, prohibitions, and the unconscious) and real orders (the sphere of lived experience and primordial sense data). In a phallocentric symbolic order that privileges the male's voice (the basis of sexist practices), *jouissance* has an upper limit of a male form. That is, whomever situates her/himself in the role (discursive subject-position) of the man assures him/herself of potentially attaining phallic *jouissance*. Situating oneself in the female discursive subject position, following Lacan, means not being able to attain full *jouissance*. One remains *pas-toute* (not all), incomplete. However, Lacan also mentions another form of *jouissance*, the *jouissance* of the body, JO. It appears at the confluence of the imaginary (the sphere of images, illusions, gestalts, stereotypes) and Lacan's real order. This form of *jouissance* is inexpressible in a male-dominated symbolic order. To return to our edgeworker, much of edgework experiences are ineffable: confronted with being immersed in the Real, it is only the momentary imaginary construction that can provide the "meaning of it all." Outsiders, however, are all too ready to provide a discursive explanation, or a resituating of the initial raw thoughts of the edgeworker into a dominant discourse, thus bringing the imaginary and symbolic domain in some form of join or connectedness.

Closely connected with each form of *jouissance* is what Lacan referred to as "*objet petit(a)*." These are various objects of desire, mostly illusory, but nevertheless with effects. The newborn who gradually enters the symbolic order finds, on the one hand, that she is irreversibly disconnected with her Real, separated, distanced, and castrated, but finds on the other that the symbolic order offers various objects of desire that for a moment can provide a sense of completion, a momentary feeling of fullness and with it, the attendant feeling of *jouissance*. Edgework can be viewed as a form of *objet petit(a)*: It has a seductive character. Those who successfully negotiate boundaries reflect about their overwhelming feeling of mastery and superhumaness. Put to an explanation, however, the edgeworker finds an uneasy accommodation between phallic and bodily *jouissance*. A conventional discourse, for example, provides signifiers (words) by which one can explain the event to self and others. In the *jouissance* of the body form, however, the experience remains more ineffable, unexplainable, and unverbalizable in the dominant discourse. Thus the edgeworker often finds difficulty in precisely locating her/himself on the $J\varphi - JO$ continuum.

Figure 2.1b suggests various forms of edgework. The five dimensions we have identified in Figure 2.1a interact in diverse ways, producing the loci for particular forms of edgework. Given the need to engage in edgework, what are the possible forms of expression, and why do they appear in the forms they do? For each expressive form of edgework, there exists an attractor, which represents its tendency in a five-dimensional state space. Thus, basejumpers could be located in terms of tendencies toward JO, greater emotional intensity, illegality, and a situatedness in the boundary of the in- and out-of-control region. These tendencies can be located within a background space of socioeconomic and historical contingencies that account for opportunities for particular forms of expression. Said in yet another way, each form of edgework appears at the intersectional region in phase space defined by at least five degrees of freedom.

Let us take "in-control" versus "out-of-control" as our primary continuum for expository purposes (see Figure 2.1b), qualified by its inherent limitation due to its linear portrayal and unidimensionality. In actuality, we would need to locate each form of edgework in some region of state space (Figure 2.1a).

On one end of the linear continuum portrayed in Figure 2.1b, in-control, we see "packaged edgework" (or "adventure;" Holyfield et al. [chapter 7 of this volume]). This is typified by the ability to have relative control of the situation. This could include amusement parks, video machines, gaming, casinos, raves, novels (i.e., detective fiction), reality TV, adventure weekends, adrenaline TV programming, game-parks for hunters, etc. In state space, we could locate it in the upper regions of Figure 2.1a.

Next we could depict "workplace edgework." This includes the various opportunities to engage in edgework at the workplace. This could include floor stock trader, participant observer researcher, police, military, fireman, ambulance driver, oil rig roughneck, rescue team member (air, land, sea), deep sea diver, smokejumper, jet pilot, crop-duster, shop-floor buzzes (i.e, racing a forklift around the warehouse, pushing some work place technology to the edge, and so forth), etc. Workplace edgework can be distinguished from extreme sport in terms of the degree of being in control by the fact that the former specifies more clearly understood boundaries between acceptable and nonacceptable behavior and thus has more rules of conduct built into the activity. The latter, however, often finds ever-new definitions of appropriate boundaries. Perhaps, too, extreme sports have their own built-in tendencies toward normalization, such as we (Ferrell, Milovanovic, and Lyng, 2001) saw with basejumpers at Bridgeday. Thus, extreme sports allow more out-of-control activity; it goes with the territory, so to speak.

Moving further toward the "out-of-control" continuum, we could identify extreme sports. This includes the various activities associated with sporting activities that demand high skills in potentially escalating adverse conditions. This would include: basejumpers, skydivers, hang glider pilots, tug pilots for hang gliders, downhill skiers, free-style rock climbers, motorcyclists, race car drivers, etc. For the extreme sport enthusiast, following Lyng's suggestive study of skydivers, it is the ability to have the utmost control in a situation of pending catastrophe that produces a rush during and after the event.

Next could be "sneaky thrills." This would include the various activities in which clandestine activities present excitement in the ability to not be detected. This would include some shoplifting, perhaps some forms of employee theft and embezzlement, hacking, graffiti writing, CIA operatives engaged in clandestine activities, etc.

Following this we could have the "badass." This would include activities whereby the person arouses extreme emotions in confronting a situation, providing a clear, visible display to others of her/his willingness to carry through on the ominous presentation being made. It would include a sense of abandonment of fearful feelings, a letting go of strong emotional states, a display of being out-of-control to create fear in the other. This would include Katz's badass, police busts, criminal justice line staff (prison, jails, probation, etc.) and their posturing, bank robbers, etc.

Next would be "righteous slaughter." Here we have moved toward the "out-of-control" end of the continuum. This would include situations where the edgeworker, often with some self-justifying rhetoric, goes over the edge into a state of chaos; here s/he is often transformed into an object, resigned to the dictates of situations constructed (Matza, 1969). Matza is especially clear on this technique in which a person has become more object than subject. It is also a situation in which subjectivity is regained by the carrying through of the event. This would include Katz's righteous slaughter, State-sponsored righteous slaughter, operatives engaged in State/governmental executions, "police actions" (Vietnam, Iraq, Afghanistan), army snipers, governmental assassins, military company pointmen, etc.

Our final form, appearing on the right end of the in- and out-of-control continuum, could be "transcendental experiences." This form is characterized by those experiences in which the subject has abandoned any sense of control and lives in the moment, more often, exclusive of the world around him/her. This would include near-death experiences, trances, religious, out-of-body ences, epiphanies, "peak experiences," dreams, drug usage, sex, psychosis,

For each particular edgework activity, at least five dimensions are needed to provide a bona fide explanation for the activity. In other words, intersecting the "in-" and "out-of-control" dimension are the four others. Four of the dimensions are immersed in the fifth, the structural dimension. Our typology includes both "street" and "suite crimes" (badass and righteous slaughterer, as well as the hacker, embezzler, and manipulator of power); lower-class and upper-class edgework (shop-floor buzzes as well as business collusions and embezzlers); organized crime and state-sponsored edgework (scams, hits, strong-arming, and racketeering, as well as capital executions, "police actions," sting operations, clandestine/covert operations, etc.). It cuts across gender, race, and class categorizations.

Consider, for example, a computer hacker. S/he has arrived at a historical and economic time where a particular technology emerged and was available to many; where legality and illegality were at times ambiguous; where great excitement in doing the act existed; where being in control is a sure recipe for minimizing detection; and where the pleasures and excitement of the doing of the act were difficult to capture in contemporary discourse. (But once apprehended, the hacker is given a dominant set of linguistic coordinate systems within which to defend her/himself in law.)

Consider a company point man in Vietnam. In "free-fire zones," definitions of crime were completely irrelevant (all that moved before him were subject to being shot immediately). The wherewithal of the "police action" could be located in political, historical, and economic determinants. The degree of excitement and adrenaline rush while on "point"—M-16 on fully automatic, intensely scanning the situations in front—was at a dizzying level. Along the in-control and out-of-control dimension, oscillation between the two poles took place: in-control while on point, moving to out-of-control while in the midst of a fire fight. And finally, the point man was hard pressed to provide a verbalization in dominant discourse about his "high" in doing "point." More often it remained a domain that found difficulty in expression.

Boundaries

We can also conceptualize boundaries that exist along each dimension. These are regions with the precise line being somewhat imperceptible. Let us look at socioeconomic and historical conditions. These can be seen as providing certain locations where dissipation and spontaneous emergents flourish. Figure 2.2 depicts this. The inner circle (core, or dominant field) represents dominant logics, the dominant paradigm of the time period, and an assumed equilibrium or homeostatic dynamic (i.e., structural functionalism). Dominant logics can be seen as the quasi cause for structural libidinal investments, a process that may be coined "axiomatization" (Holland, 1999, pp. 66–67, 104–105; Deleuze and Guattari, 1987). The outer circle (periphery, or minor field) represents

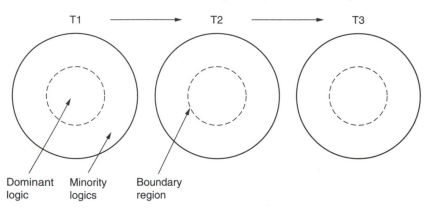

Socio-economic/historical contingencies (Real order, Lacan):

T1 ⟶ T2 ⟶ T3

Dominant   Minority   Boundary
logic   logics   region

Fig. 2.2 Structural boundaries

minority logics, emergents, contra logics, and oppositional perspectives. This is where multiplicity, heterogeneity, conflict, and spontaneous, unhindered developments unfold.

The boundary region between these two fields can be seen as representing ongoing dislocations. It is the borderland. Structural dislocations, according to Laclau and Mouffe (1985; see also Laclau, 1990) and contrary to many linear forms of historical analysis, are normal historical developments. One limited form is in Marxist's thesis-antithesis-thesis idea behind dialectical materialism; although, its logic most often follows an overly linear form. Foucault (1972; 1973), drawing from Nietzsche, has also presented the idea of genealogical analysis, which indicates nonlinear historical developments. For our purposes, following chaos theory, we depict this region as far-from-equilibrium conditions where emergents are much more likely occurrences in the form of dissipative structures. Dissipative structures are characterized by their ability to both develop some temporary form while undergoing continuous dissipation and reformation. These emergents are keenly sensitive to immediate conditions. Small perturbations may produce disproportional effects. It is in marked contrast to the rigidity of the bureaucratic form found in the dominant field.

A boundary region appears between the legal/illegal dimension; between greater/lesser emotional intensity; between in- and out-of-control; between Jϕ and JO, and between the dominant and minor field. Each of these boundaries could be fruitfully depicted by the Mandelbrot set (M-set) suggested by chaos theory (see Figure 2.3).

Note the jagged edges. Magnified thousands of fold, this boundary region shows incredible complexity and patterns that repeat. There is both order and disorder in this region. The M-set is created by taking a rather simple mathematical operation or formula, inserting some initial value, computing, plotting,

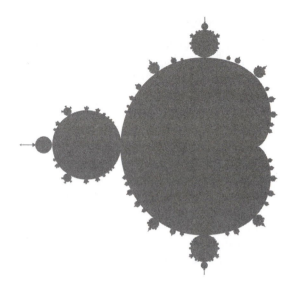

Fig. 2.3 Mandelbrot set

and determining where trajectories tend to fall. One continues to repeat this process (e.g., iteration). In other words, take the results, plug them back into the initial formula, solve, and plot. This would be done dozens to thousands of times. A pattern would emerge. Some points remain within the boundaries of the M-set and are identified as "prisoner sets." Others zoom outside, identified as the "escape set." At the boundary region, variability and indeterminacy is at its greatest. Interestingly enough, however, with ever greater and greater magnifications of the boundary region, eventually what surface are "baby M-sets," which in turn form their own boundaries. These, in turn, and *ad infinitum*, form baby, baby M-sets—the point being that within this rather "chaotic" region, stability still exists. "Stability" could represent a body of information, skills, and learned abilities that contribute to the edgeworker's propensity to safely confront the disorder within this region. Thus we have an orderly (dis)order. For the five dimensions we have developed, each encompasses a boundary that can be usefully conceptualized as the boundary regions of the M-set. It is also the loci of ineffable experiences. Thus we could locate the prisoner and escape sets for our five factors:

Prisoner Set	Boundary Region	Escape Set
legal		illegal
Jφ		JO
Lesser emotional intensity		greater emotional intensity
in-control		out-of-control
dominant field		minor field

Lines of Flight, Solitons, and Logics

Let us explore the logics within each field (see Figure 2.4). The dominant field is constituted by core logics based on rationalism. Max Weber's analysis of the forces of rationalization and the bureaucratic form is one example. Karl Marx's notion of "dialectical materialism" is another. Consider, for example, that connected with dialectical materialism is a prediction of particular modes of production following in linear form (e.g., feudalism, capitalism, socialism, communism). Hegel's notion of the "Absolute Spirit" seems to move in a similar direction. Emile Durkheim's "spontaneous division of labor" is yet another example of the dynamics predicted in the dominant field. These logics can be seen as emerging from the core region of the dominant field and spreading outward in the social formation, depicted in Figure 2.4 as the spirals.[2]

Within the minor field, a plurality of logics finds degrees of manifestation. Some emerge, some combine, some attain a relative stability, some are co-opted by the dominant field, and some cancel each other out. Elsewhere (Milovanovic, 1996; 2002; Henry and Milovanovic, 1996), it has been presented in the form of "trouser diagrams." A trouser diagram is an alternative diagramming to the privileged lines and trajectories of empirical positivistic analysis; it provides for both movement (variability, combination, dissipation, order, and disorder) and the wherewithal of emergent forms.

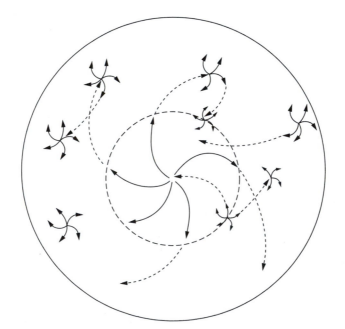

Fig. 2.4 Logics, solitons, lines of flight

In the boundary region, logics develop more spontaneously from singularities. These are short lived, more in the form of dissipative structures. To borrow from quantum mechanics, within the flux or dynamical states, quantum fluctuations may "spontaneously" produce the materialization of a logic. Indeed, singularities are unique in that at times they seem to suggest the materialization of something from nothing. In each case, we could again depict logics as solitons[3] that traverse space. In traversing space, these solitons, or following Deleuze and Guattari (1987), "lines of flight," hypercathect various relatively stabilized configurations of coupled iterative loops (developed in the next section). Set in resonance, these configurations often produce disproportional, nonlinear effects.

Coupled Iterative Loops

We want to now depict the interactions among the five factors. Here we are aided by the notion of iterative loops developed by chaos theory (Gregerson and Sailer, 1993). An iterative loop, said simply, is any circular processing phenomena (feedback, looping) where along the way some nonlinear transformational factor is negotiated, represented by squiggles (see Figure 2.5). These are "feedback loops" of a sort. However, following chaos theory, by continuous iteration (solving some formula, plugging the result back into the initial formula, reiterating, etc.) we produce nonlinear effects; indeed, disproportional effects.[4] Iterative loops appear in coupled forms. They are connected and remain "relatively autonomous." They are neither totally independent, nor totally dependant on each other. Thus we have historically

Simple iterative loop

Configurations of relatively stabilized, coupled iterative loops

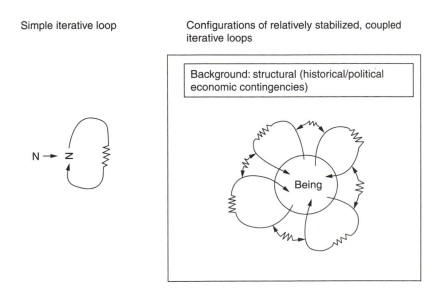

Fig. 2.5 Coupled iterative loops embedded in background space

contingent, relatively stabilized configurations of coupled iterative loops. Elsewhere (Henry and Milovanovic, 1996) we have called these "COREL sets," that is, constitutive interrelational sets.

Figure 2.5 depicts four of our factors as coupled iterative loops located within the fifth, a background space (political economy and historical conditions, i.e., dominant and minor fields). We argue that moving the loci of these interacting four factors to the dominant, minority, or boundary fields produces consequences. Hence, placed in the dominant field we suggest that the prisoner set would be the more likely events. Here, translated as the dominance of the legal, $J\varphi$, lesser sensual/emotional intensity, and in-control. Placed in the minor field, we would anticipate the escape set as being more likely: illegal, JO, greater sensual/emotional intensity, out-of-control. At the boundaries, we would have the maximum variability between the two sets.

A critical factor in understanding the effects generated by COREL sets would be the various solitons, or lines of flight, that emerge that traverse them. These traverse the social formation, hypercathecting various COREL sets, producing disproportional effects. This is akin to the Deleuzian idea of a "quasi cause" or "quasi-causal operator" (Delanda, 2002, pp. 160–161). These quasi causes put in resonance configurations of coupled iterative loops. As Delanda has said, "We should think about resonance as *positive feedback*, a generic process which implies one or other form of *mutually stimulating couplings*…inducing resonance among heterogeneous elements, as well as the *amplification of original differences*…(2002, p. 160; emphasis in original).

The boundary region, therefore, would be the crucible for the development of dissipative structures that remain extremely sensitive to their environment. Even minor perturbations elicited by solitons could bring into resonance various relatively stabilized configurations of coupled iterative loops.[5]

Klein-form and Constitutive Play: Topological Considerations

Following topology theory, let's now attempt to depict, informed by constitutive criminology, the interpenetrating effects of the various dimensions we have identified. Elizabeth Grosz, in *Volatile Bodies* (1994), has addressed the issue of the dualistic nature of subjectivity in post-Enlightenment thought (modernist thought). The Cartesian subject is said to be composed of two main forces: the body with its emotions, and the mind with its rationality and logic. Modernist thought has privileged the latter. Grosz's intriguing analysis returns us to the notion of monism, a subject reconnected to both. She depicts this by a Möbius strip. Take a rectangular piece of paper, put one twist in it, reconnect the edges, and you have a Möbius strip. One circuit around the strip indicates a continuous movement over one plane, and the object returns in inverted form. For Grosz, this represents the ongoing connectedness of the "inside" and "outside," the body and mind. Hence, monism.

Using this insight we can expand the use of topology theory in invoking a form of the Klein bottle to explain the interconnectedness of the five dimensions we have outlined. The Klein bottle is composed of two Möbius strips connected at one of their sides. We see this object in Figure 2.6. An ant placed on one of the surfaces, and which then travels around and through the bottle, would not only never negotiate a boundary, it would also never negotiate the edge (with the Möbius strip, the sides of the strip still represent an edge). The Klein bottle can only be depicted in four dimensions without intersections (where the handle curves back on itself). In three-dimensional space we have intersections.[6]

Unfortunately, the Klein bottle does not provide sufficient "room" or space for our interacting dimensions. We therefore borrow from the Klein-form, a structure based on the Klein bottle developed by Paul Ryan (1991a; 1991b) referred to as a "relational circuit." This is depicted in Figure 2.6. What it represents is three "handles" that cross *within* the object without intersection. This can only take place in four-dimensional depictions. In three-dimensional space, intersections exist. With this Klein-form we can see how various phenomena, including solitons, may interact. We could expand the number of "handles" to four, each standing for one of our dimensions, and immerse the structure within the fifth factor, the socioeconomic and historical (dominant, minor, and boundary fields). Thus depicted, we could argue that various factors

Klein bottle

Klein-form

Fig. 2.6 Klein bottle and Klein-form

may combine in a number of ways, rather imperceptibly, nonlinearly, and ulti-mately, indeterminately. This takes place with effects. And this also indicates the artificiality of boundary borders in so much as they are social constructs. The Klein-form would suggest that these five dimensions interact in complex, nonlinear ways. At the moment of doing edgework, it would be the occasion for pure duration, intensity, and immersion in the event, in what Deleuze refers to as a "smooth space," one not already mapped by the disciplinary mechanisms.

To summarize so far, we have made use of topology theory in suggesting various ways factors may interact in producing boundaries and effects. We are suggesting resituating the discussion of edgework within these emerging con-ceptualizations. We find it necessary to do so due to the rather conspicuous limitations of thought found in modernist thinking. Postmodern analysis is suggestive. Edgeworkers can be better explained within the conceptualizations provided by alternative models of being. In our next and final section, we want to draw from Deleuze and Guattari's profound insights in developing a holistic vision of edgeworkers.

BwO and Becoming

Deleuze and Guattari (1987) identify an alternative way of conceptualizing the subject and the forces within and without. This will be a critical component in understanding the edgeworker. They provide a more fluid understanding of how deeper, more-hidden dynamic states take on static form, and they are particularly concerned with developing a subject-in-process. We conclude, however, with Lacan, in indicating how these forces are rendered static. It is Deleuze and Guattari's work that suggests prescriptions for releasing the bodily forces for new and dynamic configurations. The edgeworker provides us with a momentary insight on the workings of the monistic subject and the occasion for a broader understanding of the potentialities of being and the constitution of the subject. It is at the boundary where the full potential of human variability unfolds.

One critical conceptualization of the subject Deleuze and Guattari offer is the idea of a "body without organs." The human being, the human body, is more constituted by various movements, forces, energies, flows, fluxes, inten-sities, and singularities that can potentially reconfigure themselves in infinite possible ways. This view is informed by the works of Nietzsche and Spinoza. We want to suggest that the edgeworker experiences moments of being, what Deleuze and Guattari (1987) refer to as a "body without organs" (BwO), most often more fully developed in the boundary region. It may very well be that those who populate the area closer to the core (dominant) region are most likely to be more fully integrated into the various dominant logics and find, in contemplating a deviant activity, that they are quickly provided decisive reasons for why they should not stray. Matza (1969) has already explained the heavy resources a society invests in maintaining boundaries. This is not to say that forms of edgework experienced by dominant groups, such as in the form of embezzlement, undermine our case; rather, we often find that here some of the most articulated discourses are available for temporary release from society's hold (recall Cressey's [1953] rationalizations).[7] But in many cases, the boundary region itself provides a "release" for much of this activity with minimal self-justifying verbalizations needed. However, in some cases, along the legal-illegal continuum, it is indeed the latter that paves the way for edgework. Consider Katz's righteous slaughterer, who must invoke a sense of righteousness, a moral transcendence, for what he is about to do. Consider various governmental officials working in clandestine operations undermining other governments or plotting political assassinations, invoking "national security" rhetoric. Consider Sykes and Matza's (1957) "techniques of neutralization" by which juveniles justify their deviant acts, before and after the event.

Deleuze and Guattari mention two types of BwOs. The "full" BwO is the more fluid and is more likely to be operating by "molecular processes," which realign bodily forces in a continuous way producing ever-new meanings, identities, and institutions. This is at the level of Lacan's Real order and Freud's unconscious and mnemic systems. Here desire is more playful, searching, groping, and directed toward self-actualizing the momentarily configured COREL sets; it is not a desire based on lack, as in Lacan's analysis. Desire is a quasi cause (see Dalanda, 2002, p. 160) that puts into resonance variously coupled iterative loops. The "empty" BwO is more static, more likely to operate by "molar processes," processes by which stable configuration of molecular elements are formed. Here we have such things as juridical abstractions, various social formations, ideologies, identities, and the division of classes, races, sexes, and so forth (Grosz, 1994, p. 172). We have fixed and stabilized identities. It is repetition that ensures stability and familiarity. The full BwO, however, is always a becoming-something, a becoming-child, becoming-woman, becoming-animal, becoming-comedian, becoming-Spanish-speaking, becoming- other. Left to its own logic, this is a "becoming imperceptible." All becomings work at the molecular level. We are at the same time interconnected with other becomings.

It is at the very boundaries that we would expect the greatest play of molecular processes and becoming. Here, forces, energies, speeds, movement, and intensities are continuously realigned, be it momentarily. In the boundary region of far-from-equilibrium conditions, a peak of variability arises. Yet, pockets of order (the baby M-sets) exist in the form of a distinct, contemporarily procured set of skills and knowledge needed to negotiate an impending, potentially disastrous situation. Thus order and disorder prevail. Let's consider two examples: Becoming-embezzler—an "excessive investor" in doing harm to another (harms of reduction, harms of repression [Henry and Milovanovic, 1996])—can be seen situated within our five-factor explanatory framework. This would include the structural conditions that gave rise to money institutions and paper transactions and the structural locations within which they predominantly take place; the constitution of legality in political economy; the definitions of being in control during the event, most noted in various pleadings of excuse (insanity, duress, entrapment, etc.); the form of *jouissance* experienced; and degree of emotional/sensual display. Similarly, consider becoming-basejumper. This would include the structural conditions that gave rise to basejump equipment and opportunities for its use; the construction of illegality for the event; the definitions of being-in-control during the activity, which include the ultimate test of not "bouncing"[8]; the form of *jouissance* experienced, which includes an ineffable, elusive discourse of JO; and the degree of emotion/sensual display falling short of "emotional overload" and brainlock. Therefore, the BwO experiencing a becoming in edgework experience has at least five factors at play.

The empty BwO (BwO$_e$), Deleuze and Guattari inform us, is caught in stasis, in repetition, in an emptying of its forces and intensities. The BwO$_e$ is emptied of its flows, intensities, proliferations, fluxes, and potential new configurations. The BwO$_e$ often becomes the "excessive investor" where domination of the other is central. Deleuze and Guattari (1987) give the example of the drug addict, hypochondriac, and masochist. As they argue, "the masochist has made himself a BwO under such conditions that the BwO can no longer be populated by anything but the intensities of pain, pain waves... The masochist is looking for a type of BwO that only pain can fill, or travel over" (p. 152).

Our more descriptive five-dimensional grid can now be integrated with the notion of BwO. Let us, in the final hour, speculate. The edgeworker operates within these coordinates. It is at the edge where bodily forces are realigned—some in the good sense (actualizing the full range of potentialities without becoming an excessive investor), some in the bad (excessive investor)—be it often, only temporarily. The subject is often quick to return to the stability offered by the conventional order. Thus, the conventional and unconventional are in a dialectical relationship; each constitutes the other while also being the basis of the other's undermining and undoing. Within each are the deconstructive conditions of the other. It is the internecine spaces that are created within social structure where subjects are seduced by *objet petit(a)*, the attractions of edgework. In Lacanian theory, however, the possibility of completion is only illusory: the edgeworker both negotiates the boundary and, in successfully doing so, becomes seduced by its attractive force, seeking a continuous effect while often maintaining a conventional existence; and often, in failure, provides the very evidence of why it is an everyday world that cannot be. The pursuit of *objet petit(a)* for the edgeworker is not to be seen as a "rationally" directed process; it is both mind and body at work in a dialectical and constitutive interplay.

Let us return to Grosz and one completion around the Möbius strip. At times, a rational, self-aware, goal-directed subject appears; at other times, the side most repressed, denied, de-privileged in a more materially oriented social formation, finds internecine spaces where there emerges the call of the body and its emotions. It is in this two-fold conceptualization that fuller subjectivity may materialize, one genuinely connected with the body *and* the rational, logical world.

Even though Deleuze and Guattari offer a view of a flow of forces operating on another plane, ultimately, these forces find crystallization—as Lacan argues, and with whom they agree—in the oedipalization of the subject. It is a political economic imposition of a form of organization of the body, what Deleuze refers to as "capture" (see Patton, 2000, pp. 99, 104, 109–114).[9] Lacan's theory argues that from the various, constantly fleeting imaginary and symbolic interconnections, some become knotted, forming the basis of stability.[10] Here, in the form of BwO_e, we find the more static configurations of coupled iterative loops limiting continuous variation; although, irrespective of this, they often, through iteration, produce unintended consequences that social institutions are forever vigilant in policing, channeling, redirecting, naming, and coopting. The edgeworker, the BwO_f, attests to the variability of being human and to the yearning of returning to a monistic subject, one constituted by both the rational, logical world, as well as the world of emotions, feelings, and the sensual.[11] The BwO_e, too, in a more functional way, attests to the need of maintaining boundaries; a testament to society's wish to exclude the seductions of exclusively sensual play and the excessive investor to do harm.[12] Foucault's (1977) "disciplinary mechanisms" synchronize the bodily forces into a body of utility (see also Deleuze's notion of "control societies" that generalizes Foucault's notion [1995, pp. 177–182]). It is often this to which the edgeworker reacts. At the boundary regions, bodily forces are momentarily provided a space where fleeting realignments may take place. And with each, feelings of *jouissance* emerge, some in the phallic form, but more often in the bodily form, which defies verbal expression. In contrast to the state's function of capture and the construction of a striated space in which nominalization and categorization reigns, Deleuze offers the notion of the "war-machine" that destratifies and deterritorializes, which creates smooth spaces in which continuous variability dominates (Deleuze and Guattari, 1987; Patton, 2000, chapter 6). It is in this sense that the full body without organs is a "nomadic war machine," and it is this that underlies becoming-edgeworker.

But we have heard too infrequently from edgeworkers themselves of why they do what they do. We have at best narrative reconstructions offered and imposed by various specialists that ultimately play themselves out in the rational, logical world. We need new postmodern narratives and ethnographies such as the ones described by Norman Denzin (1997). They are variously described as "experiential texts," performance-based texts," "narratives of the self," the "reflexive texts," and the "autoethnographic text." These are often "messy texts" (1997), providing only glimpses or slices of edgeworkers in action. They focus on liminal experiences and epiphanal moments (1997). It is toward this that O'Malley and Mugford's (1994) work is anticipatory in their call for a methodology focused on the "phenomenology of pleasure" in structural contexts.

Conclusion

Much has yet to be done on edgeworkers. But it provides the promise for a new understanding of the relation of the subject to structure. In this sense, understanding the edgeworker is the "royal road" to a more comprehensive understanding of what it means to be human.

Notes

1. For the vicarious pleasures of reading detective fiction, see Young (1996); for the seductions of prisons and identifications with the criminal, see Duncan (1996); for job rewards of criminal activity, see Halleck (1967); for much nonutilitarian activity of juvenile delinquents, see Cohen (1955); for engaging in crime for excitement that is subculturally situated, see Miller (1958); for raves, see Stanley (1996).

2. Let us provide some examples of these linear developments and core logics. In law, deductive logic and syllogistic reasoning is said to be the key logic for decision-making. In the economy, Marx's "commodity fetishism" has been shown to have a similar development (homologies) in the production of the legal, and linguistic forms (Pashukanis, 2002; Volosinov, 1986; Milovanovic, 2003). In other words, it is to commodity-exchange in a competitive capitalist marketplace that we need to look for the originations of phenomenal forms such as notions of freedom, equality and proprietorship interests (Pashukanis, 2002). To do law, to be logically rational, is to express fidelity to this form. All three are logics that, following a Marxian idea, work behind people's backs. They are not necessarily the result of a conspiratorial economic elite. Perhaps the notion of the "soliton" is suggestive (see note 3).

3. A soliton is usually associated with a tidal wave that has often begun with some kind of underwater disturbance. This wave can travel great distances at an incredible speed, regardless of obstacles. Similarly, adapting the notion of the soliton, we can argue that core logics traverse social space with effects. We will return to this below.

4. Consider these examples: In law, we have the dilemma of "original intent," which stands for the possibilities of current understanding of law to be traced back to the "intent" of the Constitution's founders. In eye-witness accounts in law, consider how stories of who the offender was changes over time. In self-reflection, consider how each round produces a yet new understanding of self. In textual interpretations, consider how with each interpretation, new meaning arises. In police/legal interactions, consider how with each interpretation of given law, new law is being produced, which becomes the basis of yet new interpretations and actions and interpretations, etc.

5. For a close, illuminating comparison, see Freud's analysis of the production of a dream in *The Interpretation of the Dreams* (1965).

6. This topological structure (Klein bottle) is suggestive as to indicating that boundaries are nonexistent; various boundaries we have developed are ultimately social constructs and have no real existence in themselves.

7. Consider Kennedy's (1997) analysis of judges' decision-making and the suggestion that many, faced with decisions going against their personal ideologies, are in denial and act in bad faith, but produce results that seem on the surface to reflect consistent decision-making; consider the verbalizations employed by state special forces in explaining their acts against civilian populations ("collateral damage," etc).

8. "Bouncing" is skydiver and basejumper talk for a person who dies while skydiving or BASE-jumping.

9. Consider Patton's development of Deleuze's notion of "capture":

   The state … captures flows of population, commodities, or money in order to extract from these flows a surplus which then becomes a means to maintain and enhance its own power…the essence of the state as a machine of capture [is] that it creates homogeneous and measurable or striated spaces" (Patton, 2000, pp. 104, 112–113).

10. Lacan's notion of *le sinthome* is a case in point. Lacan argues that the three orders (Symbolic, Imaginary, and Real) are normally interconnected. He portrays this in the Borromean knots. However, there are times that one of the orders gets undone, thereby undermining the stability of the psychic apparatus. It is *le sinthome* that connects the broken knots. Of course a political economy, following Foucault's notion of disciplinary mechanisms, is ubiquitous and stands ready to confront the wayward subjects. The logics emanate from the core of the dominant field in the form of solitons and traverse the diverse relatively stable configurations of coupled iterative loops.

11. This temporary breaking of knots (couplings), drawing from Lacan, as in the Borromean knot, can also be shown in play in another complex depiction, Schema I, where the imaginary becomes decoupled from the Symbolic and its otherwise induced connectedness.

12. As Patton (2000, p. 133) states: "…the state relies upon a structural or lawful violence, a violence of capture, whose institutional manifestations are juridical and penal institutions of capture and punishment such as police and prisons."

References

Becker, H. *Outsiders*. New York: Free Press, 1963.
Campbell, C. "Romanticism and the Consumer Ethic." *Sociological Analysis* 44 (1983): 279–296.
_____. *The Romantic Ethic and the Spirit of Modern Consumerism*. Oxford: Blackwell, 1987.
Cohen, A. *Delinquent Boys*. New York: Free Press, 1955.
Cressey, D. *Other People's Money*. Glencoe, IL: Free Press, 1953.
Delanda, M. *Intensive Science and Virtual Philosophy*. New York: Continuum, 2002.
Deleuze, G., and Guattari, F. *A Thousand Plateaus*. Minneapolis, MN: University of Minnesota Press, 1987.
Deleuze, G. *Negotiations*. New York: Columbia University Press, 1995.

Denzin, N. *Interpretive Ethnography*. London: Sage, 1997.
Duncan, M. *Romantic Outlaws, Beloved Prisons*. New York: New York University Press, 1996.
Elias, N. *The Civilizing Process*. Oxford: Blackwell, 1982.
Ferrell, J. *Crimes of Style*. Boston: Northeastern University Press, 1996.
Ferrell, S., Milovanovic, D., and Lyng, S. "Edgework, Media Practices, and the Elongation of Meaning." *Theoretical Criminology* 5(2) (2001): 177–202.
Foucault, M. *Archaeology of Knowledge*, A. Sheridan, translator. New York: Pantheon, 1972.
_____. *The Order of Things*, E. Gallimard, translator. New York: Vintage Books, 1973.
_____. *Discipline and Punish*, A. Sheridan, translator. New York: Pantheon Books, 1977.
Freud, S. *The Interpretation of Dreams*. New York: Avon Books, 1965.
Gregerson, H., and Sailer, L. "Chaos Theory and Its Implications for Social Science Research." *Human Relations* 46(7) (1993): 777–802.
Grosz, E. *Volatile Bodies*. Bloomington, IN: Indiana University Press, 1994.
Halleck, S. *Psychiatry and the Dilemmas of Crime*. Berkeley: University of California Press, 1967.
Henry, S., and M. Lanier. *What Is Crime?* New York: Rowman and Littlefield, 2001.
Henry, S., and Milovanovic, D. *Constitutive Criminology*. London: Sage, 1996.
Holland, E. *Deleuze and Guattari's Anti-Oedipus*. New York: Routledge, 1999.
Katz, J. *Seductions of Crime*. New York: Basic Books, 1988.
Kennedy, D. *A Critique of Adjudication*. Cambridge, MA: Harvard Univ. Press, 1997.
Lacan, J. *Ecrit*. New York: Norton, 1977.
Laclau, E., and Mouffe, C. *Hegemony and Socialist Strategy*. New York: Verso, 1985.
Laclau, E. *New Reflections on the Revolution of Our Times*. London: Verso, 1990.
Lyng, S. "Edgework: A Social Psychological Analysis of Voluntary Risk Taking." *American Journal of Sociology* 95(4) (1990): 876–921.
Matza, D. *Becoming Deviant*. Englewood Cliffs, NY: Prentice Hall, 1969.
Miller, W. "Lower Class Culture as a Generating Milieu of Gang Delinquency." *Journal of Social Issues* 14 (1958): 5–19.
Milovanovic, D. "Postmodern Criminology." *Justice Quarterly* 13(4) (1996): 201–244.
_____. (Editor) *Chaos, Criminology and Social Justice*. Westport, CT: Praeger, 1997.
_____. *Critical Criminology at the Edge*. Westport, CT: Praeger, 2002.
_____. *An Introduction to the Sociology of Law*. Monsey, NY: Criminal Justice Press, 2003.
Nietzsche, F. *Beyond Good and Evil*. New York: Vintage Books, 1966.
_____. *On the Genealogy of Morals*. New York: Vintage Books, 1968.
O'Malley, P., and Mugford, S. "Crime, Excitement, and Modernity." In *Varieties of Criminology*, edited by G. Barak. Westport, CT: Praeger, 1994.
Pashukanis, E. *The General Theory of Law and Marxism*. New Brunswick, NY: Transaction Books, 2002.
Patton, P. *Deleuze and the Political*. New York: Routledge, 2000.
Ragland, E. and Milovanovic, D., eds. *Lacan: Topologically Speaking*. New York: Other Press, 2003.
Ryan, P. "A Sign of Itself," in *On Semiotic Modeling*, edited by M. Anderson and F. Merrell. New York: Mouton De Gruyter, 1991[a].
_____. "The Earthscore Notational System for Orchestrating Perceptual Consensus About the Natural World." *Leonardo* 24(4) (1991)[b]: 457–465.
Stanley, C. *Urban Excess and the Law*. London: Cavendish, 1996.
Sykes and Matza. "Techniques of Neutralization: A Theory of Delinquency." *American Sociological Review* 22 (1957): 664–670.
Volosinov, V. *Marxism and the Philosophy of Language*. Cambridge, MA: Harvard University Press, 1986.
Wegner, T., and Tyler, R. *Fractal Creations*. Corte Madera, CA: Waite Group Press, 1993.
Young, A. *Imagining Crime*. London: Sage, 1996.

Part III

The Edgework Experience:
Anarchy and Aesthetics

3

The Only Possible Adventure:
Edgework and Anarchy

JEFF FERRELL

CONTENTS

For as long as I can remember edgework and anarchy have wound around each other like a couple of desperate lovers.

Back in the day, down in Austin, Texas, back where I guess it all began, Steve Lyng and I were deep into what you might call an integrated culture of extreme risk. Among other things, we were riding and racing stripped-down Harley-Davidsons as part of a loosely dis-organized amalgam of misfits we called, mostly kiddingly, the Maddogs. But Steve was also a jump pilot, flying the jump plane at the local skydiving center, and many of the Maddogs came from this world as well, bringing with them the skills and attitudes that defined it. The "relative work" of skydiving, for example—the experience in which skydivers join hands to form momentary formations during freefall—was offloaded onto the motorcycles, such that those of us riding separate bikes would join hands for relative work during high-speed backroad runs. Cut with the right mix of intoxicants, these sorts of extreme experiences were, to say the least, exhilarating.

Steve and I were also in graduate school in sociology at the University of Texas at Austin, and between motorcycle runs we were reading everything we could get our hands on—including Hunter S. Thompson's accounts of his own twisted exhilarations in Las Vegas and out along the open road. Reading Thompson's *Hell's Angels*, we began to see something important, to sense a weird thread running through it all. Thompson wasn't just writing about outlaw motorcyclists and the big booming Harley-Davidsons we loved to ride; he was writing about those motorcycles as a particular medium for the very sorts of extreme experiences we were discovering. Hell, reading Thompson in those days, it was like we were reading ourselves:

> But with the throttle screwed on there is only the barest margin, and no room at all for mistakes. It has to be done right … and that's when the strange music starts, when you stretch your luck so far that fear becomes exhilaration and vibrates along your arms … until the next dark stretch and another few seconds on the edge… The Edge … the edge is still Out there. Or maybe it's In. The association of motorcycles with LSD is no accident of publicity. They are both means to an end, to the place of definitions (Thompson, 1967, p. 345).

Well, indeed. Indeed we had ourselves heard that strange music whistling by at a hundred miles an hour—and indeed we had lived to tell about it, to hear the music again, because we had done it right, because we had made no mistakes, even with our throttles and our lives pegged wide open. So we stole Thompson's notion of "the edge," and began to talk and write about "edgework" as a shorthand for that uncanny blend of precision and abandon—or maybe, more to the point, as a conceptual commemoration of those moments when we found existential definition right at the edge of chaos.

But it was weirder than that.

As it happened, Steve and I were also at the time discovering the history and theory of anarchism. I was writing my master's thesis and then my doctoral dissertation on The Wobblies, the anarcho-syndicalist union that raised hell, sang songs, and won more than a few strikes a century ago. Steve and I were digging anarchist philosophers of science like Paul Feyerabend and his notion that "anything goes"; learning our anarchist chops from the early works of Michael Bakunin and Emma Goldman and Peter Kropotkin; and exploring the history of anarchist revolt as played out in the Spanish communes, as swept up with Makhno in the Russian Revolution, as betrayed by the Bolsheviks at Kronstadt and by Marx in the International. Best of all, we were beginning to see that all this was something more than graduate school history and theory—that anarchism could be what Daniel Guerin (1970) calls a "visceral revolt," maybe even a "revolution of everyday life."

And damned if Hunter Thompson wasn't seeing the same thing. Not only was he linking fast motorcycles to altered states and edgework; he was putting this linkage in the context of anarchism. For Thompson, the pursuit of the edge constituted a sort of experiential anarchy, a visceral liberation from the entrapments of everyday life. Thompson's free-associating riff on a Hell's Angels gathering even provided some historical context and perspective:

> One night about halfway through one of their weekly meetings I thought of Joe Hill on his way to face a Utah firing squad and saying his final words: "Don't mourn. Organize." It is safe to say that no Hell's Angel has ever heard of Joe Hill or would know a Wobbly from a bushmaster, but there is something very similar about the attitudes .... [The Angels'] reactions to the world they live in are rooted in the same kind of anarchic, paralegal sense of conviction that brought the armed wrath of the Establishment down on the Wobblies (1967, p. 333).

The weirdness of it all was seductive: In Thompson's writings as in our own lives and readings, the phenomenologies of anarchy and edgework seemed somehow to be intersecting time and again, in moments of individual experience and in ongoing collective behavior, in odd configurations of commitment and desire, and in some sort of political dynamic we hadn't quite figured out. This was worth pursuing.

And so we pursued it, experientially and intellectually. Steve went on to write definitively about edgework as voluntary risk taking, to explore the edgework practices of skydivers, to push his own motorcycle riding out past The Edge that Thompson described and then to write about that bone-crushing moment, too.[1] I went on to spend five years inside the underground world of hip hop graffiti writers, describing their (and my) edgy aesthetic encounters as an anarchic revolt against the everyday order of the city. Later I rode with militant bicyclists, hung out with homeless folks and homeless activists and skate punks, played music on the streets, broadcast illegally with progressive pirate radio operators—and characterized all of these groups and experiences as fluid, dis-organized attempts to reclaim the city's public spaces for a politics of pleasure and uncertainty.[2] Together with friend and fellow edgeworker Dragan Milovanovic, Steve and I recently pursued it further, investigating the moments of edgework and the ongoing anarchic ethos that define the world of high-risk BASE-jumpers—those who parachute illegally from buildings, bridges, and other fixed structures.[3]

As it's turned out, those two desperate lovers have been lost in a hell of a long embrace, swept up in repeating paroxysms of mutual desire. But what's the source of all this ongoing passion? And desperate for what, exactly?

A Passion for Self-Determination—and Self-Control

For the uninitiated, misperceptions of edgework and misunderstandings of anarchism follow a parallel course. BASE jumpers, motorcycle daredevils, graffiti writers, and other edgeworkers are often perceived as individuals dangerously out of control, misfits intent on their own imminent destruction and, along the way, the profligate destruction of others' lives and property. Immature and unfocused, they seem to wander from one nasty situation to another, too absorbed in their own bad-boy self-importance to realize the risk they pose to themselves and those around them, too intent on immediate gratification to work toward broader goals of family, career or social good. Similarly, institutional leaders and the decent folk they lead often understand anarchy and anarchism as no more than a social void, a disturbing absence of social order synonymous with chaos, destruction, violence, and ruin. For them, anarchy suggests only a nightmare of social dissolution, an abandoning of society itself.

Maybe these misperceptions are honest mistakes made by those whose lives circulate too closely between the living room sofa, the office cubicle, and the shopping mall; maybe these misperceptions are in fact ideological constructions, crafted by those leaders and authorities understandably threatened by the insubordinate potential of edgework and anarchy. In either case—and I suspect it's some of both, though more of the latter—such misperceptions miss a key dialectic that drives both edgework and anarchy, a dialectic that in fact begins to explain both their mutual attraction and their phenomenological convergence.

Both edgeworkers and anarchists share a profound passion, alright, but not simply for unthinking abandon or antisocial chaos. Rather, they're junkies for the seductive, intoxicating tension *between* artistry and abandon, for the *dialectic* of chaos and control, for that "strange music" that plays when you stretch your luck, but stretch it just right. It's this emergent interplay that defines edgework and anarchism, and the potential for human actualization that both offer. What distinguishes edgework from McDonald's work, what defines anarchy in distinction to structures of external legal authority or economic domination—that is, what edgework and anarchy both offer in place of an overdetermined and overregulated social life—is precisely this dynamic human balance. In moments of anarchy and edgework, a sort of magic emerges: You get to grab hold and let go at the same time.

Should this sound like just another intellectual abstraction—or worse, like some high-minded apologia on my part for what are in fact moments of recklessly out-of-control misbehavior—I would propose to you a series of experiential challenges, a series of empirical tests:

> In the middle of the night, down a dark alley, ducking the cops, spray paint a big hip hop graffiti mural such that the paint doesn't drip, the colors fade perfectly one into the other, the mural's outline stays sharp, and the lettering maintains a precise consistency of size, style, and dimensionality.

> Gliding up to a steeply descending set of stairs on your skateboard, kickflip your board up onto the handrail that parallels the stairs, grind the handrail all the way to the bottom, and then dismount in such a way as to avoid the protruding bolts installed by local authorities intent on stopping just such maneuvers.

From atop a towering suspension bridge, or maybe from the roof deck of a big urban skyscraper, jump off, making sure that your parachute has been packed so as to open quickly and smoothly, remembering to allow for momentary variations in wind and weather, and not forgetting to locate and steer toward a suitable landing area within the first two seconds of freefall. Add a quick forward or backward flip along the way as desired.

Blasting along in the middle of the night on a fast motorcycle, anticipate that next sharp curve in the road so that you set your line of approach well ahead of time; then lean your bike hard into the sweep of the turn, your footpegs riding just off the pavement, and finally accelerate smoothly out of the curve's centrifugal pull, all the while watching for gravel, oil spills, traffic, and cops.

If you're not dead or in jail after these empirical tests, perhaps you could get back to me with your findings on the dialectic between practiced skill and existential abandon. And if you're still having trouble understanding this dialectic, or if you still think this is all just some out-of-control bad-boy misbehavior, maybe one of the Gravity Girls can help you out.

Like the great Marta Empinotti and other female legends of the BASE-jumping underground, the Gravity Girls are a group of high-flying and highly respected women BASE-jumpers. A couple of years ago one of the Gravity Girls, having just landed a technically accomplished BASE-jump from West Virginia's 876-foot-high New River Gorge Bridge, explained the jump to me while we waited for a ride back to the top of the gorge, and in so doing explained the dialectic as well. "Once I hit the air I felt like I was home again," she told me. "You never get enough ... to just be snatched from the jaws of death ... But it isn't a death wish like everybody thinks it is. You know you're alive when you do this; every sense is working. ... You want to live so you can do it again."

So while we're at it, two more empirical tests, also about grabbing hold, letting go, and knowing you're alive:

As anarchists did in the middle of the civil war against Franco and the Fascists back in the 1930s, institute a model of "workers' self-management" at your factory or farm, figuring out on the fly a way to keep the production lines rolling and the crops growing without factory bosses or land owners, and while under relentless external attack.[4]

Or like many of the most progressive political groups today, come up with a way of "*dis-organizing*" a major street action, getting thousands of people together to fight automotive pollution or the World Trade Organization, but by intention doing so without relying on the mass media, without a central planning committee, and with no one particularly in charge.

And if you successfully complete either of these last two tests, perhaps you could write a letter to the editor of your local newspaper, asking that in the future the paper desist from using the words "anarchy" and "chaos" as interchangeable synonyms.

Come to think of it, this notion of dynamically "dis-organizing" collective anarchist action captures the edgy dialectic of agency and abandon about as well as any. As played out in the real politics of the self and the street, "disorganization" suggests not some pure form of spontaneous disorder, but rather a subversion, a subterfuge, an inside joke about the tension between structure and emergence. The dash in "dis-organization" gives the joke away: unlike "disorganization," "dis-organization" does in fact denote some degree of planning and forethought—but just enough to engender conditions conducive to collective spontaneity, conditions in which planning and forethought can be happily abandoned.

So to mention one example among many today, members of the militant bicycling movement Critical Mass dis-organize collective bike rides through rumor, word of mouth, and Web sites, and through what they call "xerocracy," a democracy of communication built on fliers, handbills, and stickers produced by anyone and everyone in the movement. They strive to keep their rides as fluid, spontaneous, and friendly as possible, and to undermine any sort of "testosterone brigade" that might try to take control of the ride and push it toward angry confrontation with automobile drivers. Out on the ride, they "cork" intersections so as to protect the riders; that is, some of them bicycle up to the next intersection and temporarily block cars from moving through it. But as Women's Critical Mass activist Caycee Cullen reminded me a while back:

> No one has the job of corking. Like there are no "control corkers." It's just like as you're going through, people will notice, wow, and speed up and jump out, and everybody appreciates that, and then the next time, you'll do it. You know, it's like an unwritten dynamic (quoted in Ferrell, 2001/2002, p. 107).[5]

Or as Critical Mass dis-organizer Beth Verdekal puts it, Critical Mass emerged, and continues to emerge, from "word of mouth, xerocracy, no leaders, everybody doing things on their own, people who were self-responsible, who could cork their own ride, who did their own thing and then came together and did it with other people" (quoted in White, 1999). The point of all this, by the way? "To live the way we wish it could be," say other Critical Mass participants, and to dig the unexpected as it unfolds during the ride. And the destination? As one Critical Mass flier put it: "To Wherever."

And to mention yet another example of this dis-organized dynamic, consider the Situationists—a movement of sorts that, a few decades before Critical Mass's emergence in the 1990s, sought the same uncertain destination.

Intellectual outlaws, epistemic anarchists, agitators for a "revolution of everyday life," the inspiration for the French upheavals of 1968 and a decade later for Johnny Rotten and the punks, the Situationists anticipated this same sense of "dis-organization," understood with uncanny insight this decentered dynamic that drives moments of edgework and anarchy. "We will only organize the detonation," they said back in 1963, five years before students and workers and intellectuals detonated in the streets of Paris. "The free explosion must escape us and other control forever" (quoted in Marcus, 1989, 179–180).[6]

Understanding this dynamic among Situationists and Critical Mass riders, glimpsing it in moments of motorcycle edgework or graffiti painting, we come full circle to the misperception of edgework and anarchy as angry, out-of-control abandon. In reality, it's more the opposite: Both edgework and anarchy operate as exercises in *self-control*. But let's be clear: It's not self-control for the sake of self-control, not some rigid self-imposed regimen. Oh hell no. It's self-control in place of control by church, state, or job, based on the understanding that if you don't control yourself, somebody else will. It's self-control for the sake of self-determination, self-control cut with big doses of randomness and spontaneity, self-control in the interest of holding on to your life while letting go of it. Ultimately, it's a kind of self-control that gets you high, that gets you hooked on the autonomy of self-invention and the collective power of dis-organization. "It's addictive," says Krypt, a West Coast hip hop graffiti writer. "It gets you high, but high on your own achievement. You did something. You created. You achieved. For a lot of cases it's the only way to achieve anything that's real in this damn world we're stuck with in the ghetto" (quoted in Walsh, 1996, p. 41).

DIY and the Rush of Direct Action

Stuck in British ghettos of their own, bored to death living in the drab "council tenancies" that The Sex Pistols howled about in "Anarchy in the U.K.," the early punks likewise got high on their own achievements. In fact, the dynamic of self-invention defined the early punk movement and continues to define punk culture today—so much so that the punks have given it a name: "do-it-yourself," or "DIY." From the first, punk was all about DIY, with punk taking shape as a cultural revolt against the conglomeration of corporate megamusic bands, prepackaged fashions, and centralized mass media. In their place, the punks dis-organized three-chord garage bands, and xerocracy-style 'zines (magazines); invented their own disreputably ripped-and-torn fashions; and threw the self-made pleasure and spastic excitement of all this back in the face of mainstream society. Today, this defiant commitment to do-it-yourself continues, with self-organized punk concerts and festivals, thousands of 'zines continuing to circulate, and features like "The DIY Files" appearing in *Punk Planet* magazine. In the words of Jamie Reid, one of punk's founding troublemakers: "Anarchy is the Key, Do-It-Yourself is the Melody."[7]

In this sense the punk/anarchist dynamic of DIY operates much the same as the edgework dynamic that Steve described in his definitive essay on edgework (Lyng, 1990). Both edgework and DIY develop as responses to a world increasingly alienated from its inhabitants, a world in which work is something we do on the orders of someone else, and our identities are something we're meant to purchase by way of paramilitaristic SUVs and glossy Gap ads. Both edgework and DIY invoke instead a dynamics of desperation, emerging as desperate attempts to construct an identity, a sense of self, outside the suffocating boredom of the office cubicle and the sugar-coated consumer shit sold at the shopping mall. But in their desperation both edgework and DIY are also moments of profound, maybe even revolutionary, humanity, as those involved dare to bring their own skills, their own hands and hearts, into the equation of their own lives.

Similar intersections of edgework and anarchy surface if we look for manifestations of DIY beyond the punks. From The Wobblies of 1910 to anti-WTO street activists of today, anarchists have long been just as committed to DIY as are the punks—it's just that they call this do-it-yourself dynamic "direct action." For anarchists, direct action embodies a defiant disavowal of secondhand living, "representational" governance, and top-down leadership of all sorts, embracing instead direct, on-the-ground activism in the situations of everyday life. In this way direct action also operates as a sort of propaganda, a "propaganda of the deed" as anarchists call it, by demonstrating directly that change can be undertaken, communities improved, lives lived with neither the help nor the permission of the authorities. Best of all, direct action sets in motion the dynamic between self-determination and spontaneity, producing moments when, as Critical Mass riders say, we get "to live the way we wish it could be," moments in which the future opens in unexpected directions and in so doing changes the way we understand the present. A Critical Mass ride, a dis-organized street protest, a day spent hammering together low-cost housing—all beat voting for one damn fool or another, and all teach lessons available only to those lost in the action itself.

I can attest to this last point; Steve and I certainly developed our understanding of edgework as much from fast, dangerous motorcycle runs and other direct actions best left undocumented as we did from quiet readings of Thompson or Bakunin in the University of Texas library. The notion of direct action further suggests, ironically, that you're only going to get so far in understanding edgework or anarchy if at some point you don't put down this damn book and get out in the streets. Or in the words of a piece of freight train graffiti, photographed and reproduced in the 'zine *The Fifth Goal* (a DIY publication documenting a DIY art form): "Get Off Your Computers. Get on a Train" (*The Fifth Goal*, Issue Four, 2001).[8]

Moreover—and assuming you're still reading—punk/anarchist notions of DIY and direct action also help explain particular phenomenologies of edgework that Steve and I and others have documented over the past decade or so.

In attempting to make sense of edgework and his personal and intellectual involvement in it, for example, Steve has argued that a pragmatist framework is necessary—that is, a framework that understands symbolic meaning not as a free-floating human accomplishment, but as an activity grounded in the demands and limitations of the physical environment. At other times I've used the term "situated meaning" to denote a similar sense of meaning and emotion as dynamics constructed within moments of lived experience, and thus dynamics fully known only by those participating in those moments. But whatever we call it, the idea is mostly the same: Edgework exists as a form of do-it-yourself direct action that constructs an emergent reality particular to its situations and to its participants.[9]

This sense of edgework as direct action suggests something else as well: that the often-heard claim as to edgework's ineffability—the claim that those not engaged in edgework activities can't really understand them—constitutes something more than individual ego or subcultural hubris. Thought of as a particularly sharp-edged form of direct action, edgework would indeed generate insights, not to mention emotions and sensual states, available only to those inside the phenomenonological moment of edgework—insights and emotions that can be neither pre-scripted nor fully accounted for otherwise, since their existence in the world depends on the direct action of edgework itself. And yet, viewed from the anarchist political perspective of direct action, this claim as to edgework's ineffability exists not as some exclusionary barrier, but as an invitation to join in an activity whose potential for liberation and self-realization can't be fully told, only experienced.

In that regard I suppose I've spent as much time as anybody investigating and writing about one of edgework's most vivid experiential and sensual states: the "adrenalin rush."[10] I first got turned on—physically and analytically—to the adrenalin rush during my years in the graffiti underground. Graffiti writer after graffiti writer kept describing the experience of doing graffiti to me in the same terms—telling me it was an addictive, euphoric adrenalin rush—and my own experiences were confirming it: I couldn't wait for the next night out painting, mostly because of the intensely altered state of excitement and awareness that accompanied it. Neon, a San Francisco graffiti writer, confirms it as well, and locates the rush in a larger edgework context: "There's just something exciting about seeing the paint flying out of the can onto the wall," he says. "A lot of people paint for the adrenalin rush, just like sky divers and snow boarders" (quoted in Walsh, 1996, p. 47).

Soon enough, I became aware of something else, something that even more clearly linked edgework with anarchy and direct action: The rush of being out an a nocturnal adventure with other writers, of seeing our art take shape on an alley wall, was one thing, but the rush of doing this when the local media was labelling us the city's worst crime threat, when the mayor was seriously pissed off by the local "graffiti problem," when the police were sweeping by with spotlights and special patrols—now, that was something else. "Right before you hit the wall, you get that rush," Voodoo told me in those days. "And right when you hit the wall, you know that you're breaking the law and that gives that extra adrenalin flow...kind of a romantic criminal act" (quoted in Ferrel, 1996, p. 82). I couldn't have said it better.

So, as it turns out, the adrenalin rush of edgework regularly incorporates even more than intense experiential pleasure and excitement. For many edge-workers, the rush exists as a moment of experiential anarchy, of experiential resistance to legal and economic authority, a moment of self-liberation accomplished through the magical, on-the-spot conversion of one's own criminalization and ostracization into an enhanced experience of euphoric excitement. In this sense, an adrenalin rush of this sort really is quite an accomplishment—not only a body blast of intense pleasure, but a subversion of social control through direct action, an inversion of the usual hierarchies that govern daily life, a phenomenology of freedom. And in this sense, both edgework and anarchism equally constitute "visceral revolts" against the order of things, sensual uprisings against boredom, tedium, alienation, and regulation. "Boredom is always counterrevolutionary," said the Situationists—and so, by the same logic, self-made excitement at least begins to counter that boredom, to ignite the revolution of everyday life.

But what if, as is often the case with graffiti writers and BASE-jumpers and others, you could undertake the adrenalin rush not just individually, but as a collective experience made all the more intense by its reverberation among other edgeworkers and anarchists? What if you could accomplish this rush time and again, so that it was forever bubbling up into your life and the lives of others, into lives unwinding along the lines of ongoing self-invention and uncertainty and excitement? What kind of endless, imperfect revolution would that be?

The Festival of the Oppressed

In 1871, the citizens of Paris tried to find out. That year they launched the largest urban insurrection of the era, an "unplanned, unguided, formless revolution" against France's National Government that came to be called the Paris Commune. Participants in the Commune dragged governmental guillotines into the street and burned them in rowdy public celebrations. They pulled down and destroyed the Vendôme Column, Paris's most prominent symbol of Napoleonic empire, as part of a festive gathering where "the excitement was so intense that people moved about as if in a dream." They held meetings where they urged "people, govern yourself directly," and the women of the Commune organized Women's Clubs where they argued for doing away with "bosses who treat the worker as a producing machine" and "all Governments as such," urging instead that "what we need today is action." Above all else, the women and men of the Commune danced, made music, laughed and played in the streets. "Would you believe it? Paris is fighting and singing," reported the poet Villiers de l'Isle-Adam. "Paris does not only have soldiers, she has singers, too.... Paris is the city of heroism and laughter." Louis Baron witnessed the same carnival of insurrectionary pleasure and excitement: "Eating and drinking their fill, making love, the Parisians ... have no energy left to imagine, even vaguely, the horrific consequences of defeat" (Edwards, 1973, pp. 10, 40, 99, 106, 107, 110, 140–144). After seventy-two days, defeat did come—but even on that day, Parisians were still fighting and singing, still partying at the end of the world. And because of this, the Paris Commune came to be called something else as well: the festival of the oppressed.

Like many other anarchists over the past 130 years, the Situationists saw in the Paris Commune a glimpse of anarchic possibility, a dis-organized detonation followed by a free explosion, "a city free of planning, a field of moments, visible and loud, the antithesis of planning: a city that was reduced to zero and then reinvented every day" (Marcus, 1989, p. 147). Here indeed was a revolution of everyday life, a revolution coming alive in moments of insurrectionary excitement, a revolution animated by a volatile mix of danger and pleasure. So the Situationists set about calling up the ghost of the Commune by dis-organizing their own revolution of everyday life, basing this revolution not on new leaders or new organizations or some new-boss-same-as-the-old-boss, but on their creation of subversive "situations" in which, at least for a moment, everyday meaning was undermined, the everyday order of things overturned. Anarchists like Hakim Bey have lately called up the same ephemeral spirit, arguing not for new institutions but for "Immediatism," for "temporary autonomous zones" in which individuals and groups can open a window into a better world.[11] And of course, here's the kicker: If it's insurrectionary moments and subversive situations and temporary autonomy that make an ongoing anarchist revolution, that animate the festival of the oppressed, some other folks have lately been joining in as well: graffiti writers, outlaw BASE-jumpers, skate punks, and edgeworkers of all sorts.

But you might well point out, the Paris Commune was defeated after only seventy-two days. Temporary autonomous zones by definition don't endure. Moments of edgework last no longer than it takes the spray paint to dry or the parachute to open. Maybe so—but then again, what revolution, what moment that subverts the order of things, does endure? Lenin and Stalin and the Soviet Union, tenured 60's "radicals" now in charge of administering academia, animal farms full of pontificating pigs—all suggest the fraudulence, not to mention the grave human danger, of revolutions that endeavor to endure, and in enduring become rotting institutionalized parodies of themselves.

Recognizing this, anarchists don't bother with the illusion of creating a better world that's guaranteed to remain in place; they fight instead for a process, for one free explosion after another, for a new order that's no order at all. "Anarchism is not...a theory of the future," said Emma Goldman. "It is a living force in the affairs of our life, constantly creating new conditions" (Goldman, 1969, p. 63). Arguing that "the passion for destruction is a creative passion, too," Michael Bakunin agrees, reminding anarchists and others that, if our lives and our revolutions are to avoid becoming prisons of past experience, they have to be torn down, rebuilt, reinvented day after day (Bakunin, 1974, p. 58). But maybe the "organizer" of a BASE-jumping event that Steve, Dragan, and I attended caught the ephemeral, open-ended nature of edgework and anarchy about as well as anybody. When we asked him if we could hang around, ask a few questions, and conduct some interviews, he offered in response an appropriately half-baked recipe for the festival of the oppressed: "You have my permission to do whatever the fuck you want."

Seen in this way, that passionate affinity that Steve and I first sensed between edgework and anarchy is no surprise. Anarchists and edgeworkers, anti-WTO protestors and skate punks and graffiti writers all passionately seek a different "place of definitions," as Hunter Thompson put it, a place where little is defined except the seeking. Desperate for a life outside the routine degradations of work and consumption and authority, determined to live before they die, they invent moments of human engagement and do-it-yourself excitement never meant to endure. Along the way, inside these moments of edgework and anarchy, they discover time and again new ways of knowing and being, and so detonate an ongoing revolution of everyday life.

Can all these moments coalesce into something more, into some broader "political" revolution for self-determination and direct action? Damned if I know; I suppose that mostly depends on what we are willing to mean by "something more." But I think there is something I do know, something I learned from all those illicit motorcycle runs that Steve and I undertook, something I learned especially from being a graffiti writer, from those moments of adrenalin-charged anarchy when our late-night graffiti adventures directly defied the campaigns to stop them. It's something the Situationists knew, too, and acted on, and converted into perhaps their best-remembered slogan. It's something members of the anarchist Reclaim the Streets movement understood back in 1996, illegally blockading a London motorway, staging an ephemeral "festival of resistance" on the reclaimed pavement, flying this same Situationist slogan on a big banner that floated above the dancers and the musicians, above ten thousand anarchists and edgeworkers lost in the possibilities of the moment:

The Society That Abolishes Every Adventure
Makes Its Own Abolition The Only Possible Adventure[12]

Notes
1. See Lyng, "Edgework"; "Dangerous Methods"; Lyng and Snow, "Vocabularies of Motive."
2. See Ferrell, *Crimes of Style*; *Tearing Down the Streets*.
3. See Ferrell, Milovanovic, and Lyng, "Edgework, Media Practices, and the Elongation of Meaning"; Ferrell, *Tearing Down the Streets*, pp. 79–87.
4. See for example Dolgoff, *The Anarchist Collectives*.

5. See pp. 106–107, 114.

6. See Debord, *Society of the Spectacle*; Dark Star Collective, *Beneath the Paving Stones: Situationists and the Beach, May 68*.

7. See McDermott, *Street Style*, pages 61–67.

8. See similarly Hamm and Ferrell, "Confessions of Danger and Humanity," pages 268–270.

9. See Lyng, "Dangerous Methods"; Ferrell, "Crimological *Verstehen*."

10. See for example Ferrell, *Crimes of Style*; *Tearing Down the Streets*; "Criminological *Verstehen*."

11. See for example Bey, "Immediatism"; "Primitives and Extropians."

12. See Jordan, "The Art of Necessity," pages 142–146.

References

Bakunin, M. *Selected Writings*, edited by A. Lehning. New York: Grove Press, 1974.

Bey, H. "Immediatism." In *Drunken Boat: Art, Rebellion, Anarchy*, edited by M. Blechman. Seattle: Autonomedia/Left Bank Books, 1994.

———. "Primitives and Extropians." *Anarchy: A Journal of Desire Armed* 14, no. 4 (1995): 39–43.

Dark Star Collective, ed. *Beneath the Paving Stones: Situationists and the Beach, May 68*. Oakland, CA: AK Press, 2002.

Debord, G. *Society of the Spectacle*. Detroit: Black and Red, 1983.

Dolgoff, S., ed. *The Anarchist Collectives: Workers' Self-Management in the Spanish Revolution, 1936–1939*. New York: Free Life Editions, 1974.

Edwards, S., ed. *The Communards of Paris, 1871*. Ithaca, NY: Cornell University Press, 1973.

Ferrell, J. *Crimes of Style: Urban Graffiti and the Politics of Criminality*. Boston: Northeastern University Press, 1996.

———. "Criminological *Verstehen*: Inside the Immediacy of Crime." *Justice Quarterly* 14(1) (1997): 3–23.

———. *Tearing Down the Streets: Adventures in Urban Anarchy*. New York: Palgrave/St. Martin's; Palgrave/MacMillan, 2001/2002.

Ferrell, J., Milovanovic, D., and Lyng, S. "Edgework, Media Practices, and the Elongation of Meaning: A Theoretical Ethnography of the Bridge Day Event," *Theoretical Criminology* 5(2) (2001): 177–202.

Feyerabend, P. *Against Method: Outline of an Anarchistic Theory of Knowledge*. London: Verso, 1975.

The Fifth Goal. 2001/2002. ('zine). P.O. Box 970085, Orem, UT, 84097.

Goldman, E. *Anarchism and Other Essays*. New York: Dover, 1969.

Guerin, D. *Anarchism*. New York: Monthly Review Press, 1970.

Hamm, M. S., and Ferrell, J. "Confessions of Danger and Humanity," In *Ethnography at the Edge: Crime, Deviance, and Field Research*, edited by J. Ferrell and M. S. Hamm. Boston: Northeastern University Press, 1998, pp. 254–272.

Jordan, J. "The Art of Necessity: The Subversive Imagination of Anti-Road Protest and Reclaim the Streets," " In *DIY Culture: Party and Protest in Nineties Britain*, edited by G. McKay. London: Verso, 1998, pp. 129–151.

Kornbluh, J., ed. *Rebel Voices: An IWW Anthology* (Expanded Edition). Chicago: Charles H. Kerr, 1988.

Lyng, S. "Edgework: A Social Psychological Analysis of Voluntary Risk Taking," *American Journal of Sociology* 95(4) (1990): pp. 876–921.

———. "Dangerous Methods: Risk Taking and the Research Process," In *Ethnography at the Edge: Crime, Deviance, and Field Research*, edited by J. Ferrell and M. S.Hamm. Boston: Northeastern University Press, 1998, pp. 221–251.

Lyng, S., and Snow, D. "Vocabularies of Motive and High-Risk Behavior: The Case of Skydiving," In *Advances in Group Processes*, edited by E. J. Lawler, Greenwich, CT: JAI, 1986, pp. 157–179.

Marcus, G. *Lipstick Traces: A Secret History of the Twentieth Century.* Cambridge, MA: Harvard
  University Press, 1989.
McDermott, C. *Street Style: British Design in the 80s.* New York: Rizzoli, 1987.
Thompson, H. S. *Hell's Angels: A Strange and Terrible Saga.* New York: Ballantine, 1967.
Walsh, M. *Graffito.* Berkeley, CA: North Atlantic Books, 1996.
White, T. *We Aren't Blocking Traffic, We Are Traffic!* (film/video). San Francisco, CA, 1999.

4

Edgework and the Aesthetic Paradigm: Resonances and High Hopes

DAVID COURTNEY

CONTENTS

"It don't mean a thing if it ain't got that swing."

Doo wop. Doo wop. Doo wop. Doo wop. Doo wop. Doo wop. Doo wop. Doo wop"[1] is the responsory of those in the intimate know.[2] That's a lot of "doo wops" for a culture that values an economy of means! But this response does not come from the dominant reality but the aesthetic/erotic reality. Herbert Marcuse, in his book *The Aesthetic Dimension: Toward a Critique of Marxist Aesthetics*, points out that the aesthetic reality (especially through its avant-garde works) indicts and contradicts the ordinary reality. The aesthetic/erotic reality, through liberation of individuals to sensuous forms, is autonomous from the given reality and its normative social relations (Marcuse, 1978).

Jazz is a denizen of this superior reality. Doo Wop jazz demands a "transaction" (Dewey, 1958) between performers and audiences contending with the musical material. Swinging with the music is a transaction well known by the musicians. Now, in the moment of sounding, the material demand on all the listeners (musicians and audience alike) is "give that rhythm everything you got!"

"Doo wop" has, minimally, three sensuous functions: First, it is a primitivist, primordial response, a nonsensical scat (non-discursive) utterance, utterly expressive.

Second, "doo wop" demands a communitarian affirmation analogous to a religious group affirming its identity and common experience.[3] Performing and listening to serious music emphasizes a shared or common perception. How else can the ensemble play as one in their new emergent identity as "the band?" The band is a *whole* greater than the sum of it's parts and a new being with its own aesthetic requirements of the players. Success depends on a *confluence between the band's and the participants' active listening* to shape an "emergent" event. The band looks for the audience to affirm and join the band's somatic/emotional response to the music. The aesthetic reality's participants now include the attentive audience.

Jazz, and its participatory cohort, seems a safe place to risk the subjective (individual) movement inward, abandoning the prescriptive social order and its analysis through disembodied symbolic systems, held at bay during the aesthetic experience (Marcuse, 1978, p. 38). Subjective feeling and unity to the feelings of the group (and music) are simultaneous realities in the aesthetic realm. There will be plenty of time later to employ cognition for an appraisal of the music, the musical event, and our sentient response.

Third, "doo wop" is the name of a style of jazz. The music is the Doo Wop style. It is a self-referencing, whole form. As such, the players and audience implement Doo Wop's musical vocabulary, which alerts them to what to listen for while attending to the embodied activities at hand. Here the universal discourse is only the gratification of the sensate (where one loses a sense of the external and a convergence with the music is complete). An example is the admonishing lyric:

It [my emphasis] don't mean a thing.

All you got to do is sing.

Doo wop. Doo wop. Doo wop. Doo wop. Doo wop. Doo wop. Doo wop. Doo wop.

All non-aesthetic concerns ("it") are negated. The action of the participant is all that is required. Perhaps it is hard to imagine that from such an abstract realm a life of optimal, authentic experience and radical new relations can be built. But this will be the claim later in a discussion of the "aesthetic paradigm."

For persons who wish to gain their volition, who desire to be self-determining and self-inventing, high art and serious music promise awareness of institutional manipulations. The aesthetic reality offers vehicles to shape an authentic self.

Further, those who make high art and serious music central to their needs, interests, and activities are able to develop and heighten their emotional and somatic ways of knowing and synthesize them to thought and self-consciousness. *The claim here is that persons who apply an aesthetic paradigm[4] for the invention of personal ontologies share a common experience with edgeworkers.*

How are edgeworkers and "competent viewers and listeners" (CV/L) alike? How do they differ? First, this essay will provide an explanation of how CV/Ls invent themselves by taking the initial action of overcoming the "narcissistic scar." Elimination of narcissism is necessary if CV/Ls are to participate in the aesthetic/erotic reality. The ability to unite with others and objects, to achieve "emergence," is essential to the aesthetic process. Second, there will be an examination of the aesthetic paradigm for both its content and usefulness in creating a radical ontology for CV/Ls. The aesthetic/erotic reality speaks truth to the lies of "the mystified (and petrified) social reality, opening the horizon of change (liberation)" (Marcuse, 1978, p. ix). Third, a discussion of how CV/Ls' undertakings resonate with and differ from those of edgeworkers will be explored. Finally, an instance of how CV/Ls transform their lives through understanding the content of artworks will be considered.

Competent Viewers and Listeners

Competent viewers and listeners intentionally pursue the understanding of aesthetic forms. For example, competent listeners know when a musical movement is in sonata form. How else will they be able to identify the recapitulation of the theme when it arrives? For less-than-competent listeners, the music floats by as lovely but incoherent, as a stream of consciousness. Competent listeners listen closely to the recapitulation for a possible variation on the melodic theme.

When considering representational art or programmatic music, competent viewers/listeners consider the sociohistorical context of the artwork to learn the meaning of its content for its intended audience. An analysis of antique artworks with modern eyes alone is the analytical sin of retrospective modernism.

John Dewey's distinction between "recognition" and "perception" is applicable here. In *Art as Experience*, Dewey distinguishes between these two concepts as follows:

> The difference between the two is immense. Recognition is perception arrested before it has a chance to develop freely. In recognition there is a beginning of an act of perception. But this beginning is not allowed to serve the development of a full perception of the thing recognized. It is arrested at the point where it will serve some *other* [his emphasis] purpose, as we recognize a man on the street in order to greet or to avoid him, not so as to see him for the sake of seeing what is there (1958, p. 35).

Casual listeners go to the concert hall to hear Beethoven's Symphony #5. As the opening motif sounds, a gleeful moment of recognition is likely. But this musical movement continues on for another seven minutes. Incompetent listeners read the program during the music, watch the conductor, check out the haircuts of the musicians, think about that schmuck their daughter is dating, and so on. Listening is abandoned.

Competent listeners know Beethoven's polyphonic music is packed with nuances. Their eyes are closed to hear all the notes of the chord, the different timbres, and the competing melodic lines. The perception of music requires listening, not mere hearing.[5]

Many sociologists reduce art to a commodity used only for establishing class identity.[6] This demeans the revolutionary character of serious art. Popular art reiterates the views and sentimentalities of the ordinary reality. High art demands the viewers *change*. While high art takes viewers through extreme emotions, it also engenders in them a de-sublimation of the social wrong, assisting viewers to a new cultural awareness, a new morality, and a better course of action.

The CV/L's personal cares must be set aside to meet the demands of listening and to understand an aesthetic/erotic reality that can inspire change. Private concerns are negated so that listeners might become part of something larger than themselves. Individual troubles that are the product of the narcissistic scar cannot appear during listening.

The Narcissistic Scar

In his text *Beyond the Pleasure Principle*, Freud contrasts the ego-instincts and the sexual instincts. "The upshot of our enquiry ... has been the drawing of a sharp distinction between the 'ego-instincts' and the sexual instincts, and the view that the former exercise pressure towards death and the latter towards a prolongation of life" (1961, p. 52). The ego-instincts include the "narcissistic scar" and the "pleasure principle," characteristics of the death instinct.

Freud writes, "Loss of love and failure leave behind them a permanent injury to self-regard in the form of a narcissistic scar" (1961, pp. 21–22). He says this problem starts for the child when s/he perceives the parents breaking expected bonds of intimacy and affection as they respond to the attention demands of others. He continues by arguing the wound is kept raw later in life by repetitive disappointments such as anger when a friend betrays us, a subordinate fails to show gratitude, repetitive love affairs come to the same conclusion, and so on.

Freud finds that the narcissistic scar is sustained as the individual acts out the same "character-traits" again and again out of a compulsion to repeat. This is exacerbated by the "pleasure principle," which regulates "mental events" that create "tension" for the human organism. The "pleasure principle" protects the organism from external pleasure and pain. The pleasure in the "pleasure principle" is, it seems, the organism successfully resisting change, maintaining the comfort of the status quo. For Freud, external forces create tension on the organism. The organism (following the dictates of the death instinct) wants to avoid and lower the tension. The pleasure principle is the mechanism for accomplishing this feat.

The outcome is disconnection from meaningful relationships because of lack of awareness of the character-traits that sabotage the life-instinct. Worse, the narcissistic scar creates a "sense of inferiority" in its bearer. Because the individual is unaware of these attributes, and because skills for ontological change are absent from the individual's consciousness, the neurosis continues unabated (1961, pp. 21–23).

For Freud, charting the course of human neuroses, the compulsion to avoid tension (found in self-expressive intimacies), through what the ego believes will provide stability, is evidence of the death instincts. Freud states:

> The dominating tendency of mental life, and perhaps of nervous life in general, is the effort to reduce, to keep constant or to remove internal tension due to stimuli—a tendency which finds expression in the plea-sure principle; and our recognition of that fact is one of our strongest reasons for believing in the existence of death instincts (1961, p. 67).

As for the "life instinct" (the sexual instinct), an elemental incentive to CV/Ls, Freud suggests the poets and philosophers have best captured the qualities of the sexual instinct through their descriptions of Eros (1961, pp. 60–61). The sexual instinct compulsively repeats in a biological attempt of the organism to combine with another organism to preserve its life. Freud says,

> [This] result is brought about by the influx of fresh amounts of stimulus. This tallies well with the hypothesis that the life process of the individual leads for internal reasons to an abolition of chemical tensions, that is to say, to death, whereas union with the living substance of a different individual increases those tensions, introducing what may be described as fresh "vital differences" which must then be lived off (1961, p. 67).

And "living off" these powerful frictions between the self and the object to which Eros directs us, liberated from the death instinct and the pleasure prin-ciple, is precisely what CV/Ls aim to do.

"Living off," reveling in the emotional and somatic tensions created by high art, is a category of experience CV/Ls yearn for. In fact, the extremeness and novelty of the emotional response are criteria CV/Ls use to evaluate the quality of the art.[7] The more extreme and unexpected the emotional response created by the catalytic artwork, the better the artwork. Art unleashes the imaginative capacity of viewers while their somatic and emotional reactions luxuriate in the sensuous realm. The self's feelingful reaction to new categories of emotions demonstrates the artwork's expressive powers. The artwork's interdependent, emotive elements, in turn, serve as an example (and a model) for the expressive potential of viewers in addressing the community around them.

CV/Ls do not care whether the emotions evoked are negative or positive; to feel deeply is the thing. Art's reflective distance from the horrors of ordinary reality reminds the viewers' memory to act upon the most tragic decisions through the emotional/rational injunction—*never again*. Freud remarks in *Beyond the Pleasure Principle*: "The artistic play and artistic imitation carried out by adults, which, unlike children's, are aimed at an audience, do not spare the spectators (for instance, in tragedy) the most painful experiences and can yet be felt by them as highly enjoyable" (1961, p. 17). Viewers who suffer throughout *Schindler's List* learn the necessity of change from attitudes of capricious bigotry toward a predisposition to egalitarianism. The catharsis and the renewed obligation are gratifying.

Whether or not Freud is empirically correct as to the reasons most persons fail to tend to the neuroses that stunt their emotional lives, he is not alone in the examination of why people have difficulty achieving meaningful, enduring, personalized intimacies and actions. The social behaviorist/philosopher George Herbert Mead, through his discussion of the "me" and the "I," offers an interesting contrast to Freud's subjectivist theory. Mead's "me" and "I" represent different phases of the individual act. The "me" is the phase of the act that represents the attitudes of others towards the self (including institutions), which constrain the "I" and its impulsive actions and responses.

Novelty is expressed in the action of the "I"; however, the "form" or structure of the self is "conventional." But Mead tells us that our attitudes can reduce the conventional form. He offers this example: "In the artist's attitude, where there is artistic creation, the emphasis upon the element of novelty is carried to the limit. This demand for the *unconventional* [my emphasis] is especially noticeable in modern art" (Mead, 1967, p. 209). This emphasis on the unconventional, as opposed to the structured "me," is the attitude essential to avant-garde artists in their resistance to mainstream, popular, hegemonic production. As Marcuse (1978, p. 9) puts it:

> Art is committed to that perception of the world which alienates individuals from their functional existence and performance in society—it is committed to an emancipation of sensibility, imagination, and reason in all spheres of subjectivity and objectivity. The aesthetic transformation becomes a vehicle of recognition and indictment.

The Western world's modern high art, and some antique art, self-consciously critiques the prescriptive view through its political art. As for modern art's abstractionist side, novelty is a necessary condition of inventive and complex human expression of aesthetic feeling. These emotions are answering to, and are generated by, the artist's and viewers' response to the artist's materials.

In the case of Jackson Pollock, he had a sheer "I" taking him where the materials demanded. He still operated inside a creative community whose work and styles had enormous influence on his. Nevertheless, no one debates the novelty of his mature work of the 1950s. Pollock's art still influences artists today, such as Brice Marden, Hermann Nitsch, Arnulf Rainer, and Susan Rothenberg. All owe a debt to the autonomy of the expressive gesture and the

Eastern aesthetic of the calligraphic form. The hand, the wrist, and the body are required to move into, and be a characteristic of, the perfecting act. Pollock himself referred to painting as the act of perfecting. What viewer among you would add or subtract a drip from his painting *Autumn Rhythm*?

The perfecting act is the locus of the superior reality of the aesthetic dimension.[8] There are those who would say of *Autumn Rhythm*, "That ain't art." This is censorship in the anti-art response of the conventional "me." Though the "me" does not determine the precise response, it can determine the sort of response. Remember the response is the act of taking on the attitudes of others in the group. As Mead states

> *Social control* [my italics] is the expression of the "me" over against the expression of the "I." It sets the limits, it gives the determination that enables the "I," so to speak, to use the "me" as the means of carrying out what is the undertaking that all are interested in. Where persons are held outside [as are CV/Ls] or beyond that sort of organized expression there arises a situation in which social control is absent (1967, pp. 210–211).

CV/Ls are social outliers, and they know it. The moment they critique or lampoon the commercial fetish, they are labeled "snobs" who are both "arrogant" and "obnoxious." These mainstream acts of stigmatizing CV/Ls and avant-garde social-comment artists distances the stigmatizers from the CV/L's (and art's) demystification of "the realm of propaganda" (Marcuse 1978, p. 37). The alienation of CV/Ls causes them to claim to understand the frustration and disgust of others subject to the arbitrary bigotry of the institutionalized popular culture. Popular culture serves as a megaphone of normative social control. And still, lurking in all of us is the desire for free, unmitigated expression and the search for situations that allow us to do so.

The arts widen the self's range of expressive emotions. High art's commitment to the presentation of extreme emotions pushes the boundaries, the edge, still further and deeper. Pablo Picasso's *Guernica* is an obvious presentation of extreme emotions. He records the villagers' perspective in the throes of the Spanish Fascists' bombing of their village.

Guernica is eleven and a half feet tall and twenty-five and a half feet wide. Most viewers stand about as close to a painting as they can get. *Guernica* is monumental and physically overwhelms them.[9] The "conventional me" tells typical viewers to stay close, keep control over the picture and then move on to the next one. But *Guernica* swallows viewers, drawing them into its realm. Will viewers adapt to the size of the painting? Will they move back so that they can see the interdependent symbolisms as an organic[10] whole? Learned viewers let the painting push them back. CV/Ls retreat from the painting to see it again from a long viewing distance. Now that they can see the painting all over at once, able viewers can dwell on its interrelated symbols. They do so to immerse themselves in the "I" of the aesthetic process. Arguably, the only way in which the experience can be improved is by sharing it with others with similar viewing attitudes.

Competent viewers each call out the imaginative, expressive self in the other, full of the expectation that the reciprocity of exchanges will leave their community transfixed in the moment of the "I" that will later transform the "me." After all, this is the CV/Ls' experience. They enjoy learning and the personal application of insight. In addition to cognitive acuity, they are ripe with the skills of listening, empathy, expressiveness (bringing words to feelings), the tactile, discipline, and focus. Even with all this, perhaps the paramount interest of CV/Ls is the enduring "I."

The "enduring 'I'" may not have the intent of object-cathexis, but the activity leaves the participant no choice once the "me" is abandoned. The first movement of Beethoven's Symphony No. 7 lasts approximately thirteen minutes. For the serious listener, those thirteen minutes are the duration of the "I." As Pierre Bourdieu (1984) demonstrated in *Distinction*, most persons will embrace art out of status needs and class-identity interests. For them, participation in the arts is essentially to satisfy the "me." But for CV/Ls, their existential security in themselves allows them to be humble before the music. They risk entrusting all of their being to the external phenomenon for as long as it sounds.

When one contemplates the aesthetic experience, it seems a scary undertaking. For one feels one's self gone, elided into the event. The experience of serious listeners is that they are gone—the ego is annihilated—until the music ends, and then the day-to-day reality, and their presence in it, floods back. The skeptic might ask, "Well! What if you don't get back?" One is tempted to answer, "Well then, erotic/aesthetic-cathexis to the object is complete and the self disappears in a puff of smoke."

The Aesthetic Paradigm

Think of the following elements as eigenvalues of the aesthetic paradigm system.[11] CV/Ls are ever mindful of these ideas in shaping their attitude for tangling with the complex external phenomena that are serious artworks. Aesthetic paradigm elements include:

Simultaneous realities
Emergence
Expression
Invention

"Simultaneous realities" is an analytical approach to phenomena, which begins with the hunt for samenesses during the analytic process. At the same moment of tragic soliloquy, Hamlet appears to be a laughable buffoon. How do these ostensibly contradictory feelings occupy the same moment? It drives one to ask: How are comedy and tragedy akin?

The pursuit of simultaneous realities is in stark contrast to most current academic activity in the liberal arts, now dedicated to professional specialization.

In *The Last Intellectuals*, Russell Jacoby (1995) writes of the demise of public intellectual discourse and its diminishing ability to pose solutions:

> [Academic] professionalization leads to privatization or depoliticiza-
> tion, a withdrawal of intellectual energy from a larger domain to a nar-
> rower discipline. Leftists who entered the university hardly invented this
> process, but they accepted, even accelerated it. Marxism itself has not
> been immune; in recent years it has become a professional "field"
> plowed by specialists (1995, p. 147).

The search for simultaneous realities is especially unlike ideology and its dependence on charting differences. Ideological analysis has a dualistic tendency as it
hopes to affirm its identity, in part, by identifying what it is not.[12] In the aesthetic reality, a landscape painting is simultaneously a representation of a place
(a three-dimensional space), and it is a painting (essentially a two-dimensional
space). The representational painter may be motivated to share his/her feeling of
the place or the unexpected harmony of the landscape and so on. But the painting is also a two-dimensional canvas—in material reality—a painting.

Because of the viewers' own history in the world, they cannot help but think
of the painting as a picture of the external world. Tutored viewers hold this view
but also know to see an arrangement of pigment over a two-dimensional plane.
The fun begins with finding the emergent qualities of the represented place and
the colored linen.

One benefit of seeing the canvas simultaneously as representational *and*
wholly abstract is that viewers learn to see as an artist sees. Conventional viewers look at a representational artwork as a presentation of a thing in the world
presented again. But when the Impressionists look out on the world, they see a
phantasmagoria of hues. If they faithfully record the colors and their shapes,
the representational elements will take care of themselves.

Wise viewers are the ones who *apply* what they have just learned. The next
time they look at an actual landscape, if they see as artists see, they will see no
trees, rocks, lichen, etc. but will see lines, colors, shapes, and forms. Those
evening television weatherpersons who say, "For the best color this October
weekend, drive to Muskegon" are absolutely right. But in fact, the winter
woods are just as loaded with color as the autumn forest. If you look for the
colors first, you will be shocked by the enormity of the panoply. The reading
of nuances is enhanced if you look for one improbable color at a time. One
does not expect to find blue in the vegetation of the winter landscape, but it
dominates the shadows of snow and the dark folds of mountains at sunset. In
such conditions, mountains of purple majesty appear.

Most of all, the Impressionist painters are presenting their aesthetic experiences so that we might live in and through their experiences again and again.[13]
Avant-garde artists make plain each element they used in the construction of
the work that we might reconstruct it and have aesthetic experiences akin to

the ones the artists had during the making. Each performance of a composer's work is, too, the happy chance to experience the work again in a manner not unlike the composer.

The complexity of a single visual artwork is so great that we feel its unity, but the exploration of how the nuances add up to the emergent effect requires viewing the work with a learned eye for long stretches with repeat visits. Informed viewing and listening occurs through a prolonged inward movement into the self. Marcuse argues that the inward experience is how we build "bulwarks" against oppressive regimes:

> The flight into inwardness and the insistence on a private sphere may well serve as bulwarks against a society which administers all dimensions of human existence. Inwardness and subjectivity may well become the inner and outer space for the subversion of experience, for the emergence of another universe (1978, p. 38).

Actively engaged viewers utilizing all of their emotional, somatic, and cognitive faculties will be exhausted after an hour in front of a single canvas. Their period of active engagement was the length of their enduring "I." For CV/Ls, it's time to move to the next treat, one that will require a different set of attending muscles and a new involvement of the transformed "me." The next experience is often a continuation of the inward musing in these terms: How does the aesthetic expression just received apply to one's own experience in the world?

The imperative of art—that the self, and hence the community the self is a part of, must change—means that a strategy will have to be undertaken in which the many others that make up the self can play out their restive, transactional parts. The artwork will require the self to form, in some measure, a new community. Mead states,

> If we take the attitude of the community over against our own responses, that is a true statement, but we must not forget this other capacity, that of replying to the community and insisting on the gesture of the community changing. We can reform the order of things; we can insist on making the community standards better standards. We are not simply bound by the community (1967, p. 168).

Marcuse reminds us that it is the estranging power of art's abstracting form that reorients us to the world and to the changes we must make to it and, simultaneously, ourselves. He says it is "the aesthetic form which gives the familiar content and the familiar experience the power of estrangement and leads to the emergence of a new consciousness and a new perception" (Marcuse 1978, p. 41).

"Simultaneous realities" is an estranging form that, in its unlikeness to conventional dualistic analysis in the ordinary reality, also creates anxieties for competent viewers. Educated eyes will need to remember all of the constituent elements (not allowing the array to fall into chaos) to fully understand the art-work. This never quite works in that any one example of high art, in its com-plexity, outstrips the ability of any participant to surround, or control, all the relationships of the elements no matter how much lifetime he or she has left.[14] Unlike edgeworkers, CV/Ls never feel in control of the aesthetic experience. For example, try calculating the balance Mondrian has supplied among the constituent elements of one of his paintings from the 1930s. The black lines of the grid are rightly read as negative spaces between the white, gray, black, and colored rectangles. The "simultaneous reality" is that the black lines are also a positive grid lying on a white ground. In the day to day reality this is a contra-diction. Nevertheless, this program doubles the number of combinations viewers must execute to determine the balance that the seemingly asymmetrical structure unexpectedly produces.

Anxiety is also the consequence of high art's reminder to CV/Ls that through art's estranging forms one is obligated to

> "struggle against the entire capitalist and state-socialist organization of work (the assembly line, Taylor system, hierarchy), in the struggle to end patriarchy, to reconstruct the destroyed life environment, and to develop and nurture a new morality and a new sensibility" (Marcuse 1978, 28).

Not coincidentally, these were the objectives of Mondrian's De Stijl compatri-ots. Through architecture and urban planning, De Stijl art sought to construct workers' housing in environments of unexpected harmony. Mondrian's paint-ings provided a formal paradigm for this new sensibility.

For CV/Ls another anxiety comes from the application of an *aesthetic exemplar's* conduct to our own values and behaviors. What are the conse-quences of adopting the bohemian Musetta's actions in *La Boheme*? She demands that the public who would judge her/me examine their own hypocri-sies first. It is a significant act of the "I" that should be undertaken with con-siderable tact. The kind of advice Musetta proffers is seldom welcome, and those receiving it may make such comments the foundation for enmity.

"Emergence" is a fundamental quality of aesthetic experience and is, in effect, the chase after shared or new, like experiences. John Dewey begins *Art as Experience* by contrasting mainstream viewers with connoisseurs. Dewey states, the "common conception" of art is that which is observed from the once removed. Untutored viewers look at art and do not spiral off into the host of emotional and ideational experiences into which we are to be lured. It does not cross their mind to have an "experience" with the object. Dewey writes,

> In common conception, the work of art is often identified with the building, book, painting or statue in its existence apart from human experience. Since the actual work of art is what the product does with and in experience, the result is not favorable to understanding (1958, p. 3).

Conventional viewers prefer low art because it affirms the values and feelings they already hold. Marcuse affirms that "popularized" art reifies "the dominant social institutions" and "the established relations" (1978, p. 7).

In contraposition Marcuse (1978, p. 49) discusses how high "art's unique truth breaks with both everyday and holiday reality, which block a whole dimension of society and nature. Art is transcendence into this dimension, where its autonomy constitutes itself as autonomy in contradiction. When art abandons this autonomy and with it the aesthetic form in which the autonomy is expressed, art succumbs to that reality which it seeks to grasp and indict."

Typical viewers have little interest in change or in a frictive high art that makes demands on them to achieve new experiences in unfamiliar (and autonomous) territory and reach some measure of comprehension of that which looms in front of them. Popular culture likes low art better as it more readily serves as a nonautonomous adjunct to a decorating scheme of indiscriminate and narcissistic taste. The oppositional high art truism is: Great art won't match your couch.

In aesthetic experience, emergence is the norm. Dewey says:

> Every successive part flows freely, without seam and without unfilled blanks, into what ensues…

> Because of continuous *merging* [my emphasis] there are no holes, mechanical junctions, and dead centers when we have an experience. There are no pauses, places of rest, but they punctuate and define the quality of movement. They sum up what has been undergone and prevent its dissipation and idle evaporation. Continued acceleration is breathless and prevents parts from gaining distinction. In a work of art, different acts, episodes occurrences melt and fuse into unity, and yet do not disappear and lose their own character as they do so—just as in a genial conversation there is continuous interchange and blending, and yet each speaker not only retains his own character but manifests it more clearly than is his wont (1958, p. 37).

A critical implication of the last sentence of this quotation is that the emergent qualities of high art can also be found in the conversation that takes place between the artwork and the audience. As witnessed in the examination of Michelangelo's *Creation of* Adam[15] and an orchestra's playing, the attitude of being a constituent element of the process is essential to the experience. Active, critical listening (don't forget to close those eyes!) is how the audience best participates in the music and drives the players to perfection.

"Expression" is the non-discursive articulation of emotional and somatic experiences, an ineffable gesture. The expressive in art is invented "so that the unspeakable is spoken, the otherwise invisible becomes visible and the unbearable explodes" (Marcuse, 1978, p. 45). Important art reliably captures the "essence" of corrupting reality and simultaneously pictures the inexpressable.

Expression is located at the simultaneous realities of chaos and order. With high art, one must assume (for the moment) that all the parts are synchronous as one feels the edge of the expressive pushing out into the unfamiliar.

Expression makes its appeal to the emotions first, with anti-entropic viewers in a state of dis-ease until their emotions are satisfied, or they perceive a rudimentary order in the stimulus. In addition, expression enslaves the body, the emotions and the cognition of the inventor's experience as s/he hopes to eke out some "gesture" to guide others to this place. It is in expression that one finds the cutting edge of novel insight. Very often the expression exists as an absolute abstraction, resistant to word language substitutions.

Johnny was in second grade art class. The teacher, hoping to liberate students to expression, encouraged them to make nonrepresentational paintings in which the artist's feelings would be directly registered through hand, wrist, body, and materials. Johnny did his painting in blacks and dark violets with a blood-red slash across the middle. The teacher was taken aback by the finished product. She took Johnny and the painting to the counselor's office. As Johnny waited in the hallway, the counselor examined the painting; he proclaimed, "This child is emotionally disturbed." They all marched to the principal's office. Once again, Johnny cooled his heels in the hallway as the principal surveyed the picture, announcing, "This child is unhinged." They invited Johnny in. The principal leaned down to Johnny saying, "Johnny, what were you trying to say in this painting?" Johnny said, "If I could have said it, I would not have painted it."

In pure abstraction (absolute music and nonrepresentational art), the "anarchic self" of "impulse" is given free reign in a sensible, nondiscursive sphere. There is no utility in this experience, no instrumental application to assist viewers to the normatively prescribed values of status, power, and wealth. Perhaps this is why a paucity of language exists to describe these experiences. Those who have a light regard for aesthetic experience might ask, "Why bother inventing words to talk about an unprofitable enterprise?" Many words are created to serve utility. Take for example words developed to describe computer operations. However, a few words do exist that can describe specifically aesthetic emotions. For example, we speak of the lyric feeling of the melody: flowing, gently undulating, and uninterrupted. "Lyric" is an aesthetic emotion.

The aesthetic emotions are not the ordinary emotions; no one begins the day by saying, "I am feeling very lyric today." But the lack of terms for the aesthetic emotions does not mean they are not there. Feelings and the body's response are real enough.

Because of the lack of descriptive terms for aesthetic expression, we are forced to borrow from the normal emotions to offer an analogy. The beginning of Beethoven's Symphony No. 5 is not the expression of anger but of…? Of aesthetic feelings, for which we have no language but the four-note motif that moves something in us. This is the artwork's autonomous expression to which we, the listeners, respond in producing the artwork's emergent quality.

It is through expression that one most easily discerns that art is an autonomous reality that simultaneously is able to indict and critique the ordinary reality. The challenge made by *l'art pour l'art* is: Can we invent a material world of complex, unexpected harmony like the material reality of an artwork? Marcuse writes,

> But in contrast to orthodox Marxist aesthetics I see the political potential of art in art itself, in the aesthetic form as such. Furthermore, I argue that by virtue of its aesthetic form, art is largely autonomous *vis a vis* the given social relations, and at the same time *transcends* [my emphasis] them. Thereby art subverts the dominant consciousness, the ordinary experience (1978, p. ix).

Through the abstracted narratives of George Grosz of Berlin Dada, one identifies the stratification of wealth and the human misery inflicted on those outside the ruling elite. Is there truth in Grosz's generalization that the moneyed elite spread their syphilitic infections with equal aplomb among working class prostitutes and their bourgeois housewives? Do Grosz's rotting and kaleidoscopic pictures best help us feel the dizzying, ferocious effects of the dominant *schweinhunden*, without conscience or communitarian commitment? It is through the abstracting characteristics that the essence of the vulgar reality is isolated and identified.

Thus art's "praxis" is more radical than the narrow ideological concern with the "class character of art" (Marcuse, 1978, p. 1). High art provides a more complete picture of both the political and subjective domains. Of representational, social-comment high art, Marcuse writes, "The truth of art lies in this: that the world really is as it appears in the work of art" (1978, p. xii). Examples he offers are the artistic styles of Expressionism and Surrealism anticipating "the destructiveness of monopoly capitalism" (1978, p. 11).[16]

"Invention" is the granting of autonomy to an artist's materials. The materials dictate the form. John Fowles says of writing his *French Lieutenant's Woman* (during the novel, through author intrusion),

> This is why we cannot plan. We know a world is an organism, not a machine. We also know that a genuinely created world must be independent of its creator; a planned world (a world that fully reveals its planning) is a dead world. It is only when our characters and events begin to disobey us that they begin to live (1969, p. 81).

Materials require serious artists[17] to know the physical history and evolution of the matter with which they choose to contend. Artists are asked to know the potential of the material and to demonstrate concrete interconnections (especially the unlikely ones) in recommending a unified vision.

Simultaneously the artist knows he or she "ain't nothing but a secretary." The artist's job is to learn the craft and record the information as quickly and accurately as possible. Two muses sing the sirens' song that drives artists: The first is inspiration. The second is the generalized other (including institutional forces), who determines much of the artist's values, norms, beliefs, and behaviors. Artists constantly struggle with prevailing social expectations in both their private and professional lives. For example, artists who begin to believe their own press can be in danger of succumbing to the narcissistic scar.

The cult of genius enlarges the ego of practitioners foolish enough to believe such cant. Fortunately, whatever they believe about themselves may have little to do with the manufacturing of the artwork.

Often, the meaning of artworks has little to do with the artist's intention. Jean-Francois Millet hoped to show us the oppression of the rural underclass in his painting *The Gleaners*. Then, and now, we see a beautiful landscape painting in which women in stooped labor look heroic in clean, idealized colors. Oops! Millet forgot how such academic paintings were, and are, seen and interpreted.

John Fowles reminds the reader (and presumably himself) that the only thing that separates the author from the readers is that s/he gets to find out how the story comes out first. And after the artwork is finished, the artist becomes just one more viewer.

Finally, explaining invention requires that we say the obvious things about the artist's need of consummate, analytical and evaluative skills to make accurate aesthetic judgments. Artists cannot rush to judgment based on what they have heard about the materials or their first impressions of them. Their works will be handmade and have no anonymous authorship like the mechanically reproduced materials that advertisers encourage us to prize. Hands and bodies, working the materials, direct the artist.

Pictures that come from beginners are slapdash and idiosyncratic. They forget that viewers are constituent elements of the work. There is no substitute for a thorough examination of the material of which the audience is a part. High art will always be about the exploration of nuances, and they will have to be supplied, even if the subtleties take the form of questions asked by viewers engaged in a dialogue with the artwork.[18]

Resonances and Differences Between Edgework Activities and the Aesthetic Paradigm

Are CV/Ls edgeworkers? Lyng tells us that edgework activities include:

1. An exploration of the border between chaos and order, form and formlessness (1990, p. 858);
2. A quest for the "transcendent," found in a "hyperreality" (1990, p. 861);
3. Valuing and developing an "impulsive self" in contrast to an "institutional self" to govern many actions (Turner, 1976);
4. The pursuit of "experiential anarchy" and reveling in the "ineffable" (Lyng, 1990, p. 861);

5. Engaging in actions that "develop a sense of oneness" with the objects in their environment (1990, p. 882);
6. A feeling of control over events (1990, p. 872).

Thus, it would appear that CV/Ls and edgeworkers share many similar attitudes and experiences. As noted above, CV/Ls look to the aesthetic experience for an opportunity to explore the border between chaos and order. They are dedicated to a hyperreality that promises transcendence, and they search out activities that encourage an impulsive self. They share edgeworkers' desire for an existential anarchy enjoined in the ineffable.

Both edgeworkers and CV/Ls resist providing words to their potent somatic/emotional experiences of the ineffable. Words have a way of reducing and subordinating the richness of the experience to the mere meanings of the utterances. Through his participant observations of edgeworkers Lyng reports,

> Although the ... discussion is based on a body of rich descriptive data reported by edgeworkers themselves, many edgework enthusiasts regard the experience as ineffable. They maintain that language simply cannot capture the essence of edgework and therefore see it a waste of time to attempt to describe the experience. Indeed, some believe that talking about edgework should be avoided because it contaminates one's subjective appreciation of the experience (1990, pp. 861–862).

The ineffable in art is delivered by the form and the non-discursive elements that evoke emotional/somatic responses of which there is little available language to describe them. "Embodied activities" and "edgework sensations" mean that the "soma" plays a dramatic part in edgework, erotic and aesthetic experience. Indeed, erotic emancipation links both forms of experience.

Historically, CV/Ls deny a distinction between the aesthetic and erotic. Sensuous forms loom large as the standard to measure all other events against. Picasso in his late eighties was still making drawings of *zaftig*, naked, middle-aged women. He reminds viewers that the sensuous, soft, round form of a woman is a delicacy to be consumed no matter the age of the voyeur or the woman. Lyng's skydivers demonstrate how the erotic floods into all areas of embodied consumption when they blurt out their mantra: "Eat, Fuck, Skydive" (Lyng and Snow, 1986). But maybe these are just the male sky divers.

Artists like Robert Mapplethorpe desublimate bondage and domination that its delights might be brought to the mainstream. Caravaggio's *Bacchus* champions androgyny in thought, word, and deed. Remember, resisting the high art exemplar proves (to those of us in the aesthetic reality) the inability of the viewer to change and to bring new attitudes and experiences to the ordinary reality. Surely men are improved by taking on the gender characteristics of compassion, caring, empathy, gentleness, diplomacy, praise, and comforting.

Both edgeworkers and CV/Ls know the feeling of oneness, object-cathexis, and new emergences. Lyng says of edgeworkers, spatial distinctions are altered, giving rise to a feeling of connectedness with one's environment. No longer capable of distinguishing between self and certain environmental objects, edgeworkers develop a sense of oneness with these objects or, in the most extreme form, feel as if they could mentally control them (1990, p. 882).

For both edgeworkers and CV/Ls, these sensations are associated with an alternative reality. "Transcendence" is the feeling or knowledge that one lives beyond the prescribed order. Edgework and aesthetic activities "remove the 'me' from the field of experience" (1990, p. 882). Time and space are no longer shaped by the ordinary reality, giving the participant a feeling of transcendence. Is the bullwhip penetrating Robert Mapplethorpe's anus (in his photographic self-portrait) a snapshot of a transcendent moment? How could it be otherwise? Edgeworkers, for a while, live beyond institutional routine. They are survivors who resist, during edgework moments, the societal reification of the notion that external forces decide who lives (1990, p. 873). The location of their self-determinancy is not found in the ordinary reality but the hyperreality.

Although fundamental similarities link the two groups, CV/Ls differ from edgeworkers because they use a system, the "aesthetic paradigm," to accomplish their existential and edgework goals. The argument here is that the aesthetic paradigm promulgates self-actualized and authentic lives. CV/Ls, in order to optimize all of their experiences, including those found in the ordinary reality, speak the truth to the established reality for the benefit of themselves and others. These actions may initially stir a dissensus that promises to break down quickly into chaos. But CV/Ls are well armed with skills and strategies to make order out of looming chaos.

In order to pursue values and attitudes that will assure them all of their affairs will have a fluid, organic, and uninterrupted quality, CV/Ls self-consciously make use of the aesthetic paradigm. In fact, they promote the aesthetic paradigm as a structure for transformation of the day-to-day reality that it might more nearly match the offerings of the superior (aesthetic) reality. Thus, CV/Ls think the ordinary reality and the magnificence of the hyperreality are unequivocally linked. Marcuse juxtaposes the two realities as follows:

Mimesis is representation through estrangement, subversion of consciousness. Experience is intensified to the breaking point; the world appears as it does for Lear and Antony, Berenice, Michael Kohlhaas, Woyzeck, as it does for the lovers of all times. They experience the world demystified. The intensification of *perception* [my emphasis] can go as far as to distort things so that the unspeakable is spoken, the otherwise invisible becomes visible, and the unbearable explodes. Thus the aesthetic transformation turns into indictment—but also into a celebration of that which resists injustice and terror, and of that which can still be saved (1978, p. 45).

The nineteenth century painter (and atheistic) Gustave Courbet made realist art to teach the viewing public that the ideal visual world was materially all about them, not the romantic ooze of popular art and novels. His art resisted the academy's view that a proper art was one of "mimesis without transformation" (Marcuse, 1978, p. 55) of the deceptive, reifying reality of the nineteenth century French power elite. Academic painters wished to join this elite society.[19] Courbet, on the other hand, made paintings to show that people need not envy the elite nor wait for heaven to see the ideal. Nor did they need turn to antique art's fantastic or derivative neoclassical forms to locate the Beautiful. The Beautiful could be found in peering at and feeling the hirsute textures of the female pudenda (Courbet's painting, *Origin of the World*) or in the diverse colors and textures found in the sculptural setting of craggy boulders. H. H. Aranason and Marla Prather says of Courbet's technique,

> [his] landscape combined a sense of observed reality with an even greater sense of the elements and materials with which the artist was working; the rectangle of the picture plane and the emphatic texture of the oil paint, which asserted its own nature at the same time that it was simulating the rough-hewn sculptural appearance of exposed rocks (1998, p. 45).

This view was foundational to the Impressionist art that would follow. Courbet practiced a self-conscious presentation of "simultaneous realities." The textures of an autonomous handmade painting and the texture of the thing observed are both captured through the same painterly gestures.

The distinction between small "b" beautiful and capital "B" Beautiful is that "beauty" is subject to fashion and the constructed artificial tastes of the market, while the "Beautiful" is forever thus and transcends taste. The Beautiful is subject to and meets the criteria for the evaluation of art.[20] The Beautiful hyperreality promises optimal *experiences*. Dewey describes "experience" this way:

> Experience occurs continuously, because the interaction of the live creature and environing conditions is involved in the very process of living. Under conditions of resistance and conflict, aspects and elements of the self and the world that are implicated in this interaction qualify experience with emotions and ideas so that conscious intent emerges (1958, p. 35).

CV/Ls are aware they will need to gain further skills to sustain their attention and maximize their experiential gratification. The aesthetic paradigm emboldens CV/Ls with a method for liberation to the nuances and the coherent, organic qualities of the event. These skills transferred to the day-to-day reality ensure a macro-analysis of the relationships of institutions and others to normative life. With the help of an aesthetic model and an understanding of complex forms, CV/Ls look to reshape their environment and relations to more approximate the kind of Beautiful seamless experience that is their experience with artworks.

There are other differences between edgework activities and the operations of the aesthetic paradigm. Reflexive self-consciousness, seeing oneself as an object on the object field, allows individuals to struggle with narcissism and contradict the vulgar reality in an informed manner. This most certainly creates "risk" for occupations and relationships. But some edgeworkers carry "risk" to the point of physical annihilation. Referring to the "paradox of edgework," Lyng writes,

> It seems odd to suggest that people who feel threatened by external social forces beyond their control seek experiences that are even more threatening to their survival, but this is precisely the dynamic that operates in edgework (1990, p. 873).

Physical "self-endangerment" is not knowingly pursued by CV/Ls. The aesthetic paradigm only reinforces the material truth that death is a misfortune. CV/Ls' sensibilities are dear to them. For them death is the end, and it is coming all too quickly. It is only the art that is transcendent; the corporeal self is not. *Ars longa, vita brevis.* Because they plan to have as many aesthetic/erotic experiences as they can, as close together as they can get them, CV/Ls feel they have too much to lose. This, in turn, mitigates (and complicates) CV/Ls' actions and may play upon their shame.

The sense of omnipotence and elitism that often accompanies repeated encounters with life-threatening edgework (Lyng, 1990, p. 860) is also foreign to those who live within the aesthetic paradigm. CV/Ls are self-mocking. They cannot but see the ironies of their positions. Interaction with the aesthetic paradigm causes estrangement to be the normative posture of CV/Ls and estrangement makes reflexivity a component of all social communication. The advantage of the aesthetic reality is that it provides a critique by broadcasting the essence of the repressive reality and supplies whole systems of perfected forms for the CV/L's instruction. Art alone makes the claim for complete, whole, interpenetrating, intersubjective, interdependent material systems of ideal existence while welcoming any critique that would point out its shortcomings. Art brings about change through the individual's memory of exhilarating experience that s/he knows is transferable to other sets and settings. As Marcuse puts it: "Art cannot change the world, but it can contribute to changing the consciousness and drives of the men and women who could change the world" (1978, pp. 32–33).

An Exemplar

In highlighting the similarities between the aesthetic experience and edgework, I have suggested that it may make sense to think of serious art patrons as risk takers—or, equally plausible, that edgeworkers may be seen as somewhat desperate seekers of the aesthetic experience. However, I have also argued that CV/Ls differ from edgeworkers in that the former can draw on an organic system to not only escape the dominant reality but also to transform it. This system, the aesthetic paradigm, serves as a vehicle of experience but also as a repository of material invention that presents us with multiple exemplars of the Beautiful and the Possible in the realm of human collective life. To underscore the importance of this last feature, I will end this essay the way I started it—with an exemplar that, like doo wop, means (some)thing because it's really got that swing.

Michelangelo Merisi Caravaggio's *Bacchus* is the transhistorical exemplar that will serve as the coda for this chapter.

Bacchus, in the immediate foreground of the painting, extends his foreshortened arm out at the viewer with a delicate, filled-to-the-brim, top-heavy wine goblet offered for our taking. As a constituent element of the action, the

Michelangelo Merisi Caravaggio, *Bacchus*, Florence, Galleria Degli Uffizi, c, 1595 oil on canvas, 95 × 85 cm.

viewer must ask herself/himself: "Shall I take the glass and cross the threshold into the unfathomable experiential universe of the gods? Or should I decline and stay safe among the mortals and the environs I know?" The additional question posed by the aesthetic reality is: "How do I move into the skin of this figure and live and make Bacchus's life my perspective and my own?" The competent viewer is hard-pressed to find reasons not to become him/her, Bacchus.

Caravaggio's *Bacchus* is absolutely a man and absolutely a woman, knowing all the sensual pleasures of each. The figure has the bicep and chest of a male, but the face, lips, hair and hands belong to the Renaissance painting vocabulary for rendering the ideal female. For example, unlike much of the rest of the painting's realism, the figure's hands are idealized, painted without vein, tendon, or knuckle. This Bacchus is Beautiful and a simultaneous reality, his/her gender indeterminate. For the conventional viewer, the figure is alarming, unable to be placed into ready categories. The question of whether to accept the cup becomes a classic struggle between the conventional "me" and the anarchic "I."[21]

CV/Ls take the goblet every time, gently, so as not to spill the delicious content and also to demonstrate the same self-mastery in hand–eye coordination as our temptor's. This ambrosia, this drug, will fling us into an altered consciousness, a hyperreality. As CV/Ls make the journey from the ordinary reality to the superior reality, they find the drug can facilitate the shift in attitude.

The iconography of this painting from 1595 is a presentation of the decisive moment. The sash that holds the drapery in place is about to be pulled, allowing the diaphanous veil to fall away. Bubbles on the surface of the carafe and ripples on the surface of the goblet's wine are to express the event is real and immediate. The still life in front recapitulates the invitation for sensual consumption of the objects in the picture. The background is nondescript so that nothing will distract us from the foreground enticement.

Caravaggio was a realist painter who probably took his model from the beautiful boys dressed as women at the private parties of Cardinal Del Monte of Rome. He and his retinue were classical revivalists. The representation of the classical bacchanalia is further reinforced by the figure being shown *all'antica* and reclining on a *triclinium* (a classical couch used for dining). As Christianity argues for the real presence of Jesus in the host ("the body of Christ, the bread of heaven"), so, too, do these parlor games create a like, real presence of all that is transhistorically the glory of Rome.[22]

The young Caravaggio learned his craft, and increased his virtuosity, by studying classical pieces. Del Monte commissioned the work and gave Caravaggio lodgings in the palace. As A. W. G. Poseq tells us, "Del Monte's palace must have seemed like a romantic vision of the Antique come true" (1990, p. 114).

Poseq goes on to speculate that the image might be homoerotic. He writes,

Considering that classic authors described the young Bacchus as an effeminate boy, and also referred to his affairs with male lovers, including the beardless satyr Ampelos for whom he invented wine in imitation of the heavenly nectar, Caravaggio's bacchic youths could perhaps impersonate the homosexual passion (1990, p. 114).

Such surmises have led art historians into debates about whether the images are sensual or sexual. To CV/Ls, these dithers reflect a neo-Victorian prudery plying a pejorative rhetoric—"bawdy," "decadent," and "licentious"—to discuss the sociohistorical context. This is both the analytic error of retrospective modernism and an act not unlike that of anthropological ethnocentrism. This is not at all a discussion of Del Monte's setting.

It is likely that at Del Monte's parties his guests are giving their imaginative capacities full sway through Eros (whatever that might engender), theatre, music and, as we see, dialogues about paintings and their subjects. Caravaggio's *Bacchus* reflects an attitude to which the pleasures of the material world are celebrated.

Likewise, Robert Mapplethorpe offers pictures of (voluntary) B&D participants. He lifts the stigma from these practitioners by recontextualizing the participants inside the history of high art exemplars. He legitimates this realm of sex practice so that, in part, viewers might consider adding these activities to their erotic vocabulary or, at the very least, refrain from condemning it. For CV/Ls, these photographs are pictures of sexual liberation. CV/Ls assume that an application of this process will increase their erotic virtuosity.

If there is a political attitude to be applied from Caravaggio's *Bacchus* and Mapplethorpe's erotic photographs for us today, it is probably the one reflected in queer politics. Many queer theorists share the CVL's attitude of inclusion, acceptance, and flexibility in understanding the perspective of the other. Transaction is a hopeful path to an objective relativism. Queer theorist Jeffrey Escoffier writes:

Queer politics offers a way of cutting across race and gender lines. It implies the rejection of a minoritarian logic of toleration or simple interest-representation. Instead, queer politics represents an expansive impulse of inclusion; specifically, it requires a resistance to regimes of the normal (1994, p. 135).

Ruth Goldman (1996) makes a similar argument in recounting her own experience as a bisexual discriminated against by many in the gay and lesbian communities. She offers the following description of "queer" from her experience.

The term "queer" emphasizes the blurring of identities, and as a young bisexual activist who had encountered a great deal of resistance to the concept of bisexuality within lesbian and gay communities, it didn't take me long to embrace all that I perceived "queer" as representing. In fact, the queer movement/community was founded on principles of inclusivity and flexibility, summed up quite nicely by Elisabeth Daumier: "in the queer universe, to be queer implies that not everybody is queer in the same way. It implies a willingness to articulate their own queerness" (1996, p. 170).

Like their Bohemian precursors, CV/Ls self-consciously arm themselves with the attitude (vis-à-vis the generalized other): "We're here, we're queer, get used to it."

And so it is that the aesthetic paradigm serves CV/Ls in their constant invention of selves that to outsiders appears chaotic and unanchored. CV/Ls' commitment to high art is to assure themselves an experience of the significant and enduring "I." The aesthetic paradigm also obligates the CV/L to the other. Dewey says, "This task is to restore continuity between the refined and intensified forms of experience that are works of art and the everyday events, doings, and sufferings that are universally recognized to constitute experience" (1958, p. 3). The narcissistic scar of the other may challenge and threaten the CV/L's best intentions. Nevertheless, it is the restorative dynamic of transcendent experiences that connects the CV/L's aesthetic paradigm and edgework.

High Hopes

Max Horkheimer and Theodor Adorno have written, "all reification is forgetting" (1972, p. 230). Aesthetic experience is difficult to forget. But its activities can be marginalized by institutional rhetorics of "elitism" whether conducted by the market or benighted Marxists that see art only as a tool of revolution for the ascending class.

The bridge to a liberated self might best be found by remembering transcendent subjective experiences. Can we expand and extend the applications of these experiences through strategies of committing more of our time to emergent experiences of astonishment and wonderment first felt through the senses? If so, would this create deep pools of memory in which embodied, subjective, sensuous activities are given priority in the organization of one's life? Marcuse's response to these questions is unequivocal:

Art fights reification by making the petrified world speak, sing, perhaps dance. Forgetting past suffering and past joy alleviates life under a repressive reality principle. In contrast, remembrance spurs the drive for the conquest of suffering and the permanence of joy. But the force of remembrance is frustrated, joy itself is overshadowed by pain. Inexorably so? The horizon of history is still open. If the remembrance of things past would become a motive power in the struggle for changing the world, the struggle would be waged for a revolution hitherto suppressed in the previous historical revolutions (1978, p. 73).

The remembering, liberated, subjective expressive self can only reply, "doo wop, doo wop, doo wop, doo wop, doo wop, doo wop, doo wop, doo wop." Edgeworkers take this step into the aesthetic paradigm without embarrassment.

Notes

1. Duke Ellington, "It Don't Mean a Thing If It Ain't Got That Swing," 1932.

2. The "Responsory" is a part of the Catholic mass in which the congregation responds to the priest's prayerful invocations to God. For example, the priest prays: "For those who fish on the high seas, keep them safe." The congregation's response: "Lord hear *our* prayer." The back and forth statement and response reinforces the oneness of the community. Gothic churches organize the architectural setting of *the choir* so that the monks might respond to each other from side to side in singing the psalms (among other prayers). The monastics are seen by the Christian community as exemplars. They trade their individual identity for that of the community gathered in a commitment to the first and greatest commandment: to love. This forming of the communitarian being is shaped in part by the ritualizing formulas that insist on the annihilation of the individual identity in favor of the communitarian identity.

3. Theologically and historically, "the church" has been defined by Catholicism as the community gathered. When the community of believers is gathered, they are, by creed, the one, holy (perfect), Catholic, and Apostolic church. (Hans Kung, *Church*, New York: Double Day, 1976.)

4. The aesthetic experience generates many values and behaviors. The argument here is that these can be transferred to experiences outside of aesthetic experience. The aesthetic paradigm and its activities provide a model for how we might act in regard to phenomena of the ordinary reality.

5. The conductor is a real edgeworker here. Her job is to keep order in what could easily break down into chaos in trying to keep one hundred musicians operating with a single interpretation. Her skill is manifested materially during the performance. Her craft is measured by the competent listeners.

6. Marcuse comments on the contention that high art is elitist:

   The fact that the artist belongs to a privileged group negates neither the truth nor the aesthetic quality of his work. What is true of 'the classics of socialism' is true also of the great artists: they break through the class limitations of their family, background, environment. Marxist theory is not family research. The progressive character of art, its contribution to the struggle for liberation cannot be measured by the artists' origins nor by the ideological horizon of their class. Neither can it be determined by the presence (or absence) of the oppressed class in their works. The criteria for the progressive character of art are given only in the work itself as a whole: in what it says and how it says it. In this sense art is 'art for art's sake' inasmuch as the aesthetic form reveals tabooed and repressed dimensions of reality: aspects of liberation. The poetry of Mallarme is an extreme example; his poems conjure up modes of perception, imagination, gestures—a feast of sensuousness which shatters everyday experience and anticipates a different reality principle (1978, pp. 18–19).

7. Other criteria for the evaluation of art include: complexity of the form, the more complex the form the better, and profundity of ideas. Profound ideas are those that bring about radical changes in behavior for the betterment of the individual and the society. See endnote 20.

8. Lyng (1990, p. 881) compares the edgework hyperreality to that of "normal social experience." Of the latter he says, "Most people dedicate heart and soul to maintaining role patterns associated with social structures that they themselves had no part in creating. Normal social life is 'unreal' in the sense that most of the individual's action contributes to a social agenda that is little understood and that often appears trivial when examined critically."

9. Painting's great advantage is that one can see all the constituent elements at once. It is not a time art like literature or music, where one has to remember that which went before. In painting all the elements are there for immediate gratification.

10. "Organic" and the analytic term "organicity," in art, refer to the interdependence and intersubjectivity of the constituent elements of an artwork. At first glance the constituent elements may appear to be disparate and unrelated. Works of high art are like plants and trees. The bark looks nothing like the roots, which look nothing like the leaves, and yet they are all part of the "organic" whole. After understanding the tree's biology, one begins to discover what the vessels that bark, root, and leaf have in common.

11. This list of elements is not complete. A more elaborate discussion of this program is better suited for another time as the focus here is the application of this model to activities of CV/Ls.

12. Ideology engenders notions such as "tolerance," "diversity," and "multidisciplinary" (or "comparative studies") rather than interdisciplinary studies. Do ideologues fall into the normative pattern of judging others by appearances and rumor rather than the content of their character? If this is so, an unreliable visual shorthand is at the ready for dismissing those who might appear to be different, and thus, a threat.

13. Paul Cezanne's art provides for two aesthetic experiences: the expected aesthetic experience gained from the completed artwork and the aesthetic experiences the artist has during the process of making the artwork. Cezanne reveals every stroke he used to build the work that we might paint it again and have the aesthetic experiences he had in painting the canvas. Many artists after him have done the same, especially those of the

absolute abstractionist's bent. Cezanne also presents multiple viewing perspectives in a still life painting. The simultaneity of all the viewing angles overcomes the fourth dimension, time. One does not have to remember how things looked from different perspectives; they are all there simultaneously. This is the formal underpinning of Cubism.

14. CV/Ls are not able, nor would they try, to subordinate the artwork to their interests.

15. In high art, the viewer (or active listener) is a constituent element of the work. Michelangelo devised the *Creation of Adam* with the viewer in mind. The artwork proper is a catalyst for dialogue. The meaning of the artwork is found in the verb of our tussle with the image. The viewer is invited to complete the process of God giving the spark of life to Adam by bringing the fingers of each together on the Sistine ceiling. The viewer is actively engaged in providing the decisive moment when the mystery of life is delivered to potent flesh. The viewer moves the narrative along. Thus, when one looks for samenesses in emergent relationships, the viewer must be counted among the appurtenances of the image if meaning is to be derived. Why else would the painting exist?

16. Marcuse's thesis is:

    The radical qualities of art, that is to say, its indictment of the established reality and its invocation of the beautiful image (*schoener Schein*) of liberation are grounded precisely in the dimensions where art *transcends* its social determination and emancipates itself from the given universe of discourse and behavior while preserving its overwhelming presence. Thereby art creates the realm in which the subversion of experience proper to art becomes possible: the world formed by art is recognized as a reality which is suppressed and distorted in the given reality. This experience culminates in extreme situations (of love and death, guilt and failure, but also joy, happiness, and fulfillment) which explode the given reality in the name of a truth normally denied or even unheard. The inner logic of the work of art terminates in the emergence of another reason, another sensibility, which defy the rationality and sensibility incorporated in the dominant social institutions" (1978, pp. 6–7).

17. "Artists" means all creative high artists in dance, music, visual art, literature, film, and so on, from Duke Ellington to Joseph Heller.

18. Conceptual art often uses words as the artwork. These words provoke the viewer to ask series of questions. What do these words mean? Do they cause me to remember parts of my own past? What do they have to do with me? Is this visual art? The process of questions and answers the viewer provides is the meaning of the work.

19. The majority of moneyed society's tastes then and now are the same as the mainstream's. Of them Marcuse says: "If it is at all meaningful to speak of a mass base for art in capitalist society, this would refer only to pop art [not the ironic Pop Art of Warhol, Lichtenstein, and Koons etc.] and bestsellers" (1978, p. 32).

20. Evaluative criteria include but are not limited to:

    1. How profound are the ideas being expressed? Are transcendent insights presented that will fundamentally change the recipient's actions? An example: Iris Murdoch's novel *The Black Prince* presents a protagonist who discovers, "Sex reveals itself as the great connective principle whereby we overcome duality, the force which made separateness an aspect of oneness at some moment of bliss in the mind of God" (1973, p. 176) Is the Iris Murdoch example a remarkable idea capable of transfiguring its readers who put the idea into practice?

    2. How extreme, novel, and wide-ranging are the emotions evoked form the learned, reflective viewer? High art will dare to show despair. Sentimental art will avoid such expressions.

    3. How complex is the artwork? Complexity is the many constituent elements working in a perfect interdependency with each other. Both the form and the ideas of high art are deeper and more complex than those of a popular art. For example, counterpoint is not pop music's strong suit.

21. I have shown this artwork to approximately 8,000 students over twenty years. Few have accepted the cup.

22. Classical Romans also thought of themselves as having embraced, and incorporated, all that was classical Greece.

References

Arnason, H. H., and Prather, M. F. *History of Modern Art*. New York: Prentice Hall, 1998.

Bourdieu, P. *Distinction*. Cambridge, MA: Harvard University Press, 1984.

Dewey, J. *Art as Experience*. New York: Minton, Balch and Company, 1934.

———. *Experience and Nature*. New York: Dover, 1958. (Original work published in 1935.)

Escoffier, J. "Under the Sign of the Queer." In *Queer Studies: A Lesbian, Gay, Bisexual and Transgender Anthology*, edited by B. Beemyn and M. Eliason. New York: New York University Press, 1996.

Fowles, J. *The French Lieutenant's Woman*. New York: Signet, 1969.

Freud, S. *Beyond the Pleasure Principle*. New York: Norton, 1961. (Original work published 1920.)

Goldman, R. "Who Is That Queer Queer? Exploring Norms Around Sexuality, Race, and Class in Queer Theory." In *Queer Studies: A Lesbian, Gay, Bisexual and Transgender Anthology*, edited by B. Beemyn and M. Eliason. New York: New York University Press, 1996.

Horkheimer, M., and Adorno, T. W. *Dialectic of Enlightenment*. New York: Herder and Herder, 1972.

Jacoby, R. *The Last Intellectuals: American Culture in the Age of Academe*. New York: Noonday, 1995.

Lyng, S. "Edgework: A Social Psychological Analysis of Voluntary Risk Taking." *American Journal of Sociology* 95 (4) (1990): 851–886.

Marcuse, H. *The Aesthetic Dimension: Toward a Critique of Marxist Aesthetics*. Boston: Beacon, 1978.

Mead, G. H. *Mind, Self and Society: From the Standpoint of a Social Behaviorist*. Chicago: University of Chicago Press, 1967. (Original work published 1934.)

Murdoch, I. *The Black Prince*. New York: Viking, 1973.

Poseq, A. W. G. "Baachic Themes in Caravaggio's Juvenile Works." *Gazette des Beaux Arts* 115 (1454) (1990): 113–121.

Turner, R. H. "The Real Self: From Institution to Impulse." *American Journal of Sociology* 81 (1976): 989–1019.

Part IV

Group Variations in Edgework Practices: Gender, Age, and Class

5

Gender and Emotion Management in the Stages of Edgework

JENNIFER LOIS

CONTENTS

If you let those concerns bother you—"Oh God, there's three kids out there freezing to death"—you're losing sight of your task. And you're jeopardizing your own safety and your team's safety by not being focused on what your task is. If you're out there searching for a plane crash, the odds are you have a [radio locator] signal. You're not looking for those three little kids, you're looking for that signal. And if you start thinking about those three little kids, you're going to get off your task. Emotions just get in the way on [search and rescue] missions.

Gary, eight-year member of Peak Volunteer Search and Rescue

Emergency situations call for effective action in the face of potentially overwhelming emotions. As Gary states above, strong feelings can "get in the way" of performing an important task. This chapter is about how male and female members of "Peak," a volunteer search and rescue group, "managed" their emotions (Hochschild, 1983) before, during, and after their most dangerous, stressful, or gruesome rescues. In the mountains of the western United States, Peak's rescuers engaged in a wide variety of risky activity during the searches and rescues (called "missions"). Missions presented many physically and emotionally threatening situations for rescuers, such as when they searched for missing skiers in avalanche-prone terrain, negotiated the rapids of rushing rivers to reach stranded rafters, were lowered down cliff faces to evacuate injured rock climbers, and extracted mutilated bodies from planes that crashed in the wilderness. These extreme conditions—the most crucial life-and-death circumstances—called for members to engage in what Lyng (1990) has termed "edgework": negotiating the boundary between life and death during voluntary risk taking.

While the prototypical edgework situation "is one in which the individual's failure to meet the challenge at hand will result in death or, at the very least, debilitating injury" (1990, p. 857), the concept also encapsulates a wider array of activities in which individuals need to negotiate the "edge," or boundary line, between two physical or mental states: "life versus death, consciousness versus unconsciousness, sanity versus insanity, an ordered sense of self and environment versus a disordered self and environment" (1990, p. 857). Thus, although the quintessential edgework experience is life threatening, the concept also has a broader application that extends beyond pure physical danger. In addition to physically risky situations, Peak's rescuers also engaged in emotional edgework, which often occurred when they encountered gruesome or upsetting accident scenes. In such cases, rescuers had to negotiate the boundary between controlled and uncontrolled emotions to make sure their feelings didn't "get in the way" of accomplishing their tasks.

In this chapter, I introduce four stages of edgework by tracing members' specific feelings and the corresponding management techniques they employed before, during, and after urgent rescues. The data reveal two gendered ways rescuers prepared for, engaged in, and reflected on edgework. After explaining the contribution that a meso-level analysis of edgework makes to the theoretical model, I discuss the four-stage model of edgework, and show how the instrumental nature of Peak's work may have led rescuers to experience edgework differently than many recreational risk takers. Finally, I analyze the differences between men's and women's understanding of their emotions, and thus, their edgework experiences.

Setting and Method

These data are drawn from a six-year ethnographic study of Peak, a volunteer search and rescue group in a Rocky Mountain resort town. Peak County consisted of 1700 square miles, 1300 of which were undeveloped national forest or wilderness area lands. Local residents and tourists alike used this "backcountry" land year-round for various recreational purposes such as hiking, camping, rock climbing, whitewater rafting/kayaking, snowmobiling, and backcountry skiing. Occasionally, recreational enthusiasts became lost or injured in these vehicle-inaccessible regions. Because the county sheriff's deputies did not have the skills or resources to venture into these remote areas, the sheriff commissioned Peak, a volunteer group of local citizens, to act as the public safety agent in the backcountry. Because these emergencies could happen at any time of the day or night, members were given pagers so that they could be notified immediately when they were needed, and respond if they were available. Frequently, this meant getting out of bed in the middle of the night to search for an overdue snowshoer or rescue an injured camper.

Peak's members had to have many specialized rescue skills to reach and help victims who were incapacitated while engaged in a wide variety of recreational activities. For example, some members were adept at riding snowmobiles and were frequently sent to search for lost snowmobilers or backcountry skiers. Others possessed extensive whitewater skills, and as such, their expertise was utilized for rafting or kayaking accidents. Many members, however, had only basic skill levels in several areas, for example, operating the rope and pulley systems used to maneuver victims and rescuers over cliffs, surviving for several days in the wilderness, and searching avalanche debris with radio signal receiving devices. Because all members were trained in these basic systems, they occasionally assisted the sheriff's department in rescues that did not take place in the backcountry, yet required a certain amount of technical expertise to reach the victims (for example, when people were trapped in cars driven over cliffs or into rivers). Of the thirty or so members in Peak, approximately twenty were men and ten were women.[1] All members were white and most were middle- to upper-middle class. Their ages ranged from 22–55, and their education levels ranged from high school to the MD degree.

Missions were run by one of five members designated as "mission coordinators." When a call came in, it was the mission coordinator's job to obtain the information, evaluate the urgency, decide whether to launch a search or rescue effort, and if so, mobilize the other members. During missions, the coordinators sent teams of rescuers into "the field" while they stayed behind and plotted the teams' progress on maps laid out in the group's base building.

I became interested in Peak after reading several local newspaper accounts of their rescues. With no specialized backcountry skill or experience, I joined the group in 1994 to study it sociologically. I began attending the biweekly business meetings, weekly training sessions, post-training social hours at the local bar, and a few missions. Through these initial interactions, I became intrigued by how members defined their participation in rescue work, as well as how these definitions affected their lives (Blumer, 1969).

Over the next year, I developed strong friendships with several group members, and was able to discuss some of my observations with them. I occasionally asked them for their interpretations of certain events, which enhanced my analysis through the perspective of everyday life (Jorgensen, 1989). During this time period, I became an "active" member (Adler and Adler, 1987) of the setting; I was given deeper access to members' thoughts and feelings as they began to trust me, both as a researcher and a rescuer.

For six years, I kept detailed field notes of the group activities in which I participated, including the business meetings, training sessions, social hours, and missions. It was my participation in the missions, however, that most helped me to identify with other rescuers' experiences. I was struck by the intense emotions I felt during searches and rescues, and once I realized that other rescuers experienced some of the same emotional patterns, I began to ask about them specifically during casual conversations. In addition to taking extensive field notes, I conducted 23 in-depth, semi-structured interviews with rescuers, focusing the questions loosely around their motivations for participating in Peak and their experiences on missions. I often probed the interviewees to elicit thick descriptions (Geertz, 1973) of their feelings on missions. Following the principles of grounded theory (Glaser and Strauss, 1967), I then studied these data, searching for patterns in members' emotional experiences. When patterns emerged, I restructured the subsequent interviews in an effort to draw out further conceptual distinctions. Some of the new data supported my working analysis, while other data countered it; I used all of this evidence to refine my analytic model accordingly, continuing the process until the data yielded no new conceptual patterns, a condition Glaser and Strauss (1967) called "theoretical saturation."

The Concept of Edgework

Peak's rescuers frequently engaged in edgework. They had to be able to complete their task under intense stress and maintain a sense of emotional and physical control throughout the ordeal. Members who demonstrated the greatest control during the riskiest situations—those who could work closest to the edge—were more often sent on challenging rescues because they were considered better suited to handle them. Although it was important for them to have the skills to accomplish the mission, it was more important that they regulate the intense feelings that arose from such dangerous or gruesome tasks. Uncontrolled feelings threatened rescuers' sense of order, making control precarious and potentially rendering them useless.

Yet despite these formidable challenges, many rescuers craved the opportunity to perform edgework. Lyng has argued that edgework is alluring because it gives individuals a feeling of control over their lives and environment while they push themselves to their physical and mental limits. On a phenomenological level, negotiating the edge leads edgeworkers to experience feelings of omnipotence and self-actualization. "Crowding the edge," or approaching their physical and mental limits, forces edgeworkers to become tightly focused on their task and to block out extraneous information. Such highly concentrated cognitive effort gives them the sensation of pure spontaneity. The immediate demands of the situation filter out much of the reflexive, social aspect of the self—the part of the self captured by Mead's (1934) concept of the "me"—leaving them feeling free from social constraints. In a society in which social constraints are increasingly experienced as oppressive and stifling to one's "true" self (see Turner, 1976), impulse and spontaneity permit edgeworkers access to what they perceive to be their authentic selves. It is this self-actualization experience on the edge that compels edgeworkers to pursue it repeatedly, each time pushing their physical and mental limits further to control the seemingly uncontrollable (Lyng, 1990; see also Palmer, 1983). Although it appears that feelings of omnipotence and self-actualization play an important role in edgeworkers' motivations to continue engaging in such high-risk activity, little consideration has been given to the prominent role of other intense emotions in edgework.

Scholars have examined how emotions operate in physically and emotionally demanding situations, such as overcoming fear on adventure ropes courses (Holyfield, 1997; Holyfield and Fine, 1997), interpreting emotions during whitewater rafting (Holyfield, 1999), dealing with death in medical settings (Smith and Kleinman, 1989), surviving rape (Konradi, 1999), counseling rape victims (Jones, 1997), and handling frantic callers to emergency hotline phone numbers (Jones, 1997; Whalen and Zimmerman, 1998). Although these works have generated a great deal of empirical evidence on crises in which emotions play a significant role, no attempt has been made to theoretically incorporate emotions into the edgework model of voluntary risk taking.

Lyng (1990) has further noted, albeit speculatively, that men tend to engage in edgework at higher rates than women do. Empirical research suggests support for this observation, illuminating, for example, the preponderance of men in high-risk occupations (see Martin, 1980; Metz, 1981; Yoder and Aniakudo, 1997) and demonstrating that men perceive risk differently, and generally as less threatening, than women (Fothergill, 1996; Harrell, 1986). Yet these works have not systematically analyzed the role of gender in edgework. Peak Volunteer Search and Rescue Unit, which was two-thirds men, one-third women, provides an excellent empirical setting in which to study the relationship between gender and edgework.

Gender, Emotions, and the Stages of Edgework

The levels of difficulty, danger, and stress varied greatly among Peak's missions. At times, members were asked to perform only slightly demanding, low-urgency tasks such as hiking a short distance up a trail to carry a hiker with a twisted ankle out to the parking lot. Other times they were asked to perform very difficult, dangerous, or gruesome tasks such as rappelling down a 200-foot rock face to recover the body of a fallen hiker, traversing known avalanche terrain to reach a hypothermic snowshoer, and bushwhacking for fifteen hours over miles of treacherous terrain in search of a lost hunter. It was these physically and emotionally demanding situations that most threatened rescuers' sense of control, requiring them to engage in edgework—to negotiate the boundary between order and chaos—not only physically, but emotionally as well.

There were four stages of edgework in Peak's missions. These stages were distinctly marked not only by the flow of rescue events, but also by the feelings members experienced in each stage. Women and men experienced edgework differently, interpreting and managing feelings in gender-specific ways while they prepared for missions, performed high-risk activities, reflected on their participation, and made sense of their actions.

Preparing for Edgework: Establishing Confidence Levels

Missions were unpredictable, sometimes chaotic events, and members were often required to use whatever resources they had to accomplish their task. Many of Peak's members, like other edgeworkers, found it exciting not to know what to expect from a rescue, and they felt challenged by the prospect of relying on their cognitive and technical skills to quickly solve any puzzle that suddenly presented itself. Yet other rescuers viewed the missions' unpredictability as stressful, and they worried in anticipation of performing under trying conditions.

One common worry was that they might be physically unable to perform a task because they did not have the skills to handle a difficult situation, even if others trusted their abilities. Maddie, a thirty-four-year-old, ten-year member and mission coordinator told me about first achieving "leader" status after being in the group for two years. The old-time members in the group had been evaluating her skills for weeks and, after a mock rescue scenario, told her she was ready to advance to this higher group position. She, however, was unsure of her abilities, and thus, of their decision:

> I kind of questioned it at the time because I didn't think my avalanche skills were there yet. I knew my knots, and I could make a [rope and pulley] system, and I could get other people to make one, but I asked Roy and Jim both, you know, "Are you sure I'm ready to do this?" They're like, "Yeah, I mean, you can definitely take a group of people and lead them through a rescue or a mission, and we know you'll get the job done, even though [those people] might not know a thing." And I went, "Oh, okay, I guess that's what it means to be [leader status]. *But please don't ever put me in that spot [laughs]*!" Only because you look at the rock jocks we had, or the really knowledgeable systems people, and it was just hard to think that I was considered their equal. For me, anyway; I didn't think that.

Other members, too, doubted their ability to perform and were apprehensive about entering risky rescue situations. On one occasion, Alex, a thirty-two-year-old British botanist, was selected to ice climb up an avalanche-prone gully to rescue some stranded hot-air balloonists whose balloon had crashed at the top of a cliff. This mission involved several organizations, including two rescue teams from other counties. Even though Alex was a highly skilled and experienced mountaineer and climber, she, along with others, doubted her abilities to climb the gully. She told me what happened at the command center as the mission coordinators organized two teams of two rescuers each:

> They were like, "We only want very experienced ice climbers. This is a big deal." So they picked out a couple of hot shots from [another rescue team], and then they picked Roy and told him to choose somebody to climb with—to bring somebody with him. I was like [*laughing and vigorously shaking her head "no"*]. And he's like, "Come on, you can do it." And anyway it was funny, apparently [the mission coordinators] said, "Oh, this hot shot team's going in. It's so-and-so from [another county] and so-and-so—he was on Everest—and then there's Roy from Peak Search and Rescue, and some chick" [*laughs*].... Robin overheard that. She said they were like reeling off [the names] and then "some chick" [*laughs*]. So anyway, having heard Robin tell me this, I was thinking "Oh, God, I'm gonna get left behind," or something. But anyway, we got in the gully, and we were fine.

While Roy knew Alex was skilled enough, others doubted her physical abilities, which increased her already existing apprehension about the rescue.

Members also worried about their ability to maintain emotional control, realizing that they could encounter a particularly upsetting scene on a mission. For example, Maddie told me that one situation she dreaded was encountering a dead victim whom she knew. She expected that this situation would be one that most threatened her emotional control, the one in which she would be most likely to go over the edge:

> I think my biggest fear has always been that [the victim] is gonna be, eventually, somebody I know. And eventually it was. With Arnie [who was killed] in an avalanche. And yet, I was okay with that. I was more okay than I thought I might be. I always *think* I'm gonna lose it but, I guess you expect for the worst, and then you usually do better. Or expect that "What would you do if you lost it?" or "How would you get it back?" And so I've planned ahead.

Worrying about what could arise on a future mission led rescuers to plan their actions ahead of time, anticipating their potential reactions to stressful events. Preparing for edgework by imagining numerous different scenarios gave them some sense of control over the unpredictable future, and through such planning, they were able to manage their uncomfortable anticipatory feelings about the unknown, a dynamic found in other research on high-risk takers (see Holyfield, 1997; Lyng, 1990).

Maddie's statement also typified another technique some rescuers used along with planning and rehearsing future scenarios: They set low expectations for themselves. Part of their planning process was to prepare for the most demanding possible situations, the ones in which they were most likely to fail. This emotion-management strategy served two functions: First it made members acutely aware of their progress toward the edge on missions. For example, Cyndi, a four-year member in her late twenties, told me that as a rescuer, "You need to know your limits…. If you start to do something and [find] 'I can't do this,' you shouldn't push yourself to do it just because everyone's like, 'Yes you can.' You should be like, 'No. I can't do this,' and work on other things that you can do." The second function of setting low expectations was that rescuers would probably perform beyond them. In this way, they set themselves up for success, remaining within their limits on a mission while feeling good about surpassing their expectations.

Brooke, a student and three-year member in her mid-twenties, also used this strategy of underestimating her ability; specifically, she reduced her anxiety by overemphasizing safety practices. She told me that if she was extra safety-conscious, she could anticipate better control in dangerous or risky situations:

> I'm Miss Safety. I am *Miss Safety*. I mean, I get two people to check my knots [that tie me into the lowering rope], and I check everybody else's knots. 'Cause I'm scared to death of heights! And [to other members] I'm like, "Wear your helmet, wear your helmet! Don't get too close to the river without a PFD [personal floatation device]!" I mean, I am Miss Safety. So hopefully [getting into a dangerous situation] won't happen to me because of my attitude towards it.

By practicing safety, Brooke felt she had better control over what might happen to her (or others) during a rescue, yet it is clear from her statement that she still did not feel overly confident; she said focusing on safety would "hopefully" keep her safe.

Anticipating a poor performance and uncontrollable conditions were common ways the women on the team prepared for the variety of situations they could encounter on a mission. Underestimating their ability was not a very common practice among the men in the group, however. When I talked to Martin, a fifty-three-year-old construction supervisor and five-year member, he told me that he never worried about his performance. He used an example from one of the team's most critical missions, a car accident with four casualties. A van had driven off the side of a dirt road and tumbled to the bottom of a 400-foot ravine. Search and rescue was called because the accident was inaccessible to the paramedics, who needed ropes to get down to the victims and a hauling system to get them out. Martin was the third rescuer to arrive on the scene and was immediately directed to join Gary (a rescuer and EMT) down at the accident site. Despite the stress and danger he experienced in this situation, Martin said he was never afraid of getting on a rescue scene and losing control:

> *Martin*: I've never had that worry at all. I've had thoughts that maybe I'd get on scene and somebody'd be hurt so bad, and I wouldn't have the training to be able to help them. But I don't think that's losing control. What if I'd been the first one down to that van accident? That was way beyond anything I could've known what to do.

> *Jen*: What do you think would've happened if you had been the first one down there?

> *Martin*: Actually, thrown into the situation, I probably would've handled it. I think, thrown into a situation, I think I could react well. I would've handled it somehow.

In contrast to many women's strategy of trepidation, most of the men in Peak used the opposite technique—building confidence—to prepare for emergency action, as Martin did.

Brooke, the mid-twenties student, commented, too, on rescuers' confidence levels, referring specifically to Gary and Nick. She claimed they were able to perform at very high levels *because* of their high expectations for themselves:

> I think that both of those guys see themselves as Superman. Which is not necessarily a good thing. They sort of see themselves as being invincible [and] I think that they might test their physical limits more than I would. They might go into a situation that I would stand back and say, "I don't think that's safe." But they're convinced that nothing's going to happen to them.... But then again, I think that has a lot to do with the mental aspect of it. You know, they see themselves as being more capable of doing something than I would. Therefore as long as they see themselves being capable of it, they are capable of it. If that makes any sense.

According to Brooke, extreme confidence was effective for Gary and Nick, yet she did not think that it was a viable emotion management technique for her to employ. She felt safer being wary of an uncertain situation, but acknowledged that Gary and Nick were safer charging into the same situation. She saw their confidence as enabling them to perform at high levels.

When I asked Gary himself about his experience in extreme situations, he responded with incredible certainty in his ability, supporting Brooke's perception of him:

> *Gary*: I like being thrown knee-deep [into challenging situations]. I like it when the shit hits the fan, and having to get my way out of it.
>
> *Jen*: Don't you get nervous that you might not be able to do that?
>
> *Gary*: Nope.
>
> *Jen*: Do you think you'll always be able to do that?
>
> *Gary*: Yup. I am a cocky, young, think-I-can-do-it-all kid. I can get out of a situation. Probably because I have never *not* done it. I perform tremendously under pressure. That's when I shine at my absolute, top of my game. And I love being put in the hot seat. That's one of the reasons I do [search and rescue].

Gary highlighted the mutually reinforcing relationship between confidence and ability: Not only did confidence enhance performance, but past performance enhanced confidence. By relying on "successful" (i.e., survived) past experiences, the men in the group became confident about almost any future performance. Patrick explained why, using this same circular rationale. He described Jim, the founding member of Peak: "Jim is very confident in what he does. For good reason, because he does a good job.... But I think that's one of the big reasons why he does things well is 'cause he has a lot of confidence in himself." Lyng (1990) noted a similar tautological relationship between skill and success in his study of skydivers. Successfully performing at high levels (surviving) served as "proof" that a skydiver had "the right stuff," while failing (dying or becoming critically injured) served as "proof" that one never really had it. Lyng designated this belief the "illusion of control," and showed how the skydivers he studied relied on it to enhance their confidence. This same form of ex post facto validation helped Peak's male rescuers interpret the relationship between their confidence and skill.

Many of Peak's members, furthermore, saw such confidence as a necessary quality in rescuers, largely because it allowed them to take risks and to be aggressive. Some linked these traits to gender. Nick, a twenty-eight-year-old, five-year member, and construction worker, told me that one reason the men in the group tended to be better at riding the snowmobiles was because they had "more guts" and "less fear" than the women. He said, "I just think with the guys it's more of an adrenaline rush, to a point. They're more risk-takers. You have to have more guts to be able to power through some of the terrain we ride, or you'll get [the snowmobile] stuck [in deep snow drifts]."

Other male rescuers also explained how confidence and a "big ego" were desirable features in rescuers, and often equated these traits with testosterone, thus linking them closely to men and masculinity via biology. Kevin, a forty-five-year-old, ten-year leader in the group explained this:

> You know, there's a number of child psychologists that say treat [boys and girls] both the same. Well, they ain't the same! … *There is a difference.* And I think it's great. And I don't think that difference makes one better than the other. Testosterone is not necessarily good. It's gotten a lot of males killed! I mean, *it's not necessarily good!* But nature did not create everyone equal. We have our strengths and weaknesses, and there is a difference between the male and the female of every species. And if that difference leads to a kinder, gentler person in the female, then that's the way it is…. I think some of it has to do with the society that they we're raised in. But I do believe there is a genetic difference in the male and the female.

I asked Kevin how he thought testosterone affects men. He laughed heartily, then answered:

> Well, in a general sense, you notice that they don't send old men into war. They send seventeen-, eighteen-, nineteen-, twenty-year-old men into areas of conflict where it's dog-eat-dog stuff because they are pumped with testosterone. I mean, it's a chemical hormone … that wanes as the years go on, and it is a drug. So you gotta play into that too. If I want somebody to rip up a hill [on a mission], I'm not gonna go for the thirty-fve-year-old guys, I'm gonna call the twenty-year-olds. 'Cause they've got the big egos—they've got something to prove. That's what they think anyway, because they're pumped up on chemicals. They're all hormone-strung-out and they're all, "Grrrrrr! Let's go!" It throws your scale off, and away you go!

Several members expressed similar beliefs about men's willingness to take risks and about women's reticence to do so. However, women's lack of confidence and their desire to minimize risk was much more accepted than men's (perhaps because men's trepidation was seen as "unnatural"). Thus, the men in the group who did not possess confidence and were not willing to take risks were ridiculed and disparaged for allegedly not having what it took to accomplish a mission. Denigration was most severe when these men insisted on staying involved in a mission, despite their unwillingness to take (what others saw as) the necessary risks.

Martin's opinion was typical of several others' when he criticized Russ, a fifty-year-old doctor and member of five years, who was fairly experienced, yet always unwilling to take the risks other men were:

> I think he's been trained as a doctor to be ultra-conservative in everything he does. And I think there may be a fear factor in there. I think the members we need and we're not getting—this is also what Shorty

thinks—are people who are willing to lay it on the line. There's gotta be a certain bit of cockiness. There's gotta be a certain bit of "I'll-take-a-chance" kind of thing. It's just because that's what we do. I mean, whether it's a man or woman, the kind of things we do are masculine things, they're testosterone things. We climb, we hike—and you can have a testosterone thing with women. It doesn't have to be men. That's the kind of people we need, that are going out and doing those kind of things. And I don't think—I'm *sure* Russ is not that kind of guy.... Russ is just too damned over-safety conscious. And that's why I think most people in the group don't trust him. He's overly safe to the point that he's gonna hurt somebody because of his safeness, ... like wasting time with an injured person when we have to get them down, or getting himself involved where he's not the best person to be doing things.... I'm not great on a snowmobile, so I keep it under control, but I see Russ on the snowmobile, and he'll go five miles per hour!

Russ' unwillingness to engage in edgework was unacceptable to many group members, who, as Martin noted, did not trust him. It was ironic that Russ was considered "too safe" for rescue work, yet that was how Peak's rescuers judged him. He did not engage in edgework, which painted him ineffective as a rescuer. Yet I rarely heard this degree of criticism about women who were unwilling to take risks, like Brooke (who dubbed herself "Miss Safety") or Cyndi (who thought rescuers should never try to do something they didn't think they could do). Thus, two very different emotional strategies were condoned for women and men during the edgework preparation stage. Women were expected to show trepidation, while men (by virtue of their "hormones," in many cases), were expected to display confidence and a willingness to take risks.

These gendered differences in preparation strategies can be explained in several different ways. First, in general, men were more experienced than women. Through their own recreation and group-related activities, men's exposure to risk was both more frequent and more hazardous than women's. Yet this gendered confidence pattern was not totally explained by differential risk exposure. For example, when I talked to equally experienced men and women, apprehension and lack of confidence still dominated women's anticipatory feelings (like Maddie's and Alex's), and most men still tended to feel confident and want to get involved. Furthermore, even when women performed well on missions, it did not seem to boost their confidence for future situations, while conversely, men's poor performances did not erode theirs.

A second factor in explaining this pattern was that Peak's group culture constructed rescue work as masculine, or "testosterone-filled." This enabled men to feel more at ease in the setting, and thus most tended to display unwavering certainty that they could handle any situation in which they might find themselves. Like the female ambulance workers in Metz's (1981) study, Peak's women felt disadvantaged by the "masculine" nature of rescue work and, taking this into account, set low expectations for themselves. In one way, their feelings were based in reality: They were aware that, on the whole, the men in the group were physically stronger, and thus able to perform harder tasks than they.

In another way, though, women's insecurities were due to cultural and group stereotypes about men's superior rescue ability. For example, the prevailing belief that men are emotionally stronger than women made women question whether they would be able to perform edgework in potentially upsetting situations, while the same stereotype enabled men to have confidence that they would maintain control in those situations (recall Maddie's fear that she would "lose it" if she encountered someone she knew and Gary's love for the "hot seat"). Yet, my observations (discussed later in this chapter) yielded no gendered pattern of emotional control during missions. Another stereotype that made women worry about their rescue ability was the belief that men were more mechanically and technically inclined than they were. This stereotype came into play during trainings and missions when the group used any kind of mechanization, such as rope and pulley systems, helicopters, snowmobiles, or whitewater rafting equipment. Cyndi told me she felt "hugely" intimidated in her first year by the technical training, yet she later became quite adept in setting up and operating rope and pulley systems. Elena told me that during her first training she looked around at "all the guys" and thought, "What am I doing here? I'm not even qualified for any of this." Cyndi and Elena's feelings of inferiority acted as "place markers" where "the emotion conveys information about the state of the social ranking system" (Clark, 1990, p. 308).

Because women were often marginalized in these ways, both their own and others' expectations of them were lower than they were for most men in the group. By remaining trepidacious and maintaining low expectations that they would often exceed, the women reaffirmed their place in the group as useful. Although they feared admitting when they would be unable to complete a task, because as Cyndi said, it meant "you're admitting to everyone else that you're not as good as them," the women in the group felt that bowing out early was preferable to failing. Cyndi said others would think, "at least they didn't fuck the mission up. They stayed, and they helped, and they did something." Thus, trepidation and confidence emerged as gendered emotional strategies used in preparing for edgework.

Performing Edgework: Suppressing Feelings

During Peak's urgent missions, effective action, a core feature of edgework (Lyng, 1990; see also Mannon, 1992; Mitchell, 1983), was seen as especially crucial. However, in such demanding situations, members' capacity for emotional and physical control was seen as more tenuous; emotions threatened to push them over the edge, preventing them from physically performing at all.

Rescuers who were easily scared, excited, or upset by a mission's events were considered undependable. There were several strategies members employed to control these feelings during missions, which allowed them to perform under pressure.

Members were particularly wary of the onset of adrenaline rushes because such potent physiological reactions threatened their composure; they felt that the emotions they experienced as a result of adrenaline rushes could "get in the way" of their performance. Although Schachter and Singer (1962) demonstrated that the physiological arousal associated with adrenaline does not signify a particular emotion in the absence of other situational information, Peak's members used the term "adrenaline rush" to refer to two distinct (and potentially problematic) emotional states: fear and urgency. Yet adrenaline was not totally undesirable; in fact, at lower levels rescuers welcomed it because it helped them focus and heightened their awareness. Mostly, though, rescuers were encouraged to see adrenaline rushes as an important physiological cue, one they should heed as a warning that they were approaching the edge and at risk of losing control.

One way rescuers talked about adrenaline impeding performance was through paralyzing fear (see Holyfield and Fine, 1997), which rendered them ineffective, increasing risk for their teammates and for the victim. Cyndi expressed a typical perspective when she explained the difference between helpful and harmful adrenaline rushes. She described a time when she was trying to cross a river on a series of slippery rocks, each of which was just beyond her comfortable step, requiring her to jump from one to the next. Other rescuers were waiting for her to cross, and she knew that they would be able to reach her if she slipped and fell into the rushing water. Nonetheless, she could not do it:

> I mean, I knew that I was perfectly safe. And I was trembling like a leaf, and my heart was racing, and there wasn't a damn thing I could do about it! I could sit there all day long [saying to myself] "You're gonna be fine, you're gonna be fine, you're gonna be fine," and I just sat there shaking. I was just kind of like in one of these sort of states: huge adrenaline rush…. There's a point where some fear is a good thing—adrenaline—and it helps you focus, because you know that you need to be careful. If you're in a situation where there is some fear, maybe an avalanche or a river, you want to get whatever it is you're doing done quickly because the faster you get out of it, the safer you are. But then there's a point where it stops being an aid and it becomes a hindrance: Fear outweighs your ability to act. I think that's the worst thing in the world you could do for a mission, just freeze and panic, where you spend more time combating your fear than thinking about the situation you're in.

Interestingly, Cyndi equated adrenaline with fear. She used these terms interchangeably, noting the edge between a useful and a detrimental physiological reaction that she experienced as fear. Her description highlighted both sides of the edge. She described the controllable side, where "some fear is a good thing" because rescuers could use their aroused feelings to create order and perform at higher levels. She also explained the other side, the chaotic side, where too much fear impeded rescuers' ability to act effectively.

Another problem that members attributed to adrenaline was that it could cause them to misinterpret routine situations as urgent. Maddie, the ten-year member, explained how feelings of urgency and excitement were problematic and had to be suppressed:

> [Members need to] realize the urgency, and manage that urgency. And that really is the big part [of participating in a mission]. I know I still get it every now and again, that adrenaline rush is really going as you're walking in to the [victim], and that can really get in the way, big time, out there. Because most of the time we're not in a rush to get that person out. We can't be, or we're gonna injure them.

Martin, the construction supervisor in his early fifties, gave an example of how an uncontrolled sense of urgency could put rescuers in danger when he explained what happened on the four-victim van-rollover mission. Several of the first rescuers on the scene (including Martin) rappelled down to the accident to tend to the victims, while the remaining rescuers began to set up a rope-and-pulley system to deliver needed supplies down to the site and to haul the victims out. The rescuers atop, however, overlooked an important safety issue. Instead of setting up the rope system to deliver people and gear next to the accident site, they set it up directly above the victims and rescuers, which caused a great deal of rockfall into the accident scene as other rescuers began to descend with supplies. Martin perceived this mistake to be the result of poor urgency-management:

> I'd just come down, and I was busy trying to help with this one woman that was badly hurt, and then all of a sudden rocks were coming down on top of us—literally two or three times we had to dive and cover the woman up…. One of those rocks came down and hit that van and put a dent probably 8 inches deep in the damn thing. That's when they were bringing the big ropes down to us. Right on top of us. It was just a mistake that we made; just an urgency without being as sharp as we could've been.

While excessive fear and urgency were seen as potentially dangerous overreactions to adrenaline, loss of control due to fear was more often associated with women's reactions, while becoming too excitable was considered more of a male phenomenon. One reason men and women might have experienced adrenaline rushes differently was because men were confident at the prospect of undertaking risk, which may have caused them to interpret their adrenaline during the missions as pleasurable and exciting. Since women reported more cautious mindsets in preparing for missions, worrying about their ability to exercise emotional and physical control in risky situations, perhaps they were more likely to define their adrenaline rushes as fearful and unpleasant.

Men and women, however, managed their feelings of urgency and fear similarly: They suppressed them. For example, Martin told me how he concentrated on his assignment, ignoring everything else that was not directly related to his task on the van-rollover mission:

> I was [attending to] that woman, getting her in the litter, being in charge of that litter, and getting that litter up the hillside. I was wrapped up in what I was doing. I mean, that was one [mission] where we really had to work. There were really bad, hurt people. [I thought], "Let's do what we can and get them back up that hill." … We were so exhausted, so by then it was just a technical problem, you know? I didn't have time to get involved with the victims.

Martin kept his cool by prioritizing his actions in the situation, taking one step at a time to achieve his goal of evacuating the victims. The demands of the mission forced him to focus his attention on his task and pour all of his time and energy into completing it. This narrowing of focus and losing awareness of factors extraneous to the risky activity itself is a common feature of edgework (Lyng, 1990) and is often interpreted as a pleasurable sensation for edgeworkers.

Cyndi told me that while on the same mission, she was in control of her emotions, successfully suppressing them, because she was working the rope systems up on the road, unable to see beyond the drop-off down to the accident site. She felt differently, however, when one of the accident victims reached the top of the hill in a panicked state. The victim, who had a broken arm, had managed to climb up the 400-foot embankment in an effort to catch up to the rescue team who was evacuating her critically injured mother. Cyndi was thrown off kilter by this sight:

> Because I was up at the top, it wasn't real. You know, I could sort of disassociate, it's like, "Okay, let's just get the job done and not think about it." But then you're meeting this person [climbing out of the accident scene] who is just out of it. I mean, she was panicked and [she had] adrenaline [rushing], and I was just kind of like, "Okay, there really are real people down there, but I'm not gonna get panicked. I need to calm this person down, because she's not gonna help rushing up to the scene, and getting in the way of the paramedics [while] trying to get to her mother."

Cyndi's emotional control was threatened when the victim emerged from the trauma scene. The sight forced her to the edge, where her ordered, controlled action was threatened by her feeling of chaotic, uncontrolled panic. She quickly narrowed her focus further, successfully managing her own impending panic by monitoring the victim's behavior. In this way she was able to keep her feelings at bay while she continued working. Yet the way Cyndi described how she narrowed her focus does not suggest that she was very adept at suppressing self-reflexivity. In fact, it seems as though the reflexive self pushed to the fore, causing Cyndi to talk to herself, evaluate her actions, and take on a new role in the social scene of the accident.

When I asked women how they suppressed their emotions, they gave me long and detailed descriptions of what they did and how they did it, as illustrated by Cyndi's response. Yet men's answers were brief. Some said that since they did not think about the risks they were taking, dangerous emotions did not arise. Nick said, "The majority of the time I just don't think about the worst part, like getting hurt or dying. I just think about getting the job done." Another experienced member commented on the phenomenon as well, saying, "Are you gonna stop and look at the risk factor every time you get paged out for a mission? Or are you just gonna go and do it?"

When men did give detailed responses to questions about suppressing emotions, their explanations still differed from women's in that they tended to describe suppressing their emotions as a process that required little conscious control, one that came almost "naturally" to them. In fact, Vince, a three-year member in his early twenties who was a paramedic, explained it this way:

> *Vince*: You tune out emotions and feelings, and focus on the task at hand.... And we deal with that on a lot of the missions. I mean, you can't walk up to a fall victim and say, "Oh my God, this guy has lost two fingers!" or, you know, "He's got a hole in his head!" That doesn't work. So I think what would otherwise probably really bother some people, it just doesn't affect me as much. And I'm sure that in some areas of both my personal life and my rescue life, that I kind of over-step those boundaries and let that "barrier," if you will, affect other areas of my life. Where I *should* be or I *could* be more sensitive or more feeling to stuff, it just doesn't bother me. So it's definitely not just in rescue work or medical training. It has infected my other areas also.

> *Jen*: So you see it as a bad thing in other areas of your life, but as a good thing in rescue work? You said it has "infected" your other areas.

> *Vince*: I did say "infected" because, yeah, sometimes I wish I could be more sensitive to things. It's just that the level of my feelings in some instances just doesn't go very deep at all. I can look at something and be like, [*shrugs*] "whatever." I just don't see things the same way [as other people]. Things are not a big deal to me. And in rescue work, I like that

aspect about myself; I think that's a good aspect to have. But it has definitely overflown into my personal life, which has its good and bad points. But I know that's just the nature of who I am.

Vince perceived his ability to suppress his emotions as innate. He saw this emotional trait as such a core part of who he was, that his feelings (or lack thereof) actually controlled him, not vice versa.

Another way emotions interfered with performance was when members were disturbed by the graphic sight of the accidents they encountered. Recovering the body of a dead victim, for example, held great potential for negative feelings, especially if the death was violent or gruesome, leaving the body in pieces, excessively bloody, or positioned unnaturally (such as having the legs bent backwards or an arm missing). Such situations could cause extreme reactions in rescuers, possibly preventing them from doing the job they were assigned. On the whole, men were assumed to be better suited for these gruesome or graphic jobs because they were perceived to be emotionally stronger than women. For example, Brooke, the student in her mid-twenties, stated that emotional strength and masculinity were intertwined. She said that, under such extreme conditions, Peak's members had to "have the balls to go in and do what needs to be done.... I think you have to be [emotionally] strong to see what you see and to deal with what you deal with in this group."

Other members stated these gendered expectations more blatantly. Maddie told me she had noticed a common pattern in the ten years she had been in the group:

I think there's an emotional consideration [to being in this group], because our society says men need to hold their emotions in check more so than women. It's expected. It's an expectation from our society. And so, in any kind of situation where emotions could come into play, you know, something that's really gruesome, [the mission coordinators] aren't gonna ask us [the women], they'll ask the guys first.

Jim, the founding twenty-year member of Peak, confirmed Maddie's suspicions when he told me that, as a mission coordinator, he tried to utilize members for jobs according to their ability, regardless of gender, except in one situation:

I do, however, hesitate to use women in body recovery-type situations ... I want to protect 'em from the exposure to that type of an incident. I can't tell you why I wanna protect 'em, but that's what it is. And I wanna protect the new members too. 'Cause I think it's a horrible deal. And, you know, my wife asks me all the time, "Why do *you* have to go do the body?" Been there. Done that. I can do that. Why subject somebody else to it?

Jim reasoned that those with less emotional strength—women and inexperienced members—should be protected from the trauma of recovering dead bodies. Women were, however, the less experienced members, so perhaps choosing experienced members also meant choosing men over women. In this way, stereotypes and experience interacted to create a strong pattern where men were much more likely than women to recover dead bodies.

Yet men, experienced or not, were not immune to the potentially disturbing effects of gruesome rescues. In fact, Martin told me that when he came upon a particularly gruesome plane crash, "I barfed my guts out." Meg, a resort worker and ten-year member in her mid-forties, told me that despite stereotypes of masculine emotional strength, she had seen experienced men who had trouble dealing with dead bodies, even though they were willing to assist in the recovery task:

> I've seen people that are very, very macho and strong and opinionated become very sheepish in those situations.... [They] march right in and as soon as they get a visual on it [the body], they're off doing something else. [They] walk away. Can't look, can't touch.... And for me, a body recovery is just like recovering a living person. You know, it's just a body of who was there, and the "who" part is gone.... So body recoveries are not so difficult for me, but for some people it's a real struggle.

Thus, even for members who were expected to be emotionally tough, emotions also "got in the way" in dead body situations, because they could cause some members to go over the edge, losing their ability to perform under stressful circumstances.

One emotion management strategy members used to combat these upset feelings was to depersonalize the victims, which Meg alluded to by saying a body is not a person because the "who" part is gone. Her husband, Kevin, the ten-year, leader-status member, told me exactly how he maintained emotional distance from the victims on a rescue, in particular, from dead bodies he had helped recover:

> [Recovering a dead body] brings out a shield or a protective-type barrier. I go in knowing it's a fatality, that the spirit is gone, this is merely the vehicle in which he or she traveled around this planet.... I try not to get emotionally attached. I feel very mechanical. It's just something that has to be done, and if I'm there, I'm part of that effort to take care of it.... I have put myself in a mission mode. I'm mission-ready, I'm focused, we're doing something here. So sometimes [in my mission mode] I become linear [and] cold.... Another interesting thing—I cannot tell you any of the names of the people I've bagged. It's my way of coping with it. I'll know the name going in, and within several days, that name is no longer accessible in my memory bank.... Good, bad, or indifferent, that's the

way I am. It's not something that I intentionally do. I have no idea where or why or how I came up with—I'm going to say—that "ability." But that's the way I do it.

Kevin referred to the same focusing of attention that Martin described when he was evacuating the victim of the van rollover, but Kevin also used his "ability" to depersonalize the victim. Such detachment has been shown to be a way people maintain instrumental control in other emotionally threatening situations as well (see DeCoster, 1997; Jones 1997; Mannon, 1992; Smith and Kleinman, 1989).

Jim, the founding member, also felt very strongly that emotions not be a part of recovering a dead body. He described one occasion when his team was extracting a drowned victim from a river:

> There is nothin' glamorous about taking somebody's human remains, stuffing 'em in a black bag, hauling 'em up the hill, and throwing 'em in the back of the sheriff's van. There is *nothin'* glamorous about that. And when I'm in those types of situations, there's a space that I have to go to in my head. And it's real no-nonsense; it's time to say, "Let's get the job done. Let's roll up our sleeves," if you will. You know, that is not the time to reflect on "What's it all about?" or "Why we're all here." It's a time to roll this *carcass* into a bag and drag it up the hill. And people on our team started with that [being philosophical during one extrication]. [So I said], "I don't wanna hear it! I want the guy *off* the log, *in* the bag, to the *top* of the hill. Are we ready to go?" And we should be, [*snaps*], ready to go.

Jim's "space" in his head helped him perform because it allowed him to depersonalize the victim (the "carcass"). In his view, the other members' choice to reflect on larger philosophical questions was poorly timed, interfering not only with the mission's efficiency, but with his own ability to suppress emotion as well. He clearly demonstrated edgeworkers' ability to filter out part of the social self when he explained that he had a special "space" in his head, and he showed how edgework was impeded when others reflected on their place in the world.

Fear, urgency, and emotional upset were some of the powerful feelings that threatened rescuers' control during missions. As a result, members worked to suppress them (women more actively than men), maintaining a demeanor of "affective neutrality" (Parsons, 1951) by focusing on their task and depersonalizing the victims. This group norm of displaying affective neutrality signified a cool-headedness that was thought to be safe and effective, and the group considered those who could achieve it in the most critical of circumstances to be those who could work closest to the edge. Thus, the best edgeworkers, and by extension, Peak's most valuable members, were those who could reliably suppress their emotions and get the job done. Roy, a mountaineer and fifteen-year member, attributed the essence of edgework to emotion management, saying, "The best thing I can call [search and rescue] is 'decision making under duress.'"

Completing Edgework: Releasing Feelings

Immediately after the missions, members' suppressed feelings began to surface. They viewed the sensations they got from successful mission outcomes, like reuniting victims with their families, as the ultimate reward, and I often witnessed them expressing these positive feelings upon hearing the news of a saved victim. They instantly discarded their objective demeanors and became jovial, slap-happy, and chatty. Like Mannon's (1992) ambulance workers, Peak's rescuers released the pent-up stress that had been tightly managed throughout the missions by shouting, high-fiving each other, making jokes, and talking about what they had been thinking and feeling throughout the mission.

Occasionally, rescuers would realize that they had been in a risky situation that could have gone awry during the mission. Reflecting back on the hazards they had undertaken and overcome during a mission made them feel ambivalent. On the one hand, they felt energized, which they generally regarded as a positive feeling of control and competence. For Lyng's (1990) skydivers, the whole point of edgework was to experience these feelings after the jump. Yet, on the other hand, these positive feelings were infused with unsettled feelings of doubt when rescuers realized how dangerous the situation had been. Kevin told me how he felt when looking back:

> I think while you're in the situation, the risk or the apparent danger isn't as highlighted—it's not quite as strong or acute as it is after you've had time to reflect through hindsight what exactly transpired.... When you're in the situation, you are doing, you are operating, you are moving, you are trying to accomplish something. You're fixated, to an extent. But after the mission, you get back and you go, "Wow, that was—" you know, "What if, what if, what if?"

Kevin recognized his ability to filter out some part of the reflexive self during the missions. Yet the risk became clearer once he reengaged the reflexive self and had the opportunity to analyze what had happened. I asked Kevin how he felt after one particular mission where he was in a helicopter during an extremely risky maneuver to reach an injured hiker. He said, "It was that night when I was sitting around the house going, 'That was insane where that helicopter was!'...[I felt] lucky. [And] a *big* adrenaline rush." Clearly, the feelings he had been suppressing had a chance to rush forward, taking him to the edge emotionally; his ordered experience became somewhat chaotic in retrospect. He described a pattern that many members experienced. While on the mission, they had maintained composure and objectivity by engaging in strategies to suppress their emotions. However, once the danger was over, they released this tight control and confronted feelings that challenged their interpretation of what just happened. During this stage of edgework, members tried to make sense of the myriad emotions that bombarded them.

Alex, the British botanist, told me more about the time she and Roy, the fifteen-year member and respected mountaineer, were chosen to ice-climb up the 800-foot, avalanche-prone gully to reach the stranded hot-air balloonists whose balloon had crashed at the top of a cliff. About an hour after they were dispatched into the field, the mission coordinator was able to contact a helicopter, which was going to be able to reach the stranded subjects sooner than Roy and Alex, who were still only halfway up the gully. The mission coordinator radioed Alex and Roy and told them to get to a stable, safe place because the wind from the incoming helicopter above them could stir up the snow, causing an avalanche into their gully. They assessed their location at the base of a seventy-five-foot frozen waterfall and thought they might be safe if they positioned themselves close to the ice (the momentum of an avalanche would propel the snow in an arc, providing a safety zone between the stream of snow and the vertical icefall). At the last minute, Alex saw an ice cave twenty feet up, behind the frozen waterfall. They decided they would be safer there so she climbed up and then pulled Roy (whose climbing footgear was falling off) up to her. She told me what happened next:

> The two of us landed in this snow cave, and just then we hear this *roar*, and we're like "Oh my God, an avalanche!" And we like, peer out from behind the ice fall, and the *balloon*, with the basket and all of the fuel tanks and everything, just came thundering down the gully, [and the basket] just *exploded* [broke into hundreds of pieces] at the bottom where we'd been standing, and just carried on down the gully. And we were just like [*shocked expression: jaw dropped, eyes wide, speechless*]. I mean, we just sort of lay there like "Oh my God." I mean, we were expecting an avalanche, not the *balloon*…. If we had not moved out of that position and got out of the gully, I mean, we'd've just gotten smack-a-roonied by the balloon. We were both pretty shaken by that one. I don't know, maybe we felt more vulnerable or something, but we were definitely shaken up…. Roy kept grabbing me and saying [*yelling*], "I can't believe that happened!" and "Oh my God!" I'd say it was definitely the closest I've come in a rescue to getting snookered.

Even when rescuers emerged from missions safely, these types of close calls could disturb them for days or weeks afterward, bringing their mortality into sharp relief. It was difficult when they realized that they were vulnerable, even if they believed it was only to freak accidents. Such events made it hard for them to maintain the "illusion of control" that many edgeworkers rely on (Lyng, 1990).

Missions with negative outcomes frequently left rescuers with even stronger and more unpleasant feelings than rescues that ended successfully, and members often reported being at home alone when they first encountered these feelings. One source of upset feelings was recurring memories of emotionally disturbing scenes, a common reaction for rescuers in other settings as well (see Moran, Britton, and Correy, 1992; Oliner and Oliner, 1988). Cyndi described to me how the visual images of her first dead body recovery (a victim with a severed arm) bothered her:

> I got home [from the mission], and I had to get up [in a couple of hours] and go to work. So I did the work thing, and then I got home, and I was by myself, and that night sitting at home I got this mental image and, um—I don't know. It was unpleasant. For the next couple or three days you get, like, these images. If I think about it, I can still see it. Yeah, so it was not pretty.

Recurring visual memories are common when people, like medical students (see Smith and Kleinman, 1989) or emergency workers (see Gibbs, Lachenmeyer, Broska, and Deucher, 1996; Mannon, 1992; Metz, 1981; Moran, Britton, and Correy, 1992), first see dead bodies. But for Peak's rescuers, these recurring memories were not always visual. One member told me that he once assisted in the body recovery of a fallen rock climber, after which he didn't sleep for three weeks. He had many upsetting flashbacks of both the sights and sounds from the scene: seeing the victim's legs broken backwards from the fall, and hearing them crack as rescuers straightened them to fit him in the body bag. Alex, the British rescuer, remembered feeling the weight of one dead body she helped carry out from the four-passenger van rollover: "I just remember how *heavy* it was. You know, they say 'dead weight'? That was one of the most memorable [missions]. That one lived with me for a while."

These upsetting flashbacks could be compounded by knowing personal information about the victim. When the rescue hit too close to home, members' confrontation with the stressful emotions was more intense. For example, on one mission three highly experienced rescuers, Tyler, Nick, and Shorty, volunteered to travel to another county to extract the dead body of a kayaker, which was stuck in the middle of a rushing river. The kayaker was killed when the front of his kayak got sucked under the water and pinned between two rocks. The force of the water behind him pushed the back of his kayak up into the air and then folded it over on top of him, snapping both of his legs backwards and trapping him in his kayak. The victims' friends were unable to reach him, and he drowned. Nick found that particular mission more difficult to deal with than other missions, causing him several disturbing flashbacks. He told me that for days afterward he had strong, negative feelings:

> *Nick*: It was really messing with my head. I mean, every time I looked at a river or just thought about rafting or kayaking or whatever, I would

just focus on the way the body looked.... I didn't think it was gonna be that beat up. It was only in the river for a day before we got to it, but it was pretty beat up.

Jen: How do you feel when you see stuff like that?

Nick: A little nauseous. Nervous about getting hurt in that situation, you know, dying in that same situation that the person was in. Especially since the week before I checked into kayaking lessons [*laughs*]!

Jen: And did you follow up on that?

Nick: No.

Nick was unable to control these intrusive images, and they bothered him because he felt vulnerable, a common feeling for rescuers at gruesome accident scenes (see Gibbs et al., 1996).

While not all rescuers were equally affected by the negative impact of dead body recoveries or of "failed" missions, it did not appear that men were immune to these feelings in the post-mission period, as many rescuers had imagined they would be. Both women and men reported having trouble dealing with feelings of vulnerability in these instances, which diluted the emotional charge they got from edgework. As a result, rescuers tried to manage the uncontrolled flow of conflicting emotions in the immediate post-mission period. In the most intense cases, they reported feeling overwhelmed with emotion, unable to control it, and needing to release it in some way, a prevalent pattern for other types of emergency workers as well (see Mannon, 1992; Metz, 1981).

There were several ways members released these feelings. One way was by crying. I talked to Elena, a hotel manager and five-year member in her early thirties, shortly after her first (and only) dead body recovery. She told me that she thought she was "okay" until she got home and was in the shower, where she started to cry. She said this was effective in releasing some of her feelings, stating that she never cried about it again, yet it did bother her for days afterward. She felt that this initial release was enough to reduce the backlog of feelings that she had suppressed while on the mission. It allowed her to regain her composure, reducing her stress and anxiety to manageable levels. In essence, she lost and regained her self-reflexivity, much like the battered wives Mills and Kleinman (1988) analyzed.

This pattern of releasing emotions by crying was gendered: Men never reported crying as a means of dealing with the emotional turmoil of missions, while women occasionally did. Although it is possible that men and women did cry with equal frequency and masculinity norms prevented men from reporting it, it was more likely that women saw this as a more acceptable emotion management technique and coped in this way more often than men.

Releasing pent-up emotions was not always the direct result of a death. Maddie told me that she was under a great deal of stress while in charge of one mission where she sent three rescuers into a highly avalanche-prone area to search for a lost skier. Although the rescuers took precautions to keep themselves safe, Maddie's high level of anxiety at the base was noticeable, at least to a local newspaper reporter who interviewed her while the other rescuers were in the field. The reporter ran a story about the mission the next day and described Maddie's "very emotional" state during the operation:

> Maddie Smith, who was in charge of the command post at the rescue headquarters, got very emotional when she discussed the dangers faced by her co-workers, and the precautions they were taking. "They all have tons of avalanche training, but there are no avalanche experts—they're all dead. You can never learn enough, that's why my ear is glued to this thing (radio), because they're my buddies," she said, in a slightly choked voice.

By this account, it appeared that Maddie was trying hard to control her emotions during the mission, though she let them go soon afterward when she and several other rescuers went to a local bar to unwind. She told me that she began sobbing on the five-minute walk from the parking lot to the bar, but by the time she arrived she had regained her composure, attributing her tears to the "pent-up stress" from being in charge of the mission. Similar to the vulnerability felt by members who retrospectively realized the danger they had been in, Maddie was confronted with a feeling of her teammates' vulnerability, compounded by the feeling of responsibility for putting them there.

After the most traumatic missions, such as one occasion when members extricated the charred remains of several forest fire fighters caught in a "fire storm" (an extremely hot, quick-moving, and dangerous type of forest fire), the group provided a professionally run "critical incident debriefing" session where they could talk about their feelings after the mission. While these sessions encouraged men (who were the ones most often involved in such intense missions) to express their feelings, there were only two of these sessions offered in my six years with Peak. As a general rule, Peak's culture did not encourage men to express their feelings after emotionally taxing rescues, a phenomenon that is common to American culture in general: Women tend to cope with emotionally threatening feelings by crying, while men tend to cope with stress by withdrawing, becoming angry, and using drugs and alcohol (Gove, Geerken, and Hughes, 1979; King, Delaronde, Dinoi, and Forsberg, 1996; Mirowsky and Ross, 1995; Moran, Britton, and Correy, 1992; Roehling, Koelbel, and Rutgers, 1996; Thoits, 1995).

It was common for Peak's members to drink alcohol after both positive- and negative-outcome missions, but they generally consumed more after negative outcomes, such as dead body recoveries, as a way of coping with anxiety and unpleasant feelings. After Tyler, Nick, and Shorty recovered the trapped kayaker's body in another county, Tyler told me that they bought a twelve-pack of beer for Nick and Shorty to drink while Tyler drove them home. In the three-hour drive, Shorty drank two of the beers, and Nick drank the remaining ten. When I asked Nick about this, he told me that he drank beer after missions to try to "calm down, to relax.... [I was tense] because I didn't think the body was gonna be that beat up. It's kinda like if you had a rough day at work, you drink a couple beers.... I think [it's] just part of releasing any tension, even if it's just adrenaline that you have stored up." In this way members used "bodily deep acting," manipulating their physiological state to change their emotional state (Hochschild, 1990), by relaxing themselves with alcohol in an effort to dampen the chaos of their surfacing feelings.

Maddie also talked about members' alcohol use after emotionally stressful missions. In her ten years with Peak, she noticed that more men than women used alcohol to release their emotions, attributing this difference to gender socialization:

> I think the guys hide [their upset] a lot better [than the women]. And deal with it by going and drinking beers. I mean, that has always been the way we deal with it—for years. And I don't think that's good. Because this post-traumatic stress, I mean, you can see it in a lot of our guys after a big, heavy-duty mission. You know, just going to the bar and drinking beers doesn't release it always. And then it starts to come out in their personal lives, and I don't think that's healthy at all.

Maddie explained men's higher alcohol consumption rate over women's in terms of cultural expectations for men to hide their feelings and appear to remain emotionally unaffected, an observation supported by social research (see Mirowsky and Ross, 1995; Thoits, 1995). Maddie also believed alcohol use to be a dysfunctional, ineffective strategy for some of the men she knew, an observation that has received inconclusive support in coping research (see Robinson and Johnson, 1997; Roehling, Koelbel, and Rutgers, 1996; Patterson and McCubbin, 1984; Sigmon, Stanton, and Snyder, 1995).

Rescuers often reported feeling more easily overwhelmed in the period after a mission, attributing it to their failure to release all of their pent-up emotions, much like the disaster volunteers Gibbs and her colleagues (1996) studied. Thus, another way they dealt with their feelings was to leave the group temporarily or quit altogether. After recovering the trapped kayaker, Nick turned off his pager so that he did not hear any calls for missions, saying that during the several weeks that followed, "I didn't go on any rescues.... I just wanted a break." And Roy explained the experience of another member, Walter, who had been in the group several years before I joined. He told me that one summer, in the span of only a few weeks, Walter had been on several stressful missions:

> He had been on a suicide, and he'd been on a couple of plane crashes. And what broke his spirit was [on the second plane crash] a tree branch caught and it threw maggots in his face. You know, into his nose and stuff. And that was it for him. He said, "This is fuckin' bullshit! This is it!" A suicide, a plane crash, another plane crash, and then you have maggots in your face? I mean, are people trying to kill him?

Walter removed himself from the emotional stress of Peak's missions by quitting the group. Roy saw this as a reasonable solution; to him, these incidents were so emotionally charged that they were not only "spirit breaking," but were actually life threatening.

Rescuers understood their emotions through what Stearns (1994) has called the "ventilation" model of emotions. During missions, they experienced an intense emotional buildup while performing physical edgework. These emotions, when released afterward, often took them over the emotional edge into disorder and chaos.

Maintaining the "Illusion of Control": Redefining Feelings

The fourth stage of edgework was marked by members' ability to regain control of their feelings and cognitively process them, retrospectively redefining and shaping their experiences, a process Kitsuse (1962) termed "retrospective interpretation." Often this involved neutralizing their post-mission negative feelings, which was important to edgework because, if left unresolved, negative emotions could destroy the positive elements of edgework, shake members' confidence, and impede their performance on future missions. In the long term, positive-outcome missions allowed rescuers to maintain the "illusion of control"; members' success served as evidence that they could push their limits next time, too. Negative outcomes, however, threatened the illusion of control, leaving members wondering if they were capable, and unsure of the risk they were willing to assume in the future. In this stage, rescuers employed another type of "deep acting" where they "visualiz[ed] a substantial portion of reality in a different way" (Hochschild, 1990, p. 121), and their emotion management techniques were aimed at cognitively changing the meaning of what happened, which transformed their feelings about it. This helped them to maximize their ability to conduct future edgework.

Guilt was a stressful emotion for rescuers in the wake of unsuccessful missions. Members could feel personally responsible for the outcome, for example, if they failed to save a victim. On one occasion, rescuers felt bothered by a mission where a kayaker died in a river race. Many of Peak's members were at the race, volunteering to act as safety agents on the riverbanks, throwing lines to any kayakers in trouble. One racer's kayak flipped upside down, and he was unable to right himself. Although many tried to reach him—fellow racers chased him down, people standing on the banks threw safety lines—no one could get to him until he floated through the finish line four minutes later. Many bystanders speculated that he must have been knocked unconscious while he was inverted and subsequently drowned. Jim told me that he went over and over the incident in his mind that night, trying to think of something he and the team could have done to reach the boater more quickly. He could find no flaws in the team's response, and yet found it difficult to accept that the boater was killed. Kevin echoed Jim's feelings when he told me that he felt compelled to return to the scene in search of an answer: "It bothered me that I wasn't able to do *something*. And I went back that night to stand by the river, to look at it, to reevaluate, and I came to the same conclusion: There was nothing I could've done, other than create a worse situation."

This incident was particularly troublesome for group members because they saw the accident and were so close; standing there on the riverbank, they felt helpless while the kayaker drowned, a situation that seriously threatened their sense of control. Two days later the local newspaper reported that the kayaker had died when, due to a genetic defect, his heart "exploded." Many members were relieved by this news because it confirmed the conclusions they had come to through their careful reanalysis: They could not have saved him. The ambulance workers in Mannon's (1992) and Palmer and Gonsoulin's (1990) studies also neutralized their negative emotions in these ways, feeling relieved when they found out that patients died from causes beyond anyone's control.

One way members neutralized their guilt was by redefining their part in missions. One technique was "denying responsibility" (Sykes and Matza, 1957) for the victim's fate. Members were often reminded that their first concern on a mission was to protect themselves, second, their teammates, and third, the victim. The rationale was that if rescuers hurt themselves on a mission, they could not be any help to anyone else. In fact, they increased the burden on their team members, who would then have to divert rescue resources to help them. Brooke demonstrated her understanding of this protocol when she told me, "The safety of the group comes first. We're volunteers and there's no reason in the world that we should put ourselves in danger to save somebody else. There is *no reason*. And it is our choice [if we decide] to do so." It was therefore irrational for members to endanger themselves to help someone else, especially since they bore no responsibility for putting them there in the first place. By encouraging members to define their part in the missions as above and beyond the normal duties of average citizens, this perspective helped members avoid feeling a sense of personal failure in the event of "failed" missions.

Another way members avoided feeling responsible for not saving people was by attributing control to a higher power. Meg told me that she relied on her "personal philosophical beliefs" to help her deal with the potentially negative feelings that could result from recovering a dead body. She used this technique to accept the reality that people die, as well as to deny any responsibility for it:

> I realize that, in what we're doing, the reality is that there are gonna be the dead bodies. That's part of what we're doing. So that part doesn't bother me. I mean, I always feel sad, and I feel bad—and there are still the situations, the really horrific things, you still can visualize, after years, you know, but that doesn't mean I dwell on that.... I guess I deal with it by saying, "Shit happens." To good people, too! ... You say, "God, that was awful," and move on. That's part of life. When it's your time, it's your time. Sometimes you go out nice and easy, and sometimes you go out pretty gory. That's the reality of it. You know, I was born and raised Catholic, I believe in God, and I think that helps. I mean, I believe that that's just a body. The spirit's gone.

Members also denied responsibility by blaming the victims themselves. Gary told me that he often said to himself, "'God, I'm glad that's not me.' It sounds selfish but it's really not.... If they're dead, they might have done something stupid to get there; that's not our fault. It's not your fault that that person out there is dead." And Alex noted that, "It's just easier to rationalize it when [you know that] he was doing something where he knew the risks." Not only did members dodge guilt using these rationalizations, but they sidestepped vulnerability, too. The victim's stupidity was the cause of death, and rescuers, who considered themselves much smarter, could avoid such a fate. Lyng's (1990) skydivers and Mitchell's (1983) mountain climbers used similar rationalizations. Through these methods, rescuers were able to temper their feelings of guilt and vulnerability, which, in turn, helped them to maintain a positive self-image as well as to maintain the illusion of control, to reassure themselves about their own ability to survive edgework.

Members also redefined their part in "failed" missions by emphasizing the positive side of negative events. For instance, although dead body recoveries were very unpleasant experiences for everyone in the group, most members were prepared to voluntarily assist in them, pointing out how their part in retrieving bodies helped the grieving families. Many reasoned that it was better for the victims' families to have "closure" to the incidents so that they could move on, as opposed to never knowing whether their loved one was alive or dead. Nick demonstrated this positive spin when he justified his general willingness to recover dead bodies, saying that he felt good when he could "help out the family by getting the body back [to them]." In this way, group members imputed important meaning to this unpleasant but routine activity, defining body recoveries instead as good deeds.

Another technique members used to counter the stress of emotionally taxing missions was to weight the successes more than the failures. Although they took great pains to separate themselves personally from failed missions, denying responsibility and downplaying the significance of those situations, members actively sought a personal connection with the successful missions, acknowledging their role in them, and allowing their participation to be meaningful and important reflections of their abilities. Personally accepting credit for successes protected rescuers by bolstering their confidence and making them feel that they had control over risky conditions, a strategy used by other edgeworkers who strive to maintain the illusion of control (see Lyng, 1990; Mannon, 1992).[2]

Meg told me about a time when she and her husband, Kevin, were on a winter search for a missing woman whom they finally found at four o'clock in the morning. She was huddled under a rock outcropping, disoriented, hypothermic, and dehydrated, and she was having trouble breathing (they later found out she had a collapsed lung). They got her warmed up and hydrated, and then helped her walk out of the field:

> We pulled her out and we hiked her down having her step across the top of our snowshoes, I mean, we went side-by-side for *miles* letting her walk on [top of] our snowshoes to get down.... She still sends us a card at the holidays. You know, "You saved my life." That one was really rewarding. It was successful; it was a good ending. They're not always that way, which leaves you feeling kind of empty. But that was one of those happy-ending ones.

I asked Meg how long she felt good about that rescue:

> I *still* feel good about that. I mean, it's [been] eight years, and I still feel good that at some point I made a difference in one person's life. If you can make a difference in one person's life, that should be enough reward. I mean, I still think about her, and I still think back on missions that have been very successful, you know, and I try and dwell on those.

By "dwelling" on the good, Meg was able to evoke and sustain her good feelings in the long run. Many members used this technique: They defined their overall participation in search and rescue as valuable, and thus next time were able to "crowd the edge" (Lyng, 1990)—risk more emotionally and physically—because the rewards outweighed the costs.

Conclusion

There were four stages of edgework that were marked not only by the flow of rescue events, but also by the corresponding emotions they evoked. Rescuers risked both their physical and emotional well-being before, during, and after the missions, and maintaining a sense of an ordered reality was a key concern in each stage. Because each of these four stages was characterized by different threatening feelings, members utilized several types of emotion management strategies as they prepared for, performed, completed, and redefined edge-work. Moreover, these feelings and management techniques were gender specific. The men in the group tended to feel confident and excited on missions and to display emotional stoicism about negative outcomes. Conversely, the women tended to feel trepidacious and fearful on the critical missions and to express their feelings in the mission's aftermath. Both genders, though, tended to maintain a positive self-image by using cognitive strategies to redefine their feelings in retrospect. Examining the role of emotions and gender in edgework provides some new ideas that expand the edgework model.

First, by focusing on the group's role in helping individual rescuers define and deal with their emotions, this research provides an analysis of edgework that has not yet been discussed in the research literature. One powerful aspect of Lyng's theoretical model is that it links the micro-sociological elements of the edgework experience, such as individuals' feelings of omnipotence and self-actualization, to the macro-sociological elements of edgework, such as postindustrial rationality and institutionalization. Yet my research clarifies an important dimension of the edgework model by presenting a meso-level analysis; it illustrates how Peak's group culture was instrumental in providing its members with the tools to understand their edgework experiences, specifically the "danger" of particular emotions and the ways they "should be" controlled. By illuminating how individual edgework experiences are socially constructed in a subcultural context, this research bridges the gap between the micro and macro levels of analysis.

Second, by concentrating on emotions, these data produce a stage model of edgework that is not explicit in Lyng's work. In discussing skydivers' emotional and cognitive states, Lyng implicitly presents three stages of edgework. The preparation stage (to use my terminology) is marked by edgeworkers' nervousness before the jump. In the performing stage, edgeworkers suspend the reflexive aspect of the self, and act without thinking. In the immediate aftermath stage, edgeworkers feel omnipotent and self-actualized (in part because they experienced a non-reflexive self in the previous stage). Clearly, emotions are an important part of edgework, and by specifically tracing edgeworkers' emotions and emotion management techniques throughout the experience, my data explicitly illuminate the stages of edgework, which, in the case of "successful" missions, tend to correspond with those Lyng has discussed.

Yet, my data also uncover a fourth stage of edgework, one previously unidentified in the edgework literature. The "redefining feelings" stage shows how rescuers were able to maintain the illusion of control—a crucial part of edgeworkers' repertoire—despite the negative feelings they were left with after "failed" rescues. This fourth stage of edgework was arguably the most important for rescuers; they had to deal with their "failure" and neutralize their threatening feelings because these managed feelings then carried over to the first phase again, in which rescuers emotionally prepared for future missions. Since emotions occur "on the template of prior expectations" (Hochschild,

1983), rescuers who could not deal with their feelings would be unable (or at least unmotivated) to pursue edgework in the future. This fourth stage of edgework, redefining feelings, was apparent in my research with Peak, suggesting that the "problematic" emotions in this stage were more prominent for rescuers than for the edgeworkers Lyng studied.

One reason that my data may have revealed this fourth stage of edgework is because of the greater potential for negative outcomes for search and rescue workers, as compared to Lyng's skydivers or other risk-taking recreationalists. In most leisure-oriented edgework, the outcomes are positive, and edgeworkers are left with feelings of omnipotence and self-actualization. Thus it makes sense that Lyng's edgework model, which is based largely on recreational risk taking, would not include this fourth stage of edgework; there would be no need to neutralize and eradicate feelings of omnipotence and self-actualization. In rare cases where the outcome was not positive, such as that of a fallen comrade, Lyng's edgeworkers used the tautological attribution of the "innate survival skill" to neutralize their negative feelings, reasoning that they themselves had been successful because they had the "right stuff." Yet perhaps some types of edgeworkers are more likely to be left with feelings of vulnerability and guilt, such as rescuers, police officers, and firefighters, whose activities are more instrumentally focused, and who, in helping others, are often not able to control the risk and outcome of their edgework. Such service-oriented situations contain many more variables, and thus, the survival of everyone involved is much less common; sometimes these edgeworkers fail. These service-oriented edgeworkers, then, might rely more heavily on the fourth stage of edgework to manage their negative emotions and regain their "illusion of control" so that they may engage in edgework again. The typical tautological justifications used by many leisure-oriented edgeworkers may not be sufficient because the "failure" involves more than just those who are taking the risk. Thus, the instrumental and service-oriented nature of Peak may explain why this fourth stage of edgework emerged from these data.

This research also provides more information on the first and second stages, preparing for and performing edgework. In Lyng's model, the "how" of edgework is explained (and perhaps understood) vaguely by the edgeworkers themselves. They believed they had a unique ability that went beyond the technical skill required to perform any particular risky activity—the innate survival instinct that allowed them to maintain control over the seemingly uncontrollable. This ability allowed them to "respond automatically without thinking," to "avoid being paralyzed by fear and ... to focus [their] attention and actions on what is most crucial for survival" (1990, p. 859). When they survived their experience on the edge, it "proved" they had this unique "edgework skill" (the "right stuff"); when they failed (died or sustained serious injury), it "proved" they did not.

Some of my data correspond with Lyng's model, while others do not, and it appears that gender is an important factor in this distinction. While Peak's culture promoted the idea that emotions were "dangerous" because they "got in the way," interfering with performance and sacrificing the efficiency of the mission, not all rescuers dealt with emotions in the same way. In illuminating the role of emotions in edgework (or, really, what rescuers perceived in retrospect to be the role of emotions), this research highlights a distinct gender difference in understanding the edgework experience.

In the first stage, preparing for edgework, male rescuers were similar to Lyng's skydivers. They tended to hold unwavering confidence about their potential edgework performances because they said they were sure that their bodies would take over, and they would not have to think about it. Thus, they did not plan and rehearse future scenarios because they were confident that, with proper training, they would be able to perform when the time came. They claimed that they never worried that their emotions would interfere. In contrast, and unlike Lyng's skydivers, female rescuers tended to display a great deal of trepidation, which they combated by rehearsing future scenarios and anticipating bowing out of tasks that were beyond their physical and emotional limits. Interestingly, both women and men tended to naturalize this gendered difference in confidence levels, often reasoning that edgework, a traditionally male domain, is connected to hormones (recall that several members mentioned the importance of testosterone) and physical strength. Thus, women said they felt out of place and worried about their ability, while men seemed to feel more comfortable at the prospect of risk. Women's understanding of themselves as "emotional deviants" (Thoits, 1990), then, sheds light on one way that ideas about gender may influence the edgework process in the preparation stage.

In the second stage, performing edgework, both male and female rescuers tended to attribute men's potential loss of control to an overdeveloped sense of urgency and women's to fear. When discussing how they controlled these emotions (and others, such as disgust) during missions, women and men also used different descriptors: Men tended to talk about their ability to suppress emotions as though it was a natural or essential part of who they were. They did not need to think about it; it just happened during edgework. These data correspond closely to Lyng's edgework model in that Peak's men saw themselves as having this innate ability to perform edgework, much as Lyng's subjects (most of whom were male) did. Yet Peak's women talked about suppressing their emotions in a much more self-reflexive way. They gave detailed accounts of how they monitored their emotions during missions, and of the ways they consciously suppressed their fear and disgust. Women's descriptions, then, were not consistent with the idea that they had some "innate" ability to perform edgework, as men's were. Rather, women tended to think that edgework did not come naturally to them, so they compensated by carefully attending to and controlling their feelings during missions.

However, if edgework is characterized by the suspension of self-reflexivity—filtering out the social part of the self characterized by Mead's concept of the "me"—then interpreting women's conscious attempts at emotion management, a highly self-reflexive phenomenon, during edgework is problematic. Emotion management cannot occur during edgework; therefore, women's accounts of their experiences do not accord with Lyng's theoretical model. Yet, their actual experiences might. Theoretically it is impossible for anyone to understand and reflect on edgework while doing it (because of the suspension of self-reflexivity), thus it stands to reason that any interpretation of the experience is necessarily retrospective. Thus, what these data demonstrate is two gendered ways of making sense of the edgework experience in hindsight; they represent the meanings male and female rescuers ascribe to their experiences after-the-fact. Peak's men described their edgework experiences as emotionless. Peak's women described it as a highly emotional and self-reflexive experience.

One explanation for these two divergent understandings of edgework may be found in the links between emotions, gender, and the self. According to Lyng's theory, the suspension of self-reflexivity during edgework causes edge-workers to experience "self-actualization," or a sense of their "true selves," which they are able to feel once they have regained their self-reflexivity after the (successful) edgework event. It seemed that Peak's men, in feeling self-actualized after the successful missions, looked back on their experiences and interpreted them as emotionless. Women, however, retrospectively interpreted their self-actualizing experiences through the lens of emotion: what emotions they were feeling and what they did (or must have done) to control them. These ideas about emotions correspond with gender norms and identity. Masculinity norms dictate that men should be emotionally tough and deny their emotions; thus traditional male gender identity is closely tied to emotional stoicism (Kimmel, 1996; Messner, 1992). Even though the emotional intensity of the edgework experience—the feelings of omnipotence and power—is one of the main reasons people pursue it, the male rescuers still denied that their emotions were part of their edgework experience. They interpreted the rescue, and thus, themselves, as emotionless quite possibly because of the strength of the masculine norm of emotional stoicism. Feminine gender norms, on the other hand, encourage women to be highly in touch with their emotions. Thus for many women, the self is found *in* emotions and feelings; traditional feminine gender identity is culturally unintelligible without them (Kanter, 1977; Hochschild, 1983; Pierce, 1995). Therefore, even though emotion management is not possible during edgework, female rescuers, in an effort to understand themselves, still interpreted their experience as one in which they were highly in touch with and were constantly monitoring their emotions. It is thus possible to conclude that women's and men's gendered understandings of emotions influenced how they understood their "authentic" selves, and hence, their edgework experiences. By illuminating the role of emotions in the social construction of the self, these data begin to map out the gendered ways of understanding the edgework experience.

Notes

1. Because Peak's membership fluctuated greatly during my six years, I am only able to estimate the number of members who possessed any particular trait at an unspecified time.

2. This strategy, known more broadly to social psychologists as the "self-serving bias," is one of the most common ways that people protect their self-esteem.

References

Adler, P. A., and Adler, P. *Membership Roles in Field Research*. Newbury Park, CA: Sage, 1987.

Blumer, H. *Symbolic Interactionism*. Englewood Cliffs, NJ: Prentice-Hall, 1969.

Clark, C. "Emotions and Micropolitics in Everyday Life: Some Patterns and Paradoxes of 'Place'" in *Research Agendas in the Sociology of Emotions*, edited by T. D. Kemper. Albany, NY: SUNY Press, 1990, 305–333.

DeCoster, V. A. "Physician Treatment of Patient Emotions: An Application of the Sociology of Emotion" in *Social Perspectives on Emotion*, Vol. 4, edited by R. J. Erickson and B. Cuthbertson-Johnson. Greenwich, CT: JAI Press, 1997, 151–177.

Fothergill, A. "Gender, Risk, and Disaster." *International Journal of Mass Emergencies and Disasters* 14 (1996): 33–56.

Geertz, C. *The Interpretation of Cultures*. New York: Basic Books, 1973.

Gibbs, M., Lachenmeyer, J. R., Broska, A., and Deucher, R. "Effects of the AVIANCA Aircrash on Disaster Workers." *International Journal of Mass Emergencies and Disasters* 14 (1996): 23–32.

Glaser, B., and Strauss, A. *The Discovery of Grounded Theory*. Chicago: Aldine, 1967.

Gove, W. R., Geerken, M., and Hughes, M. "Drug Use and Mental Health Among a Representative National Sample of Young Adults." *Social Forces* 58 (1979): 572–590.

Harrell, W. A. "Masculinity and Farming-Related Accidents." *Sex Roles* 15 (1986): 467–478.

Hochschild, A. R. *The Managed Heart*. Berkeley: University of California Press, 1983.

_____. "Ideology and Emotion Management: A Perspective and Path for Future Research" in *Research Agendas in the Sociology of Emotions*, edited by T. D. Kemper. Albany, NY: SUNY Press, 1990, 117–142.

Holyfield, L. "Generating Excitement: Experienced Emotion in Commercial Leisure" in *Social Perspectives on Emotion*, Vol. 4, edited by R. J. Erickson and B. Cuthbertson-Johnson. Greenwich, CT: JAI Press, 1997, 257–281.

_____. "Manufacturing Adventure: The Buying and Selling of Emotions." *Journal of Contemporary Ethnography* 28 (1999): 3–32.

Holyfield, L., and Fine, G. A. "Adventure as Character Work: The Collective Taming of Fear." *Symbolic Interaction* 20 (1997): 343–363.

Jones, L. C. "Both Friend and Stranger: How Crisis Volunteers Build and Manage Unpersonal Relationships with Clients" in *Social Perspectives on Emotion*, Vol. 4, edited by R. J. Erickson and B. Cuthbertson-Johnson. Greenwich, CT: JAI Press, 1997, 125–148.

Jorgensen, D. L. *Participant Observation*. Newbury Park, CA: Sage, 1989.

Kanter, R. M. *Men and Women of the Corporation*. New York: Basic Books, 1977.

Kimmel, M. *Manhood in America: A Cultural History*. New York: The Free Press, 1996.

King, G., Delaronde, S. R., Dinoi, R., and Forsberg, A. "Substance Use, Coping, and Safer Sex Practices Among Adolescents with Hemophilia and Human Immunodeficiency Virus." *Journal of Adolescent Health* 18 (1996): 435–441.

Kitsuse, J. "Societal Reactions to Deviant Behavior: Problems of Theory and Method." *Social Problems* 9 (1962): 247–256.

Konradi, A. "'I Don "t Have To Be Afraid of You': Rape Survivors' Emotion Management in Court." *Symbolic Interaction* 22 (1999): 45–77.

Lyng, S. "Edgework: A Social Psychological Analysis of Voluntary Risk Taking." *American Journal of Sociology* 95 (1990): 851–886.

Mannon, J. M. *Emergency Encounters: A Study of an Urban Ambulance Service*. Sudbury, MA: Jones and Bartlett, 1992.

Martin, S. E. *Breaking and Entering*. Berkeley: University of California Press, 1980.

Mead, G.H. *Mind, Self, and Society*, Chicago: University of Chicago Press, 1934.

Messner, M. A. *Power at Play.* Boston, MA: Beacon Press, 1992.

Metz, D. L. *Running Hot.* Cambridge, MA: Abt Books, 1981.

Mills, T., and Kleinman, S. "Emotions, Reflexivity, and Action: An Interactionist Analysis." *Social Forces* 66 (1988): 1009–1027.

Mirowsky, J., and Ross, C. E. "Sex Differences in Distress: Real or Artifact?" *American Sociological Review* 60 (1995): 449–468.

Mitchell, R. G., Jr. *Mountain Experience: The Psychology and Sociology of Adventure.* Chicago: University of Chicago Press, 1983.

Moran, C., Britton, N. R., and Correy, B. "Characterising Voluntary Emergency Responders: Report of a Pilot Study." *International Journal of Mass Emergencies and Disasters.* 10 (1992): 207–216.

Oliner, S. P., and Oliner, P. M. *The Altruistic Personality: Rescuers of Jews in Nazi Europe.* New York: Free Press, 1988.

Palmer, C. E. "'Trauma junkies' and Street Work: Occupational Behavior of Paramedics and Emergency Medical Technicians." *Urban Life* 12 (1983): 162–183.

Palmer, C. E., and Gonsoulin, S. M. "Paramedics, Protocols, and Procedures: 'Playing Doc' as Deviant Role Performance." *Deviant Behavior* 11 (1990): 207–219.

Parsons, T. *The Social System.* New York: Free Press, 1951.

Patterson, J. M., and McCubbin, H. I. "Gender Roles and Coping." *Journal of Marriage and the Family* 46 (1984): 95–104.

Pierce, J. L. *Gender Trials.* Berkeley, CA: University of California Press, 1995.

Robinson, M. D., and Johnson, J. T. "Is It Emotion or Is It Stress? Gender Stereotypes and the Perception of Subjective Experience." *Sex Roles* 36 (1997): 235–258.

Roehling, P. V., Koelbel, N., and Rutgers, C. "Codependence and Conduct Disorder: Feminine Versus Masculine Coping Responses to Abusive Parenting Practices." *Sex Roles* 35 (1996): 603–618.

Schachter, S., and Singer, J. E. "The Interactions of Cognitive and Physiological Determinants of Emotional State." *Psychological Review* 69 (1962): 379–399.

Sigmon, S. T., Stanton, A. L., and Snyder, C. R. "Gender Differences in Coping: A Further Test of Socialization and Role Constraint Theories." *Sex Roles* 33 (1995): 565–587.

Smith, A. C. III, and Kleinman, S. "Managing Emotions in Medical School: Students' Contacts with the Living and Dead." *Social Psychology Quarterly* 52 (1989): 56–69.

Stearns, P. N. *American Cool.* New York: New York University Press, 1994.

Sykes, G., and Matza, D. "Techniques of Neutralization: A Theory of Delinquency." *American Sociological Review* 22 (1957): 664–670.

Thoits, P. A. "Emotional Deviance: Research Agendas." In *Research Agendas in the Sociology of Emotions,* edited by T. D. Kemper. Albany, NY: SUNY Press, 1990, 180–203.

————. "Identity-Relevant Events and Psychological Symptoms: A Cautionary Tale." *Journal of Health and Social Behavior* 36 (1995): 72–82.

Turner, R. H. "The Real Self: From Institution to Impulse." *American Journal of Sociology* 81 (1976): 989–1016.

Whalen, J., and Zimmerman, D. H. "Observations on the Display and Management of Emotion in Naturally Occurring Activities: The Case of 'Hysteria' in Calls to 9-1-1." *Social Psychology Quarterly* 61 (1998): 141–159.

Yoder, J. D., and Aniakudo, P. "'Outsider Within' the Firehouse: Subordination and Difference in the Social Interactions of African American Women Firefighters." *Gender & Society* 11 (1997): 324–341.

6

Adolescents on the Edge: The Sensual Side of Delinquency

WILLIAM J. MILLER

CONTENTS

Introduction

As the United States enters the twenty-first century, crime and delinquency remain a permanent part of the public discourse. While crime rates have fallen over the last decade or so, the media maintains its continuous, selective, and often sensational coverage of crime. The government, the police, and politicians continue their pleas to get tougher on crime. And for the most part, academics continue to rely on old, one-dimensional explanations of crime that are too narrowly focused on the structural and rational-choice dimensions of criminal behavior. But in recent years, sociology has paid an increasing amount of attention to the social-psychological side of criminal risk taking.

Jack Katz (1988) and Stephen Lyng (1990) have been particularly influential in this area. While Lyng originally developed his theory of edgework to analyze voluntary risk taking (i.e., skydiving, rock climbing, bungee jumping, etc.), there have been several attempts to analyze various kinds of crime/deviance based on ideas related to risk taking and thrill seeking.

Lyng's work is particularly appealing because he identifies a clear connection between macro and micro elements of risk taking. On the macro level, Lyng argues that modern post-industrial society forces people to live under a variety of institutional constraints. Modern life is increasingly mechanical, bureaucratic, rigid, impersonal, and alienating. Many people feel that they have lost the ability to control their lives.

It is this perceived loss of control that leads to the micro side of Lyng's theory. "Edgework" refers to any activity whereby people explore the boundary between order and disorder (e.g., life and death, consciousness and unconsciousness, sanity and insanity, etc.). Edgeworkers engage in the activities they do because of the freedom, sense of control, and physical/emotional sensations that they derive from the experience. Edgework presents people with an opportunity for "creative, skillful, self-determining action" (Lyng, 1990, p. 877).

While edgework is a versatile concept that has been used to analyze a variety of behaviors (e.g., skydiving, graffiti writing, and motorcycle riding), it seems particularly well suited for analyzing juvenile delinquency. Adolescents, perhaps more than any other single group, occupy a marginal social position. Adults attempt to order and control nearly every aspect of their lives at home, at school, and at work. Juveniles rarely, if ever, have the chance for genuinely free, creative, exciting, self-directed behavior. For many adolescents, delinquency may be a form of edgework that provides this opportunity.

Unfortunately, despite its theoretical appeal, sociologists and criminologists have been relatively slow to develop and refine theories of crime/delinquency based on the edgework model. In fact, other than Lyng (1993), there have been no attempts to analyze crime from an edgework perspective. Even when edgework has been used to study various forms of social behavior, mostly qualitative research designs have been used (Ferrell, 1993; Grove, 1994).

This chapter begins with a review of literature related to the sensual attractions of crime and delinquency, with the goal of outlining an edgework model of delinquency. Next, the results of a self-report delinquency survey designed to analyze the relationship between anomia, edgework sensations, and juvenile delinquency are discussed. This is followed by a more detailed consideration of the structural factors that shape the experience of contemporary adolescents. Finally, the chapter concludes by discussing possible directions for future research.

The Sensual and Emotional Attractions of Crime

In his book *The Seductions of Crime: Moral and Sensual Attractions in Doing Evil* (1988), Jack Katz argues that structural explanations of crime are incomplete. His phenomenological analysis helps to demonstrate that background factors (e.g., age, race, sex, socioeconomics, etc.) and rational-choice considerations alone do not explain what motivates people to commit crime (1988, pp. 3–4).

From Katz's perspective, robust explanations of crime must pay attention to the criminal experience itself. Crime is viewed as an emotional process that offers unique rewards and sensations. Accordingly, he focuses his attention on the seductive and transformative aspects of crime that can make it so compelling.

At the same time, Katz does not ignore social structure. Instead, he suggests that crime takes place within specific structural contexts. In assessing Katz, O'Malley and Mugford write that "he is also making the claim that much crime is to be understood as an array of reactions against mundane, secular rationality and against the (especially modern) forms of social settings in which they are inextricably implicated" (1994, p. 190). The thrill of carrying out a criminal act can provide social actors with the opportunity to escape their mundane existence. In this sense, the character of modern social life makes excitement important to the self.[1]

Katz applies his phenomenological analysis to a wide range of criminal behaviors. His discussion of the righteous slaughter claims that "the impassioned assailant takes humiliation and turns it into rage... The badass, with searing purposiveness, tries to scare humiliation off; ... young vandals and shoplifters innovate games with risks of humiliation, running along the edge of shame for its exciting reverberations" (Katz, 1988, pp. 312–313). Similarly, when considering "sneaky thrills" like shoplifting, he indicates that, "quite apart from what is taken, they may regard 'getting away with it' as a thrilling demonstration of personal competence, especially if it is accomplished under the eyes of adults" (Katz, 1988, p. 9). The fear of being caught and the electricity of the "action" produce the emotional power of this thrill.[2]

From this perspective, crime is seen as a powerful, seductive, emotional experience that allows social actors to transcend their otherwise routine, mundane lives. When commenting on Katz's notion of transcendence, O'Malley and Mugford write:

> Transcendence appears to involve crossing (or at the very least "playing with") a threshold or limit between being in and out of rational control in order to experience the self in the grip of emotional and moral forces. These emotional states involve experiences unavailable to the rational consciousness in the mundane world and that therefore register as extraordinary their emotional intensity providing, literally, an excitement of experience similar in kind with those cathartic episodes often associated with religious, sexual, or deviant experiences. (1994, p. 191)

Lyng (1990) also identifies the importance of sensual experience and transcendence in his explanation of voluntary risk taking (e.g., hang gliding, skydiving, etc.). Why do people intentionally put their lives at risk? Lyng answers this question by examining the nature of institutional life and work in postindustrial society. Modern life has enormous potential for creating alienation. People, particularly workers, have less control over their lives because of increasingly complex bureaucracies, technology, etc. And it is not just the factory workers who are estranged from their work. According to Lyng:

> The general tendency toward a "deskilling" of work in economies dominated by mass-production industries and bureaucratic decision making and authority structures means that workers at many different levels, ranging from service workers to certain types of professionals, may be forced to work under alienating conditions (Lyng, 1990, p. 876).

Thus, it is alienation and the lack of control over one's daily work (life) that leads people to participate in edgework activities.

Edgeworkers are not gamblers. They believe in their ability to confront and overcome danger. They want an opportunity to exercise their skill in overcoming a serious challenge. Edgework activities are accompanied by at least four distinct sensations: (1) self-determination, (2) fear of failure, (3) excitement, and (4) hyperreality (i.e., edgework experiences feel more real than daily life experiences (Lyng, 1990, pp. 860–861). Lyng maintains that the edgework concept "allows us to view high-risk behavior as involving, most fundamentally, the problem of negotiating the boundary between chaos and order" (1990, p. 855).

While Lyng's original study of edgework focused on skydiving, his later work recognized the promise of the edgework model to explain illicit forms of behavior, including various forms of crime (Lyng, 1993). He writes, "the prominent place of chaotic, uncertain circumstances and the actors' spontaneous responses to such conditions in criminal action is a feature this activity has in common with all other behavior classified as edgework (1993, p. 117). In short, the edgework perspective moves beyond Katz's more narrow focus on criminal behavior.

Both Katz and Lyng make serious attempts to link an experiential understanding of crime with the structural conditions of modern social life. O'Malley and Mugford identify the importance of these approaches when they suggest that

> As a consequence of the inequality of resources in society, some of the ways of transcending mundane life are more open to some groups of people than to others. Skydiving, for example, may offer a transcendent experience, but it is unlikely to be available to many young black members of the urban underclass. Crack on the other hand, may provide a similarly transcending experience, but unlike skydiving is available to all, rich and poor (1994, p. 209).

Lyng and Katz both suggest that criminal activity is a process of transcendence that can provide an escape from the routine grind of everyday social life. O'Malley and Mugford attempt to amplify this observation by suggesting that this process of transcendence is peculiarly modern. They argue that "the disenchantment of the modern world generates the routinized, despiritualized world of calculative rationality, and an attendant order of time, space, and society to which Romanticism, edgework, and crime (of the kind discussed by Katz) are transcendent responses" (1994, p. 198).

The edgework model allows us to move beyond Katz's insight that the cause of some crime can be located in the criminal experience itself, "to a level of analysis which allows us to understand how these causal factors are related to the broader structures of modern American society." (Lyng 1993, p. 128) It is precisely this emphasis that makes the edgework model particularly useful for explaining juvenile delinquency.

The Sensual Side of Juvenile Delinquency

Researchers have long observed that young people often engage in delinquency just for fun or as a way to relieve boredom (Cohen, 1955; Briar and Piliavin 1965; Ferdinand 1996.) Recently, more and more attention is being given to "sensation seeking" as a motivation for criminal conduct. Sensation seeking refers to "an individual's need for varied, novel and complex sensations and experiences and the willingness to take physical and social risks for the sake of the experience" (Zuckerman, 1979, p. 10). Sensation seeking has also played an important role in other crimes including shoplifting, burglary, assault, robbery, and rape. Gove study found that many inmates experienced "a high" when they were committing a crime (1994, pp. 374–375). They felt "intensely alive and able to do anything" (1994, p. 388). These powerful sensations motivate people to continue their edgework participation in an effort to replicate these feelings (Lyng, 1993). Similarly, Ferrell (1993) reports that many graffiti artists experience a "rush" when they work. It is this rush that separates their painting experience from that of conventional artists.

The sensations described by this body of research are consistent with those outlined by Lyng. While different kinds of edgework activities may produce different sensations, common edgework sensations include nervousness, fear, excitement, exhilaration, self-determination, and a feeling of omnipotence (Lyng, 1990, p. 860). Edgework can also alter a person's perception or consciousness. "Participants in many different types of edgework report that, at the height of the experience (as they approach the edge), their perceptual field becomes highly focused: background factors recede from view, and their perception narrows to only those factors that immediately determine success or failure in negotiating the edge" (Lyng, 1990, p. 862).

In addition to describing the sensual aspects of edgework, Lyng suggests that "the illusion of control may also help to explain some of the characteristics that distinguish people who value edgework from those who have an aversion to it" and further argues that adolescents are particularly vulnerable to edgework because they "have a sense of their own immortality" (Lyng, 1990, p. 872). This makes them particularly susceptible to the illusion of control that accompanies edgework.

An Edgework Model of Delinquency

Institutional constraint, alienation, and sensation seeking are all important elements of edgework. The edgework concept is unique because it relies on both social structure and emotional processes to explain human behavior. Thus, it should be possible to build on Lyng's work to demonstrate the utility of edgework in explaining juvenile delinquency. Such an approach would direct particular attention to the relatively powerless, marginal social status occupied by juveniles. It can be suggested that this status leaves adolescents particularly vulnerable to various forms of institutional constraint (at home, in school, at work) that can create alienation.

Juveniles find themselves living in a world where all the rules are created and enforced by adults. Often, adolescents aren't invested in the conventional social order because they had no role in creating that order. From an edgework-oriented perspective, delinquency is a behavior that pushes the limits of the normative order established by adults.

Delinquency, as a form of edgework, may represent an attempt to escape an otherwise oppressive, constraining, and alienating social world. Delinquent activities can provide juveniles with a sense of excitement and personal autonomy that allows them to momentarily transcend a routine, alienated existence that is controlled by adults. It is the intense feelings of fear and excitement and the sense of control that make the edgework experience, in this case delinquency, particularly seductive.

Unfortunately, while the idea of criminal edgework has considerable theoretical appeal, very little research has been done in this area to date. The few studies that have been done (Katz, 1988; Ferrell, 1993; Gove, 1994) are qualitative in nature. While these studies have been particularly useful for describing the social-psychological dimensions of criminal edgework, quantitative research designs may produce more generalizable findings. The following section reports the results of a self-report delinquency survey designed to analyze the relationship between alienation, edgework sensations, and delinquency.

Method

While a random, representative sample of high school students would be most desirable for this kind of research, access to high school populations can be difficult. Human subjects review boards require researchers to obtain parental permission for participating students under age eighteen (DeKesseredy and Schwartz, 1998).

To deal with this problem, I elected to use a convenience sample of college students at a midwestern public university. The sample included 691 individuals, primarily freshman and sophomores, drawn from introductory sociology classes. These classes were used because they fulfilled a general-education requirement at the university. Accordingly, the sample included students with varied backgrounds and varied academic interests. Thirty-two percent of the sample was male; sixty-eight percent was female.

Students were asked to complete a sixty-two item self-administered survey that took approximately twenty minutes to complete. Participation was completely voluntary. Respondents were told, both verbally and in writing, that they could refuse to participate or choose to discontinue their participation at any time. All respondents signed consent forms. Responses were anonymous and confidential.

Measures[3]

Predictor Variables. *Alienation and Anomia:* The present research does not rely on classical definitions of alienation. Both Emile Durkheim and Karl Marx criticized the social structure, and Horton points out that

> Alienation for Marx and anomie for Durkheim were metaphors for a radical attack on the dominant institutions and values of industrial society. They attacked similar behavior, but from opposing perspectives... Marx was interested in problems of power and change, Durkheim in problems of the maintenance of order. (1964, p. 283)

While both analyses of social structure are instructive, it is Marx's macro analysis of social structure combined with George Herbert Mead's analysis of the self that creates the synthetic theoretical framework necessary for explaining edgework behavior. Lyng writes:

> ... both Marx and Mead assign priority to the role of human action in the ontogeny of self and society but differ on what forms of action deserve analytical attention, with Marx emphasizing survival behavior

structured by macro-level economic forces and Mead focusing on social interaction at the micro level (1990, p. 866).

Accordingly, any research on edgework must respect both macro and micro levels of analysis.

The edgework model of criminal behavior detailed in this chapter pays particular attention to the ways that various social institutions (e.g., family, school, and work) function to control and regulate adolescent behavior. There is also an implied connection made between this institutional constraint and the formation of alienation experienced by many adolescents.

It is important to note that Marx developed a social theory designed to explain the relationship between institutional arrangements and human behavior. And while it is essential to understand the role of institutional structures in creating alienation, it is equally important to understand the psychological side of this process (i.e., how people experience these institutions in their daily lives, their perceptions of them, their attitudes toward them, etc.).

Accordingly, this research necessarily relies on a social-psychological measure of alienation. Srole's (1956) "anomia" is a social-psychological construct used to measure social malintegration. This includes feelings of loneliness, hopelessness, and (to a lesser extent) powerlessness. (Cronbach's alpha = .654)

"Edgework Sensations" refers to the feelings people may experience during the actual commission of a criminal act, e.g., fear, excitement, freedom, personal accomplishment, etc. (Cronbach's alpha = .854)

Outcome Variables. The "Juvenile Delinquency" measure was adapted from Mazerolle's (1998) delinquency scale. Respondents reported their frequency of involvement in 24 different delinquent behaviors. The items include a wide range of behaviors such as status offenses, substance use, property crimes, and some violent crimes. A composite measure of all 24 items was used to measure general delinquency — see the Appendix. (Cronbach's alpha = .819).

Findings

The following analysis relies on three tables that represent various relationships between anomia (an indication of social malintegration), edgework sensations, and delinquency.[4] Table 6.1 illustrates the bivariate relationship between anomia and self-reported juvenile delinquency. Students experiencing high levels of anomia also report the highest levels of delinquent behavior.

A gamma value of .144 identifies a positive and statistically significant ($p.<.01$) relationship between anomia and delinquency. Accordingly, the correlation between anomia and delinquency is an important one because it demonstrates the potential importance of institutional constraint on the formation of edgework activities.[5] However, the edgework model posits that it is not alienation per se that causes crime. Rather, institutional constraints and alienation create conditions that give rise to various forms of edgework.

TABLE 6.1 Anomia by Delinquency (N = 638)

		Juvenile Delinquency			
		Low	**Moderate**	**High**	**Total Percent**
	Low	36.0	41.6	22.5	100.0
		(64)	(74)	(40)	(178)
Anomia	Moderate	29.3	43.0	27.8	100.0
		(77)	(113)	(73)	(263)
	High	28.4	35.0	36.5	100.0
		(58)	(69)	(72)	(197)

Table 6.2 illustrates the bivariate association between alienation and edge-work sensations.

The higher the person's level of alienation, the more important edgework sensations were as a motivation for their delinquent activity. Edgework sensations were least important to those students that reported the lowest levels of alienation. A gamma value of .208 identifies a positive and statistically significant (p.<.01) association between anomia and edgework sensations.

The relationships between anomia and delinquency, and anomia and edgework, are important, but they are only two pieces of the puzzle. Table 6.3 illustrates the bivariate relationship between edgework sensations and delinquency.

The relationship between edgework sensations and delinquency is particularly striking. Fifty-two percent of those who cited edgework sensations as very important reasons for their criminal conduct also had the highest levels of self-reported delinquency. A gamma value of .567 indicates a positive and statistically significant (p.<.01) association between edgework sensations and delinquency. This is the strongest of the three relationships tested.

A graphic illustration of the relationships among anomia, edgework sensations, and delinquency is shown in Figure 6.1. These relationships are important because they suggest significant relationships among key variables that would be found in any edgework theory of crime.

While the initial results are promising, it is important to remember that this study is exploratory. It relies on a small, nonrandom sample of college

TABLE 6.2 Anomia by Edgework Sensations (N = 588)

		Edgework Sensations			
		Unimportant	**Moderately Important**	**Very Important**	**Total Percent**
	Low	41.6	34.8	23.6	100.0
		(67)	(56)	(38)	(161)
Anomia	Moderate	37.6	33.6	28.8	100.0
		(94)	(84)	(742)	(250)
	High	24.9	35.6	39.5	100.0
		(44)	(63)	(70)	(177)

TABLE 6.3 Edgework Sensations by Delinquency (N = 582)

| | | \multicolumn{3}{c}{Juvenile Delinquency} | |
		Low	Moderate	High	Total Percent
	Unimportant	49.0	40.8	10.2	100.0
		(101)	(84)	(21)	(206)
Edgework Sensations	Moderately Important	17.2	48.5	34.3	100.0
		(34)	(96)	(68)	(198)
	Highly Important	10.7	37.6	51.7	100.0
		(19)	(67)	(92)	(178)

students and the analysis is limited in both its scope and its complexity. The most serious limitation of the study as an assessment of the edgework model of juvenile delinquency is the absence of structural variables in the research design. As noted above, the concept of anomia is a social-psychological construct. While it may refer to alienating conditions at the macrostructural level, it functions as a measure of individual perceptions rather than of environmental conditions. Still, these preliminary results are important because they begin to provide the empirical foundations necessary for building and refining theories of crime and delinquency that rely on the edgework concept.

The remainder of this chapter is dedicated to reviewing additional research relating to the specific macro-level structural forces that impinge on juveniles and may help to explain the appeal of edgework sensations to certain members of this population.

Anomia and the Social Position of Adolescents

The positive associations of anomia with delinquency and edgework sensations are highly suggestive, but a key implication of the edgework model is that juvenile delinquency cannot be adequately explained without examining the social status of adolescents. Status is crucially important because it frames human interactions. Regoli and Hewitt (1994) argue that status based on age has important consequences because it relegates the largest number of people in our society to a subordinate position.[6]

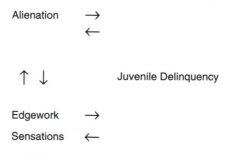

Fig. 6.1 Edgework model of delinquency

Adolescents occupy one of society's lowest-status positions. There are approximately 70 million children in America, and none of them have the right to vote. As a result of their powerless social status many children are forced to endure serious oppression (e.g., physical punishment, humiliation, unequal opportunity, physical/sexual abuse, and neglect). Furthermore, children rarely have the opportunity for authentic, self-directed behavior. For the most part, their lives are carefully controlled and ordered by adults and adult institutions.

Regoli and Hewitt examine the social position of children as well as their treatment by adults. Their theory of differential oppression is organized around the following four principles (1994, pp. 209–211):

1. Adults emphasize order in the home and at school.
2. Adults' perceptions of children establish them as inferior, subordinate, and troublemakers.
3. The imposition of adult conceptions of order on children often becomes extreme to the point of oppression.
4. Oppression leads to adaptive reactions by children, one of which includes delinquent behavior.

Delinquency is, at least in part, a symptom of a much larger problem that relates to the status children hold in society. The institutional constraints faced by young people are magnified by the unique social status they occupy.

Adolescence marks a confusing and uncertain time in a child's life. Adolescents believe that they are mentally and physically prepared for marriage and work, but they are denied both. Teenagers are told to act like adults, and yet they don't receive the respect, status, or freedom enjoyed by adults. Adolescents are left to create an identity distinct from both childhood and adulthood. This identity frequently manifests itself in teenage clothing, hairstyles, music, language, etc. (McAlexander and Schouten, 1989). For some, this identity might even be found in criminal activity.

Park (1928) and Stonequist (1937) developed the phrase "marginal man" to describe a situation encountered by first generation children of immigrants. These children were exposed to two competing cultures, one at home and one at school. At home, they were exposed to the language, values, and traditions of their parents' homeland, while at school, they were exposed to the language, values, and traditions of America. The word "marginal" is used to describe a person who is not integrated into either of two competing cultures.

It can be argued that American teenagers are marginal to the extent that they are neither children nor adults. Perhaps their position is best described by the concept of "liminality." According to Turner, liminality

... describes a condition where people slip through the network of commonly accepted and understood classifications that normally locate states and positions of status in cultural states… Liminal entities are neither here nor there; they are betwixt and between cv ccthe positions assigned and arrayed by law, custom, convention and ceremony (Turner, 1969, p. 95).

American society has no culturally accepted way of making the transition from adolescence to adulthood. Davison and Davison (1979) have described adolescence in America as a "big waiting room."

Marginal statuses are difficult to accept; see Polk (1984) for a discussion of the school's role in creating marginal youth. Cohen (1955) expanded on Merton's theory of anomie by suggesting that a large amount of delinquency behavior results from "status frustration." Cohen argued that lower class boys yearned for the same status as their middle class counterparts, but unfortunately structural barriers denied lower class boys an equal opportunity to succeed through conventional means. As a result, many of them attempted to achieve monetary success and status through delinquent activities.

Cohen's use of the term "status frustration" is useful, but perhaps too narrowly defined. His analysis is limited to lower-class boys. But to some extent, all adolescents, by nature of institutional constraints and their marginal status, experience some degree of status frustration. In other words, young people actively seek the power, privilege, and autonomy that they associate with adulthood. Since such things aren't available to them through conventional channels, delinquency can be an effective substitute.

While important, adolescents' social status is only part of the equation. Equally important is how this status influences their treatment within various social institutions that are central to their lives.

Social Structure, Social Status, Institutional Constraint, and Alienation

As noted above, Lyng's (1990) discussion of social structure focuses primarily on the dehumanizing, alienating nature of work in the postindustrial capitalist era. Any attempt to apply the edgework model to juvenile delinquency must begin with a specific examination of the social structure that constrains juveniles. While work is a significant source of constraint for adults, the family and school are important sources of constraint for children. After all, these two institutions play a dominant role in the socialization of children.

During early childhood, the family is primarily responsible for the control, discipline, and development of children. It is the family's role in creating and maintaining order that is of particular interest here. The relationship between parenting and delinquency has received considerable attention in the literature.[7] It seems clear that all child-rearing styles are oppressive to the extent that they use varying degrees of coercive power to create and maintain order. Ultimately, no matter which parenting style is adopted, children are subject to the authority/behavior of adults. Worse yet, children lack the power to change their social position, even when that change is in their best interest.

While the family is always an important agent of socialization as children age, the school plays an increasingly important role in the socialization of children. Schools are also a significant source of social constraint. Children's experiences with discipline and social order at home vary widely. But in most mainstream, American schools, children are confronted with a more authoritarian social order. At school, children are confronted with a social order that they have had little say in creating. Regoli and Hewitt (1994) maintain that the school is a serious source of oppression for children.[8]

Harry Gracey (1977) argues that from the very first day of school, children are arbitrarily judged by authoritarian adults. He further maintains that the primary purpose of kindergarten is not academic preparation. Instead, it is designed to teach children how to fit in to a bureaucratic school system. Children must be taught to do what they are told without questioning why. In other words, they must be taught the importance of following rules and submitting to authority.

Students are forced to obey a set of rules created by a group of adults who have been given "official" authority. Students may be subjected to censorship (e.g., language, newspaper content, etc.), random locker searches, dress guidelines, and suspensions/expulsions based on the subjective opinion of a given principal. (See Regoli and Hewitt, 1994, pp. 249–251 for a detailed discussion.) The school has an enormous amount of power that it uses to create standards of achievement, worth, and normality.

In addition to the institutional restraints experienced at home and in school, large numbers of adolescents also work. "Work is perhaps the most common out-of-school activity among American teenagers" (Schneider and Schmidt, 1996, p. 17). The vast majority of these teenagers work at jobs that pay minimum wage, require very little skill, and are subject to very close supervision. In fact, two-thirds of American fast-food workers are age twenty or below (Schlosser, 2002). Krisberg and Austin argue that "young people form a subservient class, alienated, powerless, and prone to economic manipulation" (1978, p. 219).

In his book *Fast Food Nation*, Schlosser (2002) paints a very disturbing picture of work behind the counters of American fast-food restaurants. The majority of these jobs have been simplified to the point that anyone can perform them. This means that workers are both cheap and easily replaceable.

According to Schlosser, managers exercise a tremendous amount of power over their employees. Obedience is the most valued trait in fast-food workers (Reiter, 1991). In addition to the close supervision and constant pressure to comply with the management's wishes, customers often feel entitled to be disrespectful fast food employees. It should come as no surprise that very few kids enjoy working behind the counter. Most high school students interviewed by Schlosser reported that the work was boring and monotonous.

Whether at home, in school, or at work, there is little doubt that adults can use their individual/institutional power and authority to create a social order that views children as subordinates who are supposed to do what they are told.

This along with their relatively marginal social status may leave adolescents particularly vulnerable to alienation.

According to Calabrese (1987), adolescence is a growth period conducive to alienation. Too often, adolescents do not develop the sense that they are valued, respected, autonomous, free, and contributing members of society. As a result, many young people have little personal investment in society or its rules. There is a rich research tradition that links alienation with various forms of delinquent behavior (Wynne, 1976; Wenz, 1979; Schaffer and Deblassie, 1984; Calabrese and Cochran, 1990; Calabrese and Adams, 1990; Krueger et al., 1994; Edwards, 1996).[9] This implies that any serious discussion of juvenile delinquency must include a discussion of adolescent alienation.

Concluding Comments

This chapter has explored the usefulness of the edgework model for understanding the sensual attractions of delinquency for adolescent members of modern society. After examining the results of a self-report delinquency survey that demonstrated significant relationships between anomia, edgework sensations, and juvenile delinquency, attention was devoted to the unique structural constraints that make adolescents particularly vulnerable to illicit edgework (i.e., delinquency). These results are exciting because they speak to the promise of edgework as an explanation for various kinds of juvenile delinquency.

This research identifies a number of interesting relationships that call for further exploration. An edgework model of delinquency suggests that constraining social institutions may give rise to alienation. Delinquency can provide an authentic, exciting way for some adolescents to escape their otherwise routine and alienating lives (that are closely controlled by adults). It is the thrilling, sensual nature of delinquency that makes it difficult for some adolescents to resist. While this research identified significant correlations between alienation, delinquency and edgework sensations, future research must clearly establish the temporal ordering of these variables.

Also, this study relied on anomia for a general measure of alienation (i.e., social malintegration). But as Gold (1969) points out, there are several different kinds of alienation (e.g., powerlessness, meaninglessness, social isolation, self-estrangement, etc.). Future research should try to specify the particular kinds of alienation that lead to illicit edgework activities. Are some kinds of alienation better predictors of edgework than others? Attempts should also be made to not only identify those parts of the social structure that foster adolescent alienation, but also to specify the institutional practices that create this alienation.

Additionally, as pointed out by Miller (1991), attempts must be made to include race, gender, and class into both theoretical and empirical examinations of edgework. There can be little question that race, gender, and class not only influence alienation, but may also influence the kinds of edgework that people pursue.

Finally, researchers need to thoroughly examine particular kinds of crime. In other words, is the edgework model of delinquency better suited for explaining certain kinds of crimes (e.g., theft, drug use, etc.), but not others (e.g., truancy, assault, etc.)? If so, why is this the case?

While edgework explanations of criminal behavior are still in their infancy, their intuitive appeal and empirical promise are undeniable. It is only through continued theoretical refinements and empirical testing that the full explanatory power of edgework will be realized.

Notes

1. For additional analysis of Katz (1988), as well as a discussion of various factors that contribute to the dilemma of the modern self (e.g., alienation, clock time, and commodification), see O'Malley and Muford (1994).

2. The usage of the term reflects Goffman's conceptualization (1967, pp. 149–270). Action is defined as behavior that is consequential for the individual and that has unpredictable, but clear-cut consequences.

3. Many self-report delinquency surveys are narrowly time-bound. These surveys ask questions such as "How many times did you steal or try to steal something worth five dollars or less during the past 90 days?" It can be reasonably assumed that answers to questions about relatively recent events improve the accuracy of the information being recalled. In other words, there should be less recall bias.

   Since this study relies on a convenience sample of college students to examine juvenile delinquency, a slightly different method was needed. To gain information about eighteen- and nineteen-year-old college students and their involvement in juvenile delinquency, the time frame for the retrospective questions needed to be much larger than the usual span. The self-report survey used in this research asked students to consider their entire high school career when answering questions. For example, a subject would have been asked to "Indicate how often you engaged in the activity described below during your high school years (grades 9–12)—Stolen or tried to steal something worth five dollars or less." The subject could then choose one of the following responses: "not at all," "once or twice," "several times," "very often" (see Appendix 1).

   Retrospective designs like this one (which are more broadly time bound) can be criticized for relying on the participants' memory of life events that may have taken place several years ago. This could increase the likelihood of recall bias.

   While this is a legitimate concern, there are several good reasons to believe that a properly designed and administered survey that asks people to recall events as far back as four or five years can produce valid results.

   First, this design is not unique. Many researchers have asked college students to retrospectively self-report their behaviors (e.g., delinquency), experiences (e.g., victimization), and attitudes (e.g., feelings toward parents) during their high school years (Mitchell, Dodder, and Norris, 1990; DeKeseredy and Schwartz, 1994; Free 1994; DeKeseredy and Schwartz, 1998; Gibbs, Giever, and Martin, 1998; Langhinrichsen-Rohling, Monson, Meyer, Caster, and Sanders, 1998).

Second, a very important difference between the method used in this study and the method used in more narrowly time bound surveys exists: Narrowly time bound surveys ask respondents to be very specific when giving an answer. Such questions typically ask "How many times have you consumed an alcoholic beverage during the last 90 days?" This design does not require such precision or accuracy on the part of the respondent.

Respondents needed only to remember whether they never did something, did it once or twice, did it several times, or did it very often. Given the lack of specificity required in the response, recall bias should not be as much of an issue.

Third, the subject matter of the self-report survey is very salient. The events in question involve, for the most part, exceptional behaviors. As such, these events are more likely to stand out in respondents' memories.

Finally, while asking college students (eighteen- and nineteen-year-olds) to remember events that took place up to four years ago may seem like a long time, it is important to remember that for them, this time period has probably been, for better or worse, the most prominent and memorable stage of their lives. Also, high school experiences can be remembered by associations with teachers, classrooms, or peers. Such associations are likely to help to make memories more reliable.

4. All tables have been percentaged by row. Due to rounding errors rows may not equal one-hundred percent.

5. It is important to note that anomia is a social-psychological construct that does not directly measure structural constraints. However, these results may allow one to infer that anomia is at least in part produced by structural constraints.

6. While all adolescents share a subordinate social position, the consequences of that position are mediated by a number of structural variables including race, ethnicity, class, and gender.

7. For additional discussion of parenting styles and their effect on adolescent development, see Baumrind (1978; 1991). Particularly strict and rigid parenting styles (e.g., authoritarian parenting styles) tend to have negative effects on children. Children of authoritarian parents tend to be less happy, moody, passively hostile, vulnerable to stress, and have low self-esteem (Belsky, 1984). Some evidence that suggests they are vulnerable to delinquency (Conger and Conger, 1994). There is also a substantial research tradition that links child maltreatment with delinquency and violence (Heck and Walsh, 2000; Kelly, Thornberry, and Smith, 1997; Thornberry, 1994; Widom, 1989).

8. See Freire (1990, p. 59) for a discussion of the oppressive teacher-student relationship in schools.

9. As pointed out by Gold (1969), alienation has at least three common meanings in the social scientific literature. Any discussion of juvenile delinquency must specify the precise meaning of alienation being used.

References

Belsky, J. *The Child in the Family.* Reading MA: Addison-Wesley, 1984.

Baumrind, D. "Parental Disciplinary Patterns and Social Competence in Children." *Youth and Society* 9 (1978): 239–276.

———. "Parenting Styles and Adolescent Development." In *The Encyclopedia of Adolescence,* edited by R. Lerner, A. Peterson, and J. Brook-Gunn. New York: Garland Publishing Company, 1991.

Briar, S. and Piliavin. "Delinquency, Situational Inducements and Commitment to Conformity." *Social Problems* 13 (1965): 35–45.

Calabrese, R. L. "Adolescence: A Growth Period Conducive to Alienation." *Adolescence* 22 (1987): 929–938.

Calabrese, R. L., and Adams, J. "Alienation: A Cause of Juvenile Delinquency." *Adolescence* 25 (1990): 435–440.

Calabrese, R. L., and Cochran, J. T. "The Relationship of Alienation to Cheating among a Sample of American Adolescents." *Journal of Research and Development in Education* 23 (1990): 65–72.

Cohen, A. K. *Delinquent Boys: The Culture of the Gang.* New York: Free Press, 1955.

Conger, K. J., and Conger, R.D. "Differential Parenting and Change in Sibling Differences in Delinquency." *Journal of Family Psychology* 8 (1994): 287–302.

Davison, P., and Davison, J. "Coming of Age in America." In *Readings in Sociology,* edited by P. Whitten. New York: Harper and Row, 1979: 52–55.

DeKeseredy, W. S., and Schwartz, M. D. "Locating a History of Some Canadian Woman Abuse in Elementary and High School Dating Relationships." *Humanity and Society* 18 (1994): 49–63.

———. *Woman Abuse on Campus: Results From The Canadian National Survey.* Thousand Oaks, CA: Sage, 1998.

Edwards, W. J. "A Measurement of Delinquency Differences between a Delinquent and Nondelinquent Sample: What Are the Implications?" *Adolescence* 31 (1996): 973–990.

Ferdinand, T. N. *Typologies of Delinquency: A Critical Analysis.* New York: Random House, 1966.

Ferrell, J. *Crimes of Style: Urban Graffiti and the Politics of Criminality.* New York: Garland, 1993.

Free, M. D., Jr. "Religiosity, Religious Conservatism, Bonds to School, and Juvenile Delinquency among Three Categories of Drug Users." *Deviant Behavior: An Interdisciplinary Journal* 15 (1994): 151–170.

Freire, P. *Pedagogy of the Oppressed.* New York: Continuum, 1990.

Gibbs, J. J., Giever, D., and Martin, J. S. "Parental Management and Self-Control: An Empirical Test of Gottfredson and Hirschi's General Theory." *Journal of Research In Crime and Delinquency* 35 (1998): 40–70.

Goffman, E. *Interaction Ritual: Essays on Face-to-Face Behavior.* New York: Anchor Books, 1967.

Gold, M. "Juvenile Delinquency as a Symptom of Alienation." *Journal of Social Issues* 15 (1969): 121–135.

Gracey, H. L. "Learning the Student Role: Kindergarten as Academic Boot Camp" In *Readings in Introductory Sociology,* 3rd ed., edited by D. H. Wrong and H. L. Gracey. New York: Macmillan, 1977: 215–226.

Gove, W. R. "Why We Do What We Do: A Biopsychosocial Theory of Human Motivation." *Social Forces* 73 (1994): 374–388.

Heck, C. and Walsh, A. "The Effects of Maltreatment and Family Structure on Minor and Serious Delinquency." *The International Journal of Offender Therapy and Comparative Criminology* 44 (2000): 178–193.

Horton, J. "The Dehumanization of Anomie and Alienation: A Problem in the Ideology of Sociology." *British Journal of Sociology* 15 (1964): 283–300.

Katz, J. *Seductions of Crime.* New York: Basic Books, 1988.

Kelly, B., Thornberry, T., and Smith, S. *In the Wake of Childhood Maltreatment.* U.S. Department of Justice, Office of Juvenile Justice and Delinquency Prevention, Juvenile Justice Bulletin (Youth Development Series). Washington, D.C.: August 1997.

Krisberg, B., and Austin, J. *Children of Ishmael: Critical Perspectives on Juvenile Justice.* Palo Alto, CA: Mayfield Publishing, 1978.

Krueger, R.F., Schmutte, P. S., Caspi, A., Moffitt, T. E., Campbell, K., and Silva, P. A. "Personality Traits Are Linked to Crime among Men and Women: Evidence from a Birth Cohort." *Journal of Abnormal Psychology* 103 (1994): 328–338.

Langhinrichsen-Rohling, J., Monson, C. M., Meyer, K. A., Caster, J., and Sanders, A. "The Associations among Family-of-Origin Violence and Young Adults' Current Depressed, Hopeless, Suicidal and Life-Threatening Behavior." *Journal of Family Violence* 13 (1998): 243–261.

Lyng, S. "Edgework: A Social Psychological Analysis of Voluntary Risk Taking." *American Journal of Sociology* 95 (1990): 851–886.

———. "Edgework Revisited: A Reply to Miller." *American Journal of Sociology* 96 (1991): 1534–1539.

———. "Dysfunctional Risk Taking: Criminal Behavior." In *Adolescent Risk Taking*, edited by N. J. Bell and R. W. Bell. Newbury Park, CA: Sage, 1993.

Mazerolle, P. "Gender, General Strain and Delinquency: An Empirical Examination." *Justice Quarterly* 15 (1998): 65–91.

McAlexander, J. H., and Schouten, J. W. "Hair Style Changes as Transition Markers." *Sociology and Social Research* 74 (1989): 58–62.

Miller, E. M. "Assessing the Risk of Inattention to Class, Race, Ethnicity, and Gender: Comment on Lyng." *American Journal of Sociology* 96 (1991): 1530–1534.

Mitchell, J., Dodder, R. A., and Norris, T. D. "Neutralization and Delinquency: A Comparison by Sex and Ethnicity." *Adolescence* 25 (1990): 487–497.

O'Malley, P., and Mugford, S. "Crime, Excitement and Modernity." In *Varieties of Criminology*, edited by G. Barak. Westport, CN: Praeger, 1994.

Park, R. E. "Human Migration and the Marginal Man." *American Journal of Sociology* 33 (1928): 893.

Polk, K. "The New Marginal Youth." *Crime and Delinquency* 30 (1984): 462–480.

Regoli, R M., and Hewitt, J. D. *Delinquency in Society: A Child-Centered Approach*. NY: McGraw-Hill, Inc., 1994.

Reiter, E. *Making Fast Food: From the Frying Pan into the Fryer*. Montreal: McGill–Queen's University Press, 1991.

Schaffer, B., and Deblassie, R. R. "Adolescent Prostitution." *Adolescence* 19 (1984): 689–696.

Schneider, B. and Schmidt, J. A. "Young Women At Work." In *Women and Work: A Handbook*, edited by P. . Dubeck and K. Borman. New York: Garland, 1996: 17–21.

Schlosser, E. *Fast Food Nation*. New York: Houghton Mifflin Company, 2002.

Srole, L. "Social Integration and Certain Corollaries." *American Sociological Review* 21 (1956): 709–716.

Stonequist, E.H. *The Marginal Man*. New York: Charles Scribner's Sons, 1937.

Thornberry, T. "Violent Families and Youth Violence." U.S. Department of Justice, Office of Juvenile Justice and Delinquency Prevention Fact Sheet. Washington, D.C.: 1994.

Turner, V. The Ritual Process: Structure and Anti-Structure. NY: Cornell University Press, 1969.

Wenz, F. V. "Sociological Correlates of Alienation Among Adolescents Suicide Attempts." *Adolescence* 14 (1979): 19–30.

Widom, C. S. "The Cycle of Violence." *Science* 244 (1989): 160–166.

Wynne, E. "Adolescent Alienation and Youth Policy." *Teacher's College Record* 78 (1976): 23–40.

Zuckerman, M. *Sensation Seeking: Beyond the Optimal Level of Arousal*. Hillsdale, N.J., L. Earlbaum Associates 1979.

Appendix

Anomia

Please indicate whether you agree or disagree with the following statements: a) Most public officials (people in public offices) are not really interested in the problems of the average person; b) Nowadays a person has to live pretty much for today and let tomorrow take care of itself; c) In spite of what some people say, the life of the average person is getting worse, not better; d) It's hardly fair to bring children into the world with the way things look for the future; e) These days a person doesn't really know whom he or she can count on; f) Most people really don't care what happens to the next person; g) Next to health, money is the most important thing; h) You sometimes can't help wondering if anything is worthwhile; i) To make money there are no right and wrong ways anymore, only easy and hard ways.

Codes: 0 = Disagree, 1 = Agree

Edgework Sensations

Listed below are several possible reasons for breaking the law; please rate the importance each had for you: a) Created a natural high; b) provided a sense of personal accomplishment; c) Enjoyment; d) the risk of being caught; e) The sense of freedom it provided; f) Challenge; g) Excitement

Codes: 0 (unimportant) – 4 (important)

Juvenile Delinquency

Please indicate how often you participated in the following: a) Stolen or tried to steal a motor vehicle such as a car or a motorcycle; b) Stolen or tried to steal something worth more than $50; c) Stolen or tried to steal things worth $5 or less; d) Stolen or tried to steal things between $5.01 and $50; e) Knowingly bought, sold, or held stolen goods or tried to do any of these things; f) Ran away from home; g) Carried a concealed weapon (other than a plain pocket knife); h) Skipped school without a legitimate excuse; i) Attacked someone with the idea of seriously hurting or killing him/her; j) Sold marijuana or hashish; k) Smoked cigarettes (and were under age 18); l) Hit or threatened to hit a teacher or other adult at school; m) Hit or threatened to hit a parent or guardian; n) Hit or threatened to hit another student; o) Broken curfew (your town's legal curfew, not a curfew imposed by your parents/guardians); p) Sold hard drugs such as heroin, cocaine, or LSD; q) Had or tried to have sexual intercourse with someone against their will; r) Had or tried to have sexual relations other than intercourse against their will; s) Used force or strong-arm methods to get money or things from other students or teachers; t) Used force or strong-arm methods to get money or things from other people (not students or teachers); u) Stolen or tried to steal something at school, such as someone's coat from a classroom, locker, or cafeteria, or a book from the library; v) Broken or tried to break into a building or vehicle to steal something or just to look around; w) Bought or drank beer, wine or liquor (without parent's/guardian's permission); x) Purposely damaged or destroyed public or private property that didn't belong to you.

Codes: 0 = not at all, 1 = once or twice, 2 = several times, 3 = very often

Part V
Mainstreaming Edgework

7

Adventure Without Risk Is Like Disneyland

*LORI HOLYFIELD, LILIAN JONAS,
AND ANNA ZAJICEK*

CONTENTS

Adventure consumption is a relatively new cultural genre. Combined with recreation (another theme for our age), it assumes broad cultural significance, both shaping and being shaped by our expanding appetites for experienced emotions. Just one alternative on a continuum (from roller coasters to ropes courses) of "packaged" adventures, commercial white water rafting provides a unique emotional frame for experiencing emotions such as fear, excitement, and spontaneity, with (more often the perception of) some level of risk. We borrow the sentence, "Adventure without Risk is like Disneyland" (Coupland, 1991) for our title, as it captures much of the paradox that we will address in this chapter.

Today's adventure consumers are a savvy lot. The past several decades their numbers have grown along with commercial outlets that serve them, creating yet another example of what some might call the "new means of consumption" (Ritzer, 2000; 2002). Spectacular fabricated worlds within bounded spaces (e.g., Six Flags, Disney, Las Vegas) simply won't do for a growing number of adventure seekers, who are quickly abandoning Disney World for experiences that are more interactive and offer the illusion of risk (Dunn and Gulbis, 1976; Holyfield, 1999; Iso-Ahola, 1988; Jonas, 1999). Moreover, commercial experiences that combine "adventure" with the "outdoors" are perceived as more natural, constituting a "deep reality" (Fine, 1992).

Lyng (1990) describes how extreme adventure or "edgework" takes place in situations most would regard as entirely uncontrollable, both physically and mentally. "Edgework," he writes, "represents one's ability to manage situations which verge upon complete chaos, lending a sense of omnipotence, self-determination, mental control over environmental objects, ineffability, and hyperreality" (1990, p. 877). Accordingly, "edgework" serves to put us in touch with emotions, sensations, and skills that are normally absent in our overly rationalized routines of modern life (O'Malley and Mugford, 1994). Ironically, the experiences we have pushed to the margins in modern times (e.g., emotions, feelings, reflection) are now the very items we crave. "Edgework" pulls all of the experiences together in one phenomenologically heated moment.

In reality, however, we are not all "serious action" seekers (Goffman, 1969). Today's adventure companies now compete to provide excitement and other intense emotions while guaranteeing the safety of those who do not wish to actually risk their lives experiencing these sensations. There is irony in this mix insofar as such persons look to the institutional realm for ways to express their "impulsive" traits (Turner, 1976), thus creating an interesting paradox for both consumer and provider. Consumers' pursuit of fateful endeavors within the "protective cocoon" (Giddens, 1991) of commercial adventure enables them to actively court risks in an otherwise uneventful world.

Achieving the *appearance* of fatefulness without the risks requires unique organizational strategies. Emotions must be managed, perceptions must be shaped, and experiences must match expectations. Similarly, commodification must be downplayed, and in its place, at least the impression of spontaneity must be created. In this chapter we draw upon data from white water rafting in the southeastern United States to illustrate how commercial adventure incorporates these opposing forces. We will focus upon both the expectations of novice white water enthusiasts, or those whom Goffman (1969) might call the "pseudo-adventurers," and the challenges and strategies faced by commercial providers. Can adventure consumers experience some of the perceived benefits of "edgework" without exercising the necessary competencies? Can companies provide commodified adventure and keep intact the risk-taking characteristics so valued in today's culture? Can the very emotions associated with risk (e.g., fear and excitement) become objects of exchange in commercial adventures?

The Sociology of Adventure

Adventure, as we use the term, includes voluntary engagement in novel, uncertain, and most often emotionally intense recreational activity. Most sociological discussions of adventure and its components have focused upon individual pursuits of adventure that incorporate skill, competence, and motivation. We view adventure as existing on a continuum, from BASE-jumping off the Sears Tower in Chicago, to riding the south's fastest roller coaster at Busch Gardens, to gambling in Las Vegas.

Talk of adventure is necessarily talk of the self in contemporary culture. An individual's pursuit of adventure is often valorized and perceived as a tool for self-work, i.e., a chance to maintain self-command under trying or uncertain circumstances. Seen as a vehicle of self-actualization, self-induced stress, control over the arousal of one's emotions, and successful completion of acts of self-endangerment are often regarded as possessing a sacred quality. Character is both created and tested in adventure (Lyman and Scott, 1989).

Discussions of adventure include the notion that voluntary risk or "fateful" action (Goffman, 1969) has a moral quality to it. Adventures become symbolically associated with uncertainty (Wanderer, 1987), interpreted as transcendent and holistic, directed by intrinsic rules (Lyman and Scott, 1989), a "quasi-hypnotic" excitement (Gans, 1962, p. 65). But it is not the actual activity that makes voluntary risk taking an adventure, Simmel argues. Instead, it is our ability to symbolically transform an emotionally intense experience into something that can be assigned positive value. Wanderer (1987, p. 25) describes this as a process of "symbolic conversion." One must first imagine an act to be adventuresome. Otherwise, it could be interpreted as burdensome (Burke, 1935, p. 82) or, worse yet, terrifying.

Thus, the consumption of adventure is shaped by cultural scripts. Moreover, adventures are now available to everyone, from novice to expert (see Ewert, 1986), from vicarious and safe positions (watching movies, reading novels, spectator events), to relatively safe group trips and outings (where "experts" guide and protect), to solo and collective adventures of extreme risk ("edgework"). Commercial facilitation has become more common, as companies capitalize upon cultural ideals of risk taking and justify its use in a variety of contexts, including mandatory adventures (e.g., ropes courses for team building, outdoor expeditions for juvenile offenders, and the like).

Commercial adventures of all sorts seek to accentuate the desired experiences and the emotions anticipated in adventure participation. Herein lies the paradox where a balance must be struck between risk and safety. For example, commercials, brochures, and newsletters are produced to accent the "wild and scenic" aspect of white water rafting, the excitement, fear, and thrill that customers can expect to experience. A quote from a company publication illustrates this point, referring to rafting on the Chattooga river as the "ride of a lifetime." Meanwhile, customers are greeted upon entry with waiver forms, life vests, and "safety talks" from staff.

While there is no literature speaking to the organization of adventure, per se, there are numerous studies that relate specifically to the ways organizations influence our emotions. Hochschild's (1983) research on the "managed heart" of flight attendants and bill collectors aids our understanding of the normative aspects of emotional conduct. Similar to the flight attendants at Delta, we found that river guides share a collective appreciation for the need to present and maintain an emotional climate for customers. They may engage in emotion management of selves or others (see also Thoits, 1996) to achieve company aims. For example, guides may feel estranged from their emotions when required to present an emotional frame that does not match their own feelings. We found also that emotion management is used by guides to inflate or deflate statuses of customers (see Holyfield and Jonas, 2003).

Hochschild (1983) examines how institutions construct emotional frames, guiding what we see and experience. Organizational "feeling rules" are espoused by managers to ensure employees gain control over others to promote organizational goals (Sutton, 1991). But leisure organizations are often considered free of managerial controls. We don't automatically think about how commercial recreation shapes our emotional experiences. Moreover, while the literature has focused upon the workplace and workers' emotions, organizational practices are important to consumers as well (Leidner, 1993). It is important to examine companies that cater to our recreational and hedonistic desires and the more implicit strategies they employ in shaping our emotional experiences.

While there are few unknown routes in river rafting today, and boat materials are stronger and safer than ever before, the danger associated with navigating white water remains alluring to both experienced and novice boaters. Accordingly, we examine how impressions of risk and management of emotions are used by guides to ensure the activity remains somewhere between the poles of boredom and anxiety, creating an experiential space along the previously described adventure continuum between vicarious adventure and true edgework. We also address the expectations customers bring with them as they serve to influence/resist the interpreted experience.

The Setting

We chose to explore these issues by focusing on data collected in a study of commercial rafting. Both the first and second author have conducted research that examines both commercial and noncommercial ("private") rafting in the southeastern (Chattooga, Nantahala, and Ocoee rivers) and the southwestern (Colorado) United States. The data we examine in this chapter were gathered by the first author on the Chattooga river (designated a "wild and scenic" river in 1974).

Primary data included in-depth interviews with forty-seven customers and staff and participant-observation (attending raft guide school, accompanying commercial and training river trips, and videotaping) over an eleven-month period. Selection of interviewees emerged via snowball sampling. Sometimes managers would suggest a guide to interview, but most guides were approached by the first author at the outpost between raft trips. While achieving a random sample was not an aim, an effort was made to be mindful of the level of experience, age, and gender of those interviewed so as to gain as wide a representation as possible. Similarly, customers were approached during or immediately after a rafting trip, and interviews were conducted on-the-spot. One group of co-workers were interviewed about their experiences two weeks after their trip. Those interviews took place at their workplace. All interviews were recorded on audiotape and transcribed for coding purposes.

Some data was generated via casual conversations with customers both before, during, and after trips and was recorded as field notes. Field notes were taken throughout the study and a journal was kept for reflections from participation. Entries were dated for chronological purpose. Whenever possible, attempts were made to consistently write up the field notes immediately following an observation. Much of the coding of field notes was ongoing, beginning early on in the research process with "jottings" and initial coding schemes. Later the notes were expanded and codes were condensed to meaningful categories for analysis (Strauss and Corbin, 1995).

White Water

White water rafting calls to mind images of big waves and fast-moving water. Rivers, more specifically those designated "wild and scenic," hold a special quality for white water enthusiasts, who understand that their experiences on a natural flowing river are, to some degree, ephemeral and ineffable. Those inclined toward "edgework" can find ample opportunity in the watery rites of passage. Some may even seek occupations that keep them embedded in risk settings to experience the "flow" (Csikszentmihalyi, 1991) that accompanies complete engagement in the act of white water boating. But for novice enthusiasts, those not inclined to learn the skills of white water boating or to take paddle-in-hand, a variety of meaningful experiences are possible.

Rafting companies have organizational cultures that serve as powerful control mechanisms, working both informally and formally at multiple levels to approve or prohibit certain behaviors (Martin and Seihl, 1983; Fine, 1984). Consumers encounter these organizational cultures with a variety of expectations. At a more superficial level, the organizational culture of commercial rafting includes jargon, office arrangements, physical items, dress codes, technology, and art, as well as habits and rites (Schien, 1981; Ott, 1989). It is at this level we see tangible evidence of company concerns for safeguarding customers from harm and protecting management from liability while also making a profit. One manager spoke of the importance of safety "at all points." Customers are "screened" via telephone, when they arrive at the outpost, during the orientation speech (when trip leaders describe the "safety rules"), and while they load the buses (raft guides watch for signs of physical problems and evidence of alcohol or other drug impairment). Raft guides often tell customers while they are signing the waiver, "The most dangerous part of your trip is over now that you're off the highway!"

The second level of organizational culture includes intangible components much harder to observe, i.e., beliefs and values. Here, beneath the visible surface of artifacts and documents, we find the "living culture" (Davis, 1984) and witness the tension between what organizations can and cannot achieve. This is where guides confront a contradiction in attempting to provide a thrilling but safe ride down the river for a wide variety of customers (or "peeps" as some guides call them out of earshot).

Raft guides share a subculture, living, working, and playing together for several months at a time. While there are some older guides, the occupation of raft guiding remains a youthful enterprise. Raft guides are a fairly homogeneous group with little variation in age, race, education, and class background. Most are white, middle- to upper-middle-class backgrounds, with at least some college education. A growing number of guides are female, but they represent a small percentage of the group. Even fewer people of color can be found in the rafting industry.

Because the work is seasonal, many outfitters employ college students eager to earn summer wages and at the same time have exhilarating outdoor experiences. The low wages are compensated by housing at the outposts, which often resemble a youth camp but with recreational use of alcohol and, in some cases, other drugs. Guides enjoy the relative isolation and freedom that their "bohemian" lifestyle affords them. For example, one guide bragged she had not read a newspaper in three months. Another was proud that he had not watched a television all summer. Though some guides are married and live away from the outposts with their families, others enjoy the less restrictive aspect of outpost living. As one guide who has since married described, "Raft guiding is for a certain type of freestyle person. It's like, open relationships or whatever. You've got to be up for that."

Maintaining a balance between spontaneity and constraint is the primary challenge guides confront in their everyday actions. When working, guides assume multiple roles. Excitement and "serious fun" are the dominant emotional frames. However, commercial involvement creates tension for river guides, many of whom could be accurately described as actual or potential "edgeworkers." Many of the guides spend their leisure time on the river engaging in challenging white water boating, pushing themselves to physical, mental, and emotional limits. On the job, however, they are required to shape the experience of customers. Rendering services to rafting customers is a means to an end for most, although some private boaters see it as "selling out." One guide illustrated the need to keep his identity separate from novice customers when he exclaimed, "I wouldn't be caught dead [as a passenger] on a commercial trip," no doubt reacting to a perceived sense that commercial rafting is not "real" rafting.

Behind-the-scenes remarks about customers are often made, demonstrating guides' need to create a symbolic distance from their "guests" (management's term for customers). The felt tension is not invisible to management. Trip leaders and outpost managers may downplay guides' disdain for customers. Sometimes guides will jokingly fight over who is going to be "stuck" with an "out of shape" customer, particularly if a customer is obese. One guide explained that, as rafting has gotten more popular, "people show up and you look at them and say, 'I don't want that person in my raft.'"

Outpost managers walk in two worlds, sometimes engaging in the banter and other times reminding the guides that the customers are their "bread and butter." The manager at one outpost explained, "If it were not for the rafting companies here, Joe Public wouldn't get the chance to enjoy what boaters of all types get to see." The commercial provider, he argued, "becomes the liaison between typical suburbanites and the yet-to-be-experienced river." The organizational norm is to offer "guests" an exciting, thrilling, and fun experience but also to manage the actual risks inherent in a wild and scenic river. As this manager explained to staff members during guide school, many of today's customers are challenged just "walking from the car to the mall."

While guides earn relatively low wages, the potential to earn good money rests upon gratuity. Thus, many guides exercise a great deal of control over the emotions and experiences of passengers in their charge and, therefore, have an excellent opportunity to employ gratuity-enhancing techniques on the river. For example, a skilled guide can choose which passengers will get sprayed with water when the raft hits a particular rapid. They can often control who will be most likely to fall out of the raft (by deciding who will occupy the "ejector seat"). When a guide has a passenger that is arrogant or bored, he/she may intentionally take a rapid sideways or backwards to "liven things up." The unsuspecting customer is likely to experience such events as frightening, which can be both good or bad, depending upon the guide's ability to transform the meaning to excitement before the trip ends.

Similar to Hochschild's flight attendants, personalities are part of the commercial transaction and thus subjected to occupational demands. Indeed, commercial guides are doing more than providing technical skills for maneuvering white water; guides have to engage in emotion labor/work as part of the commercial transaction, manipulating both their own emotions and those of others. Commercial guides are required to master emotions, especially those deemed negative in their work roles (e.g., anger, fear, and disgust).

Most often guides engage their emotions to enhance the status and well being of their customers. But as Fine (1984, p. 246) points out, organizational actors don't always operate on the basis of rational, profit-oriented models. They often assume that position which works best at the time. For example, guides may attempt to temporarily elevate their own status and deflate the statuses of their customers to reduce the felt tension of being "inauthentic" or estranged from their feelings. The result may be a reduced tip for that day. If a raft guide is regularly unpleasant to customers, he/she is likely to be fired. We have elsewhere discussed how guides' interactions and attempts at status elevation are more thinly veiled in commercial pursuits than in noncommercial trips (Holyfield and Jonas, 2003).

A delicate balance must be found in guides' social construction of danger. In calling attention to dangers that are sometimes illusory and sometimes real, guides rely on white water discourse as both a control mechanism and as a way to enhance customer satisfaction. On commercial trips, the trip leaders often display large photographs of flipped rafts to a group of customers while conducting a "safety talk."

They encourage all to listen closely so as to "avoid the dangers of the river." Humor is also injected in an attempt to keep those who are frightened from becoming too anxious. For example, during a "safety talk" a trip leader held up a picture of people falling out of a raft as the boat went over a large rapid and explained, "This is Jawbone, a nasty rapid, so listen up folks cause this could be you today!" Discussing topics that elicit fear tinged with humor is an especially effective way to maintain a balance between anxiety and boredom among customers.

Often friends or family book the trip and, therefore, many customers arrive not fully aware of the participation expected of them on a "wild and scenic" river. This is especially the case on the Chattooga, where the more cynical guides believe customers often come expecting a "Disneyland" experience. This creates some strain between guides who want customers that appreciate their river skills and are willing to "rough it" and those customers who have come for a special, extraordinary experience that includes thrill, excitement, and fun, but minimal work. A successful guide is one who employs impression management and sets an emotional tone that is responsive, but never lets the customer know it is scripted.

While the aim is to manage impressions of risk, there are limits as to how much the organization can influence the customer's experience of the river. Unanticipated events or "meso" phenomena can intervene, sometimes interrupting attempts to maintain an appropriate balance between anxiety and boredom (see Maines, 1977; Zurcher, 1985). For example, low water on a wild and scenic river can make for smaller waves, and thus be interpreted as less exciting. High water can have the opposite effect, making the experience too frightening. Trips on rainy days are often considered gloomy, and customers may not be as satisfied (most scheduled trips take place, regardless of rain, unless lightning is present). Conversely, mist rising above the water on a crisp morning can lend a sense of awe to the experience, rendering the trip memorable.

The Adventure Consumer

River guides assume that customers want to be safe and have a thrilling experience, but customers can't always articulate just what it is they expect. When asked what they want from the experience, customers' answers include a range of affective responses, such as intense excitement, and in some cases, fear. One customer recalled after his trip, "We had talked about this trip amongst ourselves for about a month, and the closer it got, the more afraid I was." While he was not able to articulate what he expected, he anticipated some degree of uncertainty. He explains, "I mean I swim, and I'm pretty athletic, but when it comes to something like this that has the element of the unknown, I'm not willing to do that. I mean I just don't do things like that." Another customer laughed when asked about her expectations, saying she "expected to be drowned, thrown in the water, having to be saved, CPR and the whole bit." Still another customer spoke of his desire to be "scared": "We said, let's do something fun, something that is really going to scare us. So, we decided to go white water rafting and to be perfectly honest with you, when we first started talking about it, I was thinking, 'I'm going to die.'"

Although guides and managers play a crucial role in symbolically constructing the white water experience, customers are also involved in negotiating the balance between spontaneity and routine. Some trends in customers' expectations have been identified in reports published in the lay press (English and Bowker, 1993), and a few guides use this knowledge to their advantage. These reported expectations include anticipation of a natural environment, quality or professional service, relative isolation from others, scenic views, big waves, and river quantity. They also desire that rivers be clean and unpolluted enough to swim in, adding to their sense of experiencing something authentic. Customers want to feel the "wildness" of the rivers and experience something extraordinary, but at the same time, they expect to have easy access to this environment. These conflicting desires generate more tension on the Chattooga because running this river requires some participation on the part of customers (e.g., carrying rafts up and down the quarter mile corridor).

Providing white water adventure to those who otherwise would not experience the river sometimes creates significant tension between the twin imperatives for safety and uncertainty. On one occasion, a guide was told just before a trip that he would be accompanying a disabled woman down section IV of the Chattooga river (the most challenging section of the river). Her wheelchair was tied down to the center of the raft and the guide, who was also the trip leader, explained his hesitation. "It wasn't that I didn't want her on the river," he explains. "The water level was two feet [the highest water level allowed for commercial trips] and about 2.5 feet in 'Five Falls' [a section of the river that contains twelve potentially dangerous rapids in less than a quarter mile]. If we took a swim I knew we were in trouble. If we flipped it would put everyone at risk, not just her." He recommended to the manager that they refund her money, but she insisted proceeding with the trip. "She didn't care. She wanted to do it so we took her down!"

The same guide went on to explain that he was later glad the passenger had the opportunity to make the trip and that he felt it was a memorable experience for her. But not all raft guides shared his ambivalent feelings. Several felt that the company should have flatly refused to accept her on the trip or should have, at the very least, scheduled her for a less dangerous section of the river. Indeed, had their raft flipped, the outcome might have been very different.

All forms of adventure consumption are experiential, in that many customers are seeking fun, amusement, stimulation, and enjoyment. Drawing on the cultural script that links adventure to heroism, guides assume that customers who feel that they are somehow engaged (however illusory) in managing the risks find deeper meaning in the experience. However, as with any transaction, some customers are easier to please than others. For example, a customer once complained at having wet feet from the point of put-in (place on river where trip is launched) to the point of take-out (end of trip when rafts are taken out). From the guide's point of view, the customer clearly had a distorted notion of a "wild and scenic" river trip.

Customers often complained about their assigned roles. Several balked at having to carry rafts and equipment. These examples demonstrate the importance of a somewhat realistic match between expectations and outcomes. Obviously, there were limited possibilities for constructing an adventure experience in these cases.

Conversely, other customers crave participation, although some prefer the *perception* of participation as opposed to actual engagement in the action. For example, one customer described his experience as something akin to "the rush that you get on a roller coaster": "It's pretty much like that all the way down, but you create it. You are making the fun versus Six Flags where you sit and wait for it." Another customer described being let down when the trip ended: "It was like, can't we go do it again? And you felt like you had made a bond, you know?" Yet another customer described what some might consider a particular form of the "flow" experience. She recalls, "Our guide would call out commands and we would start... 'Three strokes forward' and all of us would go 'One,' 'Two,' 'Three' ... it was fun. I had to sit in the front of the boat so I ate water all day. When he said paddle, they watched me and I set the rhythm because I was in front and we scooted right on down through there."

Like the private boaters, adventure consumers use their experiences to mark social differences between themselves and "others," sometimes defining the river trip as a "once-in-a-lifetime experience," and often purchasing a large photograph to document it! Indirect references to the ineffable aspects of the experience served as a persistent theme in customer comments. As one stated, "It's nature I think. Because when you aren't in the white water there's just ... I couldn't talk to be perfectly honest with you, because I was just sitting there with my mouth hanging open looking at the mountains and the trees and we went on the first ride of the day and the mist was still in the air and it just looked like a fairy land really." "It took my breath away," another explained. "Some of those rapids just, I can't describe the feeling of watching the boat ahead of you just disappear down a water fall and you know you're next."

Once again, however, too much excitement can border on fear; too little can lead to boredom and an unhappy customer. On a wild and scenic river, numerous elements can disrupt attempts to maintain the balance. For example, the first author took several "swims" (i.e., flipped out of a raft, usually in a rapid) and witnessed numerous other "swims" by customers. The staff managed each of these events by employing organizational norms of humor, especially when a customer appeared terrified. The goal was to establish a proper emotional foothold consistent with the stated aim of fun and excitement. Consequently, the staff responded to "swims" almost immediately, unless it is obvious that the flip was intended or occurred in a rapid that was not perceived to be dangerous. Taking a "swim" was sometimes fearful and other times humorous for customers, even in spots where rescue was necessary. The challenge for guides is to rescue customers without demonstrating fear. The only exceptions were "swims" taken by trainees during guide school. In this setting, guides who flipped were subjected to harassment from other guides.

Attempts to shape a "swim" experience were most often effective, but there were exceptions. On one occasion a guide recalled having four elderly people (each over 70) in her raft on a trip through a potentially dangerous section of the Chattooga river during high water. They had been misdirected by friends to purchase the section IV trip instead of section III (a milder section of the river). When they arrived the company would not refund their money so they went on the scheduled trip. She described the experience as "the worst trip I've ever had," recalling how each person was visibly afraid. And then the worst-case scenario actually occurred as one of the customers fell out of the raft in "Five Falls": "I took a bad swim with one of the women in Corkscrew," she explains. "She came up pre-clamped [fetal position]. She was biologically showing us in every possible way that she was not enjoying this and wasn't prepared to get back in the raft." Passive swimmers are most at risk in white water. The concern for this customer was that she could have been swept away quickly and away from possible rescue. While attempts are made to manage both perceptions of risks and actual risks, exceptional circumstances complicate this effort. As this example demonstrates, commercial rafting is never completely risk free.[1] Hence, the fundamental challenge faced by guides and managerial staff—the need to maintain a balance between danger and safety—is a delicate enterprise.

As these data reveal, outcomes may differ from customer expectations (typically articulated in hindsight), in part because it's difficult for novice adventurers to grasp the white water experience fully before experiencing it (Arnould and Price, 1993). Those adventure consumers who come for the spontaneity of big waves and scenic landscapes may or may not be pleased with the commercial experience. In the end, however, if they find at least some of the desired elements of culturally scripted adventure, many customers experience a form of risk taking that is meaningful and compelling (hence, the high number of return patrons).

Discussion and Conclusion

The proliferation of commercial adventure pursuits points to the popularity of such activity, but it does not answer why they are so attractive to growing numbers of consumers. Competency and skills are said to be the typical attraction to such pursuits (Ewert and Hollenhorst, 1989) yet as we have shown, white water consumers are hardly competent boaters. However, if the commercial transaction goes as planned, they may leave with the belief they could achieve those skills were they to pursue them later.

In this late modern era edgework is accompanied by pressures that have brought it under greater institutional control. A growing desire among not-so-serious adventurers (those less inclined to put themselves in harm's way) combined with a need to secure necessary resources for edgeworkers (e.g., time, money, equipment, and access) has resulted in an adventure industry. The rafting enterprise we presented in this chapter is but one example of a growing number of commercial adventures that organizations provide.

Early in this paper we posed the question of whether consumers can experience some of the perceived benefits of edgework without exercising the necessary competencies. The adventure consumers we have described are not doing edgework, but they get an idea of what it might be like. Moreover, many are able to achieve some symbolic distance between themselves and sedentary "couch potatoes." As we have shown, some of the activities will fall within the realm of the routine, and some will be interpreted as extraordinary, even terrifying. Thus, it is clear that river trips, however familiar their routes, always incorporate an element of uncertainty that leaves customers with a sense that their white water experience can never be replicated. Just as Goffman (1969) predicted, they get to enjoy some of the benefits of adventure with few of the risks.

Another question we posed in this chapter was whether companies can provide commercial experiences and keep intact the risk-taking characteristics so valued. The short answer is that it depends upon the skills of organizational members, the expectations of customers, and the physical environment. Organizations are challenged to keep perceptions of risk and uncertainty alive without giving away the company secrets of behind-the-scenes routine and managed emotions. Creating the desired mix between safety and danger requires that guides create an illusion of risk while not endangering the clients. Dealing with the contingencies of the physical environment (i.e., "meso" phenomena—weather, climate, water level) and the expectations or even resistance of customers, means guides must negotiate another kind of "edge" on the job.

As we have demonstrated here, guides employ a number of skills in constructing adventure experiences. While certain emotions are indeed harnessed or regulated, it is for the explicit purpose of generating other emotions. The activity is less relevant than the shaped meanings. Consequently, so long as uncertainly can be relatively assured, the paradox can be solved, if only temporarily.

Similar to Hochschild's flight attendants and insurance workers, we have illustrated the emotion management techniques employed by raft guides as they learn to master both their own emotions as well as those of their customers. And similar to Hochschild's examples, there exists the possibility that guides may come to feel estranged from their selves when required to present an emotional frame that is at odds with their own feelings. But unlike Hochschild's examples, which are found in the workplace, those encountering such organizational demands in their leisure pursuits may be even less inclined to expect social control over their emotions.

In commercial rafting, we believe the interactions between raft guides and their customers can be likened to the dialectic between the magician and his/her audience's own mundane everyday life experiences and the extra-mundane quality of reasoning found in magic (Nardi, 1984). The rafting trip, like the magic show, offers violations of everyday expectations, constructing an alternate reality, one that is embedded in interactions where a moderate level of uncertainty and fear is desirable. Both engage in appropriate roles for the experience to occur. Just as an audience at a magic show agrees to be entertained and tricked, the adventure consumer agrees to be excited and challenged, always anticipating an extraordinary experience. And just as the magician agrees to entertain, deceive, manipulate, and fabricate, the raft guide must provide a spontaneous, uncertain, and perceived challenge while simultaneously entertaining and protecting the customer.

In the white water rafting experience, as well as the magic exchange, there exists a level of voluntarism that may allow the commercial company to influence and penetrate even deeper than a typical commercial transaction (e.g., theme parks). The perception of risk creates for consumers the belief that raft guides will protect them in the event of danger. The assumed expertise and skill of white water boating allows the raft guides to assume a temporary level of authority over consumers not afforded in many service occupations.

With the growth of commercial adventures, perhaps the stated opposition of Turner's "institutional" and "impulsive" selves collapses. Maybe structural changes allow us to now seek uncertainty from the very institutions we once thought stifled us. Or perhaps it is the symbolic nature of the product that allows this blurring of boundaries and prohibits it from being trivialized, regardless of the organizational aim to make a profit. After all, adventure is not concrete in the sense that it can be brought back if it doesn't meet the needs of the consumer. It must be experienced in an emotional context. In the end we are both anchored to and free of our stifling institutions (Hewitt, 1991) so long as an experiential tension remains in tact. Combined with the inherent vagueness of expectations, commercial adventures may gain future importance in helping us achieve distance from our all too familiar worlds.

Notes

1. Indeed, the most hazardous outdoor recreational pursuits are those associated with moving water, as drownings average 8,000 per year (third most common cause for accidental death in the U.S.).

References

Arnould, E., and Price, L. "River Magic: Extraordinary Experience and the Extended Service Encounter." *Journal of Consumer Research* 20 (1993): 24–45.

Burke, K. *Permanence and Change: An Anatomy of Purupose.* New York: New Republic, 1935.

Colman, S. "Whitewater Parks." *Paddler Magazine.* August 14, 4 (1994): 74–81.

Coupland, D. *Generation X: Tales for an Accelerated Culture.* New York: St. Martins, 1991.

Csikszentmihalyi, Mihaly. 1991. *Flow: The Psychology of Optimal Experience.* New York: Harper Perennial.

Davis, M. "Sociology Through Humor." *Symbolic Interaction* 2 (1979): 105–110.

Davis, S. M. *Managing Corporate Culture.* Cambridge: Ballinger, 1984.

Dunn, R., and Gulbis, J. M. "The Risk Revolution." *Parks and Recreation* 11 (1976): 12–18.

English, D., and Bowker, J. M. *Final Report: 1993 River Study Pilot Data.* Knoxville, TN: America Outdoors, 1993.

Ewert A. "Managing Fear in an Outdoor Experiential Educational Setting." *Journal of Experiential Education* Spring (1986): 19–25.

Ewert, A., and Hollenhurst, S. "Testing the Adventure Model: Empirical Support for a Model of Risk Recreation." *Journal of Leisure Research* 21(2) (1989): 124–136.

Fine, G. A. "Negotiated Orders and Organizational Cultures." *Annual Review of Sociology* 10 (1984): 239–262.

————. "Wild Life: Authenticity and the Human Experience of Natural Places." In *Investigating Subjectivity: Research on Lived Experience,* edited by C. Ellis and M. G. Flaherty. Newbury Park, CA: Sage, 1992, 211–236.

Gans, H. J. *The Urban Villagers.* New York: Free Press, 1962.

Giddens, A. *Modernity and Self-Identity: Self and Society in Late Modern Age.* Stanford, CA: Stanford Press, 1991.

Goffman, E. *Where the Action Is.* London: Penguin Press, 1969.

————. *Frame Analysis.* New York: Harper and Row, 1974.

Hewitt, John. 1991. *Dilemmas of the American Self.* Philadelphia: Temple University Press.

Hochschild, A. *The Managed Heart: Commercialization of Human Feeling.* Berkeley, CA: University of California Press, 1983.

Holyfield, L. "Generating Excitement: Organizational and Social Psychological Dynamics of Adventure." PhD diss., University of Georgia, 1995.

————. "Manufactured Adventure: The Buying and Selling of Emotions." *Journal of Contemporary Ethnography* 28(1) (1999):

Holyfield, L., and Jonas, L. "From River God to Research Grunt: Identity, Emotions, and the River Guide." *Symbolic Interaction* 26(2) (2003): 285–306.

Iso-Ahola, S. "Perceived Competence as a Mediator of the Relationship Between High Risk Sports." *Journal of Leisure Research* 21(1988): 32–39.

Jonas, L. "The Making of a River Guide: The Construction of Authority in a Leisure Subculture." PhD diss., University of Denver, 1997.

————. "Making and Facing Danger: Constructing Strong Character on the River." *Symbolic Interaction* 22 (1999): 247–268.

Leidner, Robin. *Fast Food, Fast Talk: The Routinization of Everyday Life.* Berkeley: University of California Press, 1993.

Lyng, S. "Edgework: A Social Psychological Analysis of Voluntary Risk Taking." *American Journal of Sociology* 95 (1990): 851–886.

Lyng, S., and Snow, D. A. "Vocabularies of Motive and High-Risk Behavior: The Case of Skydiving." In *Advances in Group Process,* edited by E. J. Lawler. Greenwich, CT: JAI Press, 1986, 157–179.

Lyman, S. and Scott, M. *A Sociology of the Absurd,* 2nd ed. NY: General Hall, 1989.

Maines, D. "Social Organization and Social Structure in Symbolic Interactionist Thought." *Annual Review of Sociology* 3 (1977): 235–259.

Mannheim, K. *Essays on the Sociology of Culture.* NY: Oxford, 1956.

Martin, J. and Siehl, C. 1983. "Organizational Culture and Counterculture: An Uneasy Symbiosis." *Organizational Dynamics* 9:52–64.

Mead, G. H. *Philosophy of the Act.* Chicago: University of Chicago Press, 1938.

Metz, D. *Running Hot.* Cambridge, MA: Abt Books, 1981.

Nardi, P. "Toward a Social Psychology of Entertainment Magic (Conjuring)." *Symbolic Interaction* 7 (1984): 25–43.

O'Malley, P., and Mugford, S. "Crime, Excitement and Modernity." In *Varieties of Criminology,* edited by G. Barak. Westport, CN: Praeger, 1994.

Ott, S. J. *The Organizational Culture Perspective.* Pacific Grove, CA: Brooks/Cole Publishing, 1989.

Powell, C. "Humor as a Form of Social Control: A Deviance Approach." In *It's a Funny Thing, Humor,* edited by A. Chapman and H. Foot. Oxford: Pergamon Press, 1977, 53–55.

Ritzer, George. *The McDonaldization of Society.* Thousand Oakes, CA: Sage, 2000.

————. *Enchanting a Disenchanted World.* Thousand Oakes, CA: Sage, 2002.

Schein, E. H. "Does Japanese Management Style Have a Message for American Managers?" *Sloan Management Review* 23 (1981): 55–68.

Simmel, G. *Essays on Sociology, Philosophy, and Aesthetics,* edited by Kurt Wolf. New York: Harper and Row, 1959.

Strauss, A., and Corbin, S. *The Basics of Qualitative Research.* Newbury Park CA: Sage, 1995.

Sutton, R. "Maintaining Norms About Expressed Emotions: The Case of Bill Collectors." *Administrative Science Quarterly* 36 (1991): 245–268.

Thoits, Peggy. 1996. "Managing the Emotions of Others" *Symbolic Interaction* 19:85–109.

Turner, R. "The Real Self: From Institution to Impulse." *American Journal of Sociology* 81 (1976): 989–1016.

Wanderer, J. "Simmel's Forms of Experiencing: The Adventure as Symbolic Work." *Symbolic Interaction* 10 (1987): 21–28.

Zurcher, L. "The Staging of Emotions: A Dramaturgical Analysis." *Symbolic Interaction* 87 (1985): 181–206.

8
Financial Edgework: Trading in Market Currents

CHARLES W. SMITH

CONTENTS

Introduction: Expanding the Boundaries of Edgework

Lyng (1990), in his paper entitled "Edgework: A Social Psychological Analysis of Voluntary Risk Taking," defines edgework primarily in terms of voluntary risk taking.[1] While acknowledging the importance of individual feelings and sensations entailed by such action, Lyng seeks to expand our understanding of the social factors contributing to these activities. Drawing primarily upon Marx and Mead, he sees edgework in modern society as an attempt by actors to express their need for self-determination in an overly ordered and constraining world. He sees situations on the boundaries of social order and chaos as most receptive and conducive to such activities. Lyng concludes his analysis by calling for more research on the topic.

This paper answers Lyng's call. The primary activity examined, however, is not a leisure, high-risk sporting activity normally associated with Lyng's edgework, but rather the much more structured activity of financial, primarily stock market, traders. The comparisons, I would suggest, are extremely interesting in that they not only give us a different take on such financial trading, but also a different take on edgework.

Given that most financial trading involves a high degree of risk—admittedly more financial than physical, though extreme financial risk can entail physical risks, such as stress-related illness—it would seem to be an appropriate candidate for edgework analysis. It differs from most sports-related high-risk endeavors, however, in that most participants generally strive to reduce the risk entailed rather than maximize it. Most skydivers—the edgeworkers whom Lyng initially studied—and other leisure risk takers fervently embrace the risk factors of their sport. In contrast, most financial traders attempt to minimize risk, looking upon it as a necessary but hopefully controllable element of what they do. Most financial traders, in short, are not gamblers seeking the psychological rush that the risk of gambling can generate.[2] This is not to deny that traders enjoy, and even seek, an emotional high associated with their activity. It is not, I will argue, a "high" derived from the inherent risk of their activity.

A key framing technique used by financial traders to normalize their activities is to perceive their trading as part of a more encompassing process. Where skydivers and other participants in "extreme sports" generally see their activities as quite separate from whatever else they may do, financial traders normally see what they do as one aspect of the more encompassing and less risky activity of financial investment. In short, the risk aspect entailed in active trading is seen as one component of a particular, more marginal activity within the generally less risky process of financial investing. This is consistent with the position taken by Lyng that edgework flourishes on the boundary between order and chaos. What it adds is that those engaged in such boundary work may see themselves primarily in terms of the larger collectivity rather than as deviant outsiders. Framing edgework as a type of behavior within larger categories of behavior struck me as a promising way of approaching financial trading.[3]

Analysis by Analogy: Stock Market Trading and Kayaking

In pondering the various ways edgework could be framed in different situations, more particularly in sports and financial markets, I found myself captivated by kayaking. Here I should note that this was in no small way related to the fact that during the previous year I had become a sea kayak addict, spending a good deal of time not only kayaking but also taking many hours of both sea kayak and white water instruction. What I had been told during these hours of instruction over and over again was that basic kayak technique and skills were the same in all cases. What was true of one form of kayaking, therefore, should, at least structurally, be true for all forms. The only difference was that you could survive quite easily on flat water without having the kayak skills required to paddle in rough water. And what was the most basic kayaking skill that applied to all forms of kayaking? Edging. Admittedly, this could have been merely an interesting play on words, but it seemed to be worth a little more thought.

So what does "edging" mean in kayaking? It literally means putting your boat on its edge/side rather than riding with the bottom of the boat flat to the water. The term seemed to have a very similar meaning in skiing, where it entails putting one's skis on edge to the snow. How this notion of edging applied to the concept of edgework developed by Lyng, where "edgework" refers more to the edge or boundary areas in which the activities occur, was less clear. Moreover, I didn't see how either meaning applied to the stock market. Fortunately, further reflection on kayaking raised some possibilities.

In kayaking, you edge your boat to increase or maintain control by properly aligning the bottom of the kayak to currents in the water. In placid water, where there are few currents except those created in response to the propulsion of the boat, edging is used primarily to help they kayaker turn her boat by exploiting the currents generated by the kayaker herself. Such edging is not necessary to keep her afloat, since there are no external currents to which she needs to adjust.

In rapids and rough surf, however, the failure to edge properly in response to external currents will often result in the boat going over. What will happen is that the onrushing external currents will catch either the front or back end of the boat and spin the boat to put it perpendicular to the oncoming current. The boat will then be moving downstream sideways. In this position the current will likely catch the top of the boat, pushing it downwards. This will expose even more of the top of the boat to the current, which will quickly serve to tip the boat over by forcing the bottom edge to pass underneath the top edge. To avoid this happening, the paddler must edge the boat in a manner that will expose the bottom of the boat to the oncoming current. The current will then simply push the boat in front of its movement without it tipping over.

The main reason that the boat won't tip in this second situation but will tip in the first case is that in the second case, the weight of the paddler will counteract the force from the current. This prohibits the bottom edge from spinning under the top edge, whereas in the first case it will reinforce this movement. The challenge is made more difficult in both severe rapids and rough surf by the fact that the currents constantly shift, requiring the paddler to continually readjust how the boat is edged.

Taken together, the kayak analogy gives us a slightly different conception of edging and hence edgework. While edging, strictly speaking, refers to the physical act of putting a boat on its edge, its function is normally to adjust to external currents. Doing so, or more accurately being in situations that require edging (namely turbulent waters), may in and of itself entail voluntary risk taking, even high-risk taking, but its essential function is quite different. It is not meant to increase risk, but is rather a technique for managing risk. In kayaking, these risks, especially the most dangerous ones, are generated by external, often conflicting and changing, currents. Moreover, given the nature of currents, they exist primarily below the surface, and hence, they are not easy to discern. Often, the only way you know what the water is doing is by feeling its influence on your boat. And even then, you may not feel what is happening until you experience your boat reacting to the particular way you edge it.

Reframed in this way, edging in kayaking clearly falls within the meaning of edgework developed by Lyng, insofar as it occurs in boundary situations. The current metaphor, however, also transforms the notion of edge from a static boundary location to one of a dynamic, often conflicting, interface of two processes. The edge here isn't a line where one domain ends and another begins, but rather an area where two are more domains overlap (Milovanovic, this volume).

This conception of a boundary area as constituted by overlapping domains clearly describes the situations within which most market traders work. As such, it also grasps much of what research on financial markets and market traders over the last four decades (Abolafia, 1996; Knorr-Cetina and Bruegger, 2000; Smith, 1981; 1999) reveals, most particularly the extent to which traders generally operate under conditions of ambiguity. Linking the notion of edgework to the managing of ambiguity, I would suggest, allows us not only to gain some new insights into such trading, but also to reach a deeper understanding of the inherently social nature of much edgework.

Propositions

Listed below are ten propositions that will be used to structure the rest of this chapter. While I believe each statement has wide applicability, I will limit most of my comments and examples to those drawn from my own research on financial and auction markets—and kayaking. The overlap and similarities of the list presented below with Lyng's (1990) account of edgework are quite striking:

1. Boundaries, or more precisely boundary areas, are commonly created by conflicting and ever-changing currents of various sorts.
2. Boundary areas are usually intimately related to more stable interior spaces.
3. Boundary situations entail various sorts of ambiguities and uncertainties.
4. Boundary areas tend to be quite turbulent.
5. Because of these uncertainties, boundary areas are experienced as a source of risk.
6. Boundary areas generally provide only liminal knowledge.
7. Liminal knowledge requires being engaged in the situation.
8. Market edgework requires specialized skills and techniques.
9. Controlling feelings in boundary situations generates its own particular "high."
10. Edgework is inherently social.

1. Market boundaries are due to cross currents

While the concept of a boundary generally conveys a highly static image, such as a national border, a property line, or the edge of a table, in kayaking and in most financial markets, a boundary connotes a much more dynamic image. It isn't an idealized line separating two spaces, but rather a loosely defined area where different, often conflicting forces come together. In kayaking, these forces are physical currents of water. In the stock market and other auction markets, these forces tend to be flows of information and buying and selling pressures. These flows are not constant but vary in their strength both over time and in different places.

While numerous factors contribute to these variations, the less defined and structured the situation, the more likely one is to confront conflicting currents. In the middle of a lake, one is much less likely to confront conflicting currents than when caught between two merging rivers in a location populated by numerous large boulders. Similarly, market situations subject to large and sudden changes in supply and demand, consumer tastes, or grading/classification categories exhibit stronger cross currents than do more stable markets. Just as high-risk kayakers seek out such boundary areas characterized by conflicting currents in which to paddle, so market traders seek out financial instruments subject to conflicting expectations and high volatility. For both the kayaker and the market trader, however, the objective is more complex than simply trying to stay afloat. Each seeks to profit from the flux to which they subject themselves. For the kayaker the reward is likely to be an exciting and challenging outing; for the trader it is the ability to latch onto a financial instrument of one sort or another that will either appreciate or depreciate in value more rapidly than most other financial instruments, enabling him or her to profit from the transaction. For the trader and the kayaker, it is the flux created by the cross currents that create such opportunities.

2. Market boundary areas by definition are linked to more stable interior spaces

While boundary areas are generally experienced as unstable, this instability is directly related to the fact that they are connected to more-stable areas. Boundary areas are unstable exactly because they are subject to conflicting pressures coming from two or more distinct, stable areas. In financial markets each of the numerous conflicting streams of information comes from a source where it is not only generated and nurtured, but where it also reigns supreme. Likewise, buying and selling pressures emerge from locations where one segment clearly dominates another. Without these sources, there would be no market currents. This of course is consistent with Lyng's (1990) observation regarding the extent to which edgework occurs on the boundary of order and chaos.

These streams need not always be in conflict. Fundamentalists, Insiders, and Chartists—three "ideal type" stock market actors whose market behavior is governed by one of the major stock market philosophies (Smith, 1981; 1999)—may all evaluate a particular stock quite similarly. Buying and selling forces may also be in balance so that the price of a stock is very likely to be quite stable. Just as buying and selling pressures do not always fluctuate in rhythm, however, so different market orientations do not always, or even normally, evaluate stocks similarly.

It is when such interpretations differ, and when buying and selling pressures gyrate, that the price of the stock is most apt to fluctuate dramatically. It is from these situations that market traders seek to profit by using their particular skills to determine which of the various currents is likely to dominate. Among other things, one must understand the nature and character of the various currents. This, in turn, requires grasping the essential principles and character of the various more-structured components of the market.

3. Market boundary situations entail ambiguities of various sorts

That boundary situations in general are likely to entail ambiguity is implicit in much that has already been said. Financial markets and market traders not only underscore this fact; they also give the relationship a more expansive meaning. In financial markets, uncertainty is not simply a product of the turbulence and cross-currents that exist; it is itself a root factor in generating this turbulence and cross currents. Just as rapids not only generate cross currents, but are also created by them, so market turbulence not only generates ambiguities and different evaluations, but it is also created by different evaluations and ambiguities. In most financial markets, ambiguity tends to be more the cause of turbulence than the reverse. The heavy reliance on auction formats testifies to this fact insofar as auctions are normally selected because of their ability to resolve allocation and pricing under conditions of high ambiguity (Smith, 1989).

While all financial markets tend to fluctuate, instances of extreme fluctuations nearly always occur when the market is subject to high degrees of uncertainty due to intense competition between and among different interpretive frameworks. This is not to deny that multiple frameworks are normally operative simultaneously within most markets (Smith 1981; 1999), including fairly placid markets. In such placid markets, however, each framework tends to have its own zone of jurisdiction. Boundary zones, consequently, tend to be quite narrow and have relatively little impact on the majority of market practices occurring within the various distinct sectors. It is when these boundary areas expand due to greater interpenetration of explanatory frameworks that boundary practices impact on the market as a whole in a significant way. Put slightly differently, the greater the confusion and uncertainty as to what is happening because multiple interpretive frameworks are operating simultaneously, the greater the fluctuations within the market.

4. Market boundary areas tend to be quite turbulent

It follows from the preceding section that boundary areas also tend to be turbulent. Why this should be the case in financial markets, however, isn't that apparent. To assert that conflicting water currents should create water turbulence is one thing. It is quite another thing to assert that conflicting financial judgments should generate market turbulence. Even in the most placid of markets, there need to be both buyers and sellers, which would seem to imply a need for some differences of opinion. Why, then, do conflicting evaluations generate market turbulence?

The brief answer is that it is not differences of opinion per se that generate market turbulence, but rather weakly held opinions that are subject to erratic and constant change. When evaluations differ, commodities will flow toward those who value them higher. This will lead to changes in both supply and demand, and also in future evaluations. All of this will require some degree of market activity, but this activity is likely to be experienced as ordered rather than as turbulent. When the evaluations not only differ from each other but also individually undergo significant and erratic change, however, the resulting market activity is seldom experienced as ordered.

Extreme market turbulence is not only the result of evaluations changing rather than merely being different, but is also due to the fact that market evaluations, whatever they might be, also tend to have direct behavioral consequences. In this respect, market currents function very much like water currents.

The central issue here relates to the dual functions of evaluation and meaning as both signifying and legitimating structures. While signification and legitimation are closely linked, they can and often do function independently (Giddens, 1984). More specifically, people can and do evaluate all sorts of things without necessarily acting on their evaluations. The fact that we perceive some item as being very under priced, for example, doesn't mean that we will rush out and buy it anymore than we will sell something we own or not buy something we need if we judge it to be overpriced. This, however, is exactly what professional market participants are meant to do. It is this causal relationship between judgments of market value and market action that makes markets respond so turbulently to market ambiguities.

5. Market boundaries are areas of high risk

Market boundary areas tend to be areas of high risk because of a number of distinct but related factors. First, as noted above, market evaluations have direct behavioral consequences. As opinions oscillate, so do market actions. Second, erratic market actions generate erratic prices for the stocks or other financial instruments involved. What creates the high risk of danger, however, is that these fluctuations tend not to be random. While ambiguity tends to be rampant in boundary areas, at any given moment one opinion or another is likely to reign supreme, if only for a short period of time. The reason for this is that the ambiguity serves to undermine held beliefs, leading to a situation in which players become highly susceptible to the opinions of those around them. This tendency to do what others around you seem to be doing generates a type of crowd behavior that in turn can generate extremely powerful market moves (Smith, 1981; 1999). What this means is that rather than having a situation where various different opinions coexist in approximately a set ratio to each other, one or another of these opinions is apt to catch fire and become dominant for a while only to be replaced shortly thereafter by another opinion.

The volatility and strength of these market oscillations can create significant market dangers for anyone caught in the wrong place. They can also provide opportunities for those who are able to master them. In this respect, market currents provide the same sorts of risks and rewards that powerful, fast moving water currents offer skilled kayakers. There are many market aphorisms that reflect the mixed strategies that are required in such situations, such as the following:

When in doubt, get out.
Don't fight the tape.
Go with the momentum.
Avoid the crowd.

6. Market boundary areas generally provide only liminal/threshold knowledge

With all of its ambiguity and turbulence, it isn't surprising that little is clear within market boundary areas. As in kayaking, whatever knowledge actors have tends to be liminal at best. It is not only that such knowledge is difficult to formulate and primarily tacit, but also that it is inherently incomplete and somewhat beyond one's grasp. The reasons for such liminal knowledge are also similar, namely that the forces at work tend to be below the surface. As a consequence, all that is often visible is the effect that they have on other things.

In financial markets, the most visible factor is normally the price of the instruments traded. Other factors seen to be directly related to such prices, such as market opinions of important players, consequential news, alternate investment choices, and a range of related technical data, are also considered to be visible. More accurately, such visible factors are seen to explain the perceived prices. However we formulate the relationship, there normally exists a body of knowledge, even if this knowledge tends to be post facto, that participants can and do draw upon to explain market behavior.

It is precisely the lack of such a body of knowledge that characterizes boundary areas in financial markets. As such, the task confronting anyone hoping to operate in these boundary areas with some degree of rationality is to construct or infer a workable account of what is observed. This is the particular skill that the successful market trader brings to the market. Where other market professionals tend to rely on a preformulated understanding of the market to guide them in their decision-making, successful traders bring an ability to recognize which of a plurality of different accounts is operative at any given moment. By and large, they are able to do this only by observing how particular markets react under changing conditions. In relatively stable markets, where ambiguity is modest, the trader's particular skills are of more limited value. In these more stable markets, professionals with well articulated accounts, even very different types of accounts, often can function quite well. In boundary areas, however, market traders come into their own.

7. Acquisition of liminal process knowledge requires being engaged in the situation

How does one acquire knowledge when knowledge is intrinsically liminal? Behaviorally. By this I mean that to acquire knowledge, one needs to be engaged in the process. There is nothing particularly surprising about this when we realize that most, if not all, liminal knowledge tends to be practical knowledge, and such knowledge is only acquired through practice. The patterns and relationships that one hopes to grasp can only, or at least primarily, be experienced. Like riding a bicycle or recognizing whooping cough, liminal knowledge requires encountering that which is to be known directly. As nearly every market trader I have interviewed over the years has told me, "You need to develop a 'feel' for the market." These are basically the same words that I have heard every kayak instructor give when asked "How far over should the kayak be edged?" "Until it feels right."

This need to become engaged in a particular practice to get a feel for the situation seems to be endemic to nearly all forms of edgework. The reasons for this, I would suggest, are that 1) edgework by definition occurs "on the edge;" what I have defined in this paper as boundary areas; 2) such areas are characterized by ambiguities of various sorts and turbulence, and are understood in a mostly liminal manner; and 3) such situations require one to be engaged in a manner that enables one to "feel" the situation in contrast merely to cognitively knowing it. In short, the highly affective aspect of edgework is not incidental to the experience. It is rather an essential aspect of such activity. Without it, it might be possible to operate on the edge or in boundary areas, but it wouldn't be edgework since one would be lacking the type of engagement and understanding that "work" of any sort entails. One might elect to call it edge-play, perhaps, but it would not be edgework.

8. Market edgework requires special skills and techniques

Like any type of work, market edgework demands particular skills and techniques. Some of these market skills and techniques were alluded to above: avoiding the crowd, not going against the tape, trying to ride market momentum, and not taking any action when unsure. Each of these practices requires a number of more refined skills. Most traders set firm limits, for example, as to the losses that they will tolerate, and once their limits are exceeded, they will close a position even if they still believe it will work out in the long run. Most traders similarly pay close attention to most sentiment indexes. To catch market momentum, they keep a close eye on new highs and new lows. Perhaps most important, however, they stay alert to any market behavior that seems unusual. It is here that liminal knowledge comes into play. If something is happening that doesn't make sense, then they assume that some factor presently not known is likely to be at work. It might be a stock acting better than expected, or worse than expected. It might be an unexpected announcement or an expected announcement that never occurs.

For most professional traders, these skills and techniques are more than a means to an end. Obviously, market traders, like all professional market players, want to make money in whatever markets they participate in. For traders, however, making money only counts in the long run. This means making money by following trader rules. Put slightly differently, only profits made by the rules count. Money made in any other way is dangerous because it serves to undermine the trader's reliance and commitment to the rules, and it is only by relying on these rules that the trader can hope to survive in the boundary area—on the edge—in the long term.

I clearly remember an experience nearly four decades ago when in the course of my research I apprenticed under a market trader. Having worked with this trader a number of years, I found myself operating on my own when he went on a two-week vacation. A few days after he left, I closed a position prematurely. The stock had risen faster than I had expected. Rather than going with the momentum, I had nervously sold and taken a profit. Almost immediately, I realized that I had made a mistake, but the stock had moved away from me, i.e., it had gone up too high, too quickly. I then made a second basic mistake. Off balance, I established a new position in another stock that I had been following, but which had not run away on me.

When my mentor returned, he was highly critical of my actions. Closing my first position was wrong, but not nearly as bad as taking the second position. My first mistake caused me to miss taking full advantage of an outstanding opportunity that I had been able to establish. My second mistake, however, had not only put me into a much poorer position, but had also prevented me from being able to reestablish my initial position when there would be a market correction, as there always is. I clearly remember, however, that he didn't really become concerned until I began to show a profit in my second position. When I pointed out to him a few weeks later that my second position was also showing a profit, even if one not as great as the first would have produced if I had been able to reestablish my initial position, he shook his head at me and said, "This could be real trouble. I hope this doesn't set a pattern. If it does, this is going to cost you a lot of money in the long run."

What this and similar experiences over the years taught me is that simply trading financial instruments doesn't make you a market trader. It isn't even making money in the process, per se, that makes you a market trader. To be a market trader you have to discipline yourself to follow the rules of the game no matter how much your instincts tell you to do something differently. In short, you may have to develop a feel for the market, but you can't be controlled by your feelings. Edgework in the market requires mastering your feelings or "emotion management" (Hochschild, 1983).

*9. Controlling one's feelings in boundary situations
generates its own particular "high"*

In describing edgework, Lyng notes the important role that subjects give to the sensations and emotions that they encounter. If my experience with market traders can be generalized, which I believe it can be, this relationship is more complex than is often noted. While participants in all sorts of edgework might note the associated feelings engendered, I suspect that in most cases it is not the feelings that are valued, but rather the ability to maintain mastery over these feelings. The stronger the feelings are, the greater the satisfaction in maintaining mastery. Edgeworkers, be they sky-divers or market traders, seek to enhance their feeling of risks not because they value such heightened feelings per se, but because mastering such feelings gives them a heightened sense of personal control.

This accurately describes the emotional satisfaction derived from successfully kayaking in severe rapids and currents. You are clearly aware that if you allow yourself to be overcome by the fear or thrill of being lifted and turned by the rushing water about you, you will likely loose your concentration and stop paddling and edging in response to the currents about you. The results will be an upended boat. It is only by remaining focused and acting as required that you will manage not only to stay afloat, but also to properly navigate the rapids or surf. It is the awareness that you are doing this through your control of your boat despite the adrenalin rushing through your body, not the fear or thrill felt in response to the movement of your boat, that produces the sense of elation. This can also be seen as generating the sense of "oneness" and reflecting the "mental toughness" that Lyng (1990) describes.

The elation and emotional appeal of edgework, I would suggest, is not due to experiencing the disorder and chaos inherent in boundary areas, though boundary areas clearly produce such feeling. The elation is rather due to the sense of agency one experiences by virtue of maintaining control over these feelings. This is certainly the dominant case with market traders. In short, it is not the experience of chaos that is sought but control. It is one's own control over a truly turbulent external force, however, not an external control operating over oneself.

10. Edgework is inherently social

One of Lyng's central theses is that edgework has a strong social component, or at the very least deserves a sociological understanding. My research of market traders not only supports this view, but also broadens it significantly. Lyng seeks to reveal the structural components that contribute to the pursuit of edgework. As noted earlier, he focuses upon the overly constraining character of modern society that drives many edgeworkers to the edge of our more orderly society to experience the greater freedom that they encounter on the edge.

If the activities of market traders can be generalized, however, there may be more to many forms of edgework than personal escape. Even the most ordered society contains disorders of various sorts, including not only political disorder but also normative disorder, and signification disorder. From a social constructionist perspective, the social world is ripe with ambiguities and contradictions. Moreover, from a social constructionist perspective, or Giddens' (1984) structuration double hermeneutic perspective, producing and reproducing social meanings is one of the basic activities, and perhaps the only basic activity, in which we are continually engaged. Within these frameworks, edgework of the type engaged in by market traders isn't socially peripheral, but rather central. Edgework entails coping with the continuing flow of ambiguities that a complex, heterogeneous society is constantly generating due to the many differences of signification and legitimation, to use Giddens (1984) nomenclatures, that abound in such societies. It may consequently be premature to assume that most edgework will occur in leisure activity, as suggested by Lyng. As a defining feature of the "risk society" (Beck, 1992), voluntary risk taking may be happening around us in our day-to-day lives to a much greater extent than we realize.

Concluding Comments

There remains the question why such edgework is more apparent in some situations, such as with financial market traders, than others. The answer to this question, I would suggest, is tied to the locations of the dominant social boundaries. More specifically, social edgework will be most common where different social worlds overlap. Historically, most such edgework was carried out by explorers, traveling merchants, missionaries, and foreign military expeditions. The nature of this edgework clearly varied considerably from one group to another, with most more interested in imposing their particular view on others rather than exploring differences and seeking to form agreement.

Markets represent a qualitative change in this dominate-or-be-dominated style. Markets by their very nature tend to thrive as a means for resolving definitional and interpretive differences (Smith, 2000). The function of markets is to manage changing flows of goods and services in a context of individual and cultural differences in preferences and tastes, which themselves are in flux. All of this, moreover, needs to be accomplished under the aegis of highly ambiguous ideological umbrellas of varying sorts. That there appears to be a symbiotic relationship between globalization and marketization, in short, should not come as a surprise. Markets have evolved as the allocative mechanisms of choice when there do not exist any established normative guidelines to determine price and ownership. This is one of the central implications of Polanyi's (1957) discussion of markets as compared to more traditional forms of allocation. Markets are the primary mechanism for allocating goods in a normatively heterogeneous (i.e., global) world. Insofar as this is the case, financial market traders may very well be just the vanguard of a whole new breed of edgeworkers, striving to profit from their ability to navigate in turbulent global currents likely to arise in the future.

Notes

1. See also Lyng (1993; 1998) and Lyng and Snow (1986).

2. Lyng also claims that most edgeworkers shy away from "pure gambles" (1990, p. 872).

3. Other behaviors, or more accurately some forms of other behaviors, generally considered risky may also lend themselves to this more encompassing framing. There are relatively safe ways to descend a ski slope rather than schussing down a double diamond. While white water kayaking is clearly a high risk activity, lake kayaking isn't. This raises the question, of course, as to whether these more placid activities should be considered edgework.

References

Abolafia, M. Y. "Hyper-Rational Gaming." *Journal of Contemporary Ethnography* 25 (2) (1996): 226–250.

Beck, U. *The Risk Society: Towards a New Modernity.* London: Sage, 1992.

Giddens, A. *The Constitution of Society: Outline of the Theory of Structuration.* Berkeley, CA: University of California Press, 1984.

Hochschild, A. *The Managed Heart: Commercialization of Human Feeling.* Berkeley, CA: University of California Press, 1983.

Knorr-Cetina, K. and Bruegger, U. "The Market as an Object of Attachment: Exploring Postsocial Relations in Financial Markets." *Canadian Journal of Sociology* 25 (2) (2000): 141–168.

Lyng, S. "Edgework: A Social Psychological Analysis of Voluntary Risk Taking." *American Journal of Sociology* 95 (1990): 851–886.

———. "Dysfunctional Risk Taking: Criminal Behavior as Edgework." In *Adolescent Risk Taking*, edited by N. J. Bell and R. W. Bell. Newbury Park, CA: Sage, 1993: 107–130.

———. "Dangerous Methods: Risk Taking and the Research Process." In *Ethnography at the Edge*, edited by J. Ferrell and M. S. Hamm. Boston, MA: Northeastern University Press, 1998: 221–251.

Lyng, S., and Snow, D. "Vocabularies of Motive and High-Risk Behavior: The Case of Skydiving." In *Advances in Group Process*, Volume 3, edited by E. J. Lawler. Greenwich, CT: JAI Press, 1986: 157–179.

Polanyi, K. "The Economy as Instituted Process." In *Trade and Market in the Early Empires*, edited by Karl Polanyi, Conral Arensberg, and Harry Pearson Glencoe, IL: Free Press, 1957.

Smith, C. W. *The Mind of the Market: A Study of Stock Market Philosophies, Their Uses, and Implications.* Totowa, N.J.: Rowman and Littlefield, 1981.

———. *Auctions: The Social Construction of Values.* New York: Free Press, 1989.

———. *Success and Survival on Wall Street: Understanding the Mind of the Market.* Lanham, MD: Rowman and Littlefield, 1999.

———. *Market Values in American Higher Education: The Pitfalls and Promises.* Lanham: Rowman and Littlefield, 2000.

Part VI
Historicizing Edgework

9

Edgework and Insurance in Risk Societies: Some Notes on Victorian Lawyers and Mountaineers

JONATHAN SIMON

CONTENTS

Introduction: Historicizing Edgework and Insurance

Stephen Lyng's 1990 essay on the social organization of voluntary risk takers introduced the concept of "edgework" to describe the labor of these risk takers. This intervention accomplished two important departures in the still emerging enterprise one might call the sociology of risk and insurance.[1] First, in defining edgework as a positive category of social behavior worthy of study with respect to its productive aspects for individuals and societies, Lyng broke with the long tradition in modern social science (other than economics) of treating risk primarily as a problem of loss to be managed. Even economics, with its valorization of risk taking in markets, has had little to say about risk takers who deliberately operate at the margins of social institutions (including markets), and has relegated this conduct to signaling a certain tolerance for risk. By introducing noneconomic gains produced by edgework, Lyng's account presents social science with a whole set of extreme recreation enthusiasts (drug users, mountaineers, and skydivers, among others) whose behavior not only expresses a preference for risk, but also involves mentalities, communities, and technologies for managing risk.

Second, in insisting that risk be analyzed in "the broader social historical context in which risk taking occurs," Lyng broke with the dominant tendency in economics, psychology, and some areas of sociology of treating risk taking as a largely cross-cultural universal phenomenon, to be understood institutionally rather than historically (Lyng, 1990, p. 854). Even some of the best work on risk taking in the sociological and anthropological traditions has treated risk as an oddly ahistorical category. For example, while Douglas and Wildavsky intend to open up a culturally sensitive model of risk selection in their influential 1982 monograph *Risk and Culture,* their model is ultimately rooted in organizational structures that may change historically but are not historically constituted in any deep sense. In a similar way Charles Perrow's (1987) powerful analysis in *Normal Accidents* locates the acceptability of risk in organizations.

In both regards we might want to look at edgework as a long-lost cousin of an institution only slightly better studied by social science, i.e., insurance. The voluntary assumption of risk is, after all, the essence of the insurance contract. While the acceptance of risk for "recreational" purposes may seem especially deviant or even criminal, it involves a heightened awareness of lurking dangers and a self-conscious assumption of risk that is also crucial to the insurance enterprise. From this perspective we might look at the relationship between edgework and insurance as highly variegated. In some social contexts they might appear to be radically different mechanisms, while in others their common features might come to the fore. Both edgework and insurance remain under studied even by those sociologists, political scientists, and economists that have begun to analyze risk (Baker and Simon, 2002).

The picture Lyng draws of edgework places it in stark contrast to insurance practices. Studying edgeworkers in the 1980s, Lyng suggests that edgework is often the "direct antithesis of role behavior in the institutional domain" (1990, p. 864). In edgework "spontaneity and impulse" dominate behavior, while in role enactment "constraint and normative control" are a central feature. Drawing on theoretical work in the traditions of George Herbert Mead and Karl Marx, Lyng's analysis of his own empirical work among edgeworkers suggested that enthusiasm for edgework was particularly strong among those with institutional routines characterized by a high "degree of alienation and over-socialization" (1990, p. 882). This is a position that characterizes many people at various levels in the class hierarchy (1990, p. 876), but Lyng acknowledged that this account was "specific to certain types of societies or groups in a given society" (1990, p. 879).

In retrospect we might look at the 1980s (notwithstanding the growing valorization of risk taking in the economic sphere) as the last edge of a long plateau of twentieth-century governance in which the predominant approach to handling risk was one of risk prevention through centralized expert regulation and collectivist loss spreading. In such societies with what me might call a "social" or "collectivist" approach to governing risk, public policies tend to emphasize loss spreading through insurance and risk reduction through centralized regulation.

In these societies, which favor insurance as a political technology, edgework is likely to be seen as at best abberant and at worst criminal behavior. The most visible gains from edgework are likely to be concentrated on the side of personal experience, skill, and pleasure. Institutions, to the extent that they do not actively seek to suppress edgework, are likely to ignore it and are unlikely to develop mechanisms for internalizing the potential social gains of edgework to the institution. Lyng's research subjects, often weekend extreme-sports enthusiasts, were operating within the still highly dominant (even if ideologically beleaguered) structures of social risk governance. For them, edgework's most significant social gain may have been to balance the alienating qualities of work within the safety nets of a society that still tried to temper capitalism with social risk governance and insurance.

The decade since Lyng's essay has seen an explosion of popular interest in edgework activities, marketed as extreme sports. The 1990s also witnessed a significant deepening of the restructuring of the American economy. For many workers the new economy has meant the jettisoning of old values like loyalty and stability in favor of increased competition and risk taking. It is not clear that the new demands on subjects are less alienating. Indeed, by redisciplining labor, neoliberal economic strategies seem likely to increase alienation. However, the logic of "oversocialization" described by twentieth century sociology presupposes institutions seeking to claim and control risk choices. In this regard, the social psychology of the mature industrial social order, which Mead so brilliantly analyzed, may be receding into the history of our culture.[2]

In such a context the rise in popularity of extreme sports takes on a broader significance. Debates about risk taking in and around these sports almost inevitably relate to the (often undebated) risk taking valorized by neoliberal technologies of governance. Some of these narratives treat mountaineering and other forms of edgework as a form of open nostalgia for Victorian-era capitalism, with few government restrictions on the economy and many depending on the decisions of a swashbuckling few—not, in light of recent economic news, an altogether inaccurate metaphor for our current posture.

Likewise many of the basic structures of insurance protection for the ordinary worker and consumer have changed profoundly over the last decade. In areas like pensions, health insurance, and job security, basic contracts now leave much of the risk in the hands of the ordinary worker or consumer. Even private insurance today increasingly leaves ordinary insurance consumers holding much of the goods.

At such moments the kind of binary opposition between edgework enthusiasm and institutional role that Lyng (1990) describes may remain descriptive of a social order that is undergoing change. As people find the skill of edgework—the negotiation of the boundary between chaos and order—directly relevant to problems of managing social and economic expectations, the role of edgework in producing social gains becomes as important or more important than the intrapsychic gains that Lyng describes in terms of skills and sensations. The opposition between institutional life and edgework collapses. Edgework is increasingly what institutions expect of many people.[3]

At times when institutional orders are being reshaped and renegotiated, the success of larger units—families, firms, communities, industries, and maybe nations as a whole—may depend in part on the prevalence of people in those settings with skills at managing the boundary of chaos and order. In an age of pushing responsibility for risk onto individuals, which advanced capitalist economies have increasingly embraced since the 1980s, the distinction between edgework and "center work" begins to blur.

In contrast to the recently dominant mode of risk governance through insurance, both Victorian England and late modern societies appear to be remarkably "undersocialized." New technologies and economic arrangements have disembedded individuals from many of the sources of collective normative order, maintenance, and trust, e.g., family, neighborhood, gender roles, and scientific authority.[4] Likewise the response of government is increasingly to single out selected individuals for harsh treatment in the name of deterrence and moral expressionism. In such an era, the special skills of edgeworkers, skills to cope with radical normative underdetermination[5] and their knowledge of how to respond rationally to risks without the shelter of comprehensive institutional risk-spreading systems, have enormous applicability.

In the remainder of this chapter I want to develop a thicker description of one example of edgework in a risk-management paradigm undeniably different from our own, whatever one takes our current position to be: the "golden age" of mountaineering in the Alps from the 1840s through the 1870s. "Alpinism" (as it was then called) flourished and drew wide public interest during the same period when England under Queen Victoria was experiencing the emergence of perhaps the first "risk society" in history (Beck, 1992). As the most advanced economic power of the nineteenth century, England experienced a growth in financial markets, insurance products, and industrial accidents that would eventually produce the risk society all over Europe, North America, Australia, and Asia in the twentieth century.

The popularity of Alpinism, I will argue, grew at least in part because it provided an imaginary space in which the emerging principles of Victorian risk governance could be projected, experimented with, and counternarrated.

London society, fully exposed to the risk society in the form of stock-market bubbles and motorized carnage (both caused by railways), was drawn, in fantasy and varying degrees of real tourism, to the Alps and the possibilities they offered of sublime—if dangerous—experiences.

At the center of this relationship between edgework and the Victorian risk paradigm was a rising class of professionals, who found themselves simultaneously key players in the administration of Victorian risk governance and largely exempted from its harsh rules of competition. A society governed by landed gentry was increasingly also governed by physicians, scientists, academics, clergy, and growing array of professionals. This was especially true of the legal profession, solicitors, who acted as personal counselors to businesses and families, conducted transactional legal matters, and when a question of litigation arose, arranged for representation of their clients by the barristers, the elite members of the bar who held (and still hold) a monopoly on arguing in the courts of England and historically provided a large portion of the judges, parliament members, and other governing agents of England.

The Alpine Club of London, one of the earliest organizations for the promotion of edgework to emerge, was founded in 1857 and within five years had 281 members. Barristers, solicitors, clergy, and university dons made up nearly half of the entire club, and landed gentry another six percent (Fleming, 2000, p. 172). Nearly half were individuals who lacked both landed wealth and professional privilege. This group would have included illustrators and artists like Edward Whymper, who in 1865 would climb the Matterhorn in a widely covered and tragic climb that marked the emergence of Alpinism as a spectacle for debate among an increasingly media-linked European public.

These presumably more economically insecure workers seem a more surprising element of the Alpine Club than the majority, composed of professionals and landed gentry who enjoyed protected markets, high salaries, and opportunities for substantial vacations. Less clear is why professionals were drawn to the edgework side of the growing Victorian vacation industry that had made all levels of tourism possible in the Alps by the 1850s (Ring, 2000). Particularly interesting in this regard is the prominence, even among these professionals, of barristers. Members of the legal profession made up over a third of the Club's membership in 1863[6], and nearly a quarter were drawn from the class of barristers who enjoyed the greatest access to political and judicial power (Fleming, 2000, p. 172). The fifty-seven barristers who were members of the Alpine Club at its founding constituted fully 1.3 percent of the entire bar of England and Wales.[7]

I can only offer here a preliminary proposition, subject to much further assessment against the historical record, that mountaineering played a productive role in the formation of a rational system of risk management for Victorian society, and thus in a central way of Victorian liberalism itself. First, mountaineering offered professionals a practical way to engage in the embrace of risk being imposed by Victorian law on less credentialed workers and small investors, and which their own work life sheltered them from. This substitute risk was plausibly manageable and could be entertained without interrupting the close personal attention to one's clients that also defined these professions.

Second, even though professionals enjoyed the protection of legal barriers to entrance into the professions, they still faced competition with others inside the ranks who shared the major educational requirements of the profession. Professionals, especially barristers, increasingly relied on their reputation for personal judgment and integrity to undertake this kind of competition. Conquering Alpine peaks with its implicit and (often loudly) explicit narratives of courage and skill in the face of great exposure to catastrophic risk provided credible evidence of such personal traits, and thus constituted real social capital to these professionals.

Edgework and Victorian Risk Society

Since its emergence in the eighteenth and nineteenth centuries, the risk society has been dynamic, producing fundamental changes in the paradigm through which risk is governed. The relationship of edgework to insurance and other risk-management institutions of society changes with these paradigm shifts. The first self-conscious risk society arose in Victorian England when concentrations of industrialization, financial markets, and insurance markets combined to bring risk into wide public consciousness and to compel the state and legal system to address the creation and distribution of risk as a subject of public policy. The Victorian paradigm of risk emphasized individual responsibility for controlling and living with risk even while it forged some of the first mechanisms for spreading risk (Tomlins, 1993). A comparable spirit shaped the French Civil Code in the nineteenth century (Ewald, 2002, p. 276).

The Victorian paradigm, with its emphasis on responsibility, gave way in the last third of the nineteenth century to a new paradigm of socializing risk through widespread insurance. The problem of work accidents was the central arena in which battles over the adequacy of the Victorian regime would be fought and the rise of workers' compensation across Europe and eventually England and the United States marked the triumph of the general strategy of lifting risk. From Bismarck to Nixon, the leaders of advanced capitalist economies offered a domestic vision that could be fairly summarized as "more insurance for more people."

In recent work, Tom Baker and I have argued that the turn of the twenty-first century corresponded to a shift in the axis of risk as a problem for state and for society (2002). The basic structures that have managed risk in industrializing societies—insurance, central bank management of the economy, Keynesian fiscal stimulus, pensions, and health insurance—have been dramatically restructured since the 1980s. Along with that restructuring, there has been an expectation that state and corporate leaders would maintain a constant floor for the working populations of advanced capitalist societies.

Whether it's managing your 401(k) or calling specialists in your provider network to find one willing to schedule you, affluent members of wealthy Western nations (especially the United States) have increasingly been assigned new risk management responsibilities. These responsibilities had once been assigned to large institutions by a nearly unanimous consensus on the proper governance of risk from the Great Depression of the 1930s to the rise of neoliberal market-based policies in the 1980s. The breakup of large social systems for aggregating and managing risk (call it the "general welfare state")[8] has been accomplished in a strikingly wide variety of ways, from antitrust law on the one hand (e.g., the breakup of the Bell system) to "tort" reform designed to protect manufacturers from liability in catastrophic individual accidents. The common result, however, is to raise the exposure of individuals and families, not to primary risks themselves—the middle-class at least remains "covered" by a variety of insurance and insurance-like resources (e.g., HMOs)—but to the risk of (mis)managing that risk.[9]

The relationship of edgework to the other economic and social roles changes as the paradigm of risk control shifts. In times when bureaucratic institutions control a great deal of how risks are managed, these experiences may be channeled largely in the service of "self-fashioning" or shaping an identity ("I'm a plumber who's also a skydiver") or in helping to produce spiritual and sometimes social capital for some and simply ecstatic experience for others. Lyng's empirical work with edgeworkers, conducted in the 1980s, reflects the continued dominance of this paradigm even as it was beginning to be discredited at the political level by the neoliberal policies of leaders like Ronald Reagan in the United States and Margaret Thatcher in the United Kingdom.

Law and the Victorian Risk Society

The general features that accompany the rise of risk in a society have been cataloged by recent scholarship (Ewald, 1986; Porter, 1986; Simon, 1987; Kruger, Daston, and Heidelberger, 1987; Hacking, 1990). A critical role was played by the growing accumulation of official numbers (or statistics) describing general social features and conditions and advances in probability theory that allowed these numbers to be described in normative terms (Hacking, 1990). Social problems like crime and suicide, long described in terms of the social character of the classes involved, could now be talked about in terms of the dynamics of populations whose undesirable behaviors could be objectified as risks capable of being increased or diminished by various efforts to intervene in the social conditions of these classes. Risk was also popularized by the creation of sophisticated financial institutions intended to standardize and distribute risks, like insurance companies and limited-liability corporations. Finally, the dramatic rise of accidental injuries and deaths associated with industrialization and advanced technological systems like railroads and later automobiles compelled ordinary members of the working and middle classes to consider their own health and mortality as problems of family provision.

All of these ingredients came together, perhaps for the first time, in England during the middle of the nineteenth century. While other societies in Europe and North America were not far behind, Victorian England was the first society to begin to conceptualize the governance of risk as a problem for both state and private institutions. Law and lawyers played an especially dominant role in this process in England due to the political and economic prominence of the legal profession, a role that has been reproduced to lesser degrees in other societies (Sugarman, 1993). Victorian law concerning areas like the formation and liability of corporations, the liability of employers for the deaths and injuries of workers and others, and the issuance of contracts for insurance jointly constituted the first historical regime of risk governance.[10]

Victorian England between the 1840s and 1870s was the most advanced industrial and capitalist society in the world and was also the first to confront the political question of the enormous risks of industrial capitalism. The dominant Victorian responses (nuanced by succeeding Conservative and Whig or Liberal governments dominated by two of the century's outstanding politicians, Benjamin Disraeli and William Gladstone) represented the high point of a regime of risk governance that emphasized individual responsibility for handling risk (Ewald, 2002; O'Malley, 2002). Rapid industrialization was exposing English workers and urban dwellers to high levels of death and injury in industrial and railway accidents. At the same time, the popularization of financial capitalism, primarily through offerings of shares in joint-stock railway companies to the public, exposed a wide variety of people to economic losses through boom/bust cycles that were particularly harsh on inexperienced investors.

Law emphasized contract as the proper means for distributing the risks of industrial life. Victorian legal precedent held the worker to have accepted the ordinary risks of the work and a salary reflecting the market value of that risk. Courts were especially anxious to dispel the idea that employers act as insurers for their employees or for ordinary citizens who simply have the misfortune to encounter their dangerous instrumentalities. Instead people should manage their own risk, including through the purchase of private insurance contracts, an activity already heartily embraced by English business and law but largely out of the reach of the working classes.

By the end of this period, in the 1870s, proposals to rearrange the management of risk to reflect new values of solidarity and collective management were being debated across Europe. Both Germany and France moved toward revision of employers' liability laws in favor of workers' compensation insurance systems. This approach, emphasizing the social as the locus of risk spreading and regulation, dominated risk management in the twentieth century. Victorian Britain remained mistrustful of efforts to spread risk across all of society, especially through the state. Heavily influenced by the "social Darwinism" of Victorian social scientists like Herbert Spencer and Francis Galton, law and public policy emphasized an individual's responsibility for actions in a competitive world on the grounds that state-sponsored plans compromised individual freedom and ultimately the evolutionary dynamics that produced a more civilized society.

Victorian lawyers created an influential model for governing the risks of capitalist society whose central tendency was to leave losses where they fell, at least for those defined as part of an adventuring producer class (Fine, 1954). This governance strategy of minimizing interference with direct risk allocation between "contracting" parties (be they investors and corporate management or workers) came to be known through slogans like "laissez-faire" and "liberty of contract," especially to the progressive critics of this model, who championed greater efforts at regulation and insurance to reduce losses and redistribute their burdens. Yet while lawyers were the dominant figures in constructing this Victorian risk society, they constructed for themselves a much different model of risk management aimed at sheltering the legal profession from open market competition. The legal profession produced a relatively lucrative monopoly by putting up strong barriers to competition and using academic requirements to ensure both a reduced pool of legal professionals and a more docile one (Abel, 1988; Osiel, 1990). Other producers in this period came to adopt this professional model , including academics, scientists, the clergy, and medical providers.

Professionals in general and legal professionals in particular stood in a paradoxical relationship to the growing self-consciousness about risk that characterizes a risk society (including the Victorian one as an early example). On the one hand their status was increasingly tied to their ability to help businesses, and private families with wealth, to manage risk. At the same time they were increasingly successful in securing their own economic position by controlling access to participation in their fields through the establishment of educational requirements and institutional processes of selection. The rising social concern about risk in Victorian society made these professionals more and more influential articulators of how risk should be managed even as their professional status protected them from competition.

While a sophisticated body of sociology and history of Victorian law and legal professionals now exists, an effort to trace out the role they played in making risk a problem and in constructing the dominant liberal response to management of risk in this period has not been undertaken to my knowledge. While the present chapter does not count as even a preliminary step toward this goal, it does draw on the existing literature to identify the role of law and lawyers in shaping some of the major frameworks through which Victorian society began to confront itself as a risk society.

Railroads were the most dynamic force in the early phase of Victorian capitalism and consequently were at the leading edge of law to define the emerging risk society. The recent scholarship of R. W. Kostal (1994) on law and "English railway capitalism" suggests that railway law and lawyers played a distinctive role in shaping the Victorian approach to governing risk, both in terms of the corporate structure of the railway company and in the different ways of assigning liability for accidental injuries and deaths caused by the negligence of the company's employees.

Investment Risk

One of the most visible, and at times most influential, sources of risk in modern society is the financial markets. The cycle of booms and busts in markets for shares in corporations has been a privileged point within the broader financial sectors. This is seen in the enduring enthusiasm and repeated panics associated with English railways between the 1820s and the 1850s (Kostal, 1994, p. 12). In a real sense the rise of railway joint stock companies, starting in the 1830s, constituted the world's first truly popular market in corporate equity. Operating with little or no statutory law, English railway capitalists developed a system of subscription investment instruments with the feature that they committed the investor to a series of further investments at the election of the company. During this period, railway shares were advertised in newspapers, and the relatively poor and the relatively rich were drawn into a variety of markets for shares. Booms and busts occurred, although at a more modest level than in later times (Kostal, 1994, p. 32).

As popular interest in railway shares ballooned, the boom-and-bust cycle produced aggrieved losers. A parliamentary committee under future prime minister and liberal party leader William Gladstone drafted a Joint Stock Company Act that regulated share marketing for the first time. Gladstone strove to produce a limited form of government intervention that would provide light correction without interfering with contracting liberty.[11] The law emphasized disclosure by requiring two stages of registration. To obtain a preliminary recognition of a legal status as a joint-stock company, railway companies had to reveal who was involved and a detailed description of the proposed enterprise. To obtain full authorization, joint-stock companies would also have to register information about actual capitalization (Kostal, 1994, pp. 25–26).

Gladstone, then a progressive Tory under Peele, would become prime minister himself as a liberal. He was one of chief architects of the Victorian effort to govern the burgeoning capitalist economy and its risks with a minimal amount of state intervention and maximum reliance on the capacity of individuals to protect themselves through access to information. The Joint Stock Company Act of 1844 arose from this kind of analysis. Gladstone saw repeated cycles of booms and busts by railway stock companies as arising from insufficient accountability on the part of promoters. The Act required promoters to register themselves and their business partners with the government, and to provide written financial plans for their proposed ventures available for inspection by investors (Kostal, 1994, p. 25).

Within a few years it become obvious that the law was having a very different effect. Many new joint-stock companies were being set up and the market for shares was growing even more frenzied. The bubble burst in late 1845 and early 1846, leading to one of the worst financial panics in the Victorian period.[12] The law appears to have done little to dampen speculation or improve the rationality of stock-share purchases. Although by registering, individuals rendered themselves subject to fines for failures of disclosure, the fines were too low and the potential profits of stock sales too high (Kostal, 1994, p. 26).

The Joint Stock Company Act may have made things worse by creating the impression of governmental regulation and thus of legitimacy for those firms which had complied enough with the reporting requirements of the Act to receive their provisional authorization to issue stock shares. Perhaps the greatest effect of the Act was actually to create opportunities for lawyers. The law created a complicated legal regime that share-issuing companies needed to follow. Lawyers, either alone or in partnership with others, soon emerged as the most common background of promoters.

When the bubble burst, the number of companies promoted by lawyers, as opposed to those with an involvement in railways, skyrocketed. Thus the legalization of joint-stock share offerings became yet another form of protection for lawyers, bringing a large market into the reach of legal expertise. In the estimation of Kostal, "it is not surprising then, that attorneys and solicitors became recognized as *the* masters of the Joint Stock railway swindle" (1994, p. 32).[13] Between earning the legal fees for guiding others through the registration procedures, or doing it themselves and earning the high profits of early insiders, legal professionals were the chief beneficiaries of the law. "Lawyers were admirably placed to register new companies, create scrip, pocket share deposits, and rig share markets with little risk to themselves" (Kostal, 1994, p. 47).

Intended to protect investors against the new kinds of risk associated with modern financial instruments, the Joint Stock Company Act actually operated to generate business for lawyers. Indeed, by giving an organizational advantage to lawyers over others with more expertise in the substantive business of organizing and running railways, the Act "blurred the distinction between genuine enterprise and gambling speculations" (Kostal, 1994, p. 51). The panic it engendered in railway shares led to a larger depression in 1847 and probably distorted the development of English railways by wasting a good deal of investment capital and keeping much more tied up in the complex wreckage of fraudulent or misguided joint stock companies (again to the advantage of solicitors and barristers who were employed to disentangle the mess).

Railway Accidents

The rise of popular markets for joint-stock company shares epitomized one dimension of the new risk society that was emerging in Victorian England. Investors were supposed to be the kind of people who lived by objectifying and managing risk. The Joint Stock Company Act of 1844 was intended to facilitate that objectification by creating a paper trail of promoters and plans. Instead it ended up escalating the speculative nature of risk in a way that empowered professionals (here barristers) to the disadvantage of almost everyone else.

The growing toll of industrial accidents was the other dimension in which the risk society was emerging in Victorian England. Here again, the railway companies dominated the early landscape. Railway labor involved numerous opportunities for injury and death, and it exposed workers to a dependence on the degree of care taken by colleagues. Even more than factory industries, the railways also brought carnage and mayhem directly to the general public through the frighteningly common incidents of railway accidents.

This publicity and public concern was epitomized by the Pym case of 1861. In 1860, Francis Pym, a forty-one-year-old married father of nine, was killed in a derailment. The effect of his will was to leave virtually all of his considerable fortune to his eldest son, leaving the widow and other eight children with virtually no income. Because Lord Campbell's Act was interpreted by the courts as permitting recovery for all proven economic costs, the railway was ultimately held responsible for a verdict of over 13,000 pounds, a huge amount for the time. (Kostal, 1994 estimates the yearly salary of a railway worker in those years as 52 pounds.)

While railway worker injuries were confined to the working classes, passenger and passerby injuries crossed class lines to strike at middle-class and aristocratic families. Indeed, one of the features that define a risk society is when risk outstrips class privilege (Beck, 1991). The new fear of railway accident risks reached the highest levels of Victorian society. Queen Victoria herself wrote to then–Prime Minister Gladstone (who earlier had been the chief author of the Joint Stock Company Act of 1844) complaining about the dangers on the railways:

> A subject which demands the most serious attention to the Government is the very alarming and increasing insecurity of the Railroads... In no country accept ours are there so many dreadful accidents ... the Queen's own family, not to mention her servants and visitors are in perpetual danger (quoted in Kostal, 1994, p. 311, note 373).

Prompted by litigation over railroad accidents, the law drew a stark divide between financial liability for injured or killed workers and that for injured or killed passengers (or passers-by). In both cases, accidents were caused by a combination of new technology and the error of railroad employees. But in the case of injured workers, the courts declined to hold railroad companies liable for the errors of their servants committed in the course of service, leaving the victim to sue the surely judgment-proof fellow servant. In the case of passengers, the courts embraced to a generous extent, with some dissents, the seemingly unliberal doctrine of *respondeat superior,* or vicarious liability (Kostal, 1994, p. 256).

In 1846, Parliament went a step further and created a statutory cause of action for injured passengers. Lord Campbell's Act overturned a number of doctrines created by judges that had limited the liability of companies. The right to sue for personal injury was deemed personal and thus unavailable to the dead. By extending to survivors in the immediate family the right to sue the railroad for wrongful death, the Act rapidly generated the potential for enormous losses to be passed on to the railroad companies (Kostal, 1994, p. 289). The litigation opened by Lord Campbell's Act and the carnage of the railroads in the 1850s pushed the legal system into deciding the value of a human life for the first time (Kostal, 1994, p. 292). It also made litigation one of the chief financial issues facing railroads and a source of potentially calamitous risk for the business (Kostal, 1994, p. 294). In short, perhaps for the first time, litigation became a new form of risk for companies to plan around and to seek to manage.

As seen in the Pym case, the courts allowed juries to compensate victims for real economic losses that varied with the income capacity of the deceased or injured, escalating the growing wealth gap between rich and poor in the Victorian period. Railway workers, in contrast, were perceived as voluntary risk takers. *Priestley v. Fowler*, a case from 1837 involving an accident on a horse-drawn cart, held that a worker injured by the negligence of his fellow servant could not sue the owner of the van unless the heedless actions were taken at the direct order of the owner. Although largely ignored because at the time few personal injury cases were reported, Priestley came in the 1850s to be canonized as a significant precedent establishing the fellow-servant rule. In the 1850s, English High Courts adopted what Kostal describes as the most expansive reading of that doctrine in the common-law world (1994, p. 271). The House of Lords ratified this direction in 1858.

The regime of railway accident law thus opened a somewhat different circuit of Victorian risk management from that responding to stock speculation. The law, shaped by English lawyers and judges, imagined two very different subject positions that needed to be governed. There were adventurer/producers, a class consisting of the entrepreneurs and their employees. This class needed to be governed mainly to provide incentives to protect passengers and passersby, but its own injuries were deemed to be settled by the contract of employment. The second class consisted of passengers/consumers, who, although they voluntarily placed themselves on a technology known to be new and dangerous, nonetheless were protected against any negligence by the producers.

The Professions

In the nineteenth century, English lawyers and judges played a crucial role in fashioning an English approach to the problem of risk in industrial capitalism. The regime of risk governance they created was to grant to market competition a dominant role in allocating risks. The reform elements of the law focused heavily on correcting market failures through better flow of information and on protecting certain victims who were largely beyond contractual methods of allocating risk. At the same time, they built for themselves a system of controlled competition that placed heavy barriers on those seeking to offer legal services as solicitors or barristers (professions that were gateways to political and business careers).

The major vehicles introduced in the nineteenth century for controlling entry into professions involved educational and examination requirements. These replaced earlier guild-like barriers to entry into certain fields that were based on what appeared, to modern eyes, to be irrational or purely tradition based. This shift has been interpreted in Weberian terms to reflect the rise of rational bureaucratic forms of domination and a concomitant increase in the demands of public discourse for rationality. In Marxist terms, it reflects an intensification of competition and class stratification under capitalism (Abel, 1988, Osiel, 1990, p. 2010). It is not inconsistent with both to see the emerging consciousness of risk and the need to manage it as a distinct pressure to increase educational qualifications of the legal profession.

This professional model, a kind of privileged-minority regime of risk management, was readily extendable to other professionals, such as physicians, academics, and scientists, but the legal profession enjoyed the strongest protections. Barristers were the paradigm of a protected profession. Before the end of the eighteenth century, the bar was largely limited to individuals with aristocratic titles. By the nineteenth century, and earlier than other professions, the bar was dominated by a new middle class of well-educated families that had the financial resources to pay for expensive educations but lacked noble status (Abel, 1988, p. 203).

Notwithstanding its opening to the middle classes, the bar was hardly thrown open to competition by anyone. Only individuals "called to the bar" were permitted to appear before higher English courts on behalf of litigants. Constructed out of a number of specific legal categories in the nineteenth century, membership in the bar was limited to those who had completed their studies in one of a small number of "Inns of the Court." Once law schools, by the nineteenth century these institutions had become largely gentlemen's clubs, dominated by members of the bar but utilized by many London business people for their inexpensive rooms and dining facilities. Although they did not provide education in the law, the Inns allowed senior members of the bar to determine the educational qualifications of those seeking admission to the bar (Abel, 1988, p. 40). The Inns typically required an applicant to have had an English public school education followed by university study (if not matriculation). Needless to say, these educational pathways were themselves quite limited to those of considerable means.

In 1872 a mandatory exam was instituted on top of the Inns that dealt not with law but with knowledge of history and language. Nonetheless, most students could pass these exams with help from private tutors and commercial preparation courses. By controlling admission to the Inns, the bar successfully kept its membership between 3000 and 4000 members from 1850 to 1950 (Abel, 1988, pp. 482–483).

While entry barriers sheltered members of the bar from unlimited competition, the life course of a young barrister was not necessarily assured. Daniel Duman suggests that for a golden few, the bar was a "ladder of preferment" whereby well-qualified individuals moved easily, once called to the bar, into a thriving practice of briefs (perhaps after working for a well-known barrister or working as a clerk for a firm of solicitors), and then began looking for political positions as a judge, member of parliament, or government agent. For many others the reality was more like a tree with "a few intertwining branches that reached upward and many that went nowhere …" (Duman, 1983, p. 94).

Barristers were not permitted to provide their services directly to the public. Instead they were limited to accepting briefs from solicitors who were the primary providers of legal advice to the public and who in turn briefed barristers when their clients needed to go to court. Because solicitors kept their clients happy by selecting barristers who could win in court, or at least seemed to be able to give the case its best shot, those barristers with the greatest reputation for success were in the greatest demand. Young and unknown barristers could make a living in a variety of ways while waiting for their reputation to grow. One was to seek work on the circuit, i.e., during court sittings scheduled for towns outside London. During the nineteenth century these circuit sittings were limited to times when the London courts were closed, permitting both veteran and novice barristers to keep their London business while seeking additional work elsewhere. One could also move to the colonies, where barristers were in short supply. Finally, one could work as a "devil," the term used for barristers who were hired on contract to help another barrister who had more business than he could handle.

The enviability of the situation of the professional in Victorian England compared to that of to other economic actors, especially industrial workers and small investors who lacked great inherited wealth or noble title, becomes clear when we compare their exposure to the forms of risk that were becoming major public concerns in the nineteenth century. Professionals did not experience the heavy financial and physical risks of industrialization and the railways. If they were injured in a railway accident, they stood, like other passengers, to benefit from Lord Campbell's Act of 1846. Professionals were also protected from the high risks involved in all forms of financial investments during the Victorian period. Indeed, as we have seen, the main law intended to protect the investing public, the Joint Stock Company Act of 1844, actually served to expand economic opportunities for lawyers as organizers or consultants to organizers of both good faith and fraudulent joint-stock railway companies. In both regards, professionals held a form of social capital that Victorian risk governance made more valuable and more secure.

Alpine Adventure as Social Capital for the Victorian Professional Classes

Writing at the end of the nineteenth century, Francis Galton, prototypical Victorian thinker, father of eugenics, and one of the most important general theorists of what sociologists now call the "risk society" (Beck, 1992), drew an interesting metaphor in criticizing contemporary statistical science for its focus on "normal" distribution and averages.

> It is difficult to understand why statisticians commonly limit their inquiries to Averages, and do not revel in more comprehensive views. Their souls seems as dull to the charm of variety as that of the native one of our flat English counties, whose retrospect of Switzerland was that, if its mountains could be thrown into its lakes, two nuisances would be got rid of at once (quoted in Forrest, 1974, p. 1992).

Galton's reference to Switzerland still serves its point more than a century later, highlighting how great peaks and deep trenches in all sorts of social phenomena might be hidden by talk of averages. Galton was so enamored of probability theory that he confessed to seeing little normal distributions sprouting around him anywhere he looked. He dreamed of a society improved through discouragement of the reproduction of the defective and encouragement of the reproduction of the best, a society that would be all peaks and no lakes.

Yet the appearance of Switzerland and its lakes and mountains in the midst of Galton's discourse on statistics would have carried much more nuanced tones to the late Victorian public. Starting in the 1850s, Switzerland became something of an obsession for the burgeoning middle classes of England. A century of romantic arts had already remade mountains as dazzling exemplars of the sublime (Nicholson, 1959), and with the advent of commercial tourism and rail lines throughout Europe, thousands of British citizens spent their vacation days and savings obtaining views of the Alps in France, Italy, and above all Switzerland.[14] More adventuresome visitors could hire a guide to take them for a careful walk upon glacier surfaces like the famous *Mer de Glace* in Chamonix, France.

A still more selective group of Victorian visitors sought to climb the peaks themselves, with the uneasy cooperation and sometimes competition of the local guides. The numbers who climbed the peaks were tiny compared to the growing number of British tourists to Switzerland, but the growing newspaper-reading public in England and on the Continent were thrilled by their exploits. In 1857, the Alpine Club was founded in London with a seasonal outpost in Zermatt, Switzerland, to promote public knowledge of and appreciation of Alpine mountaineering (Fleming, 2000, p. 207). The Club's first publication, *Peaks, Passes, and Glaciers* (1857), generated extraordinary interest in the reading public. The essays were quite different from the already popular genre of Romantic mountain scenes in poetry and prose. Instead of giving lush descriptions of mountain scenery, the writing was pragmatic, aimed at guiding the potential visitor and interspersed with understated descriptions of dangerous portions that were so gripping as to require virtually no artistry by the writer (Willen, 1995, p. 20). The volume was an enormous success in England and Europe, leading to a second volume in 1859 and eventually to a permanent annual under the title of the *Alpine Journal*.

The attraction of Alpinism to Victorian professionals has usually been credited to the relative opportunity available. By 1860 the growing tourism industry had made travel to the Alps from London easy, and professionals enjoyed relatively greater autonomy over their time than workers or entrepreneurs. Such accounts to not provide a historical understanding of the class specific appeals of edgework to Victorian professionals and especially members of the legal profession. Here we can only offer some speculative interpretations on the connection between Victorian risk governance and Alpine mountaineering.

The cultural success of Victorian edgework, evidenced by the founding and growth of the Alpine Club, was anchored primarily in the political and sometimes economic importance of the professional classes in Victorian society. In the twentieth century, the rise of professionals would be associated with the growth of a paternalistic welfare state. Professionals served a different function in the largely unmediated capitalism unfolding in Victorian England. Instead of playing a direct role in governing, as the professional class would in the welfare state, Victorian professionals helped support the legitimacy of a new order that exposed ordinary people to increased personal risk. Legal professionals were clearly the most important in this regard, playing a direct role in crafting the doctrines and negotiating the contracts that structured Victorian risk relations. University dons and prominent doctors also lent their scientific authority in justifying the growing risks that the new economy placed on ordinary people.

Victorian law placed on workers and small investors extraordinary risks associated with death and maiming in industrial occupations and the volatile nature of the nineteenth-century market in equities. Whatever their economic condition, which varied, professionals were characterized as being sheltered from both physical risk and the risk of having one's working capital lost in a volatile market. Alpinism permitted Victorian professionals to document their own willingness to be exposed to mortal risks in the most concrete possible way. The Alpine Club and its journal, as well as the larger newspaper and publishing interest in mountain narratives, provided a powerful machinery to carry the exploits of these peril-seeking professionals to the mass public.

The pragmatic ethos that characterized most of the writing in *Peaks, Passes, and Glaciers* provided an idealized parallel to the legal world of the factory, where the ordinary worker was presumed to be perfectly capable of avoiding accidents through greater levels of care. What could better reflect the necessity of personal caution than making one's way along narrow ridges where one misstep could prove fatal, not only to the climber but to those roped to him?

The Alps thus provided a kind of twisted mirror of the emerging English risk society. Here gentlemen and well-educated professionals competed to take outrageous risk in pursuit of nothing more than sublime views and bragging rights. But as is true for the current generation of professionals attracted to mountaineering, the message of self sufficiency and risk taking was complicated by the heavy reliance of Victorian Alpinists on local guides to find their path and protect them from perils. Indeed one of the most extraordinary features of Alpinism for Victorian professionals was the degree to which it made them subordinate, at least on the mountains themselves, to guides who were far lower in terms of traditional class status than the British workers whose fates they often determined.

Victorian professionals had another reason to pursue a reputation on the peaks. The protection of professionals from open competition was tied to claims about professional prowess that were inherently unstable. Competition for the best clients and most lucrative cases was largely won by reputation. Since the clients of professionals like barristers or surgeons often achieved poor results, professional reputation was only partially related to objective outcome figures and depended also on readily visible signs of the kinds of virtuosity supposed to be central to professional excellence.

This was especially true of barristers, perhaps the oldest of all English professions and the one with the greatest influence on the legal management of risk in Victorian England. The rise of Victorian Alpinism in the middle third of the nineteenth century corresponds to a period when the bar was becoming increasingly competitive and business oriented. Nearly four out of five men called to the bar in a typical Inn of the Court during the seventeenth century came from the upper ranks of the landed classes (Prest, 1986, p. 87). Most of these upper-class barristers had little interest in practicing law. For them the prestige of the bar lent some weight to a life of leisure, gave them some practical knowledge toward managing their estates, and helped advance them toward roles in local administration of justice as justices of the peace (Duman, 1983, p. 85).

In the nineteenth century, the membership of the bar grew and became less rooted in the landed gentry, and these new barristers were far more likely to practice. Between 1590 and 1630, about 18 percent of the students passing through the Inns of the Court[15] were intent on actually practicing law, and by the 1850s the proportion was 50 percent (Duman, 1983, p. 27). These practicing barristers faced stiff competition and limited prospects for significant income in their early years. Indeed, from the 1830s through the 1850s, the economic viability of barristers declined, as marked by a reversal of earlier growth in admissions. From a high of nearly 360 new members of the bar in 1837, admissions declined to 140 in 1855 before beginning to climb again (Duman, 1983, p. 3).

Barristers were also unique in their conditions of competition. No other profession was as unregulated by the state. For much of the nineteenth century the field lacked agreed-upon educational standards and had limited means of professional discipline. These conditions were tolerable largely because the ordinary citizen was not expected to choose a barrister, who was hired instead by a solicitor acting on behalf of his client. As a result, briefs generally went to the best-known and most-respected barristers, and most novices spent years working as clerks for more established barristers (the so-called "devilling"). Bar rules forbade other kinds of work for compensation, thus limiting survival at the bar to those already wealthy or those capable of winning the support of established barristers.

Edgework provided a field within a field upon which professionals might seek an advantage against each other. A dominant consideration for 19th century professionals was the analogy between physical and professional virtues. It in this respect that we can make sense of Daniel Duman's observation that the qualification for English legal careers most frequently expounded on by commentators at the end of the eighteenth and throughout the nineteenth century was "good health and stamina" (Duman, 1983, p. 112). Thus Arthur Hobhouse, whose future would bring him eventually to the very top of the legal system as a Law Lord, explained to a friend his decision to give up a large chancery practice and accept a charity commissionership (with a secure salary) in 1866 as follows:

> I have never properly and thoroughly recovered from the shock of my health in 1863. I find myself falling again into the same state, and determined it was foolhardy to run the same amount of risk again. The question then lay between alternatives of quitting work altogether at least for a substantial time and seeking some quiet path ... the former ... would probably have involved as final a farewell to the Bar as I have now made ... (quoted in Duman, 1983, p. 112)

The opening up of a popular form of edgework via Alpine mountaineering provided a natural avenue for professionals to produce visible signs of their own virtuosity to an audience that primarily consisted of other legal professionals rather than the general public. Visiting the Alps, and especially climbing them, was an outward sign of what could not otherwise be easily discerned in the daily conduct of Victorian professionals: good health, energy, and integrity.

The danger of Alpine mountaineering was even more important as evidence of another attribute of professional virtuosity—courage. Victorian society lionized the explorers and military officers whose exploits in forbidding zones like the arctic and equatorial Africa were wildly celebrated in the first half of the century in a way that shaped the thinking of Victorian professionals who began to come into their careers after 1850. Some professionals, such as the scientists Charles Darwin and his younger cousin Francis Galton, could tie lengthy expeditions into their professional scientific interests, or at least take the time out from science without damaging their professional connections and capital in other respects.

For other professionals, especially legal professionals, lengthy expeditions would have made their client relationships unsustainable. But by the middle of the nineteenth century, the Alpine peaks could be reached by rail and coach from London to tourism centers like Chamonix and Zermatt in a couple of days. A two-week vacation could easily provide a London barrister with the chance to attain several peaks, or to make several attempts at one summit.[16] Should a business emergency occur, the barrister would be able to reach London in two days' time.

Both interpretations of the draw of edgework for Victorian professionals cry out for empirical evidence. I close with one figure whose exemplary career as both a mountaineer and a barrister suggests both possibilities. Alfred Wills was born in 1828, the son of a Birmingham justice of the peace, and was called to the bar in 1851 (Ring, 2000, p. 56). His career defines the path of success that mid-nineteenth-century barristers would hope to follow. He was appointed to a higher rank of barristers in 1872 (called "taking silk") and was appointed a High Court judge in 1884, generally the top ambition for a barrister. In 1895, at the height of his seniority as a judge, he presided over the second criminal trial of Oscar Wilde. Lord Wills excoriated the kind of conduct Wilde was charged with in his instructions to the jury, and he sentenced Wilde to two years of hard labor in prison (Foldy, 1997, pp. 45–6).

Wills' success at the bar followed his success as a climber in the 1850s. In 1854 Wills climbed the Wetterhorn, a beautiful and jagged peak then believed (falsely, it emerged) to have been unclimbed, while on his honeymoon (his bride remained safely in their hotel). His highly successful book on the climb, *Wanderings Among High Alps*, published in 1855, won him a measure of fame in society at large and considerable renown among his fellow professionals.

Wanderings was the first book to articulate the true value of Alpinism as the creation of extraordinary subjective experiences through skillful performance in the objective world of the mountains. This implicitly dismissed a long-standing tradition of writing on the mountains that insisted on the priority of science and exploration. His passage describing his arrival at the summit of the Wetterhorn is exemplary:

> The whole world seemed to lie at my feet. The next moment I was almost appalled by the awfulness of our position. The side we had come up was steep; but it was a gentle slope, compared with that which now fell away from where I stood. A few yards of glittering ice at our feet, and then, nothing between us and the green slopes of Grindelwald, nine thousand feet beneath. I am not ashamed to own that I experienced, as this sublime and wonderful prospect burst upon my view, a profound and almost irrepressible emotion—an emotion which, if I may judge by the low ejaculations of surprise, followed by a long pause of breathless silence, as each in turn stepped into the opening, was felt by others as well as myself. Balmat [his guide] told me repeatedly afterwards, that it was the most awful and startling moment he had known in the course of his long mountain experience (quoted in Ring, 2000, p. 58).

The book established a formula for subsequent best sellers and rehearsed a new kind of celebrity associated with Alpine triumph. In its vivid descriptions of the extreme exposure the climbers faced, *Wanderings* provided ordinary people with evidence that barristers in wigs and robes were as steeped in the masculine virtues that come from risk exposure as any railroad.[17] As a narrative about the experiences of its author, one may guess that it also served as a powerful advertisement of the professional virtuosity of its subject.

Conclusion

Edgework, in the form of mountaineering, provides an exceptional metaphor for the Victorian approach to governing risk. Climbers chose to expose themselves to danger on the steep slopes and ridges of the Alps. To control that danger they hired guides and acquired the best tools available. This fits with the law's treatment of workers and small investors during the unstable growth period of Victorian industrial capitalism in the 1840s through the 1870s. The working and owning classes were joined in a common bond of adventure as "responsible and liberty loving producers" in the language of Gladstone, one of the Victorian system's chief architects (Kostal, 1994, p. 182).

For a smaller class, however, mountaineering was more than a metaphor; rather it was a kind of parallel world to their professional and social lives. This was particularly true of the professionals—lawyers, doctors, clergy, and academics—who made up a disproportionate share of the membership of the Alpine Club of London. Members of this new class lacked the security of the landed aristocracy, but they were sheltered from the crushing forces of competition and risk that Victorian society provided its working classes. Mountaineering provided a new kind of endeavor that complemented the often-elusive sense of accomplishment in the professions.[18] Victorian mountaineering provided a crucial counter practice in which young professionals could engage in a highly stylized yet undeniably competitive form of risk-taking without significant danger to their increasingly important role in governing Victorian society.

Notes

1. On the sociology of risk and insurance, see Baker and Simon, 2002, pp. 12–14.

2. Jock Young (1998) suggests that late modern societies have increasingly shifted, metaphorically speaking, from cannibalism to bulimia, from seeking to absorb and coercively integrate our deviants to trying to expel them.

3. Think about the regularity with which "rogue" traders have shown up as the cause of various banking and corporate financial crises (from Barclay's Bank to Enron), while the vary same institutions seem to have employed these agents to take outlandish risks. On a less catastrophic scale (although not necessarily for the individuals defrauded), the same thing goes on massively in the life insurance business, where, as Richard Ericson and his colleagues have recently documented, life insurance agents are expected to mislead clients to get them to take on far more risk than they are aware of (cite) (Ericson and Doyle 2004).

4. This is the thesis of at least two influential sociologists of risk, Ulrich Beck (1992) and Anthony Giddens (1990).

5. A subjectivity beautifully articulated by Grateful Dead lyricist Robert Hunter in the last verse of "Ripple" (circa 1970), a song many consider an anthem to the 1960's counter version of edgework:

    You who choose to lead must follow

    but if you fall

    you fall alone

    If you should stand

    then who's to guide you?

    If I knew the way

    I would take you home. (Hunter, 1993, p. 186)

6. In the English legal system, members of the bar have exclusive license to practice before most courts of general jurisdiction but are forbidden from representing ordinary citizens or businesses directly. A second branch of the legal profession, solicitors, handle the bulk of transactional legal work (drafting contracts, wills, etc.). When litigation needs arise, solicitors arrange for a barrister to "carry the brief" and remain as an intermediary between their client and the barrister. Solicitors made up an additional 8 percent of the Alpine Club's membership in 1863, bringing the combined total of legal professionals to nearly a third of the Club's membership five years after its start.

7. Richard Abel calculates the active membership of the bar in 1863 to be 4,360 (Abel, 1988, pp. 482–483). Since this included many older barristers a truer picture of the proportion of young barristers who were Alpinists would be higher.

8. Following Sidney Fine's influential preneoliberal view of its rise (Fine, 1956).

9. Some governments in the wealthy Western nation-states have allowed the poor to drift back into something like pre-welfare state to fending for themselves (or more accurately to relying on family, ethnic, and religious networks; incarceration; and the bottom rungs of the labor force).

10. Succeeding regimes in England and other common-law–influenced societies, the social welfare state of the mid-twentiethth century, and neoliberalism since the 1980s have developed in reaction to the Victorian model.

11. Gladstone was one of the dominant influences on Victorian liberalism as a governmental philosophy. His career took him through all the major parties of the nineteenth century and the entire span of Victoria's rule in sustained pursuit of a liberal approach to government. Churchill credits him with presiding over a

    Golden Age when Liberalism was still an aggressive, unshackling force, and the doctrine of individualism and the philosophy of *laissez faire* the method; no undue extension of Government authority was needed; and the middle class at last acquired a share in the political sphere equal to their economic power. (1958, p. 286)

12. Historian R. W. Kostal writes that "January 1846 was surely one of the bleakest months in the history of English capitalism" (1994, p. 41).

13. Kostal's examination of the registration documents of complying joint-stock companies shows that prior to March of 1845, no lawyer was listed as the sole or even as a principal promoter of a joint-stock company. By the time of the crash, thirty-one of seventy-five concerns whose registration documents were examined listed a quarter or more of the promoters as lawyers. Seven consisted of only lawyers.

14. Queen Victoria placed the ultimate imprimatur on this trend in 1868 when she visited Lucerne. She wrote in her diary: "What am I to say of the glorious scenery of Switzerland; the view from this Hse. wh. is *vy high* is most wonderfully beautiful with the lake—Pilatus, the Righi & c—& I can *hardly* believe my eyes—when I look at it! It seems like a painting or decoration—*a dream!*" (quoted in Ring, 2000, p. 93).

15. The Inns were essentially lodging and dining clubs with a variable educational role and have long provided the major vehicle for organizing and disciplining barristers and the sole means of being called to the bar.

16. During his numerous attempts to climb the Matterhorn prior to his successful effort in 1865, Edward Whymper often calculated carefully. In one attempt, captured in his memoir of Alpine climbing, Whymper sat a long way up the Matterhorn waiting for a storm to pass and trying to decide how long he could stay there and still make it back to London before the end of the week to attend a meeting for his professional work as an illustrator (Fleming, 2000, p. 239).

17. There is obviously a rich intersection between class, gender, and risk taking here that remains undeveloped in the present essay, but see Pue (1999).

18. One of the most compelling portraits of working-class risk taking in industrial Britain is given in [Victorian Railway Men, provide author, publ.info], (Kingford, 1970).

References

Abel, R. L. *The Legal Profession in England and Wales*. London: Basil Blackwell, 1988.

Baker, T., and Simon, J. *Embracing Risk: The Changing Culture of Insurance and Responsibility*. Chicago: University of Chicago Press, 2002.

Douglas, M. and A. Wildavsky. Risk and Culture. Berkeley. University of California Press. 1982.

Duman, D. *The English and Colonial Bars in the Nineteenth Century*. London: Croom Helm, 1983.

Ericson, R. and A. Doyle. Uncertain Business: Risk, Insurance, and the Limits of Knowledge. Toronto: University of Toronto Press. 2004.

Ewald, F. "The Return of Descartes's Malicious Demon: An Outline of a Philosophy of Precaution." In *Embracing Risk: The Changing Culture of Insurance and Responsibility*, edited by T. Baker and J. Simon. Chicago: University of Chicago Press, 2002.

Ewald, F. *L'Etat Providence*. Paris: Grasset.

Fine, S. *Laissez Faire and the General Welfare State: A Study of Conflict in American Thought, 1865–1901*. Ann Arbor, MI: University of Michigan Press, 1954.

Fleming, F. *Killing Dragons: The Conquest of the Alps*. New York: Atlantic Monthly Press, 2000.

Foldy, M. S. *The Trials of Oscar Wilde: Deviance, Morality, and Late-Victorian Society*. New Haven, CT: Yale University Press, 1997.

Forrest, D.W. *Francis Galton: The Life and Work of a Victorian Genius.* New York: Taplinger, 1974.

Giddens, A. The Consequences of Modernity. Stanford, CA: Stanford University Press, 1990.

Hunter, R.

Kingsford, P.W. Victorian Railway Men: The Emergence and Growth of Railway Labor, 1830–1870. London: Frank Cass & Co., Ltd. 1970.

Kostal, R. W. *Law and English Railway Capitalism, 1825–1875.* Oxford: Clarendon Press, 1994.

Kruger, L., Daston L. J., and Heidelberger, M., eds. *The Probabilistic Revolution, Vol. I: Ideas in History.* Cambridge, MA: MIT Press, 1987.

Lyng, S. "Edgework: A Social Psychological Analysis of Voluntary Risk Taking." *American Journal of Sociology* 95 (1990): 851–886.

Nicolson, M. H. *Mountain Gloom and Mountain Glory: The Development of the Aesthetics of the Infinite.* Seattle, WA: University of Washington Press, 1959.

O'Malley, P. "Imagining Insurance: Risk, Thrift, and Life Insurance in Britain." In *Embracing Risk: The Changing Culture of Insurance and Responsibility,* edited by T. Baker and J. Simon. Chicago: University of Chicago Press, 2002.

Osiel, M. J. "Lawyers as Monopolists, Aristocrats, and Entrepreneurs." *Harvard Law Review* 109 (1990): 2009, 103:2009–2065.

Perrow, C. *Normal Accidents: Living with High Risk Technologies,* revised edition. New York: Basic Books, 1999.

Porter, T. M. *The Rise of Statistical Thinking 1820–1900.* Princeton, NJ: Princeton University Press, 1986.

Prest, W. G. *The Rise of the Barristers: A Social History of the English Bar, 1590–1640.* Oxford: Oxford University Press, 1986.

Pue, W. W. "British Masculinities, Canadian Lawyers: Canadian Legal Education, 1900–1930." *Law in Context* 16 (1999): 80–122.

Ring, J. How the English Made the Alps. London: John Murray, 2000.

Simon, J. "The Emergence of a Risk Society: Insurance, Law, and the State." Socialist Review 95:61–89. 1987.

Simon, J. "Taking Risks: Extreme Sports and the Embrace of Risk in Advanced Liberal Societies." In *Embracing Risk: The Changing Culture of Insurance and Responsibility,* edited by T. Baker and J. Simon. Chicago: University of Chicago Press, 2002.

Sugarman, D. "Simple Images and Complex Realities: English Lawyers and Their Relationship to Business and Politics, 1750–1950." *Law and History Review* 11 (1993): 257–301.

Tomlins, C. "A Mysterious Power: Industrial Accidents and the Legal Construction of Employment Relations in Massachusetts, 1800–1850." Law & History Review 6:375–438.

Willen, M. S. "Composing Mountaineering: The Personal Narrative and the Production of Knowledge in the Alpine Club of London and the Appalachian Mountain Club, 1858–1900." PhD diss., University of Pittsburgh, 1995.

Young, J. "Cannibalism and Bulimia." Theoretical Criminology 4(1999): 387–408.

10

On the Edge: Drugs and the Consumption of Risk in Late Modernity

GERDA REITH

CONTENTS

This paper has as its focus the fine line between "normal" and "abnormal" behavior, particularly with reference to consumption, which has, in recent years, emerged as the defining activity of late modern Western societies. It argues that, on the one hand, individuals are regulated by a set of ideological forces that caution them to exercise self-control and consume moderately in a way that maintains their well-being and enhances their identity. Failure to do so is criticized in the language of a rational-medical discourse, with transgressions regarded as "addictive," "pathological," or "irrational" behavior. On the other hand, however, a contrary force encourages individuals to "let go"—to give in to their desires and deny themselves nothing— in other words, to consume immoderately and often to excess. The tension between these two forces is the place where edgework goes on; where individuals "let go," "give in," and take risks, but also manage to "hold on" and exercise self-control. This is controlled excess and regulated risk, with the process of edgework a constant exercise in maintaining the boundary between "normal" and "abnormal" consumption, the crucial line between consumption that enriches the self and that which destroys it.

So, this chapter attempts to do two things: First, at the macro level, it examines the development of theoretical notions of "normal" and "abnormal" consumption within the structural conditions of late modernity. Second, at the micro level, it focuses on the notion of edgework within this climate and examines its social-psychological meanings for a specific group of edgeworkers: drug users.

A Culture of Consumption

Modern society is a consumer society. Our social relationships and self identities, our forms of cultural expression, and even our political and economic lives are increasingly constructed and negotiated around the consumption of a wide range of mass-produced commodities and activities. Such a trend is characteristic of broader socioeconomic changes, which have been described as the move to "post-modernity" (Baudrillard, 1998), "late" or "high" modernity (Giddens, 1991), or "reflexive" modernity (Beck, 1992). Despite differences in terminology, all describe a fundamental shift from the period of modernity and the move to an era that is characterized by a restructuring of economic and labor market processes and the diversification and fragmentation of social, familial, and community relations. It is dominated by increased insecurity, flux, and risk in social life, and by a general domination of appearances, signs, and images over reality.

It has further been argued that this late modern world has seen the replacement of traditional social hierarchies based on class, gender, race, and ethnicity with new lifestyle groups based on consumption. In other words, as Bauman (1998) puts it, we have moved from a "production ethic" to a "consumption ethic," where individuals make decisions about who and what they want to be through the possession and display of a range of consumer goods and leisure activities. In addition to satisfying material needs, commodities are appropriated as symbolic objects of fantasy and desire to create and display a carefully constructed self-image.

There are, however, problems with this approach. As well as the limitations imposed on consumption by the unequal distribution of material resources, a range of ideological forces also work to curtail such apparently "free" choice. As Bauman (1988) has noted, despite its many "freedoms," consumption is also a site of constraint, where the pressure to behave in socially acceptable ways and to conform to social norms by making the "right" choices actually creates anxiety and tension amongst consumers.

The Regulation of Consumption: The Discourse of Reason and Medicine

When we look at this tension more closely, we start to see that the whole notion of the "right" choice, as well as the definition of what constitutes "acceptable" behavior, is highly relative and historically specific. The nature of its construction is crucial for this essay since it is against the strictures of this particular form of control that the practice of edgework defines itself against.

In the modern world, the notion of "normal" behavior exists as part of a rational-medical discourse in which the former is defined in terms of rationality, moderation, and health, and in which "abnormal" behavior is defined as its opposite, in terms of irrationality, excess, addiction, and risk. This discourse has its roots in the development of modernity, a period in which the twin movements of rationalization and medicalization sought to control the world through the exercise of rational human action, founded on the tenets of self-control, moderation, and deferment of gratification. Such behavior was formed within the structural conditions of modernity, which created the conditions for the internalization of certain social norms and conventions, expressed in particular codes of conduct (Elias, 2000; Foucault, 1975; 1977). This was part of a more sophisticated process of normalization, a disciplining of bodies into standardized, controllable forms that was mediated through governmental institutions such as medicine, law, and education. Through these, what Foucault called "techniques of self management (1976)" ensured that control was carried out from within, with individuals involved in the constant monitoring of their own thoughts and behavior.

The institution of medicine was crucial for the creation of notions of acceptable behavior, and it was thanks to its influence that actions regarded as abnormal or "excessive" came to be explained by the concept of "addiction" (Berridge and Edwards, 1987; Conrad and Schneider, 1992). This was defined as a physical dependency on a substance so powerful that the urge to consume it undermined human volition and reduced the individual to a state of abject helplessness. By postulating some kind of powerful causal mechanism between the object in question—the addictive substance—and the susceptible individual, the addict, the concept of "addiction" brought the understanding of human behavior firmly into the realm of medicine. It turned the reasonable consumer on its head; with the subordination of personal agency, reason was replaced with irrationality, moderation with excess, and free will with slavery. Whereas consumers *chose* to act, addicts were *forced* to do so (Reith, 2004).

These ideas were initially worked out with reference to opium, morphine, and heroin, and were gradually expanded to include a wide range of substances and activities. This initial focus meant, however, that the paradigmatic object of addiction was drugs; its subject the drug consumer.

"Abnormal" Consumption

In the general notion of addiction, the twin discourses of reason and medicine converged, and "abnormality" was medicalized. In terms of consumption, the ideal was of highly regulated behavior that ensured the realization of the self, while its out-of-control opposite threatened the well-being of both the individual and the social body. Here we return to the original negative implications of "consumption" in the literal meaning of the verb "to consume: to destroy, cause to disappear; swallow up in destruction; to waste one's substance, ruin oneself" (Oxford English Dictionary, 1991).

It is within this rational-medical discourse of modernity that the associated idea of risk has valence. By definition, a "risk" is something that poses a threat to the self and which is also calculable and predictable, since it implies some knowledge, however partial, of potential future danger. As such, its threat lies within the boundaries of human action and so can feasibly be avoided or reduced. The problem of risk was part of the project of modernity, insofar as the latter aimed at the elimination of unpredictability from the world and the safeguarding of the individual from danger. In this context, the avoidance of unnecessary risks was of paramount importance to rational consumers, who were expected to keep themselves informed about potential dangers and regulate their behavior accordingly. Behavior that could threaten personal safety was regarded as the height of irresponsibility; anyone who would voluntarily take risks was not fulfilling their part of the social contract and, by definition, was engaging in excessive and therefore deviant and abnormal behavior.

As well as defining notions of acceptable behavior, this discourse postulated a crucial distinction between two "types" of individuals, between "normal" consumers who consumed moderately and "abnormal" ones who did so to excess, destroying themselves in the process. Its normative regulation created a highly ordered and risk-free society whose stability depended on widespread adherence to standardized, conformist patterns of behavior: what Weber (1985) called the "iron cage" of rationalist modernity.

However, having outlined the parameters of rational social action, we now run into a problem, for the fact is that consumer culture has a deeply ambivalent relation with elements that are generally regarded as excessive. Despite its portrayal as something that is abnormal or deviant, excessive behavior was and is actually widespread, both in the period of modernity just discussed, and increasingly in the more recent era of late or "post" modernity. This contradiction will be the focus of the next section, where we consider it as both a feature of the social structure, and of individual experience and action.

The Excesses of Consumer Culture

Anomie, Insatiability, and Excess

The central and problematic existence of "excessive" behavior, broadly conceived, is an ongoing theme in Emile Durkheim's and Karl Marx's classic accounts of consumer capitalism, and also in George Bataille's critique of such systems.

Durkheim was one of the first sociologists to apply ideas about excess and abnormality to consumption, albeit indirectly. For him, society was regulated by a moral force that ensured that an individual's desires and the means of attaining them were balanced and finite. However, Durkheim feared that increased industrial productivity and affluence were destroying this regulatory force, creating abnormal social forms that unleashed insatiable appetites and brought about a state of disequilibrium or "anomie." Without regulation, the constant search for fulfillment through the consumption of goods and experiences fell into "an insatiable and bottomless abyss" of desire (Durkheim, 1970, p. 247), repeated over and over again in a form of behavior that Durkheim described as pathological. This was "the longing for infinity," of which he wrote: "From top to bottom of the social ladder, greed is aroused without knowing where to find ultimate foothold.... A thirst arises for novelties, unfamiliar pleasures, nameless sensations, all of which lose their savour once known..." (Durkheim, 1970, p. 256). Because the indefinite expansion of profit was the permanent goal of economic life, there could be no end to this state of affairs, and so Durkheim's rational model of society remained troubled by the problem of excess. Instead of banishing it, as he had intended to, he unwittingly made it central to his universe, an anomaly that could not be theorized out of existence.

Marx also recognized the nonrational features of capitalism. Unlike Durkheim, however, he did not think they were anomalous or pathological and, although he also did not regard them as desirable, he did grasp the centrality of nonutilitarian desire to the process of production. He described how producers had a vested interest in cultivating "excess and intemperance" in individuals; of "feeding imaginary appetites" so that needs were replaced by "fantasy, caprice and whim" (Marx, 1972, pp. 147–148). Profit depended on the constant stimulation of appetites and the introduction of novelties and fashions that were discarded almost immediately as the consumer was presented with a new array of temptations, and the cycle begun all over again. The end result, for Marx, was the creation of "morbid appetites," the erasure of the line that separates desire from need, and the inculcation of indulgence, hedonism, and excessive consumption in the population (Marx, 1972, p. 148).

At this point, George Bataille's radical model of "excess" can be introduced as a departure from classic social theory that is able to cast fresh light on supposedly problematic consumption. Although Marx and Durkheim both found excessive consumption abnormal or artificial, for Bataille it was actually the natural state of economic life. He described how Western market economies were based on the principle of material utility, characterized by "restrained expenditure," which only recognized the "right to acquire, to conserve and to consume rationally" (Bataille, 1985, p. 117). In other words, they were based on a model of scarcity, which necessitated the rational allocation of finite resources and rewarded the "bourgeois" values of asceticism and restraint. In such systems, moderate pleasure was tolerated, but "violent pleasure is seen as *pathological*" (Bataille, 1985, p. 116). However, according to Bataille, this was not the normal state of economic life and had only developed along with the ascendance of the system of market capitalism, when "everything that was generous, orgiastic and excessive" had disappeared from social life (Bataille, 1985, p. 124). Despite the dominance of these values, Bataille insisted that human behavior was not characterized by utilitarianism and restraint, but rather by what he called "unproductive expenditures," activities that were pursued for their own sake, and whose principle was pure consumption and indulgence in excess. Widespread in traditional, non-Western cultures, they also existed in capitalist economies, where they took the form of sports, forms of "orgiastic" consumption, and activities pursued as ends in themselves. What characterized all these activities was the intensity of the affective states they induced, "states of excitation which are comparable to toxic states" (Bataille, 1985, p. 128), and their rejection of rational, productive values in favor of instantaneous, "orgiastic" gratification and indulgence in excess. The intensity with which they were pursued meant that "the danger of death is not avoided: on the contrary, it is the object of a strong unconscious attraction" (Bataille, 1985, p. 119).

Although his model drew heavily on non-Western systems, Bataille regarded the "principle of excess" as fundamental to human life in general, and in its broad explanatory framework, we can see salient features of the structure and experience of modern Western consumption elsewhere described as "pathological."

Out of these theoretically diverse accounts, certain themes emerge as constant, and an image is built up of the consumer as an individual motivated by the quest for novelty and excitement, driven to over-consumption by a basic insatiability for the luxuries and pleasures offered by consumer capitalism. So much for the self-governing, rational agent of modernity introduced earlier!

Getting Out, Taking Risks, and Letting Go

The inherent tension between the twin imperatives of abandon and restraint has been recognized in more recent writers' accounts of the tendency to "let go," take risks, or otherwise escape from the constraints of rational society.

From Elias's neofunctionalist account of the "quest for excitement," in which the cathartic release of tension through various activities results in a "controlled de-controlling of the emotions" (Elias and Dunning, 1986), to Goffman's notion of "action," through which individuals realize their selves through fateful endeavors (Goffman, 1972), there exists a general recognition of the need to express or recreate self identity through extreme or risky activities.

Recently, however, this trend has intensified with voluntary or recreational risk taking becoming increasingly tolerated and even encouraged in modern society. Lyng's notion of "edgework" articulates and expresses this trend, describing the paradox that, even as public organizations attempt to reduce the dangers of modern life, individuals nevertheless seek out risky situations in dangerous sports such as skydiving and motorcycle racing, occupations such as fire-fighting and police work, and criminal activities such as robberies. Such activities are "spontaneous, anarchic and impulsive" (Lyng, 1990, p. 864) and generate extreme experience based on the transgression of boundaries. This is the central problem of "negotiating the boundary between chaos and order" (Lyng, 1990, p. 855), or more fully, "life versus death, consciousness versus unconsciousness, sanity versus insanity, ordered sense of self and environment versus disordered sense of self and environment" (Lyng, 1990, p. 857). The control and negotiation of the high levels of danger and risk are regarded as belonging to "a special realm that transcends more conventional, institutional experience" (Lyng, 1993, p. 109). By pushing themselves to the limit but still maintaining their self-control, individuals experience sensations of transcendence and hyperreality, and in this way, the successful negotiation of the edge becomes a realm of "self determination and authenticity" (Lyng, 1990, p. 883). Perhaps the most crucial aspect of edgework is the notion of transgression, the crossing of a boundary, which can be from rational to irrational, from danger to safety, or in the context of this paper, from normal to abnormal behavior. This is fundamental in the consumption of risk, and it is from this that risk derives its appeal.

Consumption as Edgework

In late modernity, a certain amount of excess in the form of risky consumption is regarded as legitimate and, indeed, is actually commodified as an experience that can be purchased (Ritzer, 1999). As opposed to the negative features associated with exposing the self to unnecessary risk discussed earlier, this form of controlled risk is actually sanctioned and encouraged. Indeed, risk taking is frequently utilized in commercial advertising and portrayed in the media as a heroic act, with images of courageous individuals engaging in dangerous activities used to promote products that promise consumers excitement and escape. But although this represents a form of excess, it is *controlled* excess. The action goes on within strictly defined parameters; the activity has a clearly set beginning and end (frequently measured by cost), beyond which the thrills do not go.

Such a contrast is typical of wider structural forces within late modernity, where we find an emerging contradiction between two tendencies: the trend to restraint, and the trend to indulgence. Consumers themselves are central to this, as they are caught in a unique historical juncture, between modernity's legacy of asceticism and self-control, and late modernity's increasing emphasis on hedonism and personal gratification (Turner, 1996; Crawford, 1984). On the one hand, their behavior is subject to the normative regulation of the rational-medical discourse reviewed earlier, and is liable to a diagnosis of "pathology" or "addiction" should it fail to conform to its demands. On the other, suffocated by such restrictions and surrounded by the temptations of consumer capitalism, consumers feel the urge to break free and give in to emotion and desire: to indulge in what Durkheim would call "anomie," Marx "morbid appetites," and Bataille, "excess."

Such dualism lies at the heart of the experience of modern consumption. Consumers are allowed to let go; to give in to excess; to dive into the action; to escape—but not *too* much. They also have to keep a bit back and exercise self-control. They are allowed to take risks, to go to the edge, but they have to be able to step back again. This is *regulated* excess, *controlled* risk, and negotiating this boundary is the task of edgework. Consumers must negotiate "the boundary between chaos and order," between abnormal and normal consumption, between the annihilation of the self in addiction and the realization of the self in fulfilling activity.

Certain forms of consumption embody this dualism particularly well and can be defined as "liminal;" they are poised on the brink between normal and abnormal, between life-affirming risk and self-destructive chaos. Dangerous sports and extreme activities are prime examples of this, but more commonplace consumption also has this dual potential. For instance, the everyday activity of shopping can slide into "shopaholism" if pursued to excess, while eating (in its "normal" form, the route to a healthy body image) can become dysfunctional through under- or over- consumption, resulting in a diagnosis of anorexia, bulimia, "carboholism," or some other pathological form. Similarly, gambling[1] involves the pursuit of chance as well as money, and the risk of losing everything should the bet fail, while drugs can provide an escape from everyday reality and a world of Dionysian excess as well as the misery of addiction (Reith, 2004).

All of these activities exemplify the dualism of consumption and the tightrope that individuals must walk between consuming "normally" or "abnormally." But perhaps the most striking instance is to be found in drug taking, which vividly demonstrates the conflicting pressures on consumers, and which consequently provides unique opportunities for edgework.[2] The consumption of drugs exemplifies the central themes of edgework, since drug users constantly negotiate the boundary between order and chaos, consciousness and unconsciousness, an ordered and a disordered sense of self and environment, sanity and insanity, and in extreme cases, even life and death. In the following section, these features will be explored by drawing on references to empirical academic research as well as first-hand literary accounts of drug use.

On the Edge: Drugs and the Consumption of Risk

As the physical ingestion of excess, voluntary intoxication through drugs is perhaps the most dramatic and demanding instance of edgework. Since he took his first "trips to the edge" in the 1950s and 60s, many people have followed in Hunter S. Thompson's drug-fueled footsteps. Although the 1960s and 70s saw the relatively small-scale use of drugs amongst certain sub-cultures, today the use of soft drugs appears to be increasingly widespread (South, 1999). Although the consumption of (illegal)[3] drugs is still generally regarded as a deviant or marginal form of behavior, ironically, a contrary trend is appearing, the normalization—if not the legalization—of drug use in everyday life (Parker, Measham, and Aldridge, 1995; Coffield and Gofton, 1994). Amongst a significant minority of the population, soft drugs are becoming increasingly commonplace and central to the leisure habits of certain lifestyle groups.

In particular, since the late 1980s, the drug Ecstasy has come to be an integral part of the rave club scene, with its symbolism and imagery permeating the dress and music codes of youth culture. This symbolism has been commodified by various leisure industries and disseminated by the media so that representations of drugs are now firmly established in mainstream youth culture. Fashion, music, magazines, advertising, art, and even language are suffused with the iconography of drugs. T-shirts are emblazoned with the smiley face logo of Ecstasy and LSD, dance songs celebrate the high life with lyrics such as "feel the rush" and "pure XTC," and even pills themselves are named after icons of popular culture, such as Bart Simpson, Adidas, and McDonald's. As a result, recreational drugs, especially Ecstasy, have come to be seen as much as a fashion accessory, a brand name, or a logo as an object of addiction. We now have a situation in which "illegal drugs have become products which are grown, manufactured, packaged and marketed through an enterprise culture whereby the legitimate and illicit markets have merged" (Parker, Measham, and Aldridge, 1995, p. 25).

Weekend drug taking is part of the leisure habits of many thousands of young people, who frequently indulge in poly-drug use, "picking and mixing" Ecstasy, cannabis, amphetamines, LSD, and any number of other substances to get the best high (Parker and Measham, 1994). The creation, maintenance, and control of this high is a striking instance of the most demanding edgework.

Transgression

Although the nature of the high varies according to the chemistry of the drug taken—(with, for example, LSD characterized by unreality and hallucinations, stimulants by sensations of intensity and physicality, and opiates by a transcending of reality) all are united in the common feature of transgression. On taking a drug, there is an immediate and very dramatic transgression of boundaries, from order to chaos, sanity to insanity, or in terms of drugs, from "straight" to "wasted." This transgression, known as "diving in," "going up," or getting "out of it," is a desirable experience in itself, and this is the high that is the whole point of taking drugs. It is this that characterizes the intense, euphoric "rush" experienced by heroin and cocaine users, which is described as almost sexual in nature, and that overtakes the entire body as the drug takes hold. The French poet Rene Daumal experienced such a transgression that was almost physical in nature when he ingested drugs, recalling "I was hurled faster and faster toward ever-imminent annihilation ... until the moment when, letting go, I fell into a brief spell of unconsciousness" (Daumal, 1991, p. 62). A kind of fear is not uncommon in edgework, and this is similar to the fear of death, which, as Bataille (1986) stated, is not avoided in moments of excess, but is rather the object of an unconscious attraction.

Extreme Experience—The High

The high is the vortex of the drug experience, the peaking of intensity and excitement in which the outside world is blocked out in a moment of temporary oblivion. It is momentarily a "wild zone," where experience is ungoverned and disordered (Stanley, 1996). The veteran LSD voyager Albert Hofman described such experiential anarchy as a characteristic feature of hallucinogens' ability to "suspend the boundaries between the experiencing self and the outer world in an ecstatic, emotional experience" (Hofman, 1991, p. 91). Similarly with opium, whose high was described by Thomas de Quincey as an "abyss of divine enjoyment" in which he lost track of the outside world and the passage of time as he gave in to a maelstrom of emotional and affective sensation (de Quincey, 1982, p. 71). After taking a concatenation of drugs, Hunter S Thompson described the "fiendish intensity, strange glow and vibrations" (Thompson, 1972, p. 49) that assaulted him before he hit a chemical vortex of hallucinations and insanity. As with many drug users, Thompson frequently crossed the line between sanity and insanity and consciousness and unconsciousness. It is the negotiation of the fine line between these states that constitutes the thrill of drug taking, and Thompson tested that to the limit when he felt

> "a giddy, quavering sort of high that means the crash is coming. But when? How much longer? This tension is part of the high. The possibility of physical and mental collapse is very real now ... this is the moment of truth, that fine and fateful line between control and disaster" (Thompson, 1972, p. 85).

This tightrope balancing act constitutes the thrill of the high, and it is in this that the seductive appeal of drugs lies.

Hyperreality

Despite the intensity and unreality of the experiential zone they have entered, drug users often find it somehow *more* real than the one they have left. Such an intensification of reality can be one of the most vivid features of the drug experience, as Daumal outlines: "This 'world' lost all reality because I had abruptly entered another world, infinitely more real, an instantaneous and intense world of eternity...." (Daumal, 1991, p. 61). Lyng calls this phenomenon "hyper-reality," and notes that, typically, edgework participants "often describe the experience as being much more real than the circumstances of their day-to-day existence" (Lyng, 1990, p. 861).

Hyperreality also alters perceptions of time and space, and at the peak of the edgework experience, individuals' perceptual fields narrow to such an extent that "they also lose the ability to gauge the passage of time in the usual fashion. Time may pass either much faster or slower than usual ..." (Lyng, 1990, p. 861). Drug use provides the archetypal experience of the disordered temporality of edgework (Reith, 1999a). Swept up in the intensity of the high, users focus exclusively on the Here and Now, blocking out all extraneous factors in their total immersion in the experience. One narcotics user described how, "everything went kind of blurry ... when you're using [drugs] you've no concept of time passing, time just flies past" (quoted in Reith, 1999a, p. 110). This feature can apply to entire lifestyles, as well as to the singular experiences of the high. As Burroughs put it, "life telescopes down to junk, one fix and looking forward to the next" (Burroughs, 1977, p. 22). A study of heroin users found that many described a distortion in the sense of the passage of time, so that, although it appeared to pass quickly, it remained somehow "empty" and unfilled with experience (Reith, 1999a). This is the quintessential drug experience, the blocking out of the outside world, and with it, the "destruction of the bonds of linearity and time" (Cohen and Taylor, 1992, p. 147), that is an integral feature of the high.

Self-Actualization

Negotiating the edge has important consequences for individuals in terms of their sense of self and the enhancement of their status and identity. Edgework is an arena of self-actualization where "the ego is called forth in a dramatic way" (Lyng, 1990, p. 860), and where individuals experience sensations of empowerment and even omnipotence. Here, they leave their more limited, everyday personas behind and temporarily "experience themselves as instinctively acting entities, which leaves them with a purified and magnified sense of self" (Lyng, 1990, p. 860).

The zone of drug use is one of self-actualization and ego work in which users frequently report feeling invincible, exhilarated, and possessed of superhuman strength and ability. One opiate user recounted how drugs made her feel separate from the world and elevated above its routine tribulations:

"drugs alter your perception of who you are ... so you feel slightly immune or aloof to your circumstances; they don't affect you in any way, nothing can get to you ..." (quoted in Reith, 1999a, p. 107). Even more strikingly, an experiment with morphine led to a state of supreme, almost god-like omnipotence for another, who declared "soon I was Absolute, All powerful; nothing was impossible to me" (Lee, 1991, p. 16).

A sensation of transcendence or "one-ness" with the universe is frequently found in the most intense forms of edgework, which Lyng describes as "a sense of cognitive control over the essential 'objects' in the environment or a feeling of identity with these objects" (Lyng, 1990, p. 861). This sense of indissociation is highly typical of drug users, and it tends to accompany feelings of omnipotence and self-actualization, during which the magnified self sometimes appears to merge with its surroundings. After the initial rush of the high, Burroughs slipped into a transcendent state that was like "a spreading wave of relaxation ... so that you seem to float without outlines, like lying in warm salted water" (Burroughs, 1977, p. 7). The feeling of being everywhere and nowhere, of transcending bodily boundaries and achieving altered states of consciousness is a common one. At the height of his LSD trip, Hofman felt as though his very being, his ego, was merging with the external world, becoming part of it: "In the LSD state, the boundaries between the experiencing self and the outer world more or less disappear ... a portion of the self overflows into the outer world, into objects, which begin to live, to have another deeper meaning" (Hofman, 1991, p. 85). Here, the boundary between the self and the world has vanished, and the ego is actually felt to be animating the surrounding environment: "this experience of deep oneness with the exterior world can even intensify to a feeling of the self being one with the universe" (Hofman, 1991, p. 85).

Slipping through the net of "paramount reality" into what Cohen and Taylor (1992) call alternative "mindscapes" opens up whole new worlds of self discovery, mystical experience, and states of transcendence in which users of hallucinogens often report feeling at one with the world and understanding the meaning of life. These mystical experiences have frequently been the subject of classic accounts of drug use, running through the writing of Aldous Huxley, Samuel Coleridge, Thomas de Quincey, and particularly William James, who wrote of the power of drugs to stimulate those capacities "usually crushed ... by the cold facts and dry criticisms of the sober hour. Sobriety diminishes, discriminates, says no. Drunkenness expands, unites and says yes" (James, 1982, p. 387). This expansive quality often generates quasi-mystical insights into social and individual existence, and is for many one of the most meaningful aspects of drug use.

Control

Despite its apparent chaos, the drug experience itself is actually characterized by high levels of skill and control, with users exercising a range of abilities to ensure that they "get as close as possible to the edge without going over it" (Lyng, 1990, p. 862). This, then, is the essence of edgework: "the ability to maintain control over a situation that verges on complete chaos" (Lyng, 1990, p. 859), and it works on two levels. As well as the edgework that controls the immediacy of the high, it also works on a broader level to maintain a boundary between the individual's consumption of drugs in their leisure time, and their other, "straight" lives, which they return to after the experience.

Recreational users are experts at negotiating risk. These are individuals for whom consumption is not out of control; these are "day trippers" who will be back at work or back in college class again by Monday morning. Recent research found that Ecstasy users' drug-taking sessions were characterized more by careful planning and control rather than wild abandon and excess (Shewan, Dalgarno, and Reith, 2000). These users stressed the importance of rational planning and forethought before setting off on a trip. From the purchase of the drug from trustworthy dealers, to the choice of a reliable venue to take it in, to the selection of appropriate "comedown" activities for afterwards, nothing was left to chance. The ongoing experience of the drug itself was monitored closely to achieve a balance between out-of-control chaos and "boring" comfort. At one extreme are experiences whereby one individual reported: "I just lost it completely—ended up being taken to hospital by the police … I couldn't speak, didn't know my name … I felt paralyzed and paranoid" (quoted in Shewan, Dalgarno, and Reith, 2000, pp. 434–435).

At the other extreme, however, was an equally undesirable experience: "planned nights out can be boring. It's another routine, and I'm not convinced that's what drug use is supposed to be *like,* fundamentally… That's not drug taking. You can use a bit of chaos in your life" (quoted in Shewan, Dalgarno, and Reith, 2000, p. 447). These drug takers used strategic planning and meticulous preparation to control their consumption and so could determine, with some precision, the exact nature of the desired experience. True, they *did* allow themselves to get "out of it," but within carefully constructed parameters that would not interfere too much with the rational demands of the everyday world that they know they will return to. As one drug taker put it: "when I'm using drugs, I plan it in advance, just to fit in with my lifestyle. If you're going to work on Tuesday, then at the weekend, you know you can't be too many miles from home, and not have recovered fully by the time you're back [at work]" (quoted in Shewan, Dalgarno, and Reith, 2000, p. 445). There are no one-way trips here; this is always a planned release, a controlled risk.

This orientation is typical of voluntary risk-taking and of what Goffman, quoting Michael Balint, called the "safe excitement of thrills," which hovered around the "more or less confident hope that the fear can be tolerated and mastered, the danger will pass, and that one will be able to return unharmed to safety" (1972, p. 196). This is the "survival capacity" that edgeworkers regard as an "innate ability" (Lyng, 1990, p. 859), and that drug takers know they must exercise to continue their lifestyle. There is some skill involved in consuming "correctly," and users respect those who manage to achieve an authentic high without succumbing to either excessive caution or total chaos.

Drug takers can be harsh judges when they encounter others who do not manage the balance, as a study by Collinson (1996) found. His respondents described the skill in "taking it right" [maintaining control] as opposed to "going down on it" [losing control], and one recounted how he had "seen too many people go down on it... One minute they're all right lads; know the score—[the next] shivering little shits, haven't got a clue ... they're the lowest of the low" (quoted in Collinson, 1996, p. 432).

Through the exercise of these survival tactics, users avoid self destruction and instead find self realization through a form of purposive action. As well as an escape from the dull routine of everyday life, the consumption of drugs provides a form of activity that is "grounded in the immediacy of excitement and adrenaline rushes, in the situated rationality of the event" (Ferrell, Milovanovic, and Lyng, 2001, p. 178). In this, it can also confer status and create meaning. This was found in a classic study of heroin users in which the authors concluded that "the quest for heroin is the quest for a meaningful life" that derives from "accomplishing a series of challenging, exciting tasks" that requires users to be alert, flexible, resourceful and courageous (Preble and Casey, 1969, pp. 2–3). This purposive action lives out "the gratifications of skill, intentionality and self invention" (Ferrell, Milovanovic, and Lyng, 2001, p. 178) that is a mark of the successful accomplishment of skilled edgework.

Crucially, then, these drug experiences are subject to users' control and none are permanent. Every one is a temporary state that is entered into for a predetermined amount of time and left behind once again as the individual steps back across the boundary into the straight world.

Stepping over the edge—and staying there—is quite a different thing. At the other side lies the physical and mental destruction of addiction, which as we saw earlier, is anathema to the rational consumer. This is the point where self-realization, purposive action, and free will are replaced with self-destruction, chaos, and slavery. It is characterized by annihilation through the total subjugation of the self to the drug consumed—permanently. Here the individual loses his or her grip on reality, becomes disconnected from the outside world and the passage of time, and is obsessed with the desire for drugs. In the state of addiction, the slight distortions of temporal perception that are characteristic of the high are massively exaggerated and eventually overcome the individual altogether.

A crucial feature of human existence and self-perception is that it is situated in a present that is always moving dynamically toward a future; and it is this that gives it what Adam (1990) calls its character of "transcendence." However, in the state of addiction the articulation of time breaks down; the individual cannot envisage themselves as agents actively moving towards future, and so remain trapped in a "frozen present" (Reith, 1999a). When life revolves around the consumption of a drug, time ceases to matter and is only projected as far as the next hit. As Alexander Trocci put it in his autobiographical account of heroin addiction, "one is no longer grotesquely involved in the becoming. One simply is" (Trocci, 1992, p. 11). An empirical study of addiction described lifestyles that were characterized by a lack of movement, inactivity and stasis, and that were revealed in comments that life was "going nowhere" or had "stopped." One addict encapsulated the breakdown of self-perception and of the articulation of time, saying, "You're just existing, no more. There's no life, no future, and you will die" (quoted in Reith, 1999a, p. 105). As the individual's temporal narrative breaks down, so too does their sense of self as a being engaging with the world and moving toward the future. Eventually, all experience, including the perception of the self as an independent entity, becomes subsumed to the desire to take drugs.

The terminal decline of the addict through illness, poverty, homelessness, isolation, and even death that accompanies such experiential states has been well documented and describes a scenario where edgework has completely broken down. Here, rather than consumption assisting the realization of the self, it has taken over and destroyed the self. The individual has gone over the precipice and has not come back.

This is the threat that faces edgeworkers: the possibility that they will lose control and their trip will become permanent. The danger of unconsciousness, insanity, self-destruction, addiction, and even death lurks behind the most exciting and invigorating of good times. The threat of genuine risk is necessary for the experiential thrill of edgework, and the rewards of successfully managing it are the greater for it. As we saw earlier, if danger is avoided too completely, the experience becomes merely "boring." The skill lies in going as close to the edge as possible without actually going over; as Lyng reminds us, the challenge is to "control the uncontrollable (1990)."

Conclusion

The increased popularity of voluntary risk taking, and the flourishing of opportunities to engage in a wide variety of such behaviors, mirrors the climate of late modernity itself, with its contradictory demands for the regulation of rational action (and criticism of failure as addictive and abnormal), and its simultaneous emphasis on excessive consumption and self indulgence. The consumption of drugs exemplifies these features on both the structural and individual level. As the world becomes more uncertain and more oriented towards hedonism, instant gratification, and consumerism, so the activities that have the most salience, the most "cultural capital," tend to reflect its values.

In this climate we find the increasing normalization of drug use, to the point where drugs themselves are described as an integral feature of our "rave new world" (Phaphides, 1997), with consumers their "medicated followers of fashion" (Collin, 1996). In this, they both express the character of late modern society and also provide the opportunity to escape it in a very culturally appropriate way.

The consumption of drugs can be seen as a form of excessive behavior that represents a revolt against the strictures of everyday reason and the regulation of a "civilized" body. The adrenaline rush, the sensation of being close to the edge, of giving in to the chaos of the moment, is a hedonistic escape from the mundane routine of "straight" society. Successful edgework ensures that users transcend the tyranny of rationalization but without succumbing to the tyranny of medicalization, the censure of addiction. In these activities, we can see a return to Bataille's model of excess: the rejection of the "bourgeois" values of restrained expenditure and the celebration of the principle of excess in extreme, intense activities that Bataille said were comparable to—and in this case, actually *are*—toxic states.

It has been argued that such moves toward the embrace of risk at moments when rational society attempts to banish it are "a testament to human variability, desire and the possible" that offer a glimpse of "alternative, nomadic ways of being" within, but also partially outside, rational society (Ferrell, Milovanovic, and Lyng, 2001, p. 180).

However, it could also be argued that certain types of drug edgeworkers do not fit this rebellious, marginal role. In the example of the largest and most rapidly growing subcultural group of soft drug users, it appears as though consumer culture has almost tamed "excess" and turned it into a commodity that can be bought: oblivion in a pill. The very concept of "normalization" itself implies risk that is controlled, chaos that is tamed. In exchange for the opportunity to purchase an extreme experience, the consumer has to keep within the limits set out by that experience, i.e., to negotiate the boundary between chaos and order, and to ensure that they return from the edge. If they fail to do so, sanctions will be imposed, namely, the refusal of the opportunity of repeat purchases, and the diagnosis of some medical abnormality or "addiction." A program of moral repentance and medical treatment may follow. It may well be that drug edgeworkers do not so much transcend the rules of rational society as they adhere to a new (admittedly more flexible) set of structural constraints.

Either way, it can be said that the opportunities for escape and for the "controlled de-controlling of the emotions" (Elias and During, 1986) are reasonably widespread and frequently sanctioned in modern society. Crucially, the activities this involves do not destroy the individual or the social structure, but on the contrary, actually facilitate the realization of the self and the pursuit of authenticity. Van Ree (1977) highlights this point, noting the general utility of certain types of disorder and arguing that drugs act as a "chemical carnival, providing a temporary and reversible slackening of the bonds of reason." The crucial word here is "reversible," meaning that they "indirectly serve to strengthen the societal framework" (Van Ree, 1977, p. 93). In other words, they provide catharsis so that the social structure can continue—provided, of course, participants' edgework is successful.

Consideration of the wider role of drugs in the maintenance of the social structure is outside the scope of this chapter. Indeed, it is recognized that such a perspective comes dangerously close to functionalism, and this is possibly partly due to the (necessarily) general nature of the discussion of drug edge-workers presented here. What is needed is a far more detailed analysis of the experiential framework of the many different subcultural groups in all their variety and complexity. This would establish in what situations and to what extent consumers of drugs are consumers of risk: who lives on the edge, who goes over, and who negotiates the boundary.

None of these issues, however, detracts from the central experience of edge-work, in which drug users walk the tightrope between the chaos of addiction and the order of sobriety, between the urge to indulge in excessive behavior and the simultaneous need to exercise self-control. Their task: is no less than the negotiation of the boundaries of normal and abnormal consumption itself, an undertaking that means that, in late modern society, drug users are the ultimate edgeworkers.

Notes

1. Lyng (1990) is critical of the inclusion of gambling as edgework due to the lack of control it involves, and to the presence of "fate." However, it has been found that gamblers believe they *are* in control of their destiny and can influence fate. Their very feelings of omnipotence, transcen-dence, hyperreality, and the alteration of perceptions of time and space (crucial to the experience of edgework) derive from this, and this is what gives gamblers the "thrill" they pursue (Reith, 1999b). Therefore, I believe it *is* appropriate to classify gambling as edgework here.

2. It should not be assumed here that the experience of drugs is homoge-nous, as the following discussion may (falsely) imply. Rather, drug con-sumption is a heterogeneous experience that depends on many factors, such as type of drug, context of consumption, and the socioeconomic, cultural, ethnic, gendered, and political orientations of consumers. Due to constraints imposed by length, these factors are not given due atten-tion here to allow for a fuller more general concentration on what is most salient to this specific discussion, namely the exercise of edgework in the consumption of drugs in a general sense.

3. Of course, drug consumers are also edgeworkers insofar as they are engaged in criminal activity. Although consideration of this dimension is outside the scope of the present paper, see Lyng (1993) for a discussion of criminal edgework.

References

Bataille, G. *Visions of Excess*. Oxford: Manchester University Press, 1985. Trans. A. Stoekl; C.L. Lovitt and D.M. Leslie.

Baudrillard, J. *The Consumer Society: Myths and Structures*. London: Sage, 1998. Trans. C. Turner.

Bauman, Z. *Freedom*. Milton Keynes, UK: Open University Press, 1988.

———. *Work, Consumerism and the New Poor*. Buckingham, UK: Open University Press, 1998.

Beck, U. *Risk Society: Towards a New Modernity*. London: Sage, 1992. Trans-H. Ritter.

Berridge, V., and Edwards, G. *Opium and the People: Opiate Use in Nineteenth Century England*. London: Allen Lane, 1987.

Burroughs, W. *Junky*. New York: Penguin, 1977.

Cohen, S and Taylor, L. *Escape Attempts: The Theory and Practice of Resistance to Everyday Life*, 2nd ed. London: Routledge, 1992.

Coffield, F., and Goften, L. *Drugs and Young People*. London: Institute for Public Policy Research, 1994.

Collin, M. "Medicated Followers of Fashion." *Time Out*, November 1996: 12–14.

Collisan, M. "In search of the high life: drugs, crime, masculinity and consumption." *British Journal of Criminology* 36(3): 428–444, 1996.

Conrad, P., and Schneider, J. *Deviance and Medicalization: From Badness to Sickness*. Philadelphia: Temple Press, 1992.

Crawford, R. "A Cultural Account of 'Health': Control, Release and the Social Body." In *Issues in the Political Economy of Health Care*, edited by J. B. McKinlay. New York: Tavistock, 1984.

Daumal, R. "A Fundamental Experiment." In *The Drug User: Documents 1840–1960*, edited by B. Strasbaugh and D. Blaise. New York: Blast Books, 1991.

De Quincey, T. *Confessions of an English Opium Eater*. Harmondsworth, UK: Penguin, 1982.

Durkheim, E. *Suicide: A Study in Sociology*. Trans. J. A. Spaulding and G. Simpson. London: Routledge, 1970.

Elias, N. *The Civilizing Process*. Translated by E. Jephcott. London: Blackwell, 2000. (Original work published 1939.)

Elias, N., and Dunning, E. *Quest for Excitement: Sport and Leisure in the Civilizing Process*. Oxford: Basil Blackwell, 1986.

Ferrell, J., Milovanovic, D., and Lyng, S. "Edgework, Media Practices, and the Elongation of Meaning: A Theoretical Ethnography of the Bridge Day Event." *Theoretical Criminology* 5(2) (2001): 177–202.

Foucault, M. *The Birth of the Clinic*. New York: Vintage Books, 1975.

———. *Discipline and Punish: The Birth of the Prison*. London: Allen Lane, 1977. Trans A.M Sheridans Smith.

Foucault, M. "The History of Sexuality" Vol. 1. Trans. R. Hurley. Harmondsworth: Penguin, 1976.

Henderson, S. "Drugs and Culture: The Question of Gender." In *Drugs: Cultures, Controls and Everyday Life*, edited by N. South. London: Sage, 1999.

Giddens, A. "Modernity and Self Identity." Cambridge: Polity. 1991.

Goffman, E. "Where the Action Is." In *Interaction Ritual: Essays in Face to Face Behavior*. London: Penguin, 1972.

Hofman, A. "LSD: My Problem Child." In *The Drug User: Documents, 1840–1960*, edited by B. Strasbaugh and D. Blaise. New York: Blast Books, 1991.

James, W. *The Varieties of Religious Experience*. London: Penguin, 1982.

Lee, J. "The Underworld of the East" in *The Drug User: Documents 1840–1960*, edited by B. Strasbaugh and D. Blaise. New York: Blast Books, 1991.

Lupton, D. *Risk*. London: Routledge, 1999.

Lyng, S., and Snow, D. "Vocabularies of Motive and High Risk Behavior: The Case of Skydiving." In *Advances in Group Processes*, Volume 3, edited by E. Lawler. Greenwich, CT: JAI Press, 1986.

Lyng, S. "Edgework: A Social Psychological Analysis of Voluntary Risk Taking." *American Journal of Sociology* 95(4) (1990): 851–886.

———. "Dysfunctional Risk Taking: Criminal Behavior as Edgework." In *Adolescent Risk Taking*, edited by N. Bell and R. Bell. London: Sage, 1993.

Marx, K. *Economic and Philosophic Manuscripts of 1844*. Translated by M. Milligan. New York: International Publishers, 1972.

Oxford English Dictionary. Oxford: Clarendon Press, 1991.

Parker, H., and Measham, F. "Pick 'n' Mix: Changing Patterns of Illicit Drug Use Among 1990s Adolescents." *Drugs: Education, Prevention and Policy* 1(1) (1994): 5–13.

Parker, H., Measham, F., and Aldridge, J. *Drugs Futures: Changing Patterns of Drug Use Amongst English Youth*. London: Institute for the Study of Drug Dependence, 1995.

Phaphides, P. "Rave New World." *Time Out* June 1997: 11–18.

Preble, E., and Casey, J. "Taking Care of Business: The Heroin Users Life on the Street." *International Journal of the Addictions* 4(1) (1969): 1–24.

Reith, G. "In Search of Lost Time: Recall, Projection and the Phenomenology of Addiction." *Time and Society* 8(1) (1999a): 99–117.

———. *The Age of Chance: Gambling in Western Culture*. London: Routledge, 1999b/2002.

———. "Consumption and its discontent: addiction, identity and the problems of freedom." *British Journal of Sociology* 55(2): 283–300, 2004.

Ritzer, G. *Enchanting a Disenchanted World: Revolutionizing the Means of Consumption*. Thousand Oaks, CA: Pine Forge Press, 1999.

Shewan, D., Dalgarno, P., and Reith, G. "Perceived Risk and Risk Reduction Among Ecstasy Users: The Role of Drug, Set and Setting." *The International Journal of Drug Policy* 10 (2000): 431–453.

Shiner, M., and Newburn, T. "Definitely, Maybe Not? The Normalization of Recreational Drug Use Amongst Young People." *Sociology* 31(3) (1997): 511–529.

Shiner, M., and Newburn, T. "Taking Tea with Noel: The Place and Meaning of Drug Use in Everyday Life." In *Drugs: Cultures, Controls and Everyday Life*, edited by N. South. London: Sage, 1999.

South, N., ed. *Drugs: Cultures, Controls and Everyday Life*. London: Sage, 1999.

Stanley, C. *Urban Excess and the Law*. London: Cavendish, 1996.

Strasbaugh, B. and Blaise, D., eds. *The Drug User: Documents 1840–1960*. New York: Blast Books, 1991.

Thompson, H. S. *Fear and Loathing in Las Vegas*. London: Paladin, 1972.

Trocchi, A. *Cain's Book*. London: Calder, 1992.

Turner, B. *The Body in Society*, 2nd ed. London: Sage, 1996.

Van Ree, E. "Fear of Drugs." *International Journal of Drug Policy* 8(2) (1997): 93–100.

Weber, M. *The Protestant Ethic and the Spirit of Capitalism*. London: Counterpoint, 1985. (Original work published in 1930.)

Part VII
Edgework in the Academy

11

Intellectual Risk Taking, Organizations, and Academic Freedom and Tenure

GIDEON SJOBERG

CONTENTS

Introduction

In recent decades sociologists have addressed the issue of what Stephen Lyng refers to as "edgework" and what Anthony Giddens and Ulrich Beck speak of as "risk." We shall employ these concepts rather synonymously while recognizing that Lyng focuses on voluntary activities on the fringes of the social order, whereas Giddens and Beck address the risks encountered by the central political and economic arrangements of contemporary social orders.

Lyng's groundbreaking essay relied on qualitative data that he had collected on the activities of skydivers who were engaged in a voluntary leisure-time pursuit. In his essay, Lyng presses forward two interrelated themes: First, he focuses on how skydivers strive to control, through mastery of a particular set of technical procedures and knowledge, a clearly hazardous or risky set of activities. Second, Lyng finds that in the process, skydivers, through their edgework, achieve an emotional or experiential high while risking physical injury (or even death itself).

What is salient about Lyng's analysis is that these skydivers' activities are a response to, or reaction against, the routinization or standardization of every-day activities. In a sense, the participation by skydivers in edgework provides them with "meaning in life." Beck and Giddens, on the other hand, focus on the risk involved in the functioning of basic economic and political arrange-ments in what Beck refers to as "second modernity."

In this essay we take the analysis of risk or edgework in a somewhat different direction than do the aforementioned authors while remaining ever mindful of their research and theorizing. Inasmuch as we shall focus attention on a central institutional arrangement in modern social orders—notably, intellectual risk taking within academic settings—we shall address the work of Giddens and Beck rather than Lyng. Concomitantly, we also find that these differing ways of approaching risk or edgework may well serve to supplement one another as we struggle to more fully understand the nature of risk taking or edgework in late or second modernity.

Specification of Objectives

Although intellectual risk taking reflects a form of individualism, we also find, on careful sociological inspection, that this individualism is embedded within, and dependent upon, a collective or group context. In this respect we take seri-ously the theorizing of John Dewey, George Herbert Mead, and like-minded scholars. Nowadays, we find widespread celebration by many journalists, policy makers, and academics of risk taking by entrepreneurs in the economic sphere. But these journalists and other opinion makers generally fall short in informing their publics that this kind of risk taking, to be successful, requires group (indeed, organizational) support. We are thus talking about a type of risk taking that can be contrasted with that of Lyng's skydivers, who were, as noted, engaged in a leisure time pursuit somewhat on the margins of the larger institutional arrangements.

Our undergirding principle is that intellectual risk taking in modern soci-ety requires organizational support, both formal and informal. While admir-ing the work of Giddens and Beck for having isolated fundamental social processes that are essential features of advanced industrial social orders in the second modernity, we discover that these sociologists have failed to grapple with the organizational structures that serve both to enhance and to constrain risk taking. Further, without attention to these organizational issues we can-not effectively address such related matters as science and democracy.

With this background in hand, we can articulate the objectives of this essay as well as the manner in which our argument unfolds. The first section begins with an autobiographical—albeit episodic—account of my intellectual risk-taking activities during 50 plus years in academia. More narrowly, I discuss my activities within the context of the University of Texas at Austin, where I have spent those years, and I shall also to some degree consider the impact of the major political interests in the State as these have shaped university policy. As with any autobiographical account, including one that serves as a basis for elaborating upon theoretical issues relating to risk taking, one must be attentive to a number of pitfalls: those arising from vanity, exaggeration, lack of a third-party perspective, or lack of candor and objectivity. While all of these dangers are real, autobiographical accounts can potentially serve to uncover social processes that are difficult to access through any other research procedure. My own account sets out to place my definition of intellectual activities within the larger organizational setting, and, more generally, I reflect on my own intellectual activities within the context of the university and the State of Texas.

In the second section we dramatically change course. Here we address issues regarding risk taking that are more theoretical in nature. We do so by critically evaluating the work of Ulrich Beck and Anthony Giddens as we advance the thesis that these social theorists have failed to take account of the organizational setting within which risk taking occurs. Evaluating the works of these scholars provides us with a fuller understanding of risk taking in modern societies. Though Giddens and Beck have made enormous strides in delineating the issue of risk, their failure to ground their analysis in an understanding of organizations deserves to be highlighted.

With my autobiographical account and the critique of Giddens and Beck in place, we can, in the third section of this essay, examine the issues of academic freedom and tenure as these relate to risk taking. In the fourth and concluding section of this essay, we recapitulate our basic themes and link our analysis with existing scholarly work and then, in broad strokes, articulate some of the general implications of our analysis of risk taking or edgework in late modernity, most notably its relationship to science and democracy.

My Scholarly Activities and Risk Taking

My life experience serves as a basis for examining the broader theoretical issue of risk taking. Inasmuch as I have spent over half a century at the University of Texas, it will be necessary not only to examine my intellectual risk-taking activities but also to recognize that these have been articulated within the context of a complex university organization that, in turn, has been shaped by powerful interest groups that have a stake in the activities of the university. Yet examination of my own life history calls for some background data.

I received my doctorate from what is now Washington State University in 1949 and, as good fortune would have it, the university of Texas has been my employer since that date. Although I was on leave for several years in the late 1960s (and almost left UT), I have been associated with the university for over half a century. During this period, I have sought to contribute to sociology in three somewhat different spheres. The first phase of my career was dominated by a concern with the nature of the city in preindustrial civilizations. Another feature of my intellectual activity has been to examine the logic of social inquiry, or methodology. Specifically, what procedures do and should sociologists employ in examining social and cultural activities, and how objective are they? Actually, my investigation of the research process has been a major theme throughout my career. The third phase of my career has been focused on organizational and moral issues, particularly as they pertain to human rights. To keep this essay to manageable proportions, I shall emphasize the early and late phases of my career and omit any significant discussion of my metho-dological perspective.

Having briefly introduced myself, I shall now introduce the University of Texas, currently referred to as the University of Texas at Austin. Although nowadays the scope of the University is national (even international), when I first arrived it was a major regional university with a number of nationally acclaimed faculty members. In the early 1940s, a major political battle had taken place at UT (an abbreviation I shall use throughout). Homer Rainey, a political liberal for that era, was president of UT, and he was intent upon moving the university into the national orbit of academic life. In the aftermath of the Great Depression and as a result of World War II, the state had been experiencing a major transformation, moving away from its agrarian roots toward greater industrialization and urbanization. Further, we remind ourselves that Texas, though often perceived as part of the Southwest, was part of the Confederacy during the Civil War.

The core of the University, situated on the legendary "40 acres," is located within about ten blocks of the state capitol building. The physical proximity of the Tower, or the main building at UT, which houses university administrators, and the Capitol, the center of Texas politics, is emblematic of the symbiosis between politics and higher education in the state. The Tower and the Capitol, which in 1949 dominated the Austin skyline, are also emblematic of the political struggles that have evolved, particularly during the early history of the University, between Texas politics and higher education. State politicians have been keenly aware of happenings on campus, and some of the faculty have perfected the art of politics gazing.

Some years before I arrived, the president, Homer Rainey, was fired by the Board of Regents; he then ran for governor but lost. During the Rainey era, the faculty was deeply divided, and these divisions were so stark that a few of the faculty (or so I was told) were not on speaking terms with one another. Moreover, because of certain events in the early 1940s, the university had been censured by the American Association of University Professors (AAUP). Although the AAUP lacks formal power as such, its censure has typically had a negative impact on an institution's standing within the national academic community. The censure signified a problem with academic freedom. Moreover, the university, at the time I arrived, required a loyalty oath, which I signed. The Cold War was a reality that faculty and administrators understood.

What I wish to emphasize is that although the University of Texas, as an organization, provided faculty members like myself with enormous human and other resources, it also placed significant constraints on academic freedom.

By the late 1940s, the university had developed an outstanding research library, and the intellectual setting was one whose quality should not be underestimated. A fellow sociologist, Boyd Littrell, has reminded me that throughout my career the university contained within its ranks a group of major scholars who set high standards of excellence to which other faculty could aspire and by which they would come to be judged. In the social sciences, there was the economist Clarence Ayres, who made a considerable name for himself as an institutionalist (he was also an early teacher of Talcott Parsons at Amherst), the historian Walter Webb, who became world renowned for his work on the frontier, and the philosopher David Miller, who achieved national and international acclaim as an expositor of George Herbert Mead's views at a time when Mead and other pragmatists were unfashionable in American academia. And arriving the same year as I, was Winfred Lehmann, who was to become the chief architect of the Department of Linguistics, the Center for Asian Studies, and the Center for Middle Eastern Studies, while making internationally recognized contributions to linguistic scholarship.

In the sociology department, my scholarly home, I found a thriving intellectual milieu. One might say that a number of my colleagues were addressing sociological problems associated with the old Chicago School. Warner E. Gettys (the founder and chair) greatly admired the Chicago School, and Carl Rosenquist (another member of the old guard) was a Chicago graduate, while Harry Moore (the third member of the old guard) was a North Carolina product. Gettys, who devoted his career primarily to administration and textbook writing, was smart and understood the meaning of theoretically informed scholarly activities. Among the younger faculty, Ivan Belknap had attended Chicago for a short time and appreciated its contribution to sociology. Perhaps more important to my development were Stanley Taylor and Walter Firey. Taylor, a Canadian, was an instructor who later returned to Chicago to complete his doctorate. He was an avowed advocate of Hegelian theorizing and thus of the notion that the concept is the reality. Firey, in turn, wrote his dissertation at Harvard under the direction of Pitirim A. Sorokin, with Talcott Parsons on his doctoral committee, and he made a considerable name for himself through his study of urban land use, as well as the formulation of an original theory of resources. He and Taylor engaged in lengthy abstract theoretical debates regarding such concepts as the nature of rationality and institutions. Although I was a very marginal participant in the ensuing discourse, my intellectual horizons were expanded greatly by their dialogue. Unquestionably, Walter Firey has, over the years, had a considerable scholarly impact on my sociological worldview.

In addition to these faculty resources, there was a small but thriving doctoral program, and some of the graduate students have had a deep influence on my sociological journey. In particular, Leonard Cain (who remains to this day one of my most trusted critics and imaginative editors) arrived as a teaching assistant when I began as an assistant professor. And I must not overlook my wife, Andrée. As soon as we arrived she began work at UT on her MA degree in anthropology and later received the first doctorate in the fledgling program in linguistics. She then taught for forty years (1960–2000) in linguistics and, later, Asian studies. She has not only has been super editor but she also came to acquire specialized knowledge about the Turkic peoples of Central Asia and the Dravidian-speaking peoples of India. She has constantly reminded me of the need to maintain a cross-cultural and cross-national perspective, and she has possessed in-depth knowledge of peoples against which to check my reality. And because the campus was relatively small, and through my own interaction patterns as well as Andrée's networks, I came to develop a rather wide variety of intellectual links with faculty members outside the field of sociology. However individualistic I might judge my intellectual endeavors, they have in large part been made possible by the social capital (or intellectual networks) and the cultural capital (for instance, access to a great library) that resulted from my affiliation with the University of Texas.

While the University has provided me with enormous scholarly resources, I have always been sensitive to the social constraints upon me. The spillover from the Rainey era still loomed large in 1949. Rainey (1971, pp. 47–48), in his autobiographical account of this turmoil, observed that the social sciences were singled out for critical attention during his presidency. At one point colleagues such as Carl Rosenquist and Harry Moore (along with others) had their research funds, which had been approved at the university level, rejected by the Board of Regents. More generally, topics such as race and gender were skirted or avoided in one's teaching and research. Nowadays, in contrast, research on and teaching about race and ethnicity and gender are de rigeur.

Early in my association with the university, I sensed that my own and other colleagues' political and economic views were, at least indirectly, being monitored. I soon learned about an assistant professor in the department who had been forced to resign a few years before I arrived. I had at first assumed he was a casualty of the Rainey struggle but later learned that a questionnaire he distributed to undergraduate students included queries about sexual activities and that this had been a precipitating factor in his departure. Yet there is reason to believe that the latter would not have been decisive without the former. Also in my early years at UT, I heard rumblings regarding the plight of a senior colleague, Harry Moore, whose authored (or co-authored) manuscript of a community study had been repressed. Some time later I heard that the editor of the newspaper in the community Moore had studied had been able, though his political influence with the Board of Regents, to suppress publication of the manuscript. These incidents in the department predated my arrival, but they remained an integral part of the cultural milieu. Furthermore, in early 1950s the economist Clarence Ayres came under severe attack by a group of politicians in the state who wanted him fired (Dugger, 1974). Had he not been a tenured professor, the historian Lewis Gould (1998) surmises, he would likely have been dismissed. Ayres was an institutional economist who was heavily influenced by Thorstein Veblen and John Dewey. Although a critic of sorts of the economic order, he was neither a socialist nor a communist.

As the 1950s evolved, changes were evident. Logan Wilson, a prominent sociologist and administrator, was brought in as president of UT in 1953, just after steps were taken by the then-chancellor to remove the university from the AAUP blacklist (Dugger, 1974). Although Wilson was a cautious administrator, he came to champion the idea that UT should become a national research university. Still, faculty members in 1957 were reminded of the limits on academic freedom when, as a result of political pressure, president Wilson removed a black woman student, Barbara Smith, from her leading role in an opera that was being produced by the School of Fine Arts.[1] There were some counterreactions. Some members of the Faculty Council openly protested this removal, and two, Robert Williams and R. C. Stephenson, were especially critical of the administration. Williams, a tenured full professor of Romance Languages, told me and other faculty members that the President had called him into his office on a Saturday morning to severely berate him for questioning administrative actions in the Barbara Smith case. Wilson, I would suggest, was sending the message that he deemed faculty criticisms of his administrative actions to be inappropriate, in this case at least. That Williams was punished for his dissident views (and not just in the Barbara Smith case) is a matter of record, having been duly noted by the faculty members who wrote his obituary. That the issues brought to the fore in the Barbara Smith case set important boundaries on what could be effectively studied by social scientists in the realm of race relations seems evident.

The race issue has historically been a greater barrier to the University's achievement of national and international scholarly acclaim than most faculty and administrators have acknowledged. This is not to say that efforts were not made to move beyond it. For example, in 1961 Richard Colvard, an assistant professor of sociology, initiated a petition that in effect called on the general faculty of the university to support the U. S. Supreme Court's decision in Brown v. Board of Education (Minutes of the Meeting of the General Faculty, May 9, 1961). The faculty approved the resolution, but not without opposition from a dissenting minority. It is important to observe that only a few members of the sociology department signed that petition. Yet, a number of distinguished members of the faculty, including Winfred Lehmann, did sign, and they lent their scholarly reputations to this effort.

What I would emphasize is that within the department, since I arrived (and afterwards), there was considerable freedom to pursue a rather diverse range of intellectual endeavors, while simultaneously one was frequently reminded of the limits imposed on that freedom and the major risks associated with transgressing the more or less established social boundaries. For instance, during the 1960s the student movement was a major presence at UT (Rossinow, 1998); yet, in contrast to the situation at a number of major institutions, few faculty members became actively engaged in supporting the student concerns (until late in the process).[2] I have assumed that this resulted from the faculty's general acceptance of the boundaries beyond which intellectual edgework was strongly discouraged by administrators and colleagues.

Significantly, however, the ideal of academic freedom has also imposed limits on the ability of administrators and the Board of Regents to shape the course of academic endeavors. It helped to turn the university around after the Rainey debacle, and it has set limits on other external intrusions into academic decision-making. Thus, in the late 1960s, Frank Erwin, a politically well-connected and powerful member of the Board of Regents, involved himself rather directly in faculty affairs, seeking to replace the then-dean of the Law School with someone more in keeping with his views. But the Law School faculty, invoking, among other principles, the academic freedom ideal, was able to mobilize the support of an influential ex-student constituency so as to resist this stark political intervention. Although Erwin continued to intrude in a heavy-handed manner into the affairs of the university (firing, for instance, the dean of the College of Arts and Sciences), the efforts by the Law School highlighted the significance of faculty freedom and autonomy and served as a counterweight to direct political intervention and control.

The limits on academic freedom and tenure were tested in other ways as well. During the 1970s a group of professors who were active in faculty-related activities (several, for instance, being members of the Committee of Counsel on Academic Freedom and Responsibility, an official committee at UT) had their recommended salary increases cut. The recommendations had been initiated at the departmental level and approved by the dean of the college but were then rescinded at the presidential level. I was a member of the Faculty Senate Fact-Finding Committee on Salary Decisions (1976) that investigated this incident. We found no smoking gun, but the circumstantial evidence was such that it seems apparent that the faculty in question were punished for their active involvement in activities that had been, and continue to be, viewed as an integral part of academic life. Surely the resistance of the faculty to this arbitrary administrative intervention in the determination of salaries signaled a concern with the faculty's freedom to pursue more broad-based scholarly endeavors.

One reason that the "faculty activists" were singled out in the 1970s is that a few years earlier the president, Stephen Spurr, had been summarily dismissed and a new one, Lorene Rogers, installed by the Board of Regents. President Rogers had decidedly less cosmopolitan views than did her predecessor. Spurr's dismissal was condemned by a sizable segment of the faculty. The new president's action in cutting the salary recommendations of the targeted faculty appears to have been an effort to reassert the authority of administrators and the Board of Regents.

And now fast-forward to the present. We must take note of one event after 9/11. Robert Jensen, an associate professor of journalism, wrote an op-ed item for the *Houston Chronicle* in which he took a position that was defined as critical of national policy in a time of crisis. As a result Jensen was rebuked by the president of UT-Austin (Faulkner, 2001), who, in a rebuttal in the same newspaper, spoke of Jensen as a "fountainhead of foolishness," though defending his right to speak.

Several matters regarding the aforementioned episodes at UT require clarification. One, it appears that the university during the past fifty years has become more cosmopolitan and thus more tolerant of a wider range of social, political, and economic perspectives. Nonetheless, a case can be made that faculty members are more passive today regarding university activities than some decades ago. Two, I would point to a paradox of sorts. Because they respect tenure, at least in a formal sense, university administrators are freer to criticize tenured faculty members with whom they disagree. Clearly, the contention by the president of the university in 2001 that a faculty member was not speaking for the university is a legitimate one (though Jensen did not identify himself as a spokesperson for that institution). At the same time, such tough reactions by administrators to dissenting perspectives is likely to narrow dissent, especially among the more vulnerable faculty who sense they are expected to conform to a particular political perspective if they are to succeed. Three, another issue concerns problems associated with junior faculty who have yet to attain tenure. I am somewhat familiar with a case involving two members of the government department who were asked to move on in the early 1980s.[3] Both of them were theoretically inclined and had written high quality work on intellectual history. One had focused on a wing of Marxist thought and was later to achieve national acclaim for his work on Michel Foucault. In my view, their intellectual left-of-center—but far from radical—scholarship worked against them, although the situation was complicated by the fact that the department was undergoing a major transition as the dean and other administrators were intent on refocusing research, not only on American government but upon model building and empirical investigation. Although this is difficult to document in any well-defined manner, the administration at UT-Austin has shaped the worldview of social science so as to conform to the politically conservative climate of the state. In recent decades controversial social science endeavors (broadly defined) have, not surprisingly, been few at UT-Austin.

Having highlighted selected controversies regarding academic freedom and some of the boundaries on scholarly freedom during the past fifty years or so at UT, I now turn attention to my own life circumstances as these relate to risk taking and academic freedom and tenure. My main objective early in my career was to analyze the nature of the preindustrial city from a cross-cultural perspective (though my first two journal articles were concerned with methodology and with the American class system). In carrying out my work on the preindustrial city, I sought to delineate the common social patterns of cities in preindustrial civilizations in the Middle East, India, China, and Mesoamerica. In a larger sense it was a critique of the Chicago School of urban sociology. I speak of risk taking because the project could have been a failure, either with respect to the quality of my work or with respect to securing an audience (or both).

I have been asked on a number of occasions by fellow sociologists: How did you come to take on this project? I had received my BA and MA from the University of New Mexico and my doctorate from Washington State, and none of my professors ever talked about the preindustrial city. At New Mexico, Paul Walter, Jr., who helped shape my sociological orientation, was much interested in the impact of urbanization on the Spanish-speaking peoples of New Mexico. From Albuquerque, I went to Washington State College, now Washington State University. There T. H. Kennedy, known more for his imaginative administrative skills than for his scholarly abilities, was for me a great teacher in that he encouraged me to do what I could do best: read widely while educating myself on various facets of sociology. Although I internalized only a small part of what I read, I was, in my own way, steeping myself in various facets of European intellectual (especially sociological) thought. Another highly influential scholar was Allan H. Smith, an anthropologist who opened my eyes to the centrality of cross-cultural research. He discussed with me his work on the Kalispel Indians and also supervised a year's reading course on field studies in major cultural areas of the world. This was my introduction to cross-cultural investigation. In addition, I learned from Roger Nett, a fellow graduate student who was at the time more philosophically inclined than I.

After I completed my doctorate in 1949, my parents offered to buy me a car. I countered with the suggestion that they support Andrée and myself for a summer while we audited courses at the University of California, Berkeley. During that summer I attended a variety of classes while preparing to teach rural and urban sociology and statistics and research methods at the University of Texas. I listened to some of Walter Goldschmidt's lectures on American rural communities and a few of C. Daryll Forde's lectures on Africa. I also audited Wolfram Eberhard's course on nomadic and agrarian peoples in eastern and central Asia as well as historian Charles Wilbur's course on the history of China. Save for Eberhard, all of these distinguished scholars were visiting professors.

After taking up my duties in Austin in the fall, I began lecturing on comparative and cross-cultural issues in both my rural and my urban courses. And within about a year of arriving at Texas, the general outline of my project on the cross-cultural analysis of cities (and preindustrial civilizations) came into focus, so that by 1952, I had published an article in the *American Journal of Sociology* (AJS) titled "Folk and 'Feudal' Societies" that contrasted Robert Redfield's folk society with an ideal-typical construction of preindustrial civilized or "feudal" societies of which preindustrial cities were an essential component. This essay was followed by "The Preindustrial City" in the AJS in 1955, and then in 1960 by the book, *The Preindustrial City*. This was the first effort to delineate the social patterns associated with the preindustrial city. Further, this work was the first broad-based, cross-cultural critique of basic tenets of the then-dominant Chicago School of urban research. However, it received a hearing, with such scholars as Redfield being generous enough to cite my work in a rather approving manner.

Why this rather extended discussion in an essay on intellectual risk taking? The reasons are several. It is now apparent that I did not at the time understand, subjectively, the nature of my intellectual edgework or risk taking; indeed, the work of cognitive psychologists suggests that human agents experience difficulties in assessing future risks. A few years ago a fellow sociologist, Larry Reynolds, asked me: What would my academic career have been if the articles in the AJS had not been published? I strongly suspect that I would have been forced to move to a less prestigious institution, though Andrée observes that I would very likely have pursued instead my interest in stratification or even methodology. But these topics would not have been as sociologically compelling as my work on the preindustrial city.

There is another reason for highlighting my research on the preindustrial city. In the late 1950s the department at Texas had undergone a profound change as the old guard retired and a new regime recruited from the outside took over. In keeping with the temper of the times, this new leadership broke sharply with the department's past, which led to adverse ramifications for me. During this transition period I also incurred the enmity of a member of the old guard when, in a meeting with president Logan Wilson, I openly opposed his candidate for the position of chair; in my view, he did not possess the necessary scholarly credentials.

With the new guard's takeover, I soon was ostracized for a number of years (most of the isolation occurring after *The Preindustrial City* was published). My case appears to be quite extreme, underscored by a marked difference between my recognition on the national level and the local scene. Looking back, I see that I could have been more of a Goffman-like actor in coping with my new circumstances. But that was not my style. Moreover, some events were beyond my immediate control. Strangely, my "exile" resulted in part from the hue and cry that surrounded the upheaval in an honorary society, Alpha Kappa Delta (AKD), whose members included students and faculty. There were accusations of prejudice against a student because of his minority group status. Indeed, this person had been blackballed by two members of AKD (sufficient reason for exclusion in that era). Interestingly, AKD already included a member of the same ethnic group in question. The long and short of it is that all the proposed new candidates, including the incoming departmental chair, were rejected for membership. Because some of the more vocal students were identified with me, I came to be blamed by some faculty for this incident, even though I never attended any of the meetings at which these events unfolded. Further, and of considerable import, my ostracism was compounded by my sociological perspective, one that did not conform with the emerging world-view that emphasized quantification and sociology as a "hard science." The end result was that I was exiled and was not permitted to teach any graduate courses (something I had done since my arrival at UT). I was removed from my associate membership in the graduate faculty (a category that has since been abolished). My salary trajectory during this era, relative to that of other members of the department, strongly supports this account. Ironically, this ostracism was most acute just after *The Preindustrial City* was published and at a time when I was, among other things, a member of the Social Science Research Council's Committee on Urbanization and an editorial board member of the AJS.

The chair was not-so-subtly informing me that I should leave. One reason I did not do so was that Andree came to be employed as a faculty member at UT. In any event, I lost two grievance hearings, and yet I was ultimately rehabilitated.[4] There were a number of reasons for my shifting fortunes. While I can be faulted for certain errors of judgment, the starkness of my scholarly exile became apparent, locally and nationally. Moreover, in time the chair's authority was eroded by the onrush of other events. One of these involved a colleague, Reece McGee, who in 1963 wrote an article for *The Nation* on the prevalence of guns among UT students. The emotions evoked by that article, just after the Kennedy assassination, led to severe criticisms of him in the state's press. As I understand the situation, the message was conveyed to him that he had no future at Texas. My working premise is that this controversy deflected attention away from me, and the chair's reactions to the tensions generated by the McGee essay sowed doubts about his effectiveness. Furthermore, the special efforts of colleagues such as Ivan Belknap and Norval Glenn, as well as the economist Forest Hill (whom I later learned had written the dean in my behalf), were decisive in my reintegration into the department.

Why this digression in the midst of discussing my intellectual edgework, or risk taking? The sociological principle I am advancing is that it is not only a faculty member's encounter with the extra-academic environment but also the shifting intellectual fortunes within a particular discipline and within departments that generate problems for academic freedom. These patterns are seldom aired except when elite scholars somehow become involved in the conflicts. If not for academic freedom and tenure, these kinds of power struggles would be accentuated as one group or faction seeks to gain ascendancy, typically to curry favor with the administrative apparatus or external power arrangements. Academic freedom and tenure protect scholars from becoming victims of this internecine warfare, which is in large part fostered by circumstances external to the academy.

But let us return to the account of my intellectual endeavors. During the 1960s, most of my efforts were devoted to methodology. I edited a work, *Ethics, Politics, and Social Research* (the first book-length treatment of this topic within sociology), and I wrote a book with Roger Nett on methodo-logy. The methodology book's general framework is that of the sociology of knowledge, the problem of how researchers who are part of the social order they investigate can sustain "objectivity" within the context of intellectual pluralism. I shall not pursue these issues herein, except to mention that this sociology of knowledge perspective permits one to conceive of ethical and political issues as integral features of the research design. And it is the ethics of social research that led me to ask the question: Which ethical perspectives should undergird social science research? This kind of query, along with a longstanding concern with genocide, led me to the investigation of human rights and large-scale organizations.[5]

When I began working on "the sociology of ethics" in the early 1970s with Ted R. Vaughan, I was only vaguely cognizant of the intellectual risks inherent in this undertaking. By about 1976 we had a book on the sociology of ethics largely written, only to realize, in part as a result of a conversation I had with Burns Weston (a legal scholar of some stature), that we lacked proper com-mand of the human rights literature that had direct bearing on our work. We set aside that 1976 manuscript and began another, which also was roughed out, only to be set aside in 1983 as we came to realize that we needed to inte-grate organizational issues more fully into our analysis.

Through these failed efforts we gained an understanding of what we needed to do. One step was to think through our views regarding the nature of human nature. One of our theoretical moves was to reinterpret George Herbert Mead's work in a way that was at odds with conventional wisdom. For us, the social mind plays a more salient role than the social self in defining the nature of human nature (though the notion of the self is not to be dismissed). A second move was to formulate a more adequate theory of organizations, one that takes account of creative human agents and their relationships to the organi-zational structure.

Slowly, in the 1980s, we were coming to define our problem more sharply. In 1984 I, along with Ted Vaughan and Andrée F. Sjoberg, co-edited a special issue of the *Journal of Applied Behavioral Science.* We presented therein our first brief overview (from a sociological perspective) of a human rights orien-tation. That issue also includes an article I wrote with Ted Vaughan and Norma Williams entitled "Bureaucracy as a Moral Issue." By then we were in the process of concluding that a salient contribution of sociology to human rights theory and practice would be to integrate a more adequate theory of social power and of formal organizations into this major problem area.

More recently, I have (with colleagues) been able to cobble together a lengthy essay in *Social Problems* (Sjoberg et al., 2001) outlining a sociologically grounded theoretical framework for the study of human rights within a cross-cultural (or global) context. How much further it will be possible to push out the boundaries of this topic remains to be seen. However, I should never have been able to engage in such edgework or risk taking without the protection of tenure and without the track record that provided me with the legitimacy to take on a project that has been so marginal to the dominant scholarly strands within sociology, and yet so central to social discourse worldwide in the latter part of the twentieth century.

The Theoretical Grounding of Risk

At this point in our analysis we shall turn from our autobiographical account of intellectual risk taking and consider the nature of risk as defined by Giddens and Beck, before revisiting the matter of academic freedom and tenure in more general terms. As suggested earlier, Anthony Giddens (Giddens and Pierson, 1998; Giddens, 2000) and Ulrich Beck (2000; in Boyne, 2001) have been among the leading lights in sociology in advancing the concept of risk as central to understanding second modernity. Although these scholars have delineated a fundamental sociological issue, we have serious reservations about the specific manner in which they have come to define the nature of risk taking in late modernity.

In our view, Giddens and Beck conceive of risk taking in more individualistic terms than is sociologically warranted. Admittedly, our analysis cannot do justice to the overall theorizing of either sociologist. Giddens in particular has written extensively for over three decades, and the volume of secondary literature on both scholars is considerable. What we intend to do is zero in on one facet of Giddens's and Beck's theorizing on risk taking and emphasize their general neglect of large-scale organizations in interpreting how risk comes to be distributed.

Giddens's search for what he terms "structuration theory," with its roots in the philosophy of Ludwig Wittgenstein, leads him astray. In his more foundational writings, Giddens seeks to overcome the dualism between agent and structure and, in the process, champions the view that organizations are both constraining and enabling. His theorizing leads him to emphasize the role of tacit knowledge (what Giddens refers to as practical consciousness) as human agents seek to adhere to, or to rework, the rules that shape social activities. Nigel Pleasants (1999), in his critical analysis of the writings of Giddens, Jürgen Habermas, and Roy Bhaskar, advances the thesis (congruent with our own) that Giddens's theorizing is individualistic in nature, and in fact, Pleasants (1999, p. 92) lumps Giddens together with the conservative economist Frederick A. Hayek: "The ontological picture of the individual as an active, knowledgeable, autonomous agent, as portrayed by Hayek and Giddens, is deeply ingrained in our individualistic intellectual and political culture." Although we do not go as far as Pleasants in singling out the similarities between Hayek and Giddens, we nonetheless contend that Giddens's conceptualization of tacit knowledge and practical consciousness has led him away from an analysis of the social power that is embedded in large-scale organizations.

As for Beck, his somewhat idiosyncratic writings lead one to rethink one's conception of modern social life (Beck, 1992). Unquestionably his views regarding the risk society are slowly but surely filtering into American sociology, particularly in studies on the environment. Yet he, like Giddens, tends to individualize risk taking. In a recent book with Beck-Gernsheim (2002), Beck, when analyzing, for instance, the nature of inequality, contends that we must move beyond Marx and Weber. With that we agree. He reasons that inequalities do not disappear, "they merely become redefined in terms of the *individualization of social risks*. The result is that social problems are increasingly perceived in terms of psychological dispositions, as personal inadequacies… Social crises appear as individual crises" (p. 39). As we interpret Beck's agenda, he wishes to redirect the manner in which this individualization has come to be expressed in what he would regard as sociologically more constructive and creative directions. With that also we agree. Yet Beck, like Giddens, turns his sociological gaze away from the large organizations that dominate the societal and global landscape. Although Beck acknowledges their existence, he minimizes their role in our understanding of risk in second modernity.

Instead of evaluating Giddens and Beck through a critical exegesis of their texts, we shall advance our argument regarding organizations and risk taking by briefly articulating three case studies that highlight the manner in which organizations come to distribute risk taking in modernity. Neither Beck nor Giddens is capable, in our judgment, of addressing the matter of risk as it comes to the fore in these instances (as well as others).

The first case involves the World Trade Organization (WTO), an organization that has arisen in recent years to manage economic activities in the world setting. But just how is the WTO reshaping the nature of risk taking? Some significant clues can be gleaned from examining the writings of one of the godfathers of the WTO, the legal scholar John H. Jackson. Early in his career he became an expert on the legal structure of GATT, out of which the World Trade Organization emerged as a result of the Uruguay Round of international trade negotiations.

Jackson, as well as some of his staunch supporters, has observed that one of his objectives in articulating the intellectual foundations for the WTO was to provide greater stability and predictability for corporate managers in the international arena (see Howse, 1999, p. 107; Jackson, 1999). Now, with the WTO in place, the managers of large corporations would, in theory at least, find that their external environments have become somewhat less risky in that an international dispute-resolution procedure has been established. To partially clarify how the WTO works, we examine the struggles taking place globally with respect to drug patents and health. Patents, we should recall, are grounded in a legal system that provides the patent holder with a monopoly for production and distribution during a specified time frame. The evidence suggests that many drug companies have conceived of the WTO as providing them with international protection, for these pharmaceutical corporations have sought to advance their monopoly by denying companies in developing countries the opportunity to create low-priced generic drugs. However, as a result of the HIV/AIDS epidemic, a number of NGOs (non-governmental organizations) as well as several nations have sought to resist the implementation of WTO rules and regulations. What is occurring (as I write this essay) is an effort to revise the organizational structure of the WTO so as to permit the production and distribution of low-priced drugs when health needs, such as those associated with HIV/AIDS, loom large. Up to this point we have yet to see a firm resolution of this issue (Editorial, 2003; Hamburger, 2003).

A second illustrative case is grounded in a lengthy account in the *Wall Street Journal*. It raises questions as to whether deregulation has aided and abetted the recent corporate scandals involving fraud and corruption, as reflected in Enron, Worldcom, Tyco, and the like. The *Journal* reported that in 1987 in a hearing room in Washington, D.C., three bank executives lobbied the Federal Reserve Board. Their mission was to remove the regulatory walls between the business of banking and that of selling stocks and bonds. Indeed, their actions (along with other lobbying efforts) were instrumental in reconfiguring the Glass-Stengall Act, which had from the Great Depression onward constrained the activities of large financial houses. The author of this account, Jacob M. Schlesinger, observed: "The erosion of that landmark law was one of many steps that added up to a free-market sweep of Washington over the past quarter-century. Policy makers transferred onto the shoulders of investors more of the responsibility for steering financial markets and policing wrongdoing" (2002, p. A1). With this responsibility came greater risk for investors. Corporate managers, especially in the powerful financial sector, were provided with new and lucrative opportunities to maneuver, with fewer regulations imposed on them by the Securities and Exchange Commission, for instance. But this process has also meant that many individual investors, such as retirees, are being forced to absorb the risk of corporate wrongdoing, inasmuch as they lack the proper information to make informed investment decisions with respect to the way in which managers are handling their assets. We are learning about some of the social and economic liabilities of the new organizational arrangements that have permitted the managers of such corporations as Enron, Worldcom, Tyco, and the like, to shift risk from the corporate managerial sector to individuals. That some retirees have lost their life savings is indicative of the risks of an unregulated market.

A third case study focuses on intellectual property and is of a somewhat different order. We shall briefly discuss a conference of the World Intellectual Property Organization (WIPO) held in Geneva in December 1996. Its main objective was to bring world intellectual property law up to date. In this diplomatic conference, one wing of the Clinton administration was particularly intent upon advancing the interests of the entertainment industry. This conference was the latest in what has been a sustained effort by the entertainment industry to gain expanded proprietary control over texts, music, audiovisual works, and the like. What came out of this conference of the WIPO Copyright

Treaty and its Agreed Statements was an explicit effort to balance the rights of authors and of corporations against those of the larger public interest, including commitments to the enhancement of science and democracy.

The U.S. delegation at the conference sought to expand the proprietary interests of the entertainment industry in several different directions. One involved protection of the contents of databases in the new digital age. Pamela Samuelson (1997, p. 423), a legal scholar who has analyzed the proceedings of this conference at some length, wrote: "The thread that led to the unraveling of the coordinated U.S.-E.U. strategy to push for adoption of a database treaty at the December 1996 diplomatic conference was a joint letter to U.S. Secretary of Commerce Mickey Kantor from the presidents of the National Academy of Sciences, National Academy of Engineering, and National Institute of Medicine." The presidents contended that the proposed treaty and the implementing legislation would limit access to and use of scientific data by researchers and educators.

Let us consider this dispute about intellectual property within the context of risk taking. It appears that some of the proposals by the U.S. delegation, had they not been modified, would have greatly reduced the risks of the entertainment industry by expanding its proprietary controls; yet it would have done so at the expense of scientific and democratic endeavors. What comes to be elucidated in the accounts of Samuelson and others is that democratic and scientific institutions (including the organizations that support them) have a major stake in sustaining a form of "commons property" with regard to the dissemination of information. That is, how intellectual property is controlled or managed in modern society has a fundamental bearing on the foundations of science and democracy. An open society can be undermined by the expansion of, and perhaps monopolistic control of, proprietary information by powerful corporate units. The free flow of information, basic to both science and democracy, would be jeopardized by the expansion of copyright law in that those who seek to engage in the free flow of information would be at risk of violating, for instance, the legal structure that supports intellectual property and thus would be subject to some form of punishment.

We have presented three illustrative cases that underscore the centrality of organizations in distributing the nature of risk. Extrapolating from these cases, as well as other data (cf. Moss, 2002), it seems fair to assert that neither Giddens nor Beck has thought through the implications of his perspective. Neither has placed large-scale organizations at the center of his understanding of the distribution of risk taking in late modernity.[6] Those who follow in their footsteps are encouraged to carefully reexamine how their theoretical framework may unwittingly provide social justification for shifting the burden of risk from the corporate and governmental sectors onto individuals, even though the latter may lack the wherewithal to cope with the demands heaped upon them. Furthermore, shifting risk from the managerial sector of organizations onto individuals may undermine basic modern scientific and democratic processes, an issue we develop in the context of the succeeding section.[7]

Academic Freedom, Tenure, and Risk Taking

Having sketched out a set of autobiographical materials, and having critically evaluated, albeit in an adumbrated manner, the writings of Beck and Giddens, we are now able to analyze the role of academic freedom and tenure in the management of intellectual risk taking, ever mindful of the fact that large-scale organizations (such as corporations) have increased, rather than decreased, in significance, while at the same time individualism has continued to flourish. Several themes relating to academic freedom and tenure are worthy of critical reflection.

Looking through the prism of this autobiographical encounter with the University of Texas at Austin, we find that the ideal of academic freedom in practice tends to be bounded. Limits are imposed, formally or informally, on which scholarly activities are deemed feasible. Many academics have been constrained in their intellectual risk taking as they seek to avoid a frontal challenge to power arrangements within the university and the society. More generally, academic freedom and tenure often come under attack as particular interests seek to shape intellectual activities so as to enhance their own social power. This kind of contestation was much in evidence during the battle to control the University of Texas in the Rainey era. Rainey (1971), in his retrospective account, in effect conceived of the challengers to academic freedom and tenure as undermining academic life. As conservatives (of the time) defined the situation, social scientists and various legal scholars were questioning their authority and influence. Thus, conservatives on the Board of Regents reacted by limiting academic freedom as they sought to sustain and expand their own moral legitimacy within the political and economic spheres.

The case of the University of Texas is not unique. There are strong indications, for instance, based on the work of an investigative reporter for the *San Francisco Chronicle* (Rosenfeld, 2002), that Ronald Reagan, when he was governor of California, cooperated with the Federal Bureau of Investigation in an effort to reshape the nature of the University of California, Berkeley, during the turbulent 1960s. That the University at Berkeley in that era apparently harbored no communists in its midst (the faculty and administrators having screened out advocates of this perspective) speaks to the faculty's and the administration's acceptance of boundaries on academic freedom.

Despite social constraints of this sort, we must not assume that the ideals of academic freedom and tenure are irrelevant. To the contrary, at the University of Texas at Austin, political intervention in faculty affairs during the late 1960s by a leading member of the Board of Regents was thwarted by professors in the Law School and in the larger constituency that they helped to mobilize. The ideal of academic freedom, buttressed by tenure, can serve as a bulwark against the heavy-handed intrusion into academic matters by power brokers outside the academy. Nor should we assume that the protests of the faculty senate in the 1970s regarding arbitrary administrative action were irrelevant, as some might suppose. The members of the administration, as well as the Board of Regents, apparently were sensitive to local and national criticisms inasmuch as they viewed themselves as guardians of the university's efforts to attain greater scholarly recognition, nationally and globally. While I have discussed certain instances in which scholarly and other social activities of the professors at UT-Austin have been bounded, these constraints have been less drastic than they might have been because of the general commitment to the ideals of academic freedom and tenure.

But the question remains: How does one justify academic freedom and tenure sociologically? Earlier, building on a modified version of John Dewey's thinking, I reasoned (Sjoberg, 1998) that academic freedom is essential to the maintenance of science and democracy. We shall elaborate further on why this is so.

Jürgen Habermas, perhaps the foremost champion of democratic theory in the past half century, has emphasized the role of consensus formation within the context of the lifeworld (with its ideal speech community), which he regards as the foundation stone of modern democracy. Although we recognize the centrality of Habermas's communicative rationality to the enhancement of the democratic process, we contend that it is institutionalized dissent rather than consensus formation that is the cornerstone of a robust democratic order. It is only through some form of institutionalized dissent that minority views can be protected; furthermore, to institutionalize dissent requires certain organizational safeguards. Dewey championed the need for participatory democracy. But the ideal of participation requires organized support. We know that for a long period there were organized efforts in the United States to construct and maintain laws that excluded African-Americans and other minorities from voting. Organized exclusion can be readily documented. What is more difficult to articulate are the organized structures that facilitate participation. One such built-in procedure is the reliance on academic freedom and tenure. At a minimum these principles provide some members of the social order with a basis for examining issues that may threaten existing power (and knowledge) arrangements.

Currently we cannot envisage how it is possible to critically examine the risks to the planet that emanate from a range of environmental issues unless we can raise basic questions regarding the relevant social arrangements in which powerful interests have a major stake. Yet, to challenge these arrangements requires an organizational buffer between powerful interests and scientific or social scientific investigators. The assumption that scholars, as lone individuals, can confront organized power without the institutional support of academic freedom and tenure has no grounding in empirical reality. While the principles of academic freedom and tenure, when translated into practice, are not without their failings, these principles make possible a range of essential intellectual activities, a fact documented to some degree by my own experience at UT-Austin.

A fundamental requirement of late modernity is the need for openness in both science and democracy so as to cope with the problems posed by what Giddens refers to as the manufactured risks that may accompany scientific advances. We should constantly bear in mind that science has been the driving force behind modernity, for it has provided the foundational knowledge for most of the development of modern technology. But in more recent times the "dark cloud" of scientific activity has cast a shadow over humankind, made all the more evident by the knowledge revolution that has given rise to the potential for a nuclear holocaust or germ warfare. Giddens and Beck have, to a considerable extent, come to focus on the risk society because of the dangers that lie in the unanticipated consequences of scientific activities in late modernity. One of Beck's favorite illustrations is the catastrophe that arose from the malfunctioning of the nuclear power plant at Chernobyl. Beck rightly focuses on the international impact of that disaster, which dramatically displayed the risks associated with the use of nuclear energy.

To sustain modern science and democracy, it seems reasonable to assume that some members of a social order will be called upon to address issues whose implications reach well beyond the time horizon of the present and the time constraints of the market model. Kai Erikson (1994), discussing the matter of nuclear waste, observes that we are expected to cope with risks that may linger with us far longer than the history of current nation-states. Social planning within that kind of time frame is difficult to grasp, and sociologists have been lax in addressing the consequences of such a reality. Indeed, the urgent need to confront these kinds of risks highlights the place of academic freedom and tenure. Natural and social scientists are called upon not only to challenge powerful interests but also to look beyond the time frames of modern economic agents whose focus is on the present rather than on some distant, murky future. Under these precarious circumstances it becomes increasingly imperative to protect the proponents of minority perspectives, not only because these serve as a basis for challenging conventional wisdom but also because a minority's proposed solutions may become the genesis for new scientific and social initiatives decades hence.

One counter to our argument is that we can resolve environmental problems only through the discovery of scientific "laws" and "principles." But what advocates of this view fail to acknowledge is that once physicists or biologists or other natural scientists begin addressing the economic, organizational, and cultural implications of their findings, they become social scientists of sorts. Furthermore, many present-day environmental issues are likely to be resolved only through the construction of alternative social arrangements (cf. Sjoberg, Gill, and Cain, 2003). Even so, the experts require some minimal social autonomy to challenge one another's proposed solutions, as well as the attendant risks. This calls for institutionalized dissent, not only with respect to the data but also with respect to the nature of the alternative social arrangements that need to be constructed. When we talk about the environment, we are talking about the life and death of human beings on planet Earth. We would surmise that new social and cultural arrangements that address the nature of consumption and production in ways not yet formulated may well be in order.

Our analysis leads us to consider another facet of academic freedom and tenure that has attracted little or no scholarly attention. In modern democratic societies "objective knowledge"—knowledge that takes account of multiple perspectives (including competing interests)—seems essential. The university is one of the few institutions in modern society that can provide this kind of knowledge. Here again we rely upon reasoning via illustrative cases. First, consider the controversies in the early part of the twenty-first century surrounding Wall Street analysts in the employ of large financial firms who have produced data relating to the economic viability of various corporations, especially those in the telecom industry. These data have been relied upon by investors who need to make strategic decisions regarding their stock purchases. But such data, we now know, have been constructed primarily with the interest of the analysts' employers in mind. The interests of the investors who rely on these data have often been ignored, with severe consequences for a wide range of citizens, including retirees, who have lost their life savings as a result of the bankruptcy of particular corporations recommended by these analysts. Today, an influential body of investors in the United States are clamoring for analysts whose knowledge base and interpretations will be more objective, by taking account of divergent and competing interests in constructing and interpreting their data.

A second illustrative case involves disputes regarding corporate sponsorship of biomedical research. A major increase in this kind of sponsorship has fostered situations wherein clinical or experimental data are examined primarily from the perspective of the corporation providing financial support. In a survey of biomedical research, Bekelman, Li, and Gross (2003), conclude that "strong and consistent evidence shows that industry sponsored research tends to draw pro-industry conclusions." The authors also contend that "industry ties are associated with both publication delays and data withholding." Without "objective analysis" of the data—one that takes account of the perspective of patients as well as corporations—some patients may well be led to taking unacceptable risks, a situation aggravated by the fact that some universities nowadays are engaged in patent licensing. This, in turn, means that these academic institutions may have a stake in the market success of particular biomedical products without regard to the basic health needs of patients.

In a more general vein, we contend that modern societies benefit considerably from the existence of organizational structures, such as universities, wherein the research activities of natural and social scientists and other scholars are sufficiently protected through academic freedom and tenure so that they are able to create knowledge that is judged to be "fair" to a range of competing perspectives or interests. Such objectivity can hardly be approximated without organizational protection for those who may, in the process of discovering new knowledge, find themselves challenging certain powerful vested interests external to the academic setting.

Summing Up

Taking my academic career at the University of Texas as a point of departure, I have ventured forth into an exploration of intellectual edgework or risking taking. I now recapitulate my basic contentions and also contextualize this investigation with respect to the writings of Stephen Lyng as well as Anthony Giddens and Ulrich Beck.

Early on I mentioned that Lyng's research on edgework focused on leisure pursuits that are somewhat marginal to the central organizational context of modern social orders, whereas Beck and Giddens, in their analysis of risk, have focused on the core political and economic structures of second modernity. While emphasizing the work of the latter sociologists, we have considered how the processes analyzed by these sociologists appear to form part of a broader mosaic. Thus, some persons in late modernity find the routinization of activities (resulting from the demands of large-scale organizations that we have emphasized) to be deadening, and consequently seek to overcome their disenchantment through edgework activities and their resultant experiental highs, so effectively documented by Lyng. In turn, the risks addressed by Giddens and Beck are also real, in that the potential of nuclear war or other Chernobyls is also a product of late modernity and of the manufactured risk produced, for instance, by modern science and technology.

Our analysis of intellectual edgework and risk has taken us along a somewhat different path-one that, however, supplements the work of Lyng on the one hand and that of Beck and Giddens on the other. Our concern with intellectual risk has led us to consider the relationship between large-scale organizations and the allocation or distribution of risk within modern social orders. How societies are organized makes a difference as to who assumes the risks, be they managers or workers, pharmaceutical corporations or patients, and so on. Moreover, how societies in late modernity are organized may well affect the nature of disenchantment. Paradoxically, for skydivers the airplanes and skydiving gear, even the leisure time on which they rely, are at least in part products of the large-scale organizations that have perhaps led to their disenchantment and the search for meaning through edgework.

As for our own trajectory, we have challenged some of the individualistic premises on which Giddens and Beck ground their analysis. Their failure to examine the manner in which organizations allocate risk taking has led them to brush aside the fact that the managers of powerful organizations have in recent decades sought to re-allocate risks away from the managerial sector onto individuals, thereby reducing the risks associated with organized power. Yet, this general trend, which loosely speaking has been associated with the privatization movement, has come to reconstitute new "winners" and "losers" in late modernity. And, if pressed forward, it may well undermine our ability to cope with the major risks confronting humankind. One such threat is to academic freedom and tenure, which are in many respects essential for sustaining science and democracy. In good Deweyan fashion, we find intellectual edgework or risk taking to be an essential feature of science and democracy, for group support is a necessary foundation for risk taking.

The crux of our argument is that academic freedom and tenure require organizational support if modern social orders are to sustain intellectual risk taking, and this last is, in turn, basic to modern science and democracy. My autobiographical, episodic account of academic freedom and tenure at the University of Texas at Austin surely suggests that although academic freedom and tenure have been compromised on a number of occasions during the past half century or more, they have nonetheless served as a bulwark against the arbitrary use of external power.

We are not suggesting that academics should be free of public scrutiny. On the contrary, one of the dilemmas facing academia is that as a result of academic freedom and tenure scholars must be prepared to undergo intensive external scrutiny. Yet the resolution of what kinds of knowledge can be deemed "scientifically grounded" calls for some autonomous judgment by experts. One alternative to academic freedom and tenure, some suggest, is to assume that expert knowledge should be congruent with, or acceptable to, the organized power arrangements in modern society. But such a view fails to address the social issues that emerge in a risk society. Members of the academic community need to be protected so that at least some scholars can focus on long-term solutions to the risks we face, many of which are, paradoxically, a product of scientific activity itself. Thus, if intellectual or scholarly edgework or risk taking is to flower, academic freedom and tenure, in some form, are essential. After all, knowledge oriented toward the resolution of issues regarding, for instance, global warming or other potentially disastrous environmental issues seems likely to threaten power blocs within the societal or global order, power blocs supported by the large-scale organizations that dominate the current social and political landscape. A degree of autonomy thus remains essential if natural and social scientific endeavor is to prosper. Without such organizational safeguards, it is well-nigh impossible to confront ongoing life-threatening issues, matters that can be effectively addressed only where the broader scientific enterprise and democracy are sustained.

Acknowledgments

I appreciate Stephen Lyng's critical reading of an earlier version of this manuscript. His constructive comments facilitated an upgrading of the manuscript. Also, Andrée F. Sjoberg has, as she has done so often in the past, edited the manuscript with an eye to improving the clarity of what I am attempting to say.

Notes

1. In a historical account of the Barbara Smith episode at UT, Gould and Sneed (1999) speak of Logan Wilson and his administration as "polite

segregationists." That is a rather apt depiction. (This article also mentions another widely publicized incident at UT during the 1990s, a case involving a law professor, Lino Graglia, who derided the capabilities of Black and Hispanic students as compared to those of white students. The resulting controversy led to academic freedom issues that were resolved in favor of the professor in question.)

2. We can reasonably infer that far less faculty participation occurred at UT than at Berkeley in affairs deemed worthy of concern by students in the 1960s. To some degree this generalization is supported by a comparison of the work compiled by Cohen and Zelnik (2002) regarding the Free Speech Movement at Berkeley with the book by Rossinow (1998) on the New Left at the University of Texas at Austin. Moreover, the work compiled by Cohen and Zelnik relates to our analysis of academic freedom in ways that lie beyond the scope of this essay. Yet, as informative as this book is, I suspect that some sections will undergo considerable interpretive revisions as a result of recent revelations about the role of the FBI in shaping university affairs at Berkeley during the 1960s. How this intervention affected specific faculty activities remains unclear.

3. One version of the activities in the government department at UT-Austin is articulated by a dissident member of that department (Edwards, 1981)

4. Some of the social-psychological processes that accompanied my marginalization are rather difficult to assess. One pattern stands out however: Whatever my inner turmoil might have been (and it was considerable), I was constantly aware of the fact that I was called upon to sustain a proper formal presentation of self to students and faculty. In this situation, I did not allow my private troubles to become a public issue. To have comported myself otherwise would have served to justify the actions of those who marginalized me. This pattern of conduct within organizational settings is seldom analyzed by sociologists.

5. I have also engaged in my share of failed projects. For example, during the 1960s I (along with a colleague) undertook a study of the responses of American intellectuals to Hannah Arendt's *Eichmann in Jerusalem* and Rolf Hochhuth's play *The Deputy*. Although we backed out of this effort because of our inability to satisfactorily theorize the problem, in hindsight I see that we should have published a descriptive account of the materials we collected.

6. Perrow (1999), for one, recognizes a relationship between organizational power and risk (as well as catastrophe), though his work is of a different order than my own. I have a number of reservations concerning his analysis, not the least of which is that he largely ignores human agents in his analysis of organizational accidents and catastrophes.

7. My conception of organizations cannot be explored in this essay but is outlined in a chapter I have written with Elizabeth A. Gill and Joo Ean Tan (2003). In this and other writings, my colleagues and I are striving to incorporate human agency into the study of formal organizations, and our conceptualization differs from that of other sociologists.

References

Beck, U. *What Is Globalization?* London: Polity Press, 2000.

——. *The Risk Society.* London: Sage, 1992.

Beck, U., and Beck-Gernsheim, E. *Individualization.* Thousand Oaks, CA: Sage, 2002.

Bekelman, J. E., Li, Y., and Gross, C. P. "Scope and Impact of Financial Conflicts of Interest in Biomedical Research," *Journal of the American Medical Association,* 289 (2003):454–465.

Boyne, R. "Cosmopolis and Risk: A Conversation with Ulrich Beck." *Theory, Culture, and Society* 18 (2001): 47–63.

Cohen, R., and Zelnik, R. E., eds. *The Free Speech Movement.* Berkeley, CA: University of California Press, 2002.

Dugger, R. *Our Invaded Universities.* New York: W.W. Norton, 1974.

Editorial. "The Importance of Patent Remedies." *Financial Times,* January 3, 2003: 8

Edwards, D. "To Members of the Government Department Faculty." *Daily Texan,* April 24, 1981: 5.

Erikson, K. *A New Species of Trouble.* New York: W.W. Norton, 1994.

Faculty Senate Fact-Finding Committee on Salary Decisions. "Committee Report." *Documents and Proceedings of the Faculty Senate.* Austin, TX: University of Texas at Austin. (April 19, 1976. Unpaginated.)

Faulkner, L. R. "UT: Jensen's Words His Own." *Houston Chronicle,* September 19, 2001: 39A.

Giddens, A., and Pierson, C. *Conversations with Anthony Giddens.* Stanford, CA: Stanford University Press, 1998.

Giddens, A. *Runaway World.* New York: Routledge, 2000.

Gould, L. L. "Remember, Tenure Protects Academic Freedom for UT Professors." *Daily Texan,* Oct. 1 (1998): 4.

Gould, L. L., and Sneed, M. R. "Without Pride or Apology: The University of Texas at Austin Racial Integration, and the Barbara Smith Case," *Southwestern Historical Quarterly,* 103 (1999): 67–87.

Hamburger, T. "U.S. Flip on Patents Shows Drug Makers' Growing Clout." *Wall Street Journal* February 6, 2003: A4.

Howse, R. L. "The House that Jackson Built: Restructuring the GATT System." *Michigan Journal of International Law,* 20 (1999): 107–119.

Jackson, J. H. "Reflections on the MJIL Special Issue." *Michigan Journal of International Law,* 20(1999): 185–191.

Lyng, S. "Edgework: A Social Psychological Analysis of Voluntary Risk Taking." *American Journal of Sociology,* 95 (1990): 851–886.

McGee, R. "The Roots of Agony." *The Nation* 197 December 21, 1963: 427–431.

Moss, D. A. *When All Else Fails: Government as the Ultimate Risk Manager.* Cambridge, MA: Harvard University Press, 2002.

Perrow, C. *Normal Accidents: Living with High-Risk Technologies.* Princeton, NJ: Princeton University Press, 1999.

Pleasants, N. *Wittgenstein and the Idea of a Critical Theory: A Critique of Giddens, Habermas, and Bhaskar.* New York: Routledge, 1999.

Rainey, H. P. *The Tower and the Dome: A Free University Versus Political Control.* Boulder, CO: Pruett Publishing, 1971.

Rosenfeld, S. "Trouble on Campus." *San Francisco Chronicle,* June 9, 2002. Available at http://sfgate.com/cgi-bin/article.cgi?f=/c/a/2002/06/09/MNCF2.DTL (accessed June 12, 2002).

Rossinow, D. *The Politics of Authenticity.* New York: Columbia University Press, 1998.

Samuelson, P. "The U.S. Digital Agenda at WIPO." *Virginia Journal of International Law* 37(1997): 369–439.

Schlesinger, J. M. "Did Washington Help Set Stage for Current Business Turmoil?" *Wall Street Journal* October 17, 2002: A1, A12.

Sjoberg, G. "Democracy, Science, and Institutionalized Dissent: Toward a Social Justification for Academic Tenure." *Sociological Perspectives* 41 (1998): 697–722.

Sjoberg, G., Gill, E. A., and Williams, N. "A Sociology of Human Rights," *Social Problems,* 48(2001): 11–47.

Sjoberg, G., Gill, E. A., and Tan, J. E. "Social Organization." In *Handbook of Symbolic Interaction,* edited by L. T. Reynolds and N. J. Herman-Kinney. Walnut Creek, CA: AltaMira Press, 2003.

Sjoberg, G., Gill, E. A., and Cain, L. D. "Countersystem Analysis and the Construction of Alternative Futures." *Sociological Theory,* 21 (2003): 210–235.

12

Doing Terrorism Research in the Dark Ages: Confessions of a Bottom Dog

MARK S. HAMM

CONTENTS

Kurt Vonnegut once said, "I like to live pretty near the edge, without actually going over the line. I can see things more clearly there." While such an obsession has never been part of the traditional American value system, Vonnegut *does* express a recurrent theme found in the works of many post World War II artists, writers, and musicians. Examples abound.

For instance, once he got behind the wheel of a car, speed and risk were like drugs to fifties icon James Dean. Dean's contemporary, actor Montgomery Clift, was known to hang from the balcony of his hotel room in Florence, Italy, just to "challenge the edge, to see how close to danger he could come." Flirting with self-destruction was actually sacred for the angel headed hipsters, the brooding doomsday prophets of the Beat Generation. In his twenties, legendary Beat writer Jack Kerouac announced to friends his intention to drink himself to death (which he did, at age 47, in 1969). Fueled by Benzedrine and his own conflicted emotions, Allen Ginsberg carried Kerouac's tortured message a step further when he issued his famous hymn to rebellion: "I have seen the best minds of my generation destroyed by madness, starving hysterical naked,/ dragging themselves through the negro streets at dawn looking for an angry fix..." This mythopoetic statement ultimately transformed living "on the edge" from a hedonistic pleasure to a generational howling as it struck the declamatory note in an age of affluence tripping toward the apocalypse of Vietnam. Building on ruins of the Beat past, in the mid-sixties Bob Dylan's amphetamine dreams posited a future where madness became the method, the golden road to joyous rebellion where we could all forget about war, retreat to the edge, and "dance beneath the diamond sky with one hand waving free."[1]

It is not surprising, then, that during this period of profound cultural change risk taking surfaced in critical works of social research as well. Scorning a research tradition that coldly analyzed deviants, criminals, and misfits as "subjects" whose behaviors should be "measured" with "scientific methods," sociologists and criminologists like Howard Becker, Alfred Lindesmith, Ned Polsky, Walter Reckless, Ruth Horowitz, Laud Humphries, and William Chambliss risked their own personal well-being as they went inside jazz clubs, "shooting galleries," pool rooms, skid-row taverns, brothels, and "tea-rooms." This body of ethnographic research offered vivid accounts of a dangerous underworld teeming with drug addicts, hustlers, gangsters, musicians, prize-fighters, corrupt politicians, pimps, and prostitutes. Scholars had found their own glorious gaggle of angel-headed hipsters. They did so by relying not on social-scientific methodology, but on genuine human engagement with the men and women they came in contact with in the course of their studies.

The Dark Ages

As Patricia and Peter Adler (1998, xv) note, the curtain fell on this rich sociological tradition sometime during the late 1970s. The primary threat to ethnographic research came from universities themselves. Specifically, argue the Adlers, the threat came from Institutional Review Boards that "denigrated the impact of critical dimensions of fieldwork techniques ... and made ethnographic work on criminal and deviant groups almost impossible to conduct." This trend ushered in what the Adlers call "The Dark Ages." While ethnographers of the 1950s and 1960s were effectively able to police themselves, universities of The Dark Ages have reasoned that researchers are incapable of self-monitoring. Suddenly a host of research activities have been deemed unethical. These include ethnographic research involving a covert role, research on minors that does not obtain parental consent, and research on sensitive (including criminal) issues without signed consent forms. "This approach,"

Adler and Adler conclude, "puts government and institutional bureaucratic mandates ahead of the research bargains and confidences previously forged by fieldworkers" (1998, pp. xiv–xv). Adding to the constraints posed by these forces, the trend toward highly functionalist, quantitative studies in the social sciences has generated a professional disrespect for fieldwork. Ethnographic studies are rarely found in mainstream books or journals on crime and deviance. Such studies are routinely neglected in annual reviews of research, they receive only scant attention in the textbook literature, and they are wholly dismissed by government research agencies on the grounds that ethnography does not produce results of major policy significance. Such are The Dark Ages.

Yet ethnographic research has not only continued within this repressive environment, but has actually flourished. This volume testifies to that achievement. Like the artists and field researchers of the fifties and sixties, ethnographers of The Dark Ages have thrown caution to the wind; once again immersing themselves in what Jeff Ferrell and I have rather rhapsodically called "the mystery of shadows, in the power of what can't be easily seen, in the dangerous beauty of unnoticed alternatives" (1998, p. 269). But this has not been an easy task. Ethnographers must routinely negotiate their way through a veritable minefield of research dangers couched in legal, ethical, emotional, and physical considerations. And what price do we pay for going through all these changes?

The Dissidents

Often the price has been great, even though research dangers have frequently been tempered with the joy that attends all good ethnographic inquiry. One of the earliest examples of this double-edged sword of fieldwork involved my own mentor, drug researcher Alfred Lindesmith. I was fortunate enough to be one of Lindesmith's students at Indiana University in the late 1960s, at the height of his career as a sociologist and public intellectual. What initially attracted me to Lindesmith's classes was his enormous popularity among the anti-war and civil rights activists and hippies of the day, which included about everyone I knew. Lindesmith's classes were big, crowded, and lively. I also recall that he sometimes invited former heroin addicts from Chicago to sit in on his classes. These visits taught me that universities could actually be places where one could acquire hipness, the authentic wisdom eternally found at the edges and bottom of the social pyramid. In their biography of Lindesmith, David Keys and John Galliher note this aspect of his popularity:

> Lindesmith's mounting reputation [in the late sixties] continued to win him new friends and solidify unusual alliances. One of these was a friendship that developed between Lindesmith and the Beat poet Allen Ginsberg ... [T]he two men had worked together in mobilizing many national figures in the drug reform movement, [including] LSD guru and Harvard professor Dr. Timothy Leary ... and a number of writers, editors, and publishers... Their friendship was an odd combination of

a socially circumspect academic and an iconoclastic Beat hipster (2000, p. 33).

Yet what truly distinguished Lindesmith was the courage he showed in carrying on a career-long fight with the federal government over drug policy. For more than thirty years he openly rebutted federal drug enforcers and passionately advocated reforms that challenged the image of the addict as a criminal, substituting the idea that addicts suffered from a medical condition. For that, Lindesmith was routinely depreciated and harassed by the Federal Bureau of Narcotics (FBN). Essentially, this was a conflict over methodology. While the anti-drug crusaders portrayed the addict as a sex-crazed "dope fiend," Lindesmith—drawing on information obtained through field research on some seventy addicts, former criminal cohorts, and henchmen—published a series of essays arguing that the psycho-pathological paradigm did not reflect the addict's true nature. Lindesmith's research showed that addicts were *not* usually violent and, in fact, had blunted sexual drives. The most influential of these was the brief but powerful article, "Dope Fiend Mythology," published in 1940 by the *Journal of Criminal Law and Criminology*. Moreover, Lindesmith's approach advanced the viewpoint that U.S. narcotics policy had a dehumanizing effect on addicts, encouraged a lucrative black market, and sought to punish rather than rehabilitate addicts. (Decades later, these policy failures would come into full relief with the government's "war on drugs.") All of this, of course, directly contradicted FBN policies. The apex of Lindesmith's persecution came shortly after Ginsberg's visit to the Indiana University campus in 1966. It was then that FBN chief Harry Anslinger persuaded FBI Director J. Edgar Hoover that Lindesmith was a member of a communist front, an unfounded charge that nevertheless threatened his tenure in the sociology department.

Because he was regularly in trouble with the government, this friend of both the down-and-out addict and the iconoclastic bohemian was the perfect role model for students with artistic and activist leanings. Many tried to follow in Lindesmith's footsteps. According to Keys and Galliher,

> Lindesmith had no illusions regarding value-free science and education. He realized that his position as a researcher and educator were also the tools that his activism used and in this sense he was far ahead of those in sociology who came to this viewpoint when the turmoil of the 1960s aroused the profession and prompted debate. When campuses around the nation began to explode following the Berkeley Free Speech Movement in 1964, Lindesmith had been quietly building what he hoped could be an aggregate of reform-minded students for a decade and a half (2000, p. 103).

While Lindesmith left an indelible mark on his students, his story also carried a dire warning for them: When knowledge production is transformed by political considerations, the role of the intellectual is degraded. But as time went by, with The Dark Ages looming on the horizon, intellectual degradation often became the least of future dissidents' worries. Once again, examples abound.

During the 1970s, another Lindesmith protégé, William Chambliss, escaped an assassination attempt by organized crime figures in Oslo, Norway, while doing fieldwork for his book, *On the Take*.[2] In fieldwork conducted for his acclaimed book on American street gangs during the late 1980s, *Islands in the Street*, Martin Sanchez-Jankowski (1991; 1994) claims to have been the victim of more than a dozen attacks waged by antagonistic gang members; he was beaten numerous times and shot with a firearm. Perhaps the most harrowing episode in the annals of sociology is described by the editor of this volume, Stephen Lyng, who came a hair's breadth away from death in pursuit of an edgework experience in motorcycle racing (Lyng, 1998). Add to these examples a string of arrests, harassments, and intimidations experienced by other fieldworkers, and you'll get the picture: Because risk taking can lead to failure, methodology is personal; and the personal is always political.

Terrorists, Lawyers, and Academic Bureaucrats

My role in this book is to describe the dangers of doing fieldwork on a social movement existing on the extreme fringes of society, including skinheads, neo-Nazis, militias, and self-described "patriots." This cannot be done without mentioning the hazards I've encountered with two formidable gatekeepers of this research endeavor. Instead of Institutional Review Boards (which I've ignored altogether), the greatest threats to my research have come from university administrators and lawyers. My goal here is to point out these dangers and the mistakes I've made in coping with them. I hope my story will be of use to others who struggle with the perils of doing ethnographic research. Let me begin with the experience that prompted my interest in terrorism.

Hitler Youth

San Francisco's Haight-Ashbury district was the epicenter of the American counterculture movement in the late 1960s. It was perhaps the only place in the country where rebels were considered a source of civic pride. The Haight soon lost its soul, however, due to hard drugs, hard people, and gentrification. I'd been there numerous times since the late sixties, but the event I want to talk about occurred during the summer of 1985. I had just finished my dissertation, further exploring the ideas in Lindesmith's "Dope Fiend Mythology," and was on vacation from my job as a prison administrator in Arizona.

Toward sundown on a Saturday night, I was standing near 710 Ashbury, once home to the mythical Beat, Neal Cassady, and the Grateful Dead, talking to an Asian-American woman who was well known in the Haight as a prostitute and a drug addict. Research was not my top priority on this fine evening. Suddenly, from out of nowhere, two shaven-headed youths rushed me, shouting "*Nigger lover!*" One of them kicked me in the shins with steel-toed boots, and then together they bolted down the street.

This was my introduction to the skinhead subculture. As the assault lingered in my mind, the skinhead movement started to gain momentum in the press. Following the collapse of the Berlin Wall in 1989, European skinheads unleashed a reign of terror against asylum seekers, punks, anarchists, and hippies. The British Home Office released a 1990 report showing that racial violence in that country had reached an all-time high of some 70,000 incidents a year, primarily because of skinhead violence. During the Persian Gulf War, skinheads were implicated in the firebombing of some twenty mosques in the greater London area. When I traveled through Europe during this period, I saw neo-Nazi skinheads in every major city. I saw their swastika graffiti near the Holocaust Museum in Amsterdam and on Jim Morrison's tombstone in Paris. Upon returning to the States, I decided to embark on a criminological study of this raging fanaticism. I adopted the idealistic—and, in retrospect, very naïve—viewpoint expressed by the protagonist in Ernest Hemingway's short story, "Winner take Nothing": "If he wrote it, he could get rid of it. He had gotten rid of many things by writing as them (Marx, 1990, 260)."

Using the research of two widely known anti-racist watchdog groups (the Anti-Defamation League and the Southern Poverty Law Center) as a starting point, I visited several U.S. cities and was able to seek out skinheads in public places where youth were known to gather. These young people were not hard to identify: They all had shaved heads or closely cropped hair and wore traditional white power and Nazi regalia. Two skinheads were tattooed in the middle of their foreheads with the mark of the swastika. They were not hard to identify, but getting them to talk was another matter.

There are several problems common to all research on street gangs. Most importantly, researchers can potentially put gang members at risk for both arrest by police and retaliation from other members of the gang. Thus, researchers are perceived (sometimes rightly so) as threatening to the gangs. Consequently, gang members may be paranoid about interacting with the researcher, and paranoia can, in turn, lead to violence against the researcher (this was Sanchez-Jankowski's problem). As New Jersey skinhead Joe Rowan told me in 1990: "I can't trust anybody anymore. These days, if I talk to somebody I could get shot or meet an agent." He was not exaggerating. Following a 1993 white power rock concert near Milwaukee, Rowan was shot and killed by a rival gang member. Yet white supremacy groups present an additional research problem: Namely, silence and secrecy are not only part of their code of conduct, but they are also part of the mystique of right-wing extremism.

While my methods didn't constitute anything as formal as a list of do's and don'ts, for present purposes a list may be the most efficient way to present some of the lessons I learned about negotiating the dangers of ethnographic fieldwork on terrorist groups:

1. *Never lie or mislead anyone.* Although rarely covered in textbooks on research methods, I found this to be the most crucial procedure of all. I

learned this lesson from an old Bob Dylan song (1966): "To live outside the law you must be honest." Honesty not only reduces a researcher's tendency toward paranoia, but it can also embolden the fieldworker with courage. Others have used covert roles and deception, often to disastrous results.

For example, in 1992 Israeli journalist Yaron Svoray went undercover to gather information on the German skinhead movement. Using an alias, Svoray, a Jew, posed as the American representative of a fictitious neo-Nazi organization. Svoray met, and documented with hidden cameras and recording devices, a gang of skinheads at a paramilitary training camp that sent neo-Nazi fighters to support Croatian soldiers in the former Yugoslavia. Throughout the research, not only did Svoray constantly fear that his identity would be discovered, but the personal risk he endured was life threatening (Svoray and Taylor, 1994). That is, the skinheads tried to kill him.

I was able to avoid these risks, in part, by simply approaching the skinheads and introducing myself as a college professor who was writing a book on their movement. I lied to no one, and emphasized the fact that I was not affiliated with any law enforcement or social service agency. I asked the skinheads to participate in an interview and offered them $10 in return. To help gain their trust, I presented the research as an attempt to set the record straight on the skinheads and promised them complete anonymity.

2. *Go low-tech*. I conducted the interviews in face-to-face contact, using only a questionnaire and a pen. At no time were the skinheads asked to speak into a tape recorder or to pose for a photograph. This was another tactic used to reduce paranoia.

3. *Know the subculture, especially its music*. Lindesmith argued that an understanding of adjacent fields can enrich understanding of criminology. This is especially true for subcultures of crime, and music, as it turns out, is the fever of Western youth subcultures. In my case, a number of the skinheads were garage band musicians whose entree into the movement came through the music scene. Knowing this music (the names of various bands, their songs, lineups, and histories), as well as the skinhead style—symbols, catch phrases, and icons—proved to be an important icebreaker and showed the youths that I'd made a meaningful attempt to understand them. (Anthropologists have long argued that the first step in conducting research on indigenous peoples is to learn the language.)

4. *Never moralize*. The defining characteristic of white supremacy is racism. Some activists are rabid racists (often homophobic and misogynist as well) and others are moderate in their views on race. The researcher's job is to explore the social and psychological roots of prejudice, not to condemn these attitudes, no matter how distasteful they may be.

5. *Use multiple methods*. The goal of social research is to gather as much reliable data as possible. The goal is *not* to promote a methodological narcissism which values fieldwork above other approaches. In addition to fieldwork, I interviewed skinheads incarcerated in prison, interviewed them over the

telephone, and sent them questionnaires in the mail. I also explored historical and literary materials on the movement.

6. *Expect failure.* On several occasions, I traveled for miles to meet skinheads at prearranged locations and waited hours for them to show, only to be stood up. Other skinheads refused to be interviewed. Others fed me only lies. Failure is part of the territory.

7. *Make "crime" the last order of business.* The surest way to end a conversation with a political extremist is to bring up their involvement in criminal activity. Researchers who are able to develop long-term relationships with their subjects have a definite advantage over those of us who conduct interviews on the fly. Under ideal conditions, the researcher asks questions about criminal behavior *only* at the end of their involvement with a subject. As a sort of stopgap measure, I did two things. First, I spent hours interviewing these young people, and the interviews often turned into conversations that probed for answers to *why* they adapted to the problems in their lives by joining a racist subculture. As with most gang research, those answers were found in the ways their lives were structured by the learning environments and opportunities tied to their place in society, that is, by the illegitimate means available to them. Second, I sequenced the questions; starting with background issues about family, school, and work; moving to questions about the subculture; then to questions on beliefs and values; and finally, to gently probing about their involvement in violence.

So, in a nutshell, that is how the research was carried out. Using multiple methods, I was able to conduct thirty-six original skinhead interviews. I controlled for paranoia on the part of subjects by honestly presenting myself as a sociologist operating independent of law enforcement and community service agencies. The early Haight Street assault notwithstanding, I experienced no life-threatening violence by any of the skinheads in the study. Along the way, I met some intelligent and fascinating people. I also met some who were so stupid that they couldn't even tell you who Hitler was. And I met some who were truly frightening. I published the study in my first book, *American Skinheads*, and thought that I was finished with my work on white supremacy. Again, I was naive.

The Oklahoma City Bombing

On the afternoon of April 21, 1995, Timothy McVeigh was taken into custody for his role in the Oklahoma City bombing. The purpose of this terrorism—committed on April 19, 1995—was to take revenge for the government's military-style actions in the April 19, 1993 raid on David Koresh and the Branch Davidians in Waco, Texas. Asked to comment on McVeigh's motive hours after his arrest, I told a Waco television reporter that the bombing could not be separated from a wave of meanness that had swept the land through the polarizing rhetoric of right-wing politicians like then-Speaker of the House Newt Gingrich. The next day, Saturday, May 22, the president and board of trustees of Indiana State University received a fax from the Constitutional Militia of Texas, calling for my termination on the grounds that I was a political extremist, "a left-wing version of [Nazi propagandist] Josef Goebbels," said the missive. Coincidentally, on the same day I was given the university's highest award for research during graduation ceremonies. This became a pattern over the next several years of my career as a terrorism researcher: praise followed by denigration.

I began writing the first of two books on the Oklahoma City bombing almost immediately (Hamm, 1997; 2002). At the time, I thought that many scholars would be lining up for an interview with America's most deadly terrorist. But I was wrong. (McVeigh would go to his grave without speaking to a single scholar, at least not directly.) I now understand why there was such little interest in McVeigh: At least for criminologists, Timothy McVeigh's crime represented a case of ad hoc research—where the focus is a particular issue or type of crime—and ad hoc research is routinely disparaged in favor of studies that focus on general, unifying themes that can maximally advance theory.

Yet I see profound moral significance in some types of ad hoc research. During the 1940s, to cite the most dramatic example, German criminologists were studying biogenetic approaches to run-of-the-mill criminal behavior. Meanwhile, the Nazis were systematically exterminating millions of Jews (see Friedrichs, forthcoming). I saw a similar moral imperative in the Oklahoma City bombing. And the struggle to write something meaningful about McVeigh, including many attempts to get him to talk on record, represented another series of edgework experiences that proved far more difficult and dangerous than anything I'd encountered with the skinheads.

The difficulties began with McVeigh's attorney, who turned out to be an implacable obstructionist. I first "applied" for an interview with McVeigh in early 1996. After submitting letters of reference to his lawyer, my vitae, a photograph, and a detailed list of questions (which by prior understanding excluded all questions about the bombing), I was granted permission to interview McVeigh later that year while he was under heavy security in a Denver jail. When it came time for the interview, however, McVeigh's attorney backed out of his commitment. Facing a choice between abandoning the project or using alternative methods, I chose the latter.

These methods involved the job of analyzing McVeigh through what Michael Burawoy calls a "virtual participation in the lives of those one studies" (1991, p. 4). By this time I had read virtually everything written on McVeigh, including articles on his background, his journey through the anti-government underground, and his role in the Oklahoma massacre. The virtual analysis split off in two parallel directions: (1) an ethnographic study of the highways, diners, gun shows, and flea-bag motels where McVeigh stayed in the weeks and days leading up to the bombing, and (2) interviews with skinheads, neo-Nazis, and militiamen who traveled through the same tangled, violent subculture that attracted McVeigh.

The first part of this investigation put me on a trail leading straight to hell, otherwise known as Kingman, Arizona. I have already written about Kingman in another book on criminological edgework (Hamm, 1998). Suffice it to say that my experience in the Mojave Desert was a nerve-wracking one involving rattlesnakes, cheap food, bad movies, and a parade of down-and-out alcoholics, speed freaks, drifters, derelicts, crack heads, Elvis impersonators, and poor single women reduced to surviving off of $10 blowjobs. I slept in the same bed McVeigh slept in at the Imperial Hotel and experienced the worst nightmares of my life. I visited a survivalist store and was asked to leave by a steely-eyed militiaman armed with an assault rifle and dressed in Desert Storm cammos. I was accosted by a gang of redneck teenagers in a pickup truck, and told to "Get the fuck out of town, freak!" And I was bulldogged by a swastika-tattooed skinhead from Arkansas who thought I was asking questions that were "none of my damn business." I went to Kingman to find evidence of McVeigh's link to the clandestine meth labs of the Mojave, where armed patriots were preparing for the end of human history. I didn't find it; though I did find a dark side of the American experience that I didn't know existed. From the edgework perspective, the challenge was to apprehend enough of this darkness to make sense of McVeigh without being consumed by it.

But from the perspective of finding a connection between McVeigh and a broader conspiracy, I would have to wait until I fully understood the nature of my own search for community.

Bad Company

In 1998, I focused my research on a gang of neo-Nazi bank robbers called the Aryan Republican Army (ARA), and their leaders, Peter "Commander Pedro" Langan and Richard "Wild Bill" Guthrie. Langan was the son of a CIA agent who'd been involved in the 1963 assassination of South Vietnamese president Ngo Dinh Diem. Peter Langan went on to amass a lengthy criminal record, including several armed robberies and an assault with a deadly weapon against a police officer. Langan had also been the subject of a Secret Service investigation for plotting to assassinate Presidents George H. Bush and Bill Clinton. Langan broke the mold of your "typical" Aryan warrior in every way: He was extremely intelligent, deeply religious, and a preoperative transsexual known among Kansas City transvestites as "Donna McClure." Guthrie was equally eccentric, only more violent. Before being thrown out of the Navy SEALS for painting a swastika on the side of a ship and assaulting his commanding officer, Guthrie attended the Department of Defense's Redstone Arsenal in Huntsville, Alabama, where he received training in nuclear, biological, and chemical weapons. His criminal portfolio included dozens of armed robberies, assaults, fraud, and counterfeiting charges; he was also wanted by the Secret Service for plotting to kill the first President Bush. Langan, Guthrie, and the ARA were responsible for at least twenty-six bank robberies—thus breaking the record of their hero, the legendary Jesse James—the purpose of which was to support a series of terrorist attacks that included armored truck heists, sabotaging public utilities, derailing trains, and bombings—including direct support for the bombing in Oklahoma City. This discovery, of course, contradicted the government's claim that Timothy McVeigh (with limited help from Terry Nichols) was the sole perpetrator of the bombing.

I began the study by making the same aimless mistake I'd made with McVeigh, by seeking the assistance of Langan's legal counsel. After setting an appointment with the attorney, I made a six-hour drive to his office in Dayton, Ohio, only to be told that the lawyer had "forgotten" about our meeting and was unavailable. After numerous subsequent attempts to reach the lawyer, I was finally promised a package of legal materials on Langan, who was now in federal custody on charges of bank robbery and the attempted murder of two FBI agents. I waited three weeks, and no package. I waited six weeks, and no package. As the research floundered, I experienced an even more severe setback. This attack came from a wholly unexpected quarter. As my colleague, British criminologist Mike Presdee, once told me: "The skinheads may have tried to break your legs, but your colleagues tried to destroy your career."

McUniversity and the Dying Flame of Erasmus

Recently, I have come to view the workplace as an important setting for sorting out spiritual possibilities. Occupation offers the promise of wholeness, meaning, and interconnectedness. This sense of community gives "work" its spiritual dimension. The promise is especially appealing to those of us who labor in a discipline—such as criminology and sociology—that specializes in the study of social justice and human rights. Gary Marx goes straight to the heart of these matters in an outstanding essay on his life as a sociologist. "Academic work," he writes, "is publicly and correctly viewed as having a sacred quality involving the pursuit and transmission of truth. But it also involves a job or career carried out in a competitive milieu where the usual human virtues and vices are never far from the surface" (Marx, 1990, 262).

In the preceding nine years (between 1989 and 1998), I had achieved far more than I ever expected. I had published widely, winning several awards for scholarship and teaching in the areas of terrorism and human rights. I had been promoted to full professor and enjoyed the privileges of directing numerous graduate theses, chairing panels at professional meetings, and traveling to give invited lectures at universities throughout the country. Following the Oklahoma City bombing, I was interviewed by television, radio, and newspaper reporters from around the world and became a consultant on the radical right for government agencies and human rights groups in the Netherlands, Norway, Germany, England, and the United States. At Indiana State University, I was an active member of faculty government, and my performance as a faculty member was considered outstanding. But more importantly, I was happy with my work—at least I thought so—and I looked forward to completing research on the Aryan

Republican Army. This period was not one of intermingled academic success and failure; it was a straight trajectory to achievement. Then came the fall.

"There are of course variants of falls," writes Marx (1990, 265). "Some are easier to deal with than others. However poignantly felt, mine was gradual and partial. I had lots of time for hedging bets, putting out safety nets, and devising alternatives. That kind of fall is easier to respond to than one that is swift, total, and unexpected." Mine was of the second variant. It was swift, total, unexpected, and painful.

In 1998, the University implemented a new pay-for-performance policy allowing for the numerical peer ranking of faculty. My department, criminology, voted to make departmental service and professional development more important than teaching and research in the calculation of these peer rankings. Two years earlier, when decisions were made by the personnel committee and the chair, I had received the department's top ranking. But in 1998, my performance was ranked last in the department. I had more publications than the rest of the department faculty combined, my teaching evaluations were "excellent," and I served on more university and professional committees than any other professor in the department. I was the only one to win a national award and the only one to gain international media attention for the University. No matter. Suddenly, I was informed that my work was useless. Even untenured assistant professors with no publications, poor teaching evaluations, and no departmental service or professional development records were ranked above me. In the words of Texas troubadour Butch Hancock, I got "Special treatment. Very special treatment." I hit bottom. Then I hit the wall.

The hardest part of this ordeal was the humiliation of being told that my work was now meaningless. The poor review *was* worse than a beating. Yet, as I have since learned, this is a common response to professional denigration. Consider the recent case of British journalist Robert Fisk.

Following the terrorist attacks of September 11 (2001) and the subsequent allied invasion of Afghanistan, Fisk was conducting interviews with refugees along the Afghanistan-Pakistan border. There he received a savage beating. "I couldn't see the for the blood pouring down my forehead and swamping my eyes. And even then I understood," Fisk wrote. "I couldn't blame them for what they were doing... If I were the Afghan refugees ... I would have done the same to Robert Fisk. Or any other Westerner." Fisk later proved to be less forgiving, however, when a popular Hollywood actor blustered that he'd like to shoot Fisk for his vitriolic anti-Americanism. Fisk wrote that such hatred had destroyed "the walls of propriety and legality ... so that a reporter can be abused ... his life cheapened and made vulnerable ... If we want a quiet life, we will just have to tow the line" (Fisk, 2002, p. 9).

Instead of towing the line, my response was to fight the power. Completely ignoring my research, I produced a 60-page grievance, arguing that I was evaluated on criteria that I was not hired to perform. Those criteria violated the

Board of Trustees resolution on performance pay, the university mission, and the stated mission of the department (all three of which valued teaching and research above other activities). I also provided detailed evidence showing that I was treated unfairly.

I eventually "won" the grievance (if that is the correct term), but not before enduring a grueling two-month mediation proceeding. Things are usually more complicated than they seem, and during these proceedings I learned the true meaning of my scathing review. I was told that the review was meant to "send me a message," a message not about my *performance*, but about my *conformance* to a status quo that valued professionalism over critical inquiry. That was the stated message. The unstated message was that is was time for me to go. I was no longer welcomed at the university. This was a serious threat to my career because—unlike my research on terrorism—it meant that I was vulnerable to forces beyond my control.

My background is in public policy, so I understand the managerial implications of this threat. My assessment was based not on *performance*, but on characteristics of the *performer*. This was allowed to happen because of a formal policy that placed personality above knowledge production. The policy not only destroyed the limited research culture that *did* exist in the department where I'd labored for more than a decade, but it also deliberately induced interpersonal conflict. "It is not news that the flame of Erasmus is ever vulnerable," argues Marx (1990, 268), "but it is news when significant threats to that flame come from within the university." Once the flame had been extinguished by my colleagues, it created rich possibilities for behaving badly, both on their part and mine. Civility gave way to hostility. Trust was replaced by suspicion, achievement by discontent.

I won several concessions in the final mediation agreement; namely, the promise that I'd receive a fair hearing in future reviews, that research and teaching would be weighed equally with service, and—the most important concession—if I did *not* get a fair hearing in the future, then the dean would assume responsibility for any future reviews. Yet these agreements turned out to be empty promises.

Two years later, the same scenario began all over again. I reported a total of sixty-six service activities for the evaluation period. This was the highest in the department; some faculty listed as few as three, some as few as twelve. Yet I was ranked last. "*How can this be fair?*" I screamed in another written grievance. My teaching evaluations were the best in the department, but I received the worst ranking for teaching. "*How can this be fair?*" My research was totally ignored, thus violating another term of the mediation agreement. But the most crushing blow came when I implored the dean to make good on his commitment to take over future evaluations, as he had promised to do in the event that I received another unfair evaluation like the one I just received. A tired and ineffective careerist with the courage of a child and the ethics of an Enron executive, he simply refused because, in his words, "I don't want to." It was then that I lost all faith in the institution. I began to feel like the anguished character in a Neil Young song (1970):

Now that you've found yourself losing your mind

are you here again

finding that what you once thought was real

is gone … and changing?

Bottom Dog: The Redemption

By this time I'd also grown weary of growing weary. I was tired of being angry and resentful, tired of being at the odd man out, tired of walking past my colleagues in the hallways without speaking a word, both of us locked in our own venomous silence. And I was tired of filing grievances; my claims of unfair treatment had only sent the message to my colleagues that they should stay even farther away from me. So I decided to do something about it. I began meditating, studying Buddhism and the Gospels, practicing yoga, and exercising more. The results were heartbreaking. I became kinder to myself and began the heavy spiritual lifting of forgiveness. Little by little, I became less of a walking battlefield and more compassionate toward the victims of *real* suffering. I joined an international protest group seeking to close down the School of Americas (SOA) in Fort Benning, Georgia, a U.S. military installation responsible for untold atrocities throughout Latin America. I met a beautiful woman from El Salvador named Juanita Sanchez who had seen her mother, father, and six brothers and sisters killed by SOA-trained paramilitaries in the 1987 massacre of El Mozote. To make sure that her suffering was exquisite, the soldiers had hacked off one of Juanita's breasts with a machete. Juanita taught me about perspective. *She* had a problem. I had a mere inconvenience.

Today there is debate among scholars over the issue of "academic rage." In my opinion, this is now the major problem facing sociology and criminology. I'd even go so far as to paraphrase Allen Ginsberg on the subject: "I've seen the best careers of my generation destroyed by academic rage." Paradoxically, academic life at the turn of the millennium seems strangely akin to the paranoia and rage of the militia culture that attracted McVeigh and Langan. Psychologists reason that all rage begins with humiliation and some writers, such as Sheng-Mei Ma and Carey McWilliams, view their experiences with humiliation as attempts to impart to academe some degree of honesty, for it enables them to effectively map institutional reality. The process of the bottom speaking to the top can potentially yield unique insights, as cogently explained here by McWilliams:

One of the best ways to view and understand a society is to see it from the bottom looking up. To be sure, the underview is incomplete. Bottom dogs see, know, and learn a lot, but their perspective is limited. But they see more, I have come to believe, than those who occupy the middle and the upper reaches; their view is less inhibited, less circumscribed. The view from down under exposes the deceits, self-deceptions, distortions, apostasies... It offers a good, if limited, guide to what the society is really like, not what it professes to be (1973, p. vii).

Once I accepted this view of myself, I began to understand the true nature of my predicament. "Unfairness is rarely unequivocal," says Marx (1990). When I looked around from my position as a bottom dog, I saw that my professional relationships were in tatters, primarily because I'd been on the edge too long. This was my greatest mistake: I had failed to realize that life in academic departments—as in other formal bureaucracies—is intimately influenced by informal social relationships. My scholarship was discredited because I had removed myself from the informal networks established by my colleagues. "You're right from your side, and I'm right from mine," said Dylan (1964), and from *their* side I was unconcerned about them and their careers. And they were right. For them, ad hoc research conducted in the ethnographic tradition was of limited value. But more importantly, my resort to conflict had made me an outcast.

There was, of course, a logical reason for this: All of my role models have been rebels. And while they taught me that good writing was one way to battle fanaticism and human suffering, I had failed to appreciate their human side. Lindesmith may have had a profound influence on my life and career, but I did not take the time to know him personally. If I had, I would have learned that, as Keys and Galliher point out, "Lindesmith managed to maintain good relations with his colleagues, avoiding the conflict and animosity which surrounded the career[s] of ... C. Wright Mills ... and Timothy Leary [both of whom had an] inability to indulge and tolerate [their] colleagues" (2000, pp. 5–6). I also failed to realize that the dissident viewpoint is a minority viewpoint, and respecting my colleagues' opposing view helped me to create some human capital with them.

In these ways, I began to rebuild bridges that had taken me years to burn. Francis Cullen (2002, p. 3) has recently highlighted the importance of bridge building as a solution to the widespread problem of academic rage:

The answer is to make a modest attempt to 'take the role of the other'—to figure out how one's actions as a professor impact on [other faculty] in ways that diminish or enhance one's effectiveness. I know that there are times to be demanding and unyielding, but I am struck by how often the difficulties that professors experience are inadvertently created and could have been avoided by anticipating how others view their actions.

Making peace with the administration was more difficult, due to the structural contradictions of modern universities. Sheng-Mei Ma argues that "The academe, in the United States and elsewhere, is a human pyramid bound together by capitalist hypocrisy" (1966, p. 230). Under this Marxist formulation (Karl, that is), administrators justify stomping faculty into the mud because it formalizes power relations of the ruling ideology. That ideology has recently undergone monumental changes, of course, so I'll make a brief digression here to explain how it looks from a bottom dog's perspective.

The academy has traditionally taken pride in its pluralistic values. This allowed generations of scholars to rely on the academy for mutual aid and protection, the maintenance of standards, and support for pursuing value-free (and not-so-value-free) knowledge. Yet, university administrators are increasingly less interested in these traditions than they are in bringing payoffs to their institutions in the form of prestige, foundation and government grants, and an abundance of tuition-paying students. Under the traditional Ivory Tower model, individual scholars worked in isolation and, if judged successful, were rewarded with tenure, promotion, and distinguished honors. Today the team or "academic unit" is more important than the individual; thus careers rise and fall on the reputation of departments. This has paved the way for a corporate model of higher education, wherein academic units are characterized for their value as differential assets in the quest for institutional upward mobility and revenue-generating capabilities. Students are viewed as "consumers" who are encouraged to buy more of the educational "commodity" from the department with the best "competitive profile." These methods have not only led to increased competition in the academy, but the competition for consumers has also forced scholastic stratification. "Pay-for-performance," or the rank ordering of faculty as if they were racehorses, is but one of many policy artifacts of this trend.

In my case, I began a one-man campaign against pay-for-performance by speaking out against the policy whenever the opportunity arose. I presented myself as a bottom dog, as the "worst" criminology professor at the university. I argued that the stratification of faculty was counterproductive, inane, and cruel. Not only that, but it violated the pluralistic culture of liberal arts education. Engaging administrators in such a forceful manner can be difficult, but engagement is a far cry better than isolation. Then again, a bottom dog has little to lose. For me, this engagement became easier when I made two important decisions.

First, I dropped the "struggle for justice" approach to conflict resolution because my experiences had taught me that mediation was just another covert means of social control and oppression. In short, the struggle for justice is futile because the culture of trust has evaporated. As Cullen notes, many professors make this mistake, "assuming that 'justice' in a department is rooted in clearly defined policies and processes. To some extent, of course, it is, but my sense is that the dominant 'rule' of academic life is not just desserts but *reciprocity* ... scratching one another's back" (2002, p, 15). To be sure, alleviating suffering and preventing unfairness are important goals. However, both of these aims involve changing people's *situations* for the better. This assumes that university administrators have both the organizational skills and the sense of propriety necessary to bring about normative changes in those situations. I seriously question that assumption.

To accept the assumption is to make the same mistake that we activists made in the late 1960s: Once the insanity of the Vietnam War and the root causes of social injustice were exposed, we reasoned, then surely America would live up to her promises and play by her stated rules of democracy. But our political leaders were incapable of doing so. Those leaders—namely, Richard Nixon and his ilk—lacked the competence, the political will, and the personal integrity necessary to change situations for the better. They were unable to make good on the promise of democracy. Today, the corporate leaders of McUniversity share the same human failure. There are simply no limits to how administrators can lie in American universities and get away with it. And it is the transposition of that approach to faculty affairs into policy that constitutes the disgrace of the corporate university.

Therefore, instead of seeking justice, I adopted a different goal, a goal of human transformation. This approach to conflict resolution involves changing not just situations but *people* themselves.[3] The goal is to create a society in which people are not just better off, but better, more human, and more humane. Of course, this process begins at a personal level by living the values you wish to see in others. I chose to follow the wisdom of the ancients, like Lao Tzu, who wrote: "Peace and quiet are dear to the heart/And victory no cause for rejoicing."

The second decision was to make a sincere effort to reconnect with parts of the university that I'd developed a deep affection for. Cullen has it absolutely right. "Universities can be frustrating places," he writes, "but life inside them is more pleasing if they are the object of at least some kind of sentiments and not the object of complete alienation" (2002, p. 9).

So, there is something of a happy ending to this tale of woe. Like Gary Marx, I have come to terms with both winning and losing. I've also become more comfortable with the ambiguities and dilemmas that shade university life. My relationships with department colleagues have improved, and I've come to accept the fact that research is not for everyone. I now respect those who devote themselves earnestly to using their talents in pursuit of professional service. They'll go on being right from their side, and I'll go on being right from mine. But now, at least, we're on speaking terms. As for the dean and the other suits, they all left the university for greener pastures; and while the new administration has not yet eliminated pay-for-performance, they have abandoned the harsh practice of stratifying faculty on a scale from "best" to "worst." And because of my struggles with the performance policy, I've recently been elected by the faculty to the committee that arbitrates faculty grievances over performance reviews. But more to the point of this essay, I was finally able to finish my work on the Oklahoma City bombing. I did so as a bottom dog, by avoiding lawyers and ducking university administrators. I went straight to the source, to the maximum-security prisons that housed Peter Langan, Tim McVeigh, and the other men of the Aryan Republican Army. I went to the communities where they grew up, visited their hangouts, listened to their music, and watched their self-produced videotapes. I spoke to their families, their lovers and enemies, and to the FBI agents who captured them. In so doing, I went back to the basics I learned long ago from Alfred Lindesmith. I also paid attention to some of his lessons that I failed to learn the first time around.

Notes

1. The Dylan quote comes from his "Mr. Tambourine Man." *Bringing It All Back Home* (Columbia Records, 1965). Preceding sources and quotes: Allen Ginsberg, *Howl and Other Poems* (San Francisco: City Lights Books, 1956), p. 9; Ellis Amburn, *Subterranean Kerouac: The Hidden Life of Jack Kerouac* (New York: St. Martin's Press, 1998); Kevin McCarthy in *Montgomery Clift*, a documentary by Claudio Masenza; Vonnegut, quoted in *Indiana Statesman*, July 9, 2002, p. 1.

2. Author interview for the *Legends of Criminology* series, American Society of Criminology/Rutgers University, ASC Meetings, November, 1996.

3. For a full explanation, see Robert A. Baruch Bush and Joseph P. Folger, *The Promise of Mediation*. San Francisco: Jossey-Bass, 1994, 15–32.

References

Adler, P. A., and Adler, P. "Foreword: Moving Backward" n *Ethnography at the Edge: Crime, Deviance, and Field Research*, edited by Jeff Ferrell and Mark S. Hamm. Boston: Northeastern University Press, 1998, p. xv.

Amburn, E. *Subterranean Kerouac: The Hidden Life of Jack Kerouac*. New York: St. Martin's Press, 1998.

Bush, R. A. B., and Folger, J. P. *The Promise of Mediation*. San Francisco: Jossey-Bass, 1994.

Burawoy, M. "Introduction" to Burawoy et al. *Ethnography Unbound: Power and Resistance in the Modern Metropolis*. Berkeley, CA: University of California Press, 1991.

Chambliss, W. Author interview for the *Legends of Criminology* series, American Society of Criminology/Rutgers University, ASC Meetings, November, 1996.

Cullen, Francis T. "It's a Wonderful Life: Reflections on a Career in Progress." In *Lessons of Criminology*, edited by Gilbert Geis and Mary Dodge. Cincinnati, OH: Anderson, 2002.

Dylan, B. *Absolutely Sweet Marie*, Columbia Records, 1966.

———. *One Too Many Mornings*, Columbia Records, 1964.

Fisk, R. "Sticks and Stones." *The New Republic* May 27, 2002, p. 9.

Friedrichs, D. O. "September 11 and Its Aftermath: Some Questions For Consideration and Discussion." In *Teaching About September 11th: Education and Catastrophe in the Global Village*, Available at Stopviolence.com

Ginsberg, A. *Howl and Other Poems*. San Francisco: City Lights Books, 1956.

Hamm, M. S. *Apocalypse in Oklahoma: Waco and Ruby Ridge Revenged*. Boston: Northeastern University Press, 1997.

———. "The Ethnography of Terror: Timothy McVeigh and the Blue Centerlight of Evil." in *Ethnography at the Edge*, edited by J. Ferrell and M. S. Hamm. Boston: Northeastern University Press, 1998, 111–130.

———. *In Bad Company: America's Terrorist Underground*. Boston: Northeastern University Press, 2002.

Hamm, M. S. and Ferrell, J. "Confessions of Danger and Humanity." In *Ethnography at the Edge*, edited by J. Ferrell and M. S. Hamm. Boston: Northeastern University Press, 1998.

Keys, D. P., and Galliher, J. F. *Confronting the Drug Control Establishment: Alfred Lindesmith as a Public Intellectual.* Albany, NY: State University of New York Press, 2000.

Lyng, S. "Dangerous Methods: Risk Taking and the Research Process." In *Ethnography at the Edge*, edited by J. Ferrell and M. S. Hamm. Boston: Northeastern University Press, 1998, 221–251.

Marx, G. T. "Reflections on Academic Success and Failure: Making It, Forsaking It, Reshaping It." In *Authors of Their Own Lives*, edited by B. Berger. Berkeley, CA: University of California Press, 1990, 260–284.

McWilliams, C. "Introduction." to Carlos Bulusan's *America Is in the Heart.* Seattle, WA: University of Washington Press, 1973.

Sanchez-Jankowski, M. *Islands in the Street: Gangs in American Urban Society.* Berkeley, CA: University of California Press, 1994.

———. "Author meets critics" session, American Sociological Association Meetings, August, 1994.

Sheng-Mei Ma, "Second-Rate or Second-Rank: The Human Pyramid of Academe" in *Rage*, 230. In *States of Rage: Emotional Eruption, Violence, and Social Change*, edited by Renee Curry and Terry Allison. New York: New York University Press, 1996, 230–244.

Svoray, Y., and Taylor, N. *In Hitler's Shadow: An Israeli's Amazing Journey Inside Germany's Neo-Nazi Movement.* New York: Nan A. Talese/Doubleday, 1994.

Young, N. *I Believe in You*, Reprise Records, 1970.

Index